PROBLEMS OF EVERYDAY LIFE

PROBLEMS
OF
EVERYDAY LIFE

*Creating the foundations for a new society
in revolutionary Russia*

LEON TROTSKY

PATHFINDER

NEW YORK   LONDON   MONTREAL   SYDNEY

ISBN 978-0-87348-854-9
Library of Congress Catalog Card Number 79-186693
Manufactured in the United States of America

First edition, 1973
Nineteenth printing, 2021

Cover: Sketch for a decoration of the Okhtensky Bridge, Petrograd, 1918–20, by Ksenia Boguslavskaia. Watercolor and ink on paper. (State Russian Museum, St. Petersburg)
Cover design: Eric Simpson

Pathfinder
www.pathfinderpress.com
E-mail: pathfinder@pathfinderpress.com

Contents

Introduction

BY GEORGE NOVACK

"Nothing human is alien to me." This maxim, minted by the Roman playwright Terence, was a favorite of the Frenchman Montaigne and the German Karl Marx. It is likewise highly appropriate to the exceptional range and diversity of the interests of the Russian revolutionist, Leon Trotsky.

He wrote in 1935 that "politics and literature constitute in essence the contents of my personal life." This self-characterization hardly does justice to the many other areas of human experience that his probing mind, equipped with the method of Marxism, investigated.

The dramatic twists and turns of his career, its sudden ascent from obscurity to the summits of power followed by its equally precipitous drop into exile, penury, and persecution, have few parallels in the twentieth century. Consider only his biography from the Russian Revolution in 1917 through the mid-1920s, the period during which most of the pieces in this collection were written. As the president of the Petrograd Soviet and the director of its Military Revolutionary Committee, Trotsky led the October uprising that brought the Bolsheviks to power and inaugurated the postcapitalist epoch in world history. He was the first commissar of foreign affairs; then he undertook the organization and command of the Red Army. He was commissar

---

George Novack, a noted Marxist scholar, is the author of many books, including Origins of Materialism, Understanding History, *and* Humanism and Socialism.

of war from 1918 to 1925. But the tremendous burden of guiding the destiny of the workers' state with Lenin seems only to have heightened the attention Trotsky gave to every detail of its development, to matters that others might have thought were so far afield from the responsibilities of state as to warrant little attention from a leader of Trotsky's stature. But Trotsky's concern for the revolution touched every aspect of Russian life.

The connection between culture and the socialist revolution is the axis of these writings. Trotsky construed culture in a very broad sense. He contrasted culture, as the totality of the works of humankind, with whatever belonged to nature in the raw. Culture encompassed all facets of social life in its historical development, from the processes of producing wealth to customs, morals, law, religion, literature, art, science, and philosophy.

The subsoil of culture was the economy, the ways in which people produced and exchanged the necessities and comforts of existence. The multifarious aspects and achievements of cultural activity grew out of this material foundation.

There is much misunderstanding about the Marxist position on the relations between the mode of production and the other elements in the social structure. "The opinion that economics presumably determines directly and immediately the creativeness of a composer or even the verdict of a judge, represents a hoary caricature of Marxism which the bourgeois professordom of all countries has circulated time out of end to mask their intellectual impotence," Trotsky declared (*In Defense of Marxism*, Pathfinder Press, 1942, 1995, p. 210 [2009 printing]).

The economic foundation of a given social formation is organically related to and continuously interacting with its political-cultural superstructure and determines the character and course of its development *in the last analysis*. According to historical materialism, economics is the principal factor shaping the conditions of life, the habits and consciousness of a people.

At the same time, inherited traditions and institutions, bound up with the uneven development of the historic process, can generate deep disparities among the constituent parts of a specific society or nation. These contradictions are especially striking and acute in a revolutionary period, when the old regime is being overthrown and broken up and relations corresponding to the demands of the new order are being formed slowly and under difficult circumstances.

That was the situation confronting the Bolsheviks in the years immediately following the consolidation of the young Soviet republic after the intervention ended in 1920. All the problems of culture were raised in theory and in practical life by the first proletarian victory in a backward country. The Communist leaders not only had to cope with immense political, military, diplomatic, and economic problems, but were also called upon to provide answers to questions of education, literacy, scientific development, architecture, family relations, and a host of other pressing matters.

Throughout this period Trotsky took on a variety of jobs. He was cofounder with Lenin of the Third International and wrote the most important manifestos and resolutions of its first four congresses. At the end of the civil war, he reorganized the shattered railroad system.

He became the chief intellectual inspirer and literary critic of postrevolutionary Russia. Despite his many government assignments, he managed to produce a remarkable literary output. In the summers of 1922 and 1923 he completed a book, *Literature and Revolution*, which presented views on cultural policy he held in common with Lenin. After participating in discussions with Communist propagandists meeting in Moscow, he wrote a series of articles for *Pravda* on various aspects of manners and morals. These were published under the title of *Problems of Everyday Life* and make up the first nine chapters of this collection.

After being relieved of his duties as commissar of war as a result of the intensifying factional conflict, he headed the Board for Electrotechnical Development and the Committee for Industry and Technology, where he oversaw the progress of Soviet scientific work. "I assiduously visited many laboratories, watched experiments with great interest, listened to explanations given by the foremost scientists, in my spare time studied text-books on chemistry and hydro-dynamics, and felt that I was half-administrator and half-student," he wrote in *My Life* (Pathfinder Press, 1970 p. 675 [2010 printing]). His reflections on these questions found expression in a set of addresses he delivered in 1925 and 1926 on the relations between science and society and on the Marxist approach to science.

Many of the articles and speeches belonging to this fruitful period of his intellectual activity are included in this collection. They were gathered, together with some other articles, in the twenty-first volume of Trotsky's *Sochinenia* (Collected Works), under the title *Culture in the Transitional Epoch* (the period of the transition from capitalism to socialism). This book, published in the Soviet Union in 1927, was among the last of Trotsky's writings to be issued in the USSR under the official imprimatur.

Trotsky, together with Lenin and other Communist theoreticians, suggested the proper course to be pursued in several domains of cultural policy—without, however, taking the attitude of imperious command that the Stalinist authorities subsequently took. The early Communist leaders wanted to leave ample room for experimentation, innovation, and competition in the wholly new undertaking of fashioning a culture of, for, and by the working masses under revolutionary auspices.

"History gives nothing free of cost. Having made a reduction on one point—in politics—it makes us pay the more on another—in culture," Trotsky observed in 1923 in *Problems of Everyday Life*. However, he was then unable to foresee what became increasingly evident not long afterwards: how cruelly heavy a price Russia's backwardness was to exact, not only in culture but in politics as well.

Because of the setbacks to the international revolution, the prolonged isolation of the beleaguered workers' state in a hostile imperialist environment, and its material and cultural poverty, the Soviet Union took a different path from that envisaged by its chief architects. The program, the high ideals and aspirations that had animated and guided the early years of the revolution were perverted, trampled upon, and discarded by the bureaucratic reaction that took over the Communist Party, usurped power in the country, and blighted all aspects of Soviet life.

The bulk of the articles and speeches in this book were composed in the mid-twenties, during the factional struggle inside the Russian Communist Party that Lenin initiated just before his death. Trotsky carried on this struggle when he formed the Left Opposition, which tried to maintain the revolutionary character of the party against the growth of a conservative privileged bureaucracy led by Stalin. During most of this four-year struggle, Trotsky was prohibited from voicing his political criticisms publicly. But in his discussions of cultural and scientific questions, he dealt with the dangers of bureaucratism and of narrow-mindedness, conservatism, and pettiness, warning his listeners to defend and extend the gains of their revolution. Virtually every article in this book contains a veiled discussion of the struggle against bureaucracy. The Stalin leadership was infuriated by these articles but was unable to prevent their publication until 1927, when it felt strong enough to expel Trotsky and other Oppositionists from the party.

Cultural advancement was a prime casualty of this degenerative process of the 1920s and 1930s. Thanks to the conquests of the revolution, the Soviet Union was enabled to make considerable headway in bringing the elementary prerequisites of modern culture to the broad masses that had been denied them under czarism. The spread of literacy, the growth of educational facilities and opportunities, the promotion of science and technology, the formation of an extensive intelligentsia, the improvement of the skills of the working class, the increase in opportunities for women, the establishment of state social security and medical care, raised the Soviet Union closer to the technical and cultural levels of the advanced capitalist countries.

But the totalitarian practices of the new ruling caste had the most pernicious effects upon the rights and freedoms of the Soviet people. This retrogression was manifested, for example, in the sphere of the family, where instead of providing social equivalents for family housekeeping functions in order to lessen the servitude of women, Stalin revived the cult of the family, withdrew the right of abortion, and gave incentives to wives to become brood sows. Trotsky took note of the degeneration with respect to the family in *The Revolution Betrayed*, written in 1936. The selection is included in this anthology.

The dictatorship of the bureaucracy built schools, universities, and technical institutes, issued papers and magazines by the millions, set up radio and TV networks, made films—and pressed down upon all this a deadly uniformity that nonconformist minds found more and more intolerable. "Permitting and encouraging the development of economic individualism (piecework, private land allotments, premiums, decorations) [the bureaucracy] at the same time ruthlessly suppresses the progressive side of individualism in the realm of spiritual culture (critical views, the development of one's own opinion, the cultivation of personal dignity)," wrote Trotsky in 1936 (*The Revolution Betrayed*, Pathfinder Press, 1937, 1972, p. 185 [2009 printing]).

But the triumph of Stalinism does not invalidate the views expounded by Trotsky in this collection. Quite the contrary. What he had to say on cultural matters stands out all the more forcefully and favorably by contrast with the anti-Marxist policies of Stalin and his imitators. His ideas retain their full value in clarifying the complex problems of culture encountered in the transition from capitalism to socialism.

Trotsky never claimed originality for his theoretical and political positions. From his conversion to the doctrines of Marxism as a youth in 1898 to his assassination in 1940, he was a Marxist in the classical tradition extending from Marx and Engels to Lenin. This did not prevent—indeed it made it possible—his enrichment of the Marxist treasury of thought through the formulation of the theory of the permanent revolution and the law of uneven and combined development.

In this collection, Trotsky focuses the searchlight of dialectical materialism upon the big and the little tasks involved in building a new society on the debris of the old. What an abundance of ideas is spread before the reader in these brilliant observations! Trotsky takes up philosophy, science, technology, bibliography, stenography, library work, religion, social and individual psychology, literature, the role of the cinema, the position and prospects of women, the purification of speech as an instrument of clear thought, mass initiative, and much more.

How often do the adversaries of Marxism charge that its "dogmatic" outlook blinkers the sight, blunts sympathies and sensitivities, constricts the interests of its adherents. These pages should help dispose of such allegations. They show how a master of Marxist method deals with the problems of culture and science in a realistic and flexible manner, always keeping in view their connection with the struggle for socialism against capitalist domination and bureaucratic corruption.

NOVEMBER 7, 1972

Part 1

Problems of everyday life

Not by politics alone

[PUBLISHED JULY 10, 1923]
This simple thought should be thoroughly grasped and borne in mind by all who speak or write for propaganda purposes. Changed times bring changed tunes. The prerevolutionary history of our party was a history of revolutionary politics. Party literature, party organizations—everything was ruled by politics in the direct and narrow sense of that word. The revolutionary crisis has intensified political interests and problems to a still greater degree. The party had to win over the most politically active elements of the working class. At present the working class is perfectly aware of the *funda-*

The first nine articles in this collection were published in an English translation by Z. Vergerova in 1924 under the title Problems of Life. *The book arose out of a series of articles written during 1923 for* Pravda, *the official newspaper of the Communist Party of the Soviet Union. The articles themselves were based on discussions with Communist propagandists meeting in Moscow.*

"Not by Politics Alone" *is from* Pravda, *July 10, 1923.*

mental results of the revolution. It is quite unnecessary to go on repeating over and over the story of these results. It does not any longer stir the minds of the workers, and is more likely even to wipe out in the workers' minds the lessons of the past. With the conquest of power and its consolidation as a result of the civil war, our chief problems have shifted to the needs of culture and economic reconstruction. They have become more complicated, more detailed and in a way more prosaic. Yet, in order to justify all the past struggle and all the sacrifices, we must learn to grasp these fragmentary problems of culture, and solve each of them separately.

Now, what has the working class actually gained and secured for itself as a result of the revolution?

1. The dictatorship of the proletariat (represented by the workers' and peasants' government under the leadership of the Communist Party).

2. The Red Army—a firm support of the dictatorship of the proletariat.

3. The nationalization of the chief means of production, without which the dictatorship of the proletariat would have become a form void of substance.

4. The monopoly of foreign trade, which is the necessary condition of socialist state structure in a capitalist environment.

These four things, definitely won, form the steel frame of all our work; and every success we achieve in economics or culture—provided it is a real achievement and not a sham—becomes in this framework a necessary part of the socialist structure.

And what is our problem now? What have we to learn in the first place? What should we strive for? We must learn to work efficiently: accurately, punctually, economically. We need culture in work, culture in life, in the conditions of life. After a long preliminary period of struggle we have succeeded in overthrowing the rule of the exploiters by armed revolt. No such means exists, however, to create culture all at once. The working class must undergo a long process of self-education, and so must the peasantry, either along with the workers or following them. Lenin speaks about this shift in focus of our aims and efforts in his article on cooperation:

> We have to admit [he says] that there has been a radical modification in our whole outlook on socialism. The radical modification is this: formerly we placed, and had to place, the main emphasis on the political struggle, on revolution, on winning political power, etc. Now the emphasis is changing and shifting to peaceful, organizational, "cultural" work. I should say that emphasis is shifting to educational work, were it not for our international relations, were it not for the fact that we have to fight for our position on a world scale. If we leave that aside, however, and confine ourselves to internal economic relations, the emphasis in our work is certainly shifting to education. ["On Cooperation," in Lenin's *Collected Works*, Vol. 33 (Progress Publishers, Moscow, 1966)]

I consider it of some interest to quote here a passage on the epoch of the struggle for culture, out of my *Thoughts about the Party:*[1]

> In its practical realization, the revolution is, so to speak, "broken up" into partial tasks: it is necessary to repair bridges, learn to read and write, reduce the cost of production of shoes in Soviet factories, combat filth, catch swindlers, extend power cables into the countryside, and so on. Some vulgarians from the intelligentsia, from the category of persons who wear their brains askew (for that very reason they consider themselves poets or philosophers), have already taken to talking about the revolution in a tone of the most magnificent

condescension: learning to trade, ha, ha! and to sew on buttons, heh, heh! But let these windbags yelp into the empty air. . . .

But purely practical everyday work in the field of Soviet cultural and economic construction (even in Soviet retail trade!) is not at all a practice of "petty jobs," and does not necessarily involve a hairsplitting mentality. There are plenty of petty jobs, unrelated to any big jobs, in man's life. But history knows of no big jobs without petty jobs. It would be more precise to say—petty jobs in a great epoch, that is, as component parts of a big task, cease to be "petty jobs."

. . . It is perfectly obvious that it is quite a different sort of topical demands and partial tasks that call for our attention today. Our concern is with the constructive work of a working class which is for the first time building for itself and according to its own plan. This historic plan, though as yet extremely imperfect and lacking in consistency, must embrace all sections and parts of the work, all its nooks and crannies, in the unity of a great creative conception. . . .

Socialist construction is planned construction on the largest scale. And through all the ebbs and flows, mistakes and turns, through all the twists and turns of NEP,[2] the party pursues its great plan, educates the youth in the spirit of this plan, teaches everyone to link his particular function with the common task, which today demands sewing on Soviet buttons, and tomorrow readiness to die fearlessly under the banner of communism. . . .

We must, and shall, demand serious and thorough specialized training for our young people, and so, their emancipation from the basic sin of our generation—that of being know-it-alls and jacks of all trades—but specialization in the service of a common plan grasped and thought out by every individual. . . .

Nothing, therefore, but the problems of our international position keeps us, as Lenin tells us, from the struggle for culture. Now these problems, as we shall see presently, are not altogether of a different order. Our international position largely depends on the strength of our self-defense—that is to say, on the efficiency of the Red Army—and, in this vital aspect of our existence as a state, our problem consists almost entirely of work for culture: we must raise the level of the army and teach every single soldier to read and to write. The men must be taught to read books, to use manuals and maps; they must acquire habits of tidiness, punctuality, and thrift. It cannot be done all at once by some miraculous means. After the civil war and during the transitional period of our work, attempts were made to save the situation by a specially invented "proletarian military doctrine," but it was quite lacking in any real understanding of our actual problems. The same thing happened in regard to the ambitious plan for creating an artificial "proletarian culture." [3] All such quests for the philosophers' stone combine despair at our deficiency in culture with a faith in miracles. We have, however, no reason to despair, and as to miracles and childish quackeries like "proletarian culture" or "proletarian military doctrine," it is high time to give such things up. We must see to the development of culture within the framework of the dictatorship of the proletariat, and this alone can assure the socialist content of the revolutionary conquests. Whoever fails to see this will play a reactionary part in the development of party thought and party work.

When Lenin says that at the present moment our work is less concerned with politics than with culture, we must be quite clear about the terms he uses, so as not to misinterpret his meaning. In a certain sense politics always ranks first. Even the advice of Lenin to shift our interests from politics to culture is a piece of political advice. When the labor party of a country comes to decide that at some given moment the economic problem and not the political should take first place, the decision itself is political. It is quite obvious that the word "politics" is used here in two different meanings: firstly, in a wide materialist and dialectical sense, as the totality of all guiding principles, methods, systems that determine collective activities in all domains of public life; and, on the other hand, in a restricted sense, specifying a definite part of public activity, directly concerned with the struggle for power and opposed to economic work, to the struggle for culture, etc. Speaking of politics as concentrated economics, Lenin meant politics in the wider philosophic sense. But when he urged: "Let us have less politics and more economics," he referred to politics in the restricted and special sense. Both ways of using the word are sanctioned by tradition and are justified.

The Communist Party is political in the wide historical or, we may also say, philosophic sense. The other parties are political only in the restricted sense of the word. The shifting of the interests of our party to the struggle for *culture* does not therefore weaken the *political* importance of the party. The party will concentrate its activity on the work for culture, and take the leading part in this work—this will constitute its historically leading, i.e., political part. A great many more years of socialist work, successful within and secure from without, are still needed before the party could do away with its shell of party structure and dissolve in a socialist community. This is still so very distant that it is of no use to look so far ahead. In the immediate future the party must preserve in full its fundamental characteristics: unity of purpose, centralization, discipline, and, as a result of it, fitness for the fight. But under present conditions it needs a very sound economic base to preserve and to develop these priceless assets of Communist Party spirit. Economic problems, therefore, rank first in our politics, and only in conformity with them does the party concentrate and distribute its forces and educate the young generation. In other words, politics in the broader sense requires that all the work of propaganda, distribution of forces, teaching, and education should be based at present on the problems of economics and culture, and not on politics in the restricted and special sense of the word.

The proletariat is a powerful social unity which manifests its strength fully during the periods of intense revolutionary struggle for the aims of the whole class. But within this unity we observe a great variety of types. Between the obtuse illiterate village shepherd and the highly qualified engine-driver there lie a great many different states of culture and habits of life. Every class, moreover, every trade, every group consists of people of different ages, different temperaments, and with a different past. But for this variety, the work of the Communist Party might have been easy. The example of Western Europe shows, however, how difficult this work is in reality.

One might say that the richer the history of a country, and at the same time of its working class, the greater within it the accumulation of memories, traditions, habits, the larger the number of old groupings—the harder it is to achieve a revolutionary unity of the working class. The Russian proletariat is poor in class history and class traditions. This has undoubtedly facilitated its revolutionary education leading up to October. On the other hand, it causes difficulty in constructive work after October.

The Russian worker—except the very top of the class—usually lacks the most elementary habits and notions of culture (in regard to tidiness, instruction, punctuality, etc.). The Western European worker possesses these habits. He has acquired them by a long and slow process, under the bourgeois regime. This explains why in Western Europe the working class—its superior elements, at any rate—is so strongly attached to the bourgeois regime with its democracy, freedom of the capitalist press, and all the other blessings. The belated bourgeois regime in Russia had no time to do any good to the working class, and the Russian proletariat broke from the bourgeoisie all the more easily, and overthrew the bourgeois regime without regret. But for the very same reason the Russian proletariat is only just beginning to acquire and to accumulate the simplest habits of culture, doing it already in the conditions of a socialist workers' state.

History gives nothing free of cost. Having made a reduction on one point—in politics—it makes us pay the more on another—in culture. The more easily (comparatively, of course) did the Russian proletariat pass through the revolutionary crisis, the harder becomes now its socialist constructive work. But, on the other hand, the framework of our new social structure, marked by the four characteristics mentioned above, gives an objectively socialist content to all conscientious and rationally directed efforts in the domain of economics and culture. Under the bourgeois regime the workman, with no desire or intention on his part, was continually enriching the bourgeoisie, and did it all the more, the better his work was. In the Soviet state a conscientious and good worker, whether he cares to do it or not (in case he is not in the party and keeps away from politics) achieves socialist results and increases the wealth of the working class. This is the doing of the October Revolution, and the NEP has not changed anything in this respect.

Workers who do not belong to the party, who are deeply devoted to production, to the technical side of their work, are many in Russia, but they are not altogether "apolitical," not indifferent to politics. In all the grave and difficult moments of the revolution, they were with us. The overwhelming majority of them were not frightened by October, did not desert, were not traitors. During the civil war many of them fought on the different fronts; others worked for the army, supplying the munitions. They may be described as "nonpolitical," but in the sense that in peacetime they care more for their professional work or their families than for politics. They all want to be good workers, to get more and more efficient each in his particular job, to rise to a higher position—partly for the benefit of their families, but also for the gratification of their perfectly legitimate professional ambition. Implicitly, every one of them, as I said before, does socialist work without even being aware of it. But as the Communist Party, we want these workers consciously to connect their individual productive work with the problems of socialist construction as a whole. The interests of socialism will be better secured by such united activities, and the individual builders of socialism will get a higher moral satisfaction out of their work.

But how is this to be achieved? To approach this type of worker on purely political lines is very difficult. He has heard all the speeches that were spoken and does not care for more. He is not inclined to join the party. His thoughts are centered on his work, and he is not particularly satisfied with the present conditions in the workshop, in the factory, in the trust. Such workers generally try to get at the bottom of things themselves, they are not communicative, and are just the class which produces self-taught inventors. They are not responsive to politics—at least not wholeheartedly—but they might and should be approached on matters concerning production and technique.

One of the members of the Moscow conference of mass propagandists,[4] Comrade Kolzov, has pointed to the extreme shortage of manuals, handbooks, and guides published in Soviet Russia for the study of different trades and handicrafts. The old books of such a kind are mostly sold out, and besides, many of them are technically behind the time, whereas politically they are usually imbued with an exploiting capitalist spirit. New technical handbooks are very few and very difficult to get, having been published at random by different publishers or state departments without any general plan. From the technical point of view they are not always satisfactory; some of them are too abstract, too academic, and usually colorless politically, being, in fact, slightly disguised translations of foreign books. What we really want is a series of new handbooks—for the Soviet locksmith, the Soviet cabinetmaker, the Soviet electrician, etc. The handbooks must be adapted to our up-to-date techniques and economics, must take into account our poverty, and on the other hand, our big possibilities; they must try to introduce new methods and new habits into our industrial life. They must—as far as possible anyhow—reveal socialist vistas corresponding to the wants and interests of technical development (this includes problems of standardization, electrification, economic planning). Socialist principles and conclusions must not be mere propaganda in such books. They must form an integral part of the practical teaching. Such books are very much needed, considering the shortage of qualified workers, the desire of the workers themselves to become more efficient, and considering also their interrupted industrial experience in conjunction with the long years of imperialist and civil war. We are faced here with an extremely gratifying and important task.

It is not an easy matter, of course, to create such a series of handbooks. Good practical workers do not write handbooks, and the theorists who do the writing usually have no experience of the practical side of work. Very few of them, moreover, have socialist views. The problem can be solved nevertheless—yet not by "simple," i.e., routine methods, but by combined efforts. The joint work of, say, three authors is necessary to write, or at least to edit, a handbook. There should be a specialist with a thorough technical training, one who knows the conditions of our present production in the given trade or is able to get the necessary information; the other two should include a highly qualified worker of that particular trade, one who is interested in production, and if possible has some inventive aptitudes; and a professional writer, a Marxist, a politician with industrial and technical interests and knowledge. In this or some similar way, we must manage to create a model library of technical handbooks on industrial production. The books must, of course, be well printed, well stitched, of a handy size, and inexpensive. Such a library would be useful in two ways; it would raise the standard of work and contribute thereby to the success of socialist state construction, and on the other hand it would attach a very valuable group of industrial workers to Soviet economics as a whole, and consequently to the Communist Party.

To possess a series of handbooks is, of course, not all we want. I have dealt at some length with this particular question just to give an example of the new methods required by the new problems of the present day. There is much more to do in the interests of the "nonpolitical" industrial workers. Trade journals should be published, and technical societies ought to be started. A good half of our professional press should cater for the industrial worker of that "nonpolitical" but efficient type, if it wants to have readers outside the mere staff of the trade unions. The most telling political arguments, however, for the workers of that type are our practical achievements in industrial matters—every casual success in the management of our factories and workshops, every efficient effort of the party in this direction.

The political views of the industrial worker, who matters most for us now, might be best illustrated by the following attempt to formulate approximately his rarely expressed thoughts.

"Well," he would say, "all that business of the revolution and the overthrowing of the bourgeoisie is right enough. Nothing to be said against it. It's done once and forever. We have no use for the bourgeoisie. Nor do we need its Mensheviks or other helpmates. As to the 'freedom of the press'—that does not matter. That is not the point either. But what about economics? You communists have undertaken to manage it all. Your aims and plans are excellent—we know that. Don't go on repeating what they are. We know all about it, we agree with you and are ready to back you—but how are you actually going to do things? Up till now—why not tell the truth?—you often did the wrong things. Well, yes. We know that it cannot all be done at once, that you have to learn the job, and mistakes and blunders can't be avoided. That is all quite true And since we have stood the crimes of the bourgeoisie, we must bear with the mistakes of the revolution. But there is a limit to everything. In your communist ranks there are also all sorts of people just as among us poor sinners. Some do actually learn their jobs, are honestly intent on work, try to achieve practical results, but many more get off with idle talk. And they are doing much harm because with them business is simply slipping away through their fingers. . . ."

That is how they reason, the workers of that type—clever, efficient locksmiths, or cabinetmakers, or founders, not excitable, rather of passive disposition in politics, but serious, critical, somewhat skeptical, yet always faithful to their class—proletarians of a high standard. In the present stage of our work the party must take this type of worker most specially into account. Our hold on them—in economics, production, technique—will be the most telling political sign of our success in the work for culture in the final sense of the word, in the sense in which it is used by Lenin.

Our special interest in the efficient worker is in no way opposed to the other most important problem of the party—the great interest in the younger generation of the proletariat. The younger generation grows up in the conditions of the given moment, grows sound and strong according to the way in which certain well-determined problems are solved. We want our younger generation, in the first place, to develop into good, highly qualified workers, devoted to their work. They must grow up with the firm conviction that their productive work is at the same time work for socialism. Interest in professional training, and desire for efficiency, will naturally give great authority in the eyes of our young proletarians to "the old men," who are experts in their trade and who, as I said above, stand usually outside the party. We see, in consequence, that our interest in good, honest, and efficient workers serves the cause of a thorough education of the growing younger generation; without it there would be no onward march to socialism.

Habit and custom

[PUBLISHED JULY 11, 1923]

In the study of life it is peculiarly manifest to what an extent individual man is the product of environment rather than its creator. Daily life, i.e., conditions and customs, are, more than economics, "evolved behind men's backs," in the words of Marx. Conscious creativeness in the domain of custom and habit occupies but a negligible place in the history of man. Custom is accumulated from the elemental experience of men; it is transformed in the same elemental way under the pressure of technical progress or the occasional stimulus of revolutionary struggle. But in the main, it reflects more of the past of human society than of its present.

Our proletariat is not old and has no ancestry. It has emerged in the last ten years partly from the petty towns-people and chiefly from the peasantry. The life of our proletariat clearly reflects its social origin. We have only to recall

From Pravda, July 11, 1923.

The Morals of Rasteryaev Street, by Gleb Uspensky. What are the main characteristics of the Rasteryaevs, i.e., the Tula workmen of the last quarter of the last century? They are all townsmen or peasants who, having lost all hope of becoming independent men, formed a combination of the uneducated petty bourgeoisie and the destitute. Since then the proletariat has made a big stride, but more in politics than in life and morals. Life is conservative. In its primitive aspect, of course, Rasteryaev Street no longer exists. The brutal treatment accorded to apprentices, the servility practiced before employers, the vicious drunkenness, and the street hooliganism have vanished. But in the relations of husband and wife, parents and children, in the domestic life of the family, fenced off from the whole world, Rasteryaevism is still firmly implanted. We need years and decades of economic growth and culture to banish Rasteryaevism from its last refuge—individual and family life—recreating it from top to bottom in the spirit of collectivism.

Problems of family life were the subject of a particularly heated discussion at a conference of the Moscow propagandists, which we have already mentioned. In regard to this everyone had some grievance. Impressions, observations, and questions, especially, were numerous; but there was no answer to them, for the very questions remain semi-articulate, never reaching the press or being aired at meetings. The life of the ordinary workers and the life of the communists, and the line of contact between the two, provide such a big field for observation, deduction, and practical application!

Our literature does not help us in this respect. Art, by nature, is conservative; it is removed from life and is little able to catch events on the wing as they happen. *The Week,* by Libedinsky, excited a burst of enthusiasm among some of our comrades, an enthusiasm which appeared to me excessive, and dangerous for the young author.[5] In regard to its form, *The Week,* notwithstanding its marks of talent, has the characteristics of the work of a schoolboy. It is only by much persistent, detailed work that Libedinsky can become an artist. I should like to think that he will do so. However, this is not the aspect which interests us at the moment. *The Week* gave the impression of being something new and significant not because of its artistic achievements but because of the "communist" section of life with which it dealt. But in this respect especially, the matter of the book is not profound. The "gubkom" is presented to us with too much of the laboratory method; it has no deeper roots and is not organic. Hence, the whole of *The Week* becomes an episodic digression, a novel of revolutionary emigrants drawn from the life. It is, of course, interesting and instructive to depict the life of the "gubkom" but the difficulty and significance come when the life of communist organization enters into the everyday life of the people. Here, a firm grip is required. The Communist Party at the present moment is the principal lever of every conscious forward movement. Hence, its unity with the masses of the people becomes the root of historic action, reaction, and resistance.

Communist theory is some dozen years in advance of our everyday Russian actuality—in some spheres perhaps even a century in advance. Were this not so, the Communist Party would be no great revolutionary power in history. Communist theory, by means of its realism and dialectical acuteness, finds the political methods for securing the influence of the party in any given situation. But the political idea is one thing, and the popular conception of morals is another. Politics change rapidly, but morals cling tenaciously to the past.

This explains many of the conflicts among the working class, where fresh knowledge struggles against tradition. These conflicts are the more severe in that they do not find their expression in the publicity of social life. Literature and the press do not speak of them. The new literary tendencies, anxious to keep pace with the revolution, do not concern themselves with the usages and customs based on the existing conception of morals, for they want to transform life, not describe it! But new morals cannot be produced out of nothing; they must be arrived at with the aid of elements already existing, but capable of development. It is therefore necessary to recognize what are these elements. This applies not only to the transformation of morals, but to every form of conscious human activity. It is therefore necessary first to know what already exists, and in what manner its change of form is proceeding, if we are to cooperate in the re-creation of morals.

We must first see what is really going on in the factory, among the workers, in the cooperative, the club, the school, the tavern, and the street. All this we have to understand; that is, we must recognize the remnants of the past and the seeds of the future. We must call upon our authors and journalists to work in this direction. They must describe life for us as it emerges from the tempest of revolution.

It is not hard to surmise, however, that appeals alone will not redirect the attentions of our writers. We need proper organization of this matter and proper leadership. The study and enlightenment of working class life must, in the first place, be made the foremost task of journalists—of those, at any rate, who possess eyes and ears. In an organized way we must put them on this work, instruct, correct, lead, and educate them thus to become revolutionary writers, who will write of everyday life. At the same time, we must broaden the angle of outlook of working class newspaper correspondents. Certainly almost any of them could produce more interesting and entertaining correspondence than we have nowadays. For this purpose, we must deliberately formulate questions, set proper tasks, stimulate discussion, and help to sustain it.

In order to reach a higher stage of culture, the working

class—and above all its vanguard—must consciously study its life. To do this, it must know this life. Before the bourgeoisie came to power, it had fulfilled this task to a wide extent through its intellectuals. When the bourgeoisie was still an oppositional class, there were poets, painters, and writers already thinking for it.

In France, the eighteenth century, which has been named the century of enlightenment, was precisely the period in which the bourgeois philosophers were changing the conception of social and private morals, and were endeavoring to subordinate morals to the rule of reason. They occupied themselves with political questions, with the church, with the relations between man and woman, with education, etc. There is no doubt but that the mere fact of the discussion of these problems greatly contributed to the raising of the mental level of culture among the bourgeoisie. But all the efforts made by the eighteenth century philosophers towards subordinating social and private relations to the rule of reason were wrecked on one fact—the fact that the means of production were in private hands, and that this was the basis upon which society was to be built up according to the tenets of reason. For private property signifies free play to economic forces which are by no means controlled by reason. These economic conditions determine morals, and so long as the needs of the commodity market rule society, so long is it impossible to subordinate popular morals to reason. This explains the very slight practical results yielded by the ideas of the eighteenth century philosophers, despite the ingenuity and boldness of their conclusions.

In Germany, the period of enlightenment and criticism came about the middle of the last century. "Young Germany," under the leadership of Heine and Boerne, placed itself at the head of the movement.[6] We here see the work of criticism accomplished by the left wing of the bourgeoisie, which declared war on the spirit of servility, on petty-bourgeois anti-enlightenment education, and on the prejudices of war, and which attempted to establish the rule of reason with even greater skepticism than its French predecessor. This movement amalgamated later with the petty-bourgeois revolution of 1848, which, far from transforming all human life, was not even capable of sweeping away the many little German dynasties.

In our backward Russia, the enlightenment and the criticism of the existing state of society did not reach any stage of importance until the second half of the nineteenth century. Chernyshevsky, Pisarev, and Dobrolyubov, educated in the Belinsky school, directed their criticism much more against the backwardness and reactionary Asiatic character of morals than against economic conditions.[7] They opposed the new realistic human being to the traditional type of man, the new human being who is determined to live according to reason, and who becomes a personality provided with the weapon of critical thought. This movement, connected with the so-called "popular" evolutionists (Narodniks) had but slight cultural significance.[8] For if the French thinkers of the eighteenth century were only able to gain a slight influence over morals—these being ruled by the economic conditions and not by philosophy—and if the immediate cultural influence of the German critics of society was even less, the direct influence exercised by this Russian movement on popular morals was quite insignificant. The historical role played by these Russian thinkers, including the Narodniks, consisted in preparing for the formation of the party of the revolutionary proletariat.

It is only the seizure of power by the working class which creates the premises for a complete transformation of morals. Morals cannot be rationalized—that is, made congruous with the demands of reason—unless production is rationalized at the same time, for the roots of morals lie in production. Socialism aims at subordinating all production to human reason. But even the most advanced bourgeois thinkers have confined themselves to the ideas of rationalizing technique on the one hand (by the application of natural science, technology, chemistry, invention, machines), and politics on the other (by parliamentarism); but they have not sought to rationalize economics, which has remained the prey of blind competition. Thus the morals of bourgeois society remain dependent on a blind and non-rational element. When the working class takes power, it sets itself the task of subordinating the economic principles of social conditions to a control and to a conscious order. By this means, and only by this means, is there a possibility of consciously transforming morals.

The successes that we gain in this direction are dependent on our success in the sphere of economics. But even in our present economic situation we could introduce much more criticism, initiative, and reason into our morals than we actually do. This is one of the tasks of our time. It is of course obvious that the complete change of morals—the emancipation of woman from household slavery, the social education of children, the emancipation of marriage from all economic compulsion, etc.—will only be able to follow on a long period of development, and will come about in proportion to the extent to which the economic forces of socialism win the upper hand over the forces of capitalism.

The critical transformation of morals is necessary so that the conservative traditional forms of life may not continue to exist in spite of the possibilities for progress which are already offered us today by our sources of economic aid, or will at least be offered tomorrow. On the other hand, even the slightest successes in the sphere of morals, by raising the cultural level of the working man and woman, enhance our capacity for rationalizing production, and promoting socialist accumulation. This again gives us the possibility of making fresh conquests in the sphere of morals. Thus a dialectical dependence exists between the two spheres. The economic conditions are the fundamental factor of history, but we, as a Communist Party and as a workers' state, can only influence economics with the aid of the working class, and to attain this we must work unceasingly to promote the technical and cultural capacity of the individual element of the working class. In the workers' state culture works for socialism and socialism again offers the possibility of creating a new culture for humanity, one which knows nothing of class difference.

Vodka, the church,
and the cinema

[PUBLISHED JULY 12, 1923]
There are two big facts which have set a new stamp on working class life. The one is the advent of the eight-hour working day; the other, the prohibition of the sale of vodka. The
liquidation of the vodka monopoly, for which the war was
responsible, preceded the revolution. The war demanded
such enormous means that czarism was able to renounce
the drink revenue as a negligible quantity, a billion rubles
more or less making no very great difference. The revolution inherited the liquidation of the vodka monopoly as a
fact; it adopted the fact, but was actuated by considerations
of principle. It was only with the conquest of power by the
working class, which became the conscious creator of the
new economic order, that the combating of alcoholism by
the country, by education and prohibition, was able to receive its due historic significance. The circumstance that the

From Pravda, July 12, 1923.

"drunkards'" budget was abandoned during the imperialist war does not alter the fundamental fact that the abolition of the system by which the country encouraged people to drink is one of the iron assets of the revolution.

As regards the eight-hour working day, that was a direct conquest of the revolution. As a fact in itself, the eight-hour working day produced a radical change in the life of the worker, setting free two-thirds of the day from factory duties. This provides a foundation for a radical change of life for development and culture, social education, and so on, but a foundation only. The chief significance of the October Revolution consists in the fact that the economic betterment of every worker automatically raises the material well-being and culture of the working class as a whole.

"Eight hours work, eight hours sleep, eight hours play," says the old formula of the workers' movement. In our circumstances, it assumes a new meaning. The more profitably the eight hours work is utilized, the better, more cleanly, and more hygienically can the eight hours sleep be arranged for, and the fuller and more cultured can the eight hours of leisure become.

The question of amusements in this connection becomes of greatly enhanced importance in regard to culture and education. The character of a child is revealed and formed in its play. The character of an adult is clearly manifested in his play and amusements. But in forming the character of a whole class, when this class is young and moves ahead, like the proletariat, amusements and play ought to occupy a prominent position. The great French utopian reformer, Fourier,[9] repudiating Christian asceticism and the suppression of the natural instincts, constructed his *phalansterie* (the communes of the future) on the correct and rational utilization and combination of human instincts and passions. The idea is a profound one. The working class state is neither a spiritual order nor a monastery. We take people as they have been made by nature, and as they have been in part educated and in part distorted by the old order. We seek a point of support in this vital human material for the application of our party and revolutionary state lever. The longing for amusement, distraction, sight-seeing, and laughter is the most legitimate desire of human nature. We are able, and indeed obliged, to give the satisfaction of this desire a higher artistic quality, at the same time making amusement a weapon of collective education, freed from the guardianship of the pedagogue and the tiresome habit of moralizing.

The most important weapon in this respect, a weapon excelling any other, is at present the cinema. This amazing spectacular innovation has cut into human life with a successful rapidity never experienced in the past. In the daily life of capitalist towns, the cinema has become just such an integral part of life as the bath, the beer-hall, the church, and other indispensable institutions, commendable and otherwise. The passion for the cinema is rooted in the desire for distraction, the desire to see something new and improbable, to laugh and to cry, not at your own, but at other people's misfortunes. The cinema satisfies these demands in a very direct, visual, picturesque, and vital way, requiring nothing from the audience; it does not even require them to be literate. That is why the audience bears such a grateful love to the cinema, that inexhaustible fount of impressions and emotions. This provides a point, and not merely a point, but a huge square, for the application of our socialist educational energies.

The fact that we have so far, i.e., in nearly six years, not taken possession of the cinema shows how slow and uneducated we are, not to say, frankly, stupid. This weapon, which cries out to be used, is the best instrument for propaganda, technical, educational, and industrial propaganda, propaganda against alcohol, propaganda for sanitation, political propaganda, any kind of propaganda you please, a propaganda which is accessible to everyone, which is attractive, which cuts into the memory and may be made a possible source of revenue.

In attracting and amusing, the cinema already rivals the beer-hall and the tavern. I do not know whether New York or Paris possesses at the present time more cinemas or taverns, or which of these enterprises yields more revenue. But it is manifest that, above everything, the cinema competes with the tavern in the matter of how the eight leisure hours are to be filled. Can we secure this incomparable weapon? Why not? The government of the czar, in a few years, established an intricate net of state barrooms. The business yielded a yearly revenue of almost a billion gold rubles. Why should not the government of the workers establish a net of state cinemas? This apparatus of amusement and education could more and more be made to become an integral part of national life. Used to combat alcoholism, it could at the same time be made into a revenue-yielding concern. Is it practicable? Why not? It is, of course, not easy. It would be, at any rate, more natural and more in keeping with the organizing energies and abilities of a workers' state than, let us say, the attempt to restore the vodka monopoly.

The cinema competes not only with the tavern but also with the church. And this rivalry may become fatal for the church if we make up for the separation of the church from the socialist state by the fusion of the socialist state and the cinema.

Religiousness among the Russian working classes practically does not exist. It actually never existed. The Orthodox Church was a daily custom and a government institution. It never was successful in penetrating deeply into the consciousness of the masses, nor in blending its dogmas and canons with the inner emotions of the people. The reason for this is the same—the uncultured condition of old Russia, including her church. Hence, when awakened for culture, the Russian worker easily throws off his purely external relation to the church, a relation which grew on him by habit. For the peasant, certainly, this becomes harder, not because the peasant has more profoundly and intimately entered into the church teaching—this has, of course, never been the case—but because the inertia and monotony of his life are closely bound up with the inertia and monotony of church practices.

The workers' relation to the church (I am speaking of the nonparty mass worker) holds mostly by the thread of habit, the habit of women in particular. Icons still hang in the home because they are there. Icons decorate the walls; it would be bare without them; people would not be used to it. A worker will not trouble to buy new icons, but has not sufficient will to discard the old ones. In what way can the spring festival be celebrated if not by Easter cake? And Easter cake must be blessed by the priest, otherwise it will be so meaningless. As for church-going, the people do not go because they are religious; the church is brilliantly lighted, crowded with men and women in their best clothes, the singing is good—a range of social-aesthetic attractions not provided by the factory, the family, or the workaday street. There is no faith or practically none. At any rate, there is no respect for the clergy or belief in the magic force of ritual. But there is no active will to break it all. The elements of distraction, pleasure, and amusement play a large part in church rites. By theatrical methods the church works on the sight, the sense of smell (through incense), and through them on the imagination. Man's desire for the theatrical, a desire to see and hear the unusual, the striking, a desire for a break in the ordinary monotony of life, is great and ineradicable; it persists from early childhood to advanced old age. In order to liberate the common masses from ritual and the ecclesiasticism acquired by habit, antireligious propaganda alone is not enough. Of course, it is necessary; but its direct practical influence is limited to a small minority of the more courageous in spirit. The bulk of the people are not affected by antireligious propaganda; but that is not because their spiritual relation to religion is so profound. On the contrary, there is no spiritual relation at all; there is only a formless, inert, mechanical relation, which has not passed through the consciousness; a relation like that of the street sight-seer, who on occasion does not object to joining in a procession or a pompous ceremony, or listening to singing, or waving his arms.

Meaningless ritual, which lies on the consciousness like an inert burden, cannot be destroyed by criticism alone; it can be supplanted by new forms of life, new amusements, new and more cultured theaters. Here again, thoughts go naturally to the most powerful—because it is the most democratic—instrument of the theater: the cinema. Having no need of a clergy in brocade, etc., the cinema unfolds on the white screen spectacular images of greater grip than are provided by the richest church, grown wise in the experience of a thousand years, or by mosque or synagogue. In church only one drama is performed, and always one and the same, year in, year out; while in the cinema next door you will be shown the Easters of heathen, Jew, and Christian, in their historic sequence, with their similarity of ritual. The cinema amuses, educates, strikes the imagination by images, and liberates you from the need of crossing the church door. The cinema is a great competitor not only of the tavern but also of the church. Here is an instrument which we must secure at all costs!

From the old family
to the new

[PUBLISHED JULY 13, 1923]
The inner relations and happenings within the family are
by their very nature the most difficult to investigate, the
least subject to statistics. It is not easy, therefore, to say how
far family ties are more easily and frequently broken nowadays (in actual life, not merely on paper) than formerly. To
a great extent we must be content to judge by eye. The difference, moreover, between prerevolutionary times and the
present day is that formerly all the troubles and dramatic
conflicts in working class families used to pass unnoticed
by the workers themselves; whereas now a large upper part
of the workers occupy responsible posts, their life is much
more in the limelight, and every domestic tragedy in their
life becomes a subject of much comment and sometimes of
idle gossip.

Subject to this serious reservation, there is no denying,

From Pravda, *July 13, 1923.*

however, that family relations, those of the proletarian class included, are shattered. This was stated as a firmly established fact at the conference of Moscow party propagandists, and no one contested it. They were only differently impressed by it—all in their own way. Some viewed it with great misgivings, others with reserve, and still others seemed perplexed. It was, anyhow, clear to all that some great process was going on, very chaotically assuming alternatively morbid or revolting, ridiculous or tragic forms, and which had not yet had time to disclose its hidden possibilities of inaugurating a new and higher order of family life.

Some information about the disintegration of the family has crept into the press, but just occasionally, and in very vague, general terms. In an article on the subject, I had read that the disintegration of the family in the working class was represented as a case of "bourgeois influence on the proletariat."

It is not so simple as this. The root of the question lies deeper and is more complicated. The influence of the bourgeois past and the bourgeois present is there, but the main process consists in a painful evolution of the proletarian family itself, an evolution leading up to a crisis, and we are witnessing now the first chaotic stages of the process.

The deeply destructive influence of the war on the family is well known. To begin with, war dissolves the family automatically, separating people for a long time or bringing people together by chance. This influence of the war was continued and strengthened by the revolution. The years of the war shattered all that had stood only by the inertia of historic tradition. They shattered the power of czardom, class privileges, the old traditional family. The revolution began by building up the new state and has achieved thereby its simplest and most urgent aim.

The economic part of its problem proved much more complicated. The war shook the old economic order; the revolution overthrew it. Now we are constructing a new economic state—doing it as yet mostly from the old elements, reorganizing them in new ways. In the domain of economics we have but recently emerged from the destructive period and begun to ascend. Our progress is still very slow, and the achievement of new socialistic forms of economic life are still very distant. But we are definitely out of the period of destruction and ruin. The lowest point was reached in the years 1920-21.

The first destructive period is still far from being over in the life of the family. The disintegrating process is still in full swing. We must bear that in mind. Family and domestic life are still passing, so to speak, their 1920-21 period and have not reached the 1923 standard. Domestic life is more conservative than economic, and one of the reasons is that it is still less conscious than the latter. In politics and economics the working class acts as a whole and pushes on to the front rank its vanguard, the Communist Party, accomplishing through its medium the historic aims of the proletariat. In domestic life the working class is split into cells constituted by families. The change of political regime, the change even of the economic order of the state—the passing of the factories and mills into the hands of the workers—all this has certainly had some influence on family conditions, but only indirectly and externally, and without touching on the forms of domestic traditions inherited from the past.

A radical reform of the family and, more generally, of the whole order of domestic life requires a great conscious effort on the part of the whole mass of the working class, and presumes the existence in the class itself of a powerful molecular force of inner desire for culture and progress. A deep-going plough is needed to turn up heavy clods of soil. To institute the political equality of men and women in the Soviet state was one problem and the simplest. A much more difficult one was the next—that of instituting the industrial equality of men and women workers in the factories, the mills, and the trade unions, and of doing it in such a way that the men should not put the women to disadvantage. But to achieve the actual equality of man and woman within the family is an infinitely more arduous problem. All our domestic habits must be revolutionized before that can happen. And yet it is quite obvious that unless there is actual equality of husband and wife in the family, in a normal sense as well as in the conditions of life, we cannot speak seriously of their equality in social work or even in politics. As long as woman is chained to her housework, the care of the family, the cooking and sewing, all her chances of participation in social and political life are cut down in the extreme.

The easiest problem was that of assuming power. Yet just that problem alone absorbed all our forces in the early period of the revolution. It demanded endless sacrifices. The civil war necessitated measures of the utmost severity. Philistine vulgarians cried out about the barbarization of morality, about the proletariat becoming bloody and depraved, and so on. What was actually happening was that the proletariat, using the means of revolutionary violence forced into its hands, started to fight for a new culture, for genuine human values.

In the first four or five years we have passed economically through a period of terrific breakdown. The productivity of labor collapsed, and the products were of an appallingly low quality. Enemies saw, or chose to see, in such a situation a sign of the rottenness of the Soviet regime. In reality, however, it was but the inevitable stage of the destruction of the old economic forms and of the first unaided attempts at the creation of new ones.

In regard to family relations and forms of individual life in general, there must also be an inevitable period of disintegration of things as they were, of the traditions, inherited from the past, which had not passed under the control of thought. But in this domain of domestic life the period of criticism and destruction begins later, lasts very long, and assumes morbid and painful forms, which, however, are complex and not always perceptible to superficial observation. These progressive landmarks of critical change in state conditions, in economics and life in general, ought to be very clearly defined to prevent our getting alarmed by the phenomena we observed. We must learn to judge them in their right light, to understand their proper place in the development of the working class, and consciously to direct the new conditions towards socialist forms of life.

The warning is a necessary one, as we already hear voices expressing alarm. At the conference of the Moscow party propagandists some comrades spoke with great and natural anxiety of the ease with which old family ties are broken for the sake of new ones as fleeting as the old. The victims in all cases are the mother and children. On the other hand, who in our midst has not heard in private conversations complaints, not to say lamentations, about the "collapse" of morality among Soviet youth, in particular among Young Communists? Not everything in these complaints is exaggeration—there is also truth in them. We certainly must and will fight the dark sides of this truth—this being a fight for higher culture and the ascent of human personality. But in order to begin our work, to tackle the ABC of the problem without reactionary moralizing or sentimental downheartedness, we must first make sure of the facts and begin to see clearly what is actually happening.

Gigantic events, as we said above, have descended on the family in its old shape, the war and the revolution. And following them came creeping slowly the underground mole—critical thought, the conscious study and evaluation of family relations and the forms of life. It was the mechanical force of great events combined with the critical force of the awakened mind that generated the destructive period in family relations that we are witnessing now. The Russian worker must now, after the conquest of power, make his first conscious steps towards culture in many departments of his life. Under the impulse of great collisions, his personality shakes off for the first time all traditional forms of life, all domestic habits, church practices, and relationships.

No wonder that, in the beginning, the protest of the individual, his revolt against the traditional past, is assuming anarchic, or to put it more crudely, dissolute forms. We have witnessed it in politics, in military affairs, in economics; here anarchic individualism took on every form of extremism, partisanship, public-meeting rhetoric. And no wonder also that this process reacts in the most intimate and hence most painful way on family relationships. There the awakened personality, wanting to reorganize in a new way, removed from the old beaten tracks, resorts to "dissipation," "wickedness," and all the sins denounced in the Moscow conference.

The husband, torn away from his usual surroundings by mobilization, changed into a revolutionary citizen at the civic front. A momentous change. His outlook is wider, his spiritual aspirations higher and of a more complicated order. He is a different man. And then he returns to find everything there practically unchanged. The old harmony and understanding with the people at home in family relationship is gone. No new understanding arises. The mutual wondering changes into mutual discontent, then into ill will. The family is broken up.

The husband is a communist. He lives an active life, is engaged in social work, his mind grows, his personal life is absorbed by his work. But his wife is also a communist. She wants to join in social work, attend public meetings, work in the soviet or the union. Home life becomes practically nonexistent before they are aware of it, or the missing of home atmosphere results in continual collisions. Husband and wife disagree. The family is broken up.

The husband is a communist, the wife is nonparty. The husband is absorbed by his work; the wife, as before, only looks after her home. Relations are "peaceful," based, in fact, on customary estrangement. But the husband's committee—the communist "cell"—decrees that he should take away the icons hanging in his house. He is quite willing to obey, finding it but natural. For his wife it is a catastrophe. Just such a small occurrence exposes the abyss that separates the minds of husband and wife. Relations are spoiled. The family is broken up.

An old family. Ten to fifteen years of common life. The husband is a good worker, devoted to his family; the wife lives also for her home, giving it all her energy. But just by chance she comes in touch with a communist women's organization. A new world opens before her eyes. Her energy finds a new and wider object. The family is neglected. The husband is irritated. The wife is hurt in her newly awakened civic consciousness. The family is broken up.

Examples of such domestic tragedies, all leading to one end—the breaking up of the family—could be multiplied endlessly. We have indicated the most typical cases. In all our examples the tragedy is due to a collision between communist and nonparty elements. But the breaking up of the family, that is to say, of the old-type family, is not confined to just the top of the class as the one most exposed to the influence of new conditions. The disintegrating movement in family relationships penetrates deeper. The communist vanguard merely passes sooner and more violently through what is inevitable for the class as a whole. The censorious attitude towards old conditions, the new claims upon the family, extend far beyond the border line between the communist and the working class as a whole.

The institution of civil marriage was already a heavy blow to the traditional consecrated family which lived a great deal for appearances. The less personal attachment there was in the old marriage ties, the greater was the binding power of the external forces, social traditions, and more particularly religious rites. The blow to the power of the church was also a blow to the family. Rites, deprived of binding significance and of state recognition, still remain in use through inertia, serving as one of the props to the tottering family. But when there is no inner bond within the family, when nothing but inertia keeps the family itself from complete collapse, then every push from outside is likely to shatter it to pieces, while, at the same time, it is a blow at the adherence to church rites. And pushes from the outside are infinitely more likely to come now than ever before. That is the reason why the family totters and fails to recover and then tumbles again. Life sits in judgment on its conditions and does it by the cruel and painful condemnation of the family. History fells the old wood—and the chips fly in the wind.

But is life evolving any elements of a new type of family? Undoubtedly. We must only conceive clearly the nature of these elements and the process of their formation. As in other cases, we must separate the physical conditions from the psychological, the general from the individual. Psychologically the evolution of the new family, of new human relationships in general, for us means the advancement in culture of the working class, the development of the individual, a raising of the standard of his requirements and inner discipline. From this aspect, the revolution in itself has meant, of course, a big step forward, and the worst phenomena of the disintegrating family signify merely an expression, painful in form, of the awakening of the class and of the individual within the class. All our work relating to culture, the work we are doing and the work we ought to be doing, becomes, from this viewpoint, a preparation for new relationships and a new family. Without a raising of the standard of the culture of the individual working man and woman, there cannot be a new, higher type of family, for in this domain we can only, of course, speak of inner discipline and not of external compulsion. The force then of the inner discipline of the individual in the family is conditioned by the tenor of the inner life, the scope and value of the ties that unite husband and wife.

The physical preparations for the conditions of the new life and the new family, again, cannot fundamentally be separated from the general work of socialist construction. The workers' state must become wealthier in order that it may be possible seriously to tackle the public education of children and the releasing of the family from the burden of the kitchen and the laundry. Socialization of family housekeeping and public education of children are unthinkable without a marked improvement in our economics as a whole. We need more socialist economic forms. Only under such conditions can we free the family from the functions and cares that now oppress and disintegrate it. Washing must be done by a public laundry, catering by a public restaurant, sewing by a public workshop. Children must be educated by good public teachers who have a real vocation for the work. Then the bond between husband and wife would be freed from everything external and accidental, and the one would cease to absorb the life of the other. Genuine equality would at last be established. The bond will depend on mutual attachment. And on that account particularly, it will acquire inner stability, not the same, of course, for everyone, but compulsory for no one.

Thus, the way to the new family is twofold: (a) the raising of the standard of culture and education of the working class and the individuals composing the class; (b) an improvement in the material conditions of the class organized by the state. The two processes are intimately connected with one another.

The above statements do not, of course, imply that at a given moment in material betterment the family of the future will instantly step into its rights. No. A certain advance towards the new family is possible even now. It is true that the state cannot as yet undertake either the education of children or the establishment of public kitchens that would be an improvement on the family kitchen, or the establishment of public laundries where the clothes would not be torn or stolen. But this does not mean that the more enterprising and progressive families cannot group themselves even now into collective housekeeping units. Experiments of this kind must, of course, be made carefully; the technical equipment of the collective unit must answer to the interests and requirements of the group itself, and should give manifest advantages to every one of its members, even though they be modest at first.

"This task," Comrade Semashko [10] recently wrote of the necessity of reconstructing our family life,

> is best performed practically; decrees and moralizing alone will have little effect. But an example, an illustration of a new form, will do more than a thousand excellent pamphlets. This practical propaganda is best conducted on the method surgeons in their practice call transplantation. When a big surface is bare of skin either as the result of wound or burn, and there is no hope that the skin will grow sufficiently to cover it, pieces of skin are cut off from healthy places of the body and attached in islets on the bare surface; these islets adhere and grow until the whole surface is covered with skin.
>
> The same thing happens in practical propaganda. When one factory or works adopts communist forms, other factories will follow. [N. Semashko, "The Dead Holds on to the Living," *Izvestia*, no. 81, April 14, 1923]

The experience of such collective family housekeeping units representing the first, still very incomplete approximations to a communist way of life, should be carefully studied and given attentive thought. The combination of private initiative with support by the state power—above all, by the local soviets and economic bodies—should have priority. The building of new houses—and, after all, we are going to build houses!—must be regulated by the requirements of the family group communities. The first apparent and indisputable success in this direction, however slight and limited in extent, will inevitably arouse a desire in more widespread groups to organize their life on similar lines. For a thought-out scheme, initiated from above, the time is not yet ripe, either from the point of view of the material resources of the state or from that of the preparation of the proletariat itself. We can escape the deadlock at present only by the creation of model communities. The ground beneath our feet must be strengthened step by step; there must be no rushing too far ahead or lapsing into bureaucratic fanciful experiments. At a given moment, the state will be able, with the help of local soviets, cooperative units, and so on, to socialize the work done, to widen and deepen it. In this way the human family, in the words of Engels, will "jump from the realm of necessity to the realm of freedom."

The family and ceremony

[PUBLISHED JULY 14, 1923]
Church ceremonial enslaves even the worker of little or no religious belief in the three great moments of the life of man—birth, marriage, and death. The workers' state has rejected church ceremony, and informed its citizens that they have the right to be born, to marry, and to die without the mysterious gestures and exhortations of persons clad in cassocks, gowns, and other ecclesiastical vestments. But custom finds it harder to discard ceremony than the state. The life of the working family is too monotonous, and it is this monotony that wears out the nervous system. Hence comes the desire for alcohol—a small flask containing a whole world of images. Hence comes the need for the church and her ritual. How is a marriage to be celebrated, or the birth of a child in the family? How is one to pay the tribute of affection to the beloved dead? It is on this need of marking

From Pravda, *July 14, 1923.*

and decorating the principal signposts along the road of life that church ritual depends.

What can we set against it? Superstition, which lies at the root of ritual, must, of course, be opposed by rationalistic criticism, by an atheistic, realistic attitude to nature and her forces. But this question of a scientific, critical propaganda does not exhaust the subject; in the first place it appeals only to a minority, while even this minority feels the need of enriching, improving, and ennobling its individual life; at any rate, the more salient events of it.

The workers' state already has its festivals, processions, reviews, and parades, symbolic spectacles—the new theatrical ceremonies of state. It is true that in the main they are too closely allied to the old forms, which they imitate and perpetuate. But on the whole, the revolutionary symbolism of the workers' state is novel, distinct, and forcible—the red flag, red star, worker, peasant, comrade, International. But within the shut cages of family life the new has not penetrated, or at least, has done so but little, while individual life is closely bound up with the family. This explains why in the matter of icons, christenings, church funerals, etc., the balance is in favor of custom. The revolutionary members of the family have nothing to offer in place of them. Theoretical arguments act on the mind only. Spectacular ceremony acts on the senses and imagination. The influence of the latter, consequently, is much more widespread. In the most communist of circles a need has arisen to oppose old practices by new forms, new symbols, not merely in the domain of state life, where this has largely been done, but in the domain of the family.

There is a tendency among workers to celebrate the birthday instead of the patron saint's day, and to name newborn infants by some name symbolizing new and intimate events and ideas, rather than by the name of a saint. At the deliberations of the Moscow propagandists I first learned that the novel girl's name of Octobrina has come to be associated with the right of citizenship.

There is the name Ninel (Lenin spelled backwards) and Rem (Revolution, Electrification, *Mir*—peace). Infants, too, are given the Christian name of Vladimir, Ilyich, and even Lenin, also Rosa (in honor of Rosa Luxemburg) and so on, showing a desire to link up with the revolution.

There have been cases where the birth of a child has been celebrated by a mock ceremonial "inspection" with the participation of fabzavkom, with a special protocol decree adding the infant's name to the list of RSFSR citizens.[11] This was followed by a feast. In a working family the apprenticeship of a boy is also celebrated as a festival. It is an event of real importance, bearing as it does on the choice of a trade, a course of life. This is a fitting occasion for the intervention of the trade union. On the whole, the trade unions ought to play a more important part in the creation of the forms of the new life. The guilds of the Middle Ages were powerful, because they hemmed in the life of the apprentice, laborer, and mechanic on all sides. They greeted the child on the day of its birth, led it to the school door, and to church when it married, and buried it when it had fulfilled the duties of its calling. The guilds were not merely trade federations; they were the organized life of the community. It is on these lines that our industrial unions are largely developing, with this difference, certainly, that in opposition to the medieval, the forms of the new life will be free from the church and her superstition and imbued with an aspiration to utilize every conquest of science and machinery for the enrichment and beautifying of life.

Marriage, if you like, more easily dispenses with ceremonial. Though, even in this respect, how many "misunderstandings" and exclusions from the party have there been on account of church weddings? Custom refuses to be reconciled to the mere marriage, unbeautified by a spectacular ceremony.

The question of burial is an infinitely more difficult one. To be laid in the ground without the due funeral service is as unusual, disgraceful, and monstrous as to grow up without baptism. In cases where the standing of the dead has called for a funeral of a political character, the stage has been set for the new spectacular ceremony, imbued with the symbolism of the revolution—the red flag, the revolutionary funeral march, the farewell rifle salute. Some of the members of the Moscow conference emphasized the need for a speedy adoption of cremation, proposing to set an example by cremating the bodies of prominent revolutionary workers. They justly regarded this as a powerful weapon to be used for anti-church and anti-religious propaganda. But cremation, which it is high time we adopted, does not mean giving up processions, speechmaking, marches, the rifle salute. The need for an outer manifestation of emotion is strong and legitimate. If the spectacular has in the past been closely connected with the church, there is no reason, as we have already said, why it cannot be separated from her. The theater separated earlier from the church than the church from the state. In early days the church fought very much against the "worldly" theater, fully realizing that it was a dangerous rival in the matter of spectacular sights. The theater died except as a special spectacle shut within four walls. But daily custom, which used the spectacular form, was instrumental in preserving the church. The church had other rivals in this respect, in the form of secret societies like the freemasons. But they were permeated through and through with a worldly priesthood. The creation of the revolutionary "ceremonial" of custom (we use the word "ceremonial" for want of a better), and setting it against the "ceremonial" of the church, is possible not only on public or state occasions, but in the relationships of family life. Even now a band playing a funeral march competes successfully with the church funeral music. And we must, of course, make an ally of the band in the struggle against church ritual, which is based on a slavish belief in another world, where you will be repaid a hundredfold for the miseries and evils of this. A still more powerful ally is the cinema.

The creation of new forms of life and new spectacular customs will move apace with the spread of education and the growth of economic security. We have every cause to watch this process with the utmost care. There cannot, of course, be any question of compulsion from above, i.e., the bureaucratizing of newborn customs. It is only by the creativity of the general masses of the population, assisted by creative imagination and artistic initiative, that we can, in the course of years and decades come out on the road of spiritualized, ennobled forms of life. Without regulating this creative process, we must, nevertheless, help it in every way. For this purpose, first of all, the tendency to blindness must give place to sight. We must carefully watch all that happens in the working family in this respect, and the Soviet family in general. Every new form, whether abortive or a mere approach to one, must be recorded in the press and brought to the knowledge of the general public, in order to stimulate imagination and interest, and give the impulse to further collective creation of new customs.

The Communist League of Youth has an honorable place in this work. Not every invention is successful, not every project takes on. What does it matter? The proper choice will come in due course. The new life will adopt the forms most after its own heart. As a result life will be richer, broader, more full of color and harmony. This is the essence of the problem.

Civility and politeness
as a necessary lubricant
in daily relations

During the many discussions on the question of our state machinery, Comrade Kiselev, the president of the Subsidiary Council of People's Commissars, brought forward, or at least recalled to mind, one side of the question that is of vast importance. In what manner does the machinery of the state come in direct contact with the population? How does it "deal" with the population? How does it treat a caller, a person with a grievance, the "petitioner" of old? How does it regard the individual? How does it address him, if it addresses him at all? This, too, is an important component part of "life."

In this matter, however, we must discriminate between two aspects—form and substance.

In all civilized democratic countries the bureaucracy, of course, "serves" the people. This does not prevent it from raising itself above the people as a closely united professional caste. If it actually serves the capitalist magnates, that is, cringes before them, it treats the workman and peasant arrogantly, whether it be in France, Switzerland, or America. But in the civilized "democracies" the fact is clothed in certain forms of civility and politeness, in greater or lesser degree in the different countries. But when necessary (and such occasions occur daily) the cloak of civility is easily thrust aside by the policeman's fist; strikers are beaten in police stations in Paris, New York, and other centers of the world. In the main, however, "democratic" civility in the relations of the bureaucracy with the population is a product and a heritage of bourgeois revolutions. The exploitation of man by man has remained, but the form of it is different, less "brutal," adorned with the cloak of equality and polished politeness.

Our Soviet bureaucratic machine is unique, complex, containing as it does the traditions of different epochs together with the germs of future relationships. With us, civility, as a general rule, does not exist. But of rudeness, inherited from the past, we have as much as you please. But our rudeness itself is not homogeneous. There is the simple rudeness of peasant origin, which is unattractive, certainly, but not degrading. It becomes unbearable and objectively reactionary only when our young novelists boast of it as of some extremely "artistic" acquisition. The foremost elements of the workers regard such false simplicity with instinctive hostility, for they justly see in the coarseness of speech and conduct a mark of the old slavery, and aspire to acquire a cultured speech with its inner discipline. But this is beside the point. . . .

Side by side with this simple kind, the habitual passive rudeness of the peasant, we have another, a special kind—the revolutionary—a rudeness of the leaders, due to impatience, to an over-ardent desire to better things, to the irritation caused by our indifference, to a creditable nervous tension.

This rudeness, too, if taken by itself, is, of course, not attractive, and we dissociate ourselves from it; but at bottom, it is often nourished at the same revolutionary moral fount, which, on more than one occasion in these years, has been able to move mountains. In this case what must be changed is not the substance, which is on the whole healthy, creative, and progressive, but the distorted form. . . .

We still have, however—and herein is the chief stumbling block—the rudeness of the old aristocracy, with the touch of feudalism about it. This kind is vile and vicious throughout. It is still with us, uneradicated, and is not easy to eradicate.

In the Moscow departments, especially in the more important of them, this aristocratic rudeness is not manifested in the aggressive form of shouting and shaking a fist at a petitioner's nose; it is more often shown in a heartless formality. Of course, the latter is not the only cause of "red tape"; a very vital one is the complete indifference to the living human being and his living work. If we could take an impression on a sensitive plate of the manners, replies, explanations, orders, and signatures of all the cells of the bureaucratic organism, be it only in Moscow for a single day, the result obtained would be one of extraordinary confusion. And it is worse in the provinces, particularly along the borderline where town and country meet, the borderline that is most vital of all.

"Red tape" is a complex, by no means homogeneous phenomenon; it is rather a conglomeration of phenomena and processes of different historical origins. The principles that maintain and nourish "red tape" are also varied. Foremost among them is the condition of our culture—the backwardness and illiteracy of a large proportion of our population. The general muddle resulting from a state machinery in continuous process of reconstruction, inevitable during a period of revolution, is in itself the cause of much superfluous friction, which plays an important part in the manufacture of "red tape." It is the heterogeneity of class in the Soviet machine—the admixture of aristocratic, bourgeois, and Soviet tradition—that is responsible for the more repulsive of its forms.

Consequently the struggle against "red tape" cannot but have a diversified character. At bottom there is the struggle against the low conditions of culture, illiteracy, dirt, and poverty. The technical improvement of the machine, the decrease of staffs, the introduction of greater order, thoroughness, and accuracy in the work, and other measures of a similar nature, do not, of course, exhaust the historic problem, but they help to weaken the more negative sides of "red tape." Great importance is attached to the education of a new type of Soviet bureaucrat—the new "spets" [specialists]. But in this also we must not deceive ourselves. The difficulties of educating thousands of new workers in the new ways, i.e., in the spirit of service, simplicity, and humanity, under transitional conditions and with preceptors inherited from the past, are great. They are great, but not insuperable. They cannot be overcome at once, but only gradually, by the appearance of a more and more improved "edition" of Soviet youth.

The measures enumerated will take comparatively long years of accomplishment, but they by no means exclude an immediate remorseless struggle against "red tape," against the official contempt for the living human being and his affairs, the truly corrupting nihilism which conceals a dead indifference to everything on earth, a cowardly helplessness which refuses to acknowledge its own dependence, a conscious sabotage, or the instinctive hatred of a deposed aristocracy towards the class that deposed it. These are the main causes of rudeness which await the application of the revolutionary lever.

We must attain a condition in which the average colorless individual of the working masses will cease to fear the government departments he has to come in contact with. The greater his helplessness, i.e., the greater his ignorance and illiteracy, the greater attention should be accorded him. It is an essential principle that he should really be helped and not merely be got rid of. For this purpose, in addition to other measures, it is essential that our Soviet public opinion should keep the matter constantly in the foreground, regarding it from as broad an angle as possible, particularly the real Soviet, revolutionary, communist, sensitive elements of the state machine of which, happily, there are many: for they are the ones who maintain it and move it forward.

The press can play a decisive part in this respect.

Unfortunately, our newspapers in general give but little instructive matter relating to everyday life. If such matter is given at all it is often in stereotyped reports, such as "We have a works called so and so. At the works there is a works committee and a director. The works committee does so and so, the director directs." While at the same time our actual life is full of color and rich in instructive episodes, particularly along the borderline where the machinery of the state comes in contact with the masses of the population. You have only to roll up your sleeves. . . .

Of course, an illuminating, instructive task of this kind must guard itself sevenfold against intrigue, must cleanse itself of cant and every form of demagogy.

An exemplary "calendar program" would be to single out a hundred civil servants—single them out thoroughly and impartially—a hundred who showed a rooted contempt in their duties for the working masses, and publicly, perhaps by trial, chuck them out of the state machine, so that they could never come back again. It would be a good beginning. Miracles must not be expected to happen as a result. But a small change from the old to the new is a practical step in advance, which is of greater value than the biggest talk.

The struggle for cultured speech

MAY 15, 1923
I read lately in one of our papers that at a general meeting of
the workers at the "Paris Commune" shoe factory, a resolution was carried to abstain from swearing, to impose fines
for bad language, etc.

This is a small incident in the turmoil of the present day—
but a very telling small incident. Its importance, however,
depends on the response the initiative of the shoe factory is
going to meet with in the working class.

Abusive language and swearing are a legacy of slavery,
humiliation, and disrespect for human dignity—one's own
and that of other people. This is particularly the case with
swearing in Russia. I should like to hear from our philolo-
gists, our linguists and experts in folklore, whether they
know of such loose, sticky, and low terms of abuse in any
other language than Russian. As far as I know, there is noth-

From Pravda, May 16, 1923.

ing, or nearly nothing, of the kind outside Russia. Russian swearing in "the lower depths" was the result of despair, embitterment and, above all, slavery without hope, without escape. The swearing of the upper classes, on the other hand, the swearing that came out of the throats of the gentry, the authorities, was the outcome of class rule, slaveowner's pride, unshakable power. Proverbs are supposed to contain the wisdom of the masses—Russian proverbs show besides the ignorant and the superstitious mind of the masses and their slavishness. "Abuse does not stick to the collar," says an old Russian proverb, not only accepting slavery as a fact, but submitting to the humiliation of it. Two streams of Russian abuse—that of the masters, the officials, the police, replete and fatty, and the other, the hungry, desperate, tormented swearing of the masses—have colored the whole of Russian life with despicable patterns of abusive terms. Such was the legacy the revolution received among others from the past.

But the revolution is in the first place an awakening of human personality in the masses—who were supposed to possess no personality. In spite of occasional cruelty and the sanguinary relentlessness of its methods, the revolution is, before and above all, the awakening of humanity, its onward march, and is marked with a growing respect for the personal dignity of every individual, with an ever-increasing concern for those who are weak. A revolution does not deserve its name if, with all its might and all the means at its disposal, it does not help the woman—twofold and threefold enslaved as she has been in the past—to get out on the road of individual and social progress. A revolution does not deserve its name, if it does not take the greatest care possible of the children—the future race for whose benefit the revolution has been made. And how could one create day by day, if only by little bits, a new life based on mutual consideration, on self-respect, on the real equality of women, looked upon as fellow workers, on the efficient care of the children—in an atmosphere poisoned with the roaring, rolling, ringing, and resounding swearing of masters and slaves, that swearing which spares no one and stops at nothing? The struggle against "bad language" is a condition of intellectual culture, just as the fight against filth and vermin is a condition of physical culture.

To do away radically with abusive speech is not an easy thing, considering that unrestrained speech has psychological roots and is an outcome of uncultured surroundings. We certainly welcome the initiative of the shoe factory, and above all we wish the promoters of the new movement much perseverance. Psychological habits which come down from generation to generation and saturate the whole atmosphere of life are very tenacious, and on the other hand it often happens with us in Russia that we just make a violent rush forward, strain our forces, and then let things drift in the old way.

Let us hope that the working women—those of the Communist ranks, in the first place—will support the initiative of the "Paris Commune" factory. As a rule—which has exceptions, of course—men who use bad language scorn women, and have no regard for children. This does not apply only to the uncultured masses, but also to the advanced and even the so-called responsible elements of the present social order. There is no denying that the old prerevolutionary forms of language are still in use at the present time, six years after October, and are quite the fashion at the "top." When away from town, particularly from Moscow, our dignitaries consider it in a way their duty to use strong language. They evidently think it a means of getting into closer contact with the peasantry.

Our life in Russia is made up of the most striking contrasts—in economics as well as in everything else. In the very center of the country, close to Moscow, there are miles of swamps, of impassable roads—and close by you might suddenly see a factory which would impress a European or American engineer by its technical equipment. Similar contrasts abound in our national life. Side by side with some old-fashioned type of domineering rapacious profiteer, who has come to life again in the present generation, who has passed through revolution and expropriation, engaged in swindling and in masked and legalized profiteering, preserving intact all the while his suburban vulgarity and greediness—we see the best type of communists of the working class who devote their lives day by day to the interests of the world's proletariat, and are ready to fight at any given moment for the cause of the revolution in any country, even one they would be unable perhaps to locate on the map.

In addition to such social contrasts—obtuse bestiality and the highest revolutionary idealism—we often witness psychological contrasts in the same mind. A man is a sound communist devoted to the cause, but women are for him just "females," not to be taken seriously in any way. Or it happens that an otherwise reliable communist, when discussing nationalistic matters, starts talking hopelessly reactionary stuff. To account for that we must remember that different parts of the human consciousness do not change and develop simultaneously and on parallel lines. There is a certain economy in the process. Human psychology is very conservative by nature, and the change due to the demands and the push of life affects in the first place those parts of the mind which are directly concerned in the case.

In Russia the social and political development of the last decades proceeded in quite an unusual way, in astounding leaps and bounds, and this accounts for our present disorganization and muddle, which is not confined only to economics and politics. The same defects show in the minds of many people, resulting in a rather curious blending of advanced, well-pondered political views with moods, habits, and to some extent ideas that are a direct legacy from ancestral domestic laws. The correct formula for education and self-education in general, and above all for our party, beginning at the top, should be to straighten out the ideological front, that is, to rework all the areas of consciousness, using the Marxist method. But there again the problem is extremely complicated and could not be solved by school-teaching and books alone: the roots of contradictions and psychological inconsistencies lie in the disorganization and muddle of the conditions in which people live. Psychology, after all, is determined by life. But the dependency is not purely mechanical and automatic: it is active and reciprocal. The problem in consequence must be approached in many different ways—that of the "Paris Commune" factory men is one of them. Let us wish them all possible success.

The fight against bad language is also a part of a struggle for the purity, clearness, and beauty of Russian speech.

Reactionary blockheads maintain that the revolution, if it hasn't altogether ruined it, is in the process of spoiling the Russian language. There is actually an enormous quantity of words in use now that have originated by chance, many of them perfectly needless, provincial expressions, some contrary to the spirit of our language. And yet the reactionary blockheads are quite mistaken about the future of the Russian language—as about all the rest. Out of the revolutionary turmoil our language will come strengthened, rejuvenated, with an increased flexibility and delicacy. Our prerevolutionary, obviously ossified bureaucratic and liberal press language is already considerably enriched by new descriptive forms, by new, much more precise and dynamic expressions. But during all these stormy years our language has certainly become greatly obstructed, and part of our progress in culture will show, among other things, in our casting out of our speech all useless words and expressions, and those which are not in keeping with the spirit of the language, while preserving the unquestionable and invaluable linguistic acquisitions of the revolutionary epoch.

Language is the instrument of thought. Precision and correctness of speech are indispensable conditions of correct and precise thinking. In our country, the working class has come to power for the first time in history. The working class possesses a rich store of work and life experience and a language based on that experience. But our proletariat has not had sufficient schooling in elementary reading and writing, not to speak of literary education. And this is the reason that the now governing working class, which is in itself and by its social nature a powerful safeguard of the integrity and greatness of the Russian language in the future, does not, nevertheless, stand up now with the necessary energy against the intrusion of needless, corrupt, and sometimes hideous new words and expressions.

When people say, "a pair of weeks," "a pair of months" (instead of several weeks, several months), this is stupid and ugly. Instead of enriching the language it impoverishes it: the word "pair" loses in the process its real meaning (in the sense of "a pair of shoes"). Faulty words and expressions have come into use because of the intrusion of mispronounced foreign words. Proletarian speakers, even those who should know better, say, for instance, "incindent" instead of "incident," or they say "instict" instead of "instinct" or "legularly" instead of "regularly." Such misspellings were not infrequent also in the past, before the revolution. But now they seem to acquire a sort of right of citizenship.

No one corrects such defective expressions out of a sort of false pride. That is wrong. The struggle for education and culture will provide the advanced elements of the working class with all the resources of the Russian language in its extreme richness, subtlety and refinement. To preserve the greatness of the language, all faulty words and expressions must be weeded out of daily speech. Speech is also in need of hygiene. And the working class needs a healthy language not less but rather more than the other classes: for the first time in history it begins to think independently about nature, about life, and its foundations—and to do the thinking it needs the instrument of a clear incisive language.

Against bureaucracy,
progressive and unprogressive

AUGUST 6, 1923

I have to speak again, probably not for the last time, about the problems of life of the working class. My object is to defend the increasing and to my mind most valuable interest of the masses in these problems against the attacks of more bureaucratic than progressive critics.

Progressive bureaucracy disapproves of all discussions on problems of life in the press, at meetings, and in clubs. What is the use, they say, of wasting time in discussions? Let the authorities start running communal kitchens, nurseries, laundries, hostels, etc. Bureaucratic dullards usually add (or rather imply, or say in whispers—they prefer that to open speech): "It is all words, and nothing more." The bureaucrat hopes (I wonder whether he has some brilliant financial

From Pravda, *August 14, 1923. Half of this article was omitted from the 1924 edition of* Problems of Life. *It has been translated for this volume from the Russian by Marilyn Vogt.*

plan handy) that when we get rich, we shall, without further words, present the proletariat with cultured conditions of life as with a sort of birthday gift.

It is curious that comrades speaking out against such rigid mechanical responses on one occasion are guilty of the same offense in reverse. This happened in the case of Comrade Vinogradskaya, when she responded in *Pravda*, no. 164, to my article about everyday life. The author attacks the "leadership"—the inert Soviet bureaucracy—with the arguments of the enlightened bureaucracy. It is necessary to dwell for a moment on Vinogradskaya's article, because her mistakes bring grist to the mill of that same inert sector against which the article is aiming its fire. The respectable and responsible "millers" of inertness could not wish for a better critic.

Vinogradskaya's general argument is the following:

1) Our task is not to hold our ways of life up to the light, since "as we know (?) our way of life in general is still about nine-tenths the same as it was during the time of our ancestors"; but rather the task is to change everyday life by appropriate measures on the part of the authorities.

2) It is impossible to demand of novelists that they reproduce life in their works "inasmuch as our way of life is still in the process of becoming, i.e., everything is in motion, full of contradictions, motley, and heterogeneous."

3) And this [demand] would be uncalled for anyway: "For our party, the corresponding problems were theoretically and programmatically resolved long ago. As far as the proletarian masses are concerned, there is no need to agitate among them. The organization of the labor process itself will create a spirit of comradeship and a sense of community among the workers."

4) The whole trouble is that "we" know perfectly well what must be done but we are not doing it because of the inertia of the Soviet organs and their leaders.

5) But it is necessary to reorganize daily habits and customs as quickly as possible. Otherwise NEP will overwhelm us: "The petty-bourgeois and bureaucratic way of life will promote the internal degeneration of the ruling class and its party."

The theses of the article as we can see are in clear contradiction to one another. First, we find out that it is not necessary to have conscious knowledge of everyday habits and customs since *nine-tenths* of them are the same as in the time of our ancestors. Then they tell us that we can't demand a portrayal of life from our novelists since "everything is in motion, full of contradictions, motley, and heterogeneous." And, finally, at the last moment we find out that NEP threatens to instill in the working class a petty-bourgeois way of life, i.e., that same way of life that already holds sway over "nine-tenths" of our present daily life.

The author of the article is thinking too schematically, and hence falls into these contradictions. The material foundations inherited from the past are part of our way of life, but so is a new psychological attitude. The culinary-domestic aspect of things is part of the concept of the family, but so are the mutual relationships between husband, wife, and child as they are taking shape in the circumstances of Soviet society—with new tasks, goals, rights, and obligations for the husbands and children.

The whole problem lies in the contradiction between the basis that everyday life has in material production and the new tasks, needs, and functions which have also become a part of everyday life and play a huge role, at least for the proletarian vanguard. The object of acquiring conscious knowledge of everyday life is precisely so as to be able to disclose graphically, concretely, and cogently before the eyes of the working masses themselves the contradictions between the outgrown material shell of the way of life and the new relationships and needs which have arisen.

But "we" know this perfectly well, Comrade Vinogradskaya repeats several times. For us these problems were solved "theoretically and programmatically" long ago. And is anyone proposing that we change our theoretical and programmatic resolution on this question? No, we must help the masses through their vanguard elements to examine their way of life, to think about it critically, to *understand* the need for change and to firmly *want* to change. When they tell us there is no need to "agitate" among the working masses because the organization of the labor process itself creates a sense of community among them, we can only throw up our hands in despair. If the "sense of community" which is created by the organization of the labor process is enough to solve the problems of socialism, what is the Communist Party for anyway? The fact of the matter is that between the vague sense of community and the determination to consciously reconstruct the mode of life is an enormously long historical road. And it is on this very road that the activity of our party finds its place.

If "we" know all this perfectly well, if these problems have been theoretically and programmatically solved, if there is no need to agitate among the masses since the productive process will foster their sense of community, then why in the world is nine-tenths of our life still the same as it was for our ancestors?

Vinogradskaya's answer is extremely simple: "The inert, conservative 'leaders' of Soviet institutions *are to blame.*"

I am in no way inclined to come to their defense on this question. But why are Soviet institutions inert? Why were they *allowed* to be inert? They don't exist in a vacuum: there is the party; there are the trade unions. Finally, besides the "upper echelons," i.e., the central governing bodies, there are the local, city, and regional Soviets which are closely linked with the masses. Why is it that "we know what must be done but haven't taken even the first step forward?"

It is not true that "we" know all these problems perfectly well. How could we? These problems have never been subjected to analyses. From our program, perhaps? But the program was written in 1919 on the basis of general historical considerations and predictions. It did not and could not predict the characteristics of everyday life in 1923.

"But don't the workers themselves know their own mode of life?" one may object. That is like saying: "The workers themselves, even without Marx, knew they were being exploited." They knew it empirically but they needed to think over and draw theoretical conclusions about the fact of their exploitation. This holds true for their everyday life as well.

Has this work been done? Not to the slightest degree. I remember an extremely interesting remark by Comrade Osipov at a Moscow meeting:

> We communists don't know our own families. How can we talk about anyone else's? You leave early and come home late. You seldom see your wife and almost never see your children. And only now, when the problems of the family are posed as the subject of party discussion, do you begin to vaguely recollect, link, and tie together something or other about it in order to express an opinion.

I was quoting from memory.

Marx actually said once—and he said it rather well—that the world had been interpreted enough; it was finally time to change it. But Comrade Vinogradskaya, I believe, did not understand these words of Marx as an argument against "an idealistic interpretation" of problems of everyday life. Marx's idea, in fact, is that philosophical or programmatic solutions to problems of the universe—including "inert leaders"—are absolutely inadequate. The masses must take these problems into their own hands in their actual setting.

A critical idea, having captivated the inmost sensibilities of the masses, will become a revolutionary force which the inertia of the most inert leaders cannot withstand. A critical disclosure of the contradictions in everyday life is precisely what distinguished Marx's method.

"But is it not clear that we need to build community dining halls, laundries, and nurseries?" Vinogradskaya answers.

"But why have these not been built?" we ask.

Precisely because the vague sense of community which the working masses have is totally inadequate as a basis for the systematic reconstruction of the mode of life. The view that the whole problem is merely the dullness of the Soviet upper echelons is a bureaucratic view—although in reverse.

No government, even the most active and enterprising, can possibly transform life without the broadest initiative of the masses. The state can organize conditions of life down to the last cell of the community, the family, but unless these cells combine by their own choice and will into a commonwealth no serious and radical changes can possibly be achieved in economic conditions and home life.

The problem in our case does not amount *only* to the lack of new life institutions, such as communal kitchens, nurseries, houses run as communes. We know very well that many women have refused to give their children to be looked after in the nurseries. Nor would they do it now, hidebound as they are by inertia and prejudice against all innovations. Many houses which had been allotted to families living in communes got into filthy conditions and became uninhabitable. People living in them did not consider communistic housing as a beginning of new conditions—they looked upon their dwellings as upon barracks provided by the state. As a result of unpreparedness, hasty methods, lack of self-discipline, and want of culture, the communes very often have proved an utter failure. The problems of life require a thorough critical study, and well-pondered, careful methods are needed to deal with them. The onward march must have a well-secured rear in *an increased consciousness of home conditions and increased demands of cultured life on the part of the men and women of the working class—especially the women.*

Let me point to a few recent cases, which illustrate the relation between the initiative of the state and that of the masses in regard to the problems of life. At the present time, and thanks to the energy of Comrade Kerzhentsev,[12] a very important element of life—*punctuality*—has become an object of organized attention. Looking upon that problem from a bureaucratic point of view, one might say: "Why bother to discuss it at all? What is the use of carrying on propaganda, founding a league with badges for the members, etc? Let the authorities enforce punctuality by a decree and have penalties attached for infringements."

But such a decree exists already. About three years ago I had—with the strong support of Comrade Lenin—a regulation about punctual attendance at business meetings, committees, etc., passed and duly ratified by the party and the soviets. There were also, as usual, penalties attached for infringements of the decree. Some good *was* done by the regulation, but unfortunately not much. Very responsible workers continue up to the present time to be half an hour and more late for committee meetings. They honestly believe that it comes from having too many engagements but in reality their unpunctuality is due to carelessness and lack of regard for time—their own and other people's. A man who is always late because he is "frightfully busy," works as a rule less and less efficiently than another who comes on time wherever he is due. It is rather curious that during the debates about the "League of Time" people seemed simply to have forgotten that such a decree existed. I, on my part, have never seen it mentioned in the press. This shows how difficult it is to reform bad habits by legislation alone. The above-mentioned decree ought certainly to be rescued from oblivion, and used as a support of the "League of Time." But unless we are helped by the efforts of the advanced labor elements to achieve punctuality and efficiency, administrative measures will not accomplish much good. The "responsible" workers ought to be put into the limelight of public control—then perhaps they will be careful not to steal the time of hundreds and thousands of workers.

Take now another case. The "authorities" have been fighting for several years against bad printing, bad proofreading, bad stitching and folding of books and papers. Some improvement has been achieved, but not much. And these shortcomings in our printing and publishing are certainly not due to our technical deficiency. The fault is with the readers who are not sufficiently exacting, not sufficiently cultured. *Rabochaya Gazeta*—to take one instance out of many—is folded—who knows why?—across the width of the page, not the length. Before starting out to read, the reader has to refold the paper in the right way and to put the turned-in page in its right place. To do it all, say in a tramcar, is not an easy matter. No bourgeois publisher would dare to present a paper to his readers like that. *Rabochaya Moskva* is published with its eight pages uncut. Readers have to cut the pages with whatever happens to be there, usually with the band, tearing more often than not part of the text. The paper gets crumpled and into no condition to be passed on to another reader after being read by the first.

Why should such carelessness be tolerated? Progressive bureaucracy, of course, would put all the blame on the inertia of the publishers. Their inertia *is* bad. We fight against it—even using such weapons as resolutions of party conferences. But worse still is the passivity of the readers, their disregard for their own comfort—their lack of cultured habits. Had they just once or twice thumped with their fists (in some cultured way, I mean) on the publisher's table, he never would dare to issue his paper uncut. That is why even such minor matters as the cutting of the pages of a paper and the stitching of books should be carefully investigated and widely discussed in public. This is an educational means of raising the standard of culture of the masses.

And still more does this apply to the complicated net of inner relations in personal and family life. No one actually imagines that the Soviet government is going to create admirably furnished houses—communes provided with all sorts of comforts—and invite the proletariat to give up the places where they live now and to move into new conditions. Supposing even such a gigantic enterprise could have been effected (which, of course, is out of question)—that would not really help things. People cannot be made to move into new habits of life—they must grow into them gradually, as they grew into their old ways of living. Or they must deliberately and consciously create a new life—as they will do in the future. The reorganization of life can and should be started with the means already provided by the wages paid under our Soviet conditions. Whatever these wages are, housekeeping in common is more practical than for each family separately. One kitchen in a large room which has been made bigger at the expense of one or two rooms next to it, is a more profitable arrangement than five, not to speak of ten, separate kitchens.

But if changes are to be achieved by the initiative of the masses—with the support of the authorities—it is obvious that just a vague "sense of socialness" alone will not do it. There must be a clear understanding of things as they are and as they ought to be. We know how enormously the development of the working class has profited by the changes from individual to collective bargaining, and what detailed work had to be done by the trade unions, how carefully the matter and all the technical details had to be discussed and agreed upon at the endless delegates' and other meetings.

The change from the separate households to housekeeping in common for many families is much more complicated, and of a much greater importance. The old secluded type of family life has developed behind people's backs, whereas the new life on a communal basis cannot come into existence unless helped by conscious effort on the part of all who participate in the change. The first step towards a new order of things must, in consequence, be the showing-up of the contradiction between the new requirements of life and the old habits—a contradiction which becomes more and more unbearable.

This is what the revolutionary party has to do. The working class must become aware of the contradictions in its home life, must get at the core of the problem with full understanding, and when this is done, if only by the very advanced elements of the class, no inertia of Soviet bureaucrats will stand against the enlightened will of the proletariat.

Let me wind up my polemics against bureaucratic views on the problems of life by a very illustrative story of Comrade Kartchevsky, who had tried to tackle the problem of reformed housekeeping by cooperative methods. "On the day of international cooperation," writes Comrade Kartchevsky (I am quoting his letter to me), "I had a talk with my next-door neighbors—poor people of the working class.

"It did not look promising at first. 'Bother the cooperatives,' they said. 'What is the use of them? They charge higher prices than the market—and you have to walk miles to get to the cooperative stores.' And so on.

"I tried another method. 'Well,' I said, 'suppose our cooperative system is 90 percent wrong. But let us analyze the idea and the aims of cooperation, and for the sake of better understanding and making allowance for our habits of ownership, let us consider in the first place our own interests and wants.' They all, of course, agreed that we want a club, a nursery, a communal kitchen, a school, a laundry, a playground for the children, etc. Let us see how we could manage to have it all.

"Then one of them shouted, losing his temper: 'You said we were to have a commune fitted up, but we don't see anything of it yet.'

"I stopped him, 'Who are the *you?* All of us here have agreed to the necessity of having these institutions organized. Did you not complain just now that the children suffer from the dampness in your basement flat, and your wife is tied like a slave to her kitchen? A change of such conditions is the common interest of all of us. Let us manage things in some improved way. How shall we do it? There are eight flats in our house. The inner court is small. There is no room for many things, and whatever we might be able to organize will be very expensive.' We started discussing the matter. I made one suggestion: 'Why not have a larger community, the district, to join us in our scheme?'

"After that suggestions began to pour in, and all sorts of possibilities were discussed. A very characteristic offer came from a man with rather bourgeois views on property: 'Private ownership of houses is abolished,' he said. 'Let us pull down the fences and make a cesspool for the whole district to prevent the poisoning of the air.' And another added: 'Let us have a playground for the children in the middle.' Then a third came with a suggestion: 'Let us ask the Soviet authorities to give us a big house in our district, or at the worst, let us make shift in some way to have room for a club and a school.' More and more demands and suggestions followed: 'What about a communal kitchen? And a nursery? You men think only about yourselves'—that came from the women—'you have no thought for us.'

"Now every time I meet them, they ask—the women particularly: 'What about your plan? Do let us start things. Won't it be nice?' They propose to call a district meeting on the matter. Every district has some ten or twenty com-

munists living in it, and I hope that with the support of the
party and Soviet institutions we shall be able to do something. . . ."

This case falls in with the general idea I have expounded,
and it clearly shows that it is well to have the problems of life
ground in the mill of collective proletarian thought. The mill
is strong, and will master anything it is given to grind.

And there is another lesson in the story.

"You only think about yourselves," said the women to
Comrade Kartchevsky, "and you have no thought for us." It
is quite true that there are no limits to masculine egotism
in ordinary life. In order to change the conditions of life we
must learn to see them through the eyes of women. This,
however, is another story, and I hope to have a talk about
the matter on some other occasion.

How to begin

AUGUST 8, 1923
Problems of working class life, especially of family life, have begun to interest, we might say to absorb, working class newspaper correspondents. The interest, to a great extent, has come unexpectedly.

The average worker correspondent experiences great difficulties in his attempts to describe life. How is he to tackle the problem? How to begin? To what should he draw attention? The difficulty is not one of literary style—that is a problem in itself—but arises from the fact that the party has not yet specifically considered the problems relating to the daily life of the working masses. We have never thrashed out these questions concretely as, at different times, we have thrashed out the question of wages, fines, the length of the working day, police persecution, the constitution of the state, the ownership of land, and so on. We have as yet done noth-

From Pravda, *August 17, 1923.*

ing of the kind in regard to the family and the private life of the individual worker generally. At the same time, the problem is not an inconsiderable one, if for no other reason than that it absorbs two-thirds of life—sixteen of the twenty-four hours in the day. We already observe, in this respect, the danger of a clumsy, almost brutal, attempt at interference in the private life of the individual. On some occasions—fortunately they are rare ones—worker correspondents treat questions of family life as they do those of production in the factory; i.e., when writing of the life of this or that family, every member of it is mentioned by name. This habit is wrong, dangerous, and inexcusable. A worker-director performs a public function. So does a member of a works committee. Holders of these offices are continually in the public eye, and are subject to free criticism. It is another thing with family life.

Of course the family, too, fulfills a public function. It perpetuates the population and partly educates the new generation. Regarded from this angle, the workers' state has a perfect right to hold the reins of control and regulation in the life of the family in matters relating to hygiene and education. But the state must use great caution in its incursions into family life; it must exercise great tact and moderation; its interference must be solely concerned with according the family more normal and dignified conditions of life; it must guarantee the sanitary and other interests of the workers, thus laying the foundations for healthier and happier generations.

As for the press, its casual and arbitrary incursion into family life, when the family does not evince any desire for it, is perfectly intolerable.

Without careful explanations, the clumsy, untimely interference on the part of the press in the private life of people connected by family ties can only increase the amount of confusion and do great harm. Moreover, as information of this kind is practically not subject to control, owing to the extreme privacy of family life, newspaper reporting on this subject may, in unscrupulous hands, become a means for the settling of private accounts, a means of ridicule, extortion, revenge, and so on.

In some of the numerous articles recently published on questions of family life, I have come across the idea, frequently repeated, that not only are the public activities of the individual member important for the party, but his private life as well. This is an indisputable fact. The more so in that the conditions of the individual life are reflected in a man's public activities. The question is how to react in the individual life. If material conditions, standard of culture, international arrangements prevent the introduction of a radical change in life, then a public exposure of given families, parents, husbands, wives, and so on, will bring no practical results and will threaten to swamp the party with cant—a disease that is dangerous and catching. The disease of cant, like typhoid, has various forms. Cant sometimes springs from the highest motives and from a sincere but mistaken solicitude about party interests; but it sometimes happens that party interests are used as a cloak for other interests—group interests, departmental, and personal interests. To arouse public interest in questions of family life by preaching would undoubtedly poison the movement with the noxious poison of cant. A careful investigation on our part into the domain of family custom must have as an objective the enlightenment of the party. It must psychologically improve the individual and make for a new orientation in state institutions, trade unions, and cooperative units. Under no conditions must it encourage cant.

How under these circumstances shall we enlighten the family? How shall we begin?

There are two fundamental ways. The first is by means of popular articles or stories. Every mature and thinking worker has a sum of impressions of family life stored in his memory. These are refreshed by daily observations. With this material as a foundation we can produce articles dealing with family life as a whole, with its changes, as well as with particular sides of it, giving the more striking examples without mentioning the name of a single family or person. Where names of families and places have to be mentioned, they should be fictitious ones, so that no particular person or family could be associated with them. On this pattern, many interesting and valuable articles have recently appeared in *Pravda* and in provincial publications.

The second method is to take an actual family, this time by name, according to the figure it cuts in public opinion. It is the catastrophes in a family that bring it within the sphere of public opinion and judgment, i.e., murders, suicides, law cases, as a result of jealousy, cruelty, parental despotism, and so on. Just as the strata of a mountain are better seen in a landslide, so the catastrophes in a family bring into greater relief the characteristics that are common to thousands of families who have managed to escape them. We have already mentioned in passing that our press has no right to ignore the occurrences that justly agitate our human beehive. When a deserted wife appeals to the court to compel her husband to contribute towards the support of his children; when a wife seeks public protection from the cruelty and violence of her husband; when the cruelty of parents towards their children becomes a question of public consideration; or vice versa, when ailing parents complain of the cruelty of their children; the press not only has a right, but is duty bound to take up the business and throw light on such sides of it as the court or other public institution does not devote sufficient attention to. Facts brought to light as a result of court proceedings have not been sufficiently used in tackling the problems of life. Nevertheless, they deserve an important place. In a period of upheaval and reconstruction in the daily relationships of life, the Soviet tribunal ought to become an important factor in the organization of the new forms of life, in the evolution of new conceptions of right and wrong, false and true. The press should follow the doings of the court; it should throw light on and supplement its work, and in a certain sense direct it. This provides a large field for educational activities. Our best journalists ought to provide a kind of sketch of court proceedings.

Of course, the usual patent methods of journalism are out of place here. We want imagination and we want conscience. A communistic, i.e., a broad, revolutionary public treatment of questions of the family by no means excludes psychology and the consideration of the individual and his inner world.

I will cite here a small example from the provinces which has lately come to my notice. In Piatigorsk a young girl of seventeen shot herself because her mother refused her consent to her marriage with a Red Army commander. In commenting on the event the local paper, *Terek*, unexpectedly ended its remarks by reproaching the Red Army commander for being prepared—O reader—to connect himself with a girl of so backward a family! I had meant to write a letter to the editor, expressing my indignation, not only for the sake of the Red Army commander, whom I did not know, but to ask for a proper statement of the case. I was absolved from the necessity of sending a letter, however, by the fact that some two or three days later an article on the subject appeared in the same paper, which treated the question in a more proper manner.

New daily relationships must be built with the human material we have at our disposal; the Red Army commander is not excluded from this material. Parents, naturally, have a right to interest themselves in the fate of their children and to influence their fate by their experience and advice; but young people are under no obligation to submit to their parents, particularly in their choice of a friend or a partner for life. The despotism of parents must not be combated by suicide, but by rallying the young, by mutual support, and so on. It is all very elementary, but perfectly true. There is no doubt that an article of the kind, coming on top of the poignant event which excited the little town, contributed more towards stimulating the thought and feeling of the reader, especially of the young reader, than the irritating phrases about petty-bourgeois elements, etc.

The comrades who hold that "throwing light" on questions of family life is immaterial, since we know and have already solved the questions long ago, are cruelly deceived. They simply forget that politically we have much untilled land! The older generation, which is more and more diminishing, learned communism in the course of a class struggle; but the new generation is destined to learn it in the elements of construction, the elements of construction of everyday life. The formulas of our program are, in principle, true. But we must continually prove them, renew them, make them concrete in living experience, and spread them in a wider sphere.

The laying of new foundations in custom will take a long time and will demand greater concreteness and specialization. Just as we have our army agitators, our industrial agitators, our antireligious propagandists, so must we educate propagandists and agitators in questions of custom. As the women are the more helpless by their present limitations, and custom presses more heavily on their shoulders and backs, we may presume that the best agitators on these questions will come from their ranks. We want enthusiasts, we want zealots, we want people whose horizon is sufficiently broad, who will know how to reckon with the tenacity of custom, who will bring a creative consideration to every peculiarity, every little thing and detail in the bonds of family custom, invisible to the naked eye. Such people are sure to come, for the needs and the questions of the hour are of too burning a nature. This does not imply that mountains will be moved at once. No; material conditions cannot be escaped. Nevertheless, all that can be attained within the limitations of present conditions will come when we can break the prison-like silence surrounding our present-day customs.

We must speed up the education of agitators against custom and make their work easier. We must institute a library in which we must collect everything we possess relating to the customs of everyday life—classic works on the evolution of the family and popular writings on the history of custom—making an investigation into the different sides of our daily life. We ought to translate from foreign languages anything of value that has appeared on the subject in recent years. Later on we can develop and expound corresponding sections in our newspapers. Who knows? Perhaps in a year or two we may have to institute a course of lectures on questions relating to the customs of everyday life.

But all this merely touches education, propaganda, the press, literature. What are we to do on the practical side? Some comrades advocate the immediate formation of a league for the inauguration of the new forms of life. The idea seems to me premature. The soil has not been sufficiently prepared; the general conditions are not yet propitious enough. Generally speaking, the formation of such an organizing instrument will become inevitable some time or other. We cannot afford to wait for everything to happen from above, as a result of government initiative. The new social structure must proceed simultaneously on all sides. The proletarian state is the structural timber, not the structure itself. The importance of a revolutionary government in a period of transition is immeasurable; even the best section of international anarchists have begun to understand this, as a result of our experience. It does not mean that all the work of building will be performed by the state. The fetish of the state, even though it be a proletarian state, does not become us as Marxists. Even in the domain of armaments, a more definite province of the state, we have had to resort (and successfully) to the voluntary initiative of worker and peasant. The preliminary work in the development of aviation has also been done on this basis. There is no doubt that the "Society of Friends of the Air Force" has a big future in front of it. The voluntary groups and associations of a local or federal character in the domain of industry, national economy, particularly in the domain of daily custom, are destined to play as big a part. Already we can see a tendency towards free cooperation on the part of Red directors, worker correspondents, proletarian and peasant writers, etc. A league has lately been formed for the purpose of studying the Soviet Union, with the ulterior motive of influencing what we call the national character. It is thought, for instance, that sooner or later—sooner rather than later—the State Cinema Department will be aided by a newly constituted "Society of Friends of the Red Cinema," destined to become a powerful revolutionary institution.

Voluntary associations of this kind can only be welcomed. They mark the awakening of the public activities of different sections of the community. Of course the socialist structure is above all a structure according to plan. Not an a priori, all-seeing, preconceived plan with all the details worked out before the commencement of operations; but a plan that, while being prepared in all the essentials, is verified and improved in the building, growing more vital and concrete in the degree to which the public initiative has gone towards its evolution and drawing up. In the general compass of the state plan there opens up a vast field for the activities of voluntary associations and cooperative units. Among the many millions of our population there are countless interests, forces, energies, a hundredth part of which cannot be utilized by the state, but which, given the requisite form for their organizing abilities, can be made to do excellent work, side by side with the state. A genuine leadership of creative organizing, especially in our "culture period," must aim at discovering suitable ways of utilizing the constructive energies of individual groups, persons, and cooperative units, and must base itself on the increasing independent activities of the masses. Many of these voluntary associations will collapse or change, but on the whole their number will increase as our work deepens and expands. The league for the inauguration of the new forms of life will doubtless occupy the foremost place among them, working in conjunction with the state, local soviets, trade unions, and particularly with cooperative units. For the time being, the formation of such an organization is premature, however. It would be far better to form local groups in factories for the study of questions relating to working class life, the activities of these groups to have a purely voluntary character.

Greater attention must be paid to the facts of everyday life. Central experiments must be tried where material and ideal conditions would make for their success. The widening of boundaries in a block of flats, a group of houses, a district, will all make for practical progress. The initiatory associations should have a local character. They should set themselves definite tasks, such as the establishment of nurseries, laundries, common kitchens for groups of houses. A wider scope of activity will follow greater experience and the improvement of material conditions. To sum up, we want initiative, competition, efficiency!

The primary task, the one that is most acute and urgent, is to break the silence surrounding the problems relating to daily life.

Attention to trifles!

[PUBLISHED OCTOBER 1, 1921]
The ruined economy must be reconstructed. We must build, produce, patch up, repair. We are operating the economy on a new basis that will ensure the well-being of all working people. But the meaning of economic production, reduced to its essentials, is the struggle of humanity against the hostile forces of nature, and the rational utilization of the natural wealth to serve humanity's own ends. The general trend of policies, decrees, and instructions can only regulate economic activity. The actual satisfaction of human needs

Volume 21 of Trotsky's Collected Works, *entitled "Culture in the Transitional Period," was published in 1927—the final work by Trotsky to be published in the Soviet Union. In the section of Volume 21 entitled "Problems of Everyday Life," Trotsky included the previous nine articles, as well as the following two, "Attention to Trifles!" and "'Thou' and 'You' in the Red Army," which are printed here for the first time in English.*

"Attention to Trifles!" is from Pravda, *October 1, 1921. Translated for this volume from Trotsky's* Collected Works, *Vol. 21, by Marilyn Vogt.*

can be achieved only by the production of material values through systematic, persistent, and stubborn effort.

The economic process is the composite product of innumerable elements and parts, of countless details, particulars, and trifles. The reconstruction of the economy is possible only by focusing the greatest attention on such trifles. This we have not done, or, at best, we have done only very, very little. The central task of education and self-education in economics is to arouse, stimulate, and sharpen attention to these particular, trivial, everyday needs of the economy. Let nothing slip by; take note of everything; take the appropriate steps at the appropriate time; and demand that others do the same. This task stands squarely before us in all areas of our government activity and economic work.

Supplying the army with boots and uniforms under existing conditions in industry is no easy task. Our distribution apparatus is frequently subject to long delays. At the same time, we see almost no attention or concern for the preservation of existing uniforms and boots or their timely repair. Our boots are hardly ever polished. When you ask why, you receive the most varied answers: sometimes there is no boot wax; sometimes it was not delivered in time; sometimes the boots are yellow and the wax is black; and so on, and so on. But the main reason is the absence of a businesslike attitude toward things on the part of either the rank-and-file Red Army soldiers, or the commanding officers and commissars.

Unpolished boots, particularly when they get wet, dry up and wear out after several weeks. The factory falls behind and begins to do a sloppy job sewing. The new boots wear out quicker than ever. It is a vicious circle. Meanwhile, there is a solution, and it is a very simple one: the boots should be polished regularly; and they should be properly laced, or else they will get out of shape and get split or worn through more quickly. We quite often spoil a good American boot simply because we have no laces for it. It is possible to get them if you keep insisting; and if there are no laces, it is because no one is paying attention to such economic trifles. But it is from such trifles that the whole is created. The same applies to the rifle, and to an even greater degree. It is a difficult item to make, but an easy one to ruin. It should be cared for—cleaned and oiled. And this demands tireless and persistent attention. This demands training and education.

Trifles, accumulating and combining, can constitute something great—or destroy something great. Slightly damaged areas in a paved road, if not repaired in time, become larger; small holes turn into deep ruts and ditches. They make travel on the road more difficult. They cause damage to wagons, shake automobiles and trucks to pieces, and ruin tires. A bad road gives rise to expenses ten times greater than the cost of repairing the road itself. It is precisely in this way that petty details cause the destruction of machinery, factory buildings, and houses. To maintain them requires tireless, day-to-day attention to trifles and details. We lack this active vigilance because we lack the appropriate economic and cultural training. It is necessary to get a very clear idea of this, our main shortcoming.

We often confuse concern over details and trifles with bureaucratism. To do this is the greatest blunder. Bureaucratism is concentration on hollow form at the expense of content and the business at hand. Bureaucratism wallows in formalism, in hairsplitting, but not in practical details. On the contrary, bureaucratism usually side-steps business details, those matters of which the business itself is composed, anxious only to see that everything adds up on paper.

The rule against spitting or dropping cigarette butts in public corridors and stairways is a "trifle," a petty rule. Nevertheless, it has great cultural and economic significance. A person who spits on the floor or stairway in passing is a dissolute slob. We can never revive the economy on the basis of the likes of these. Such an individual breaks glass out of sheer carelessness, never polishes a boot, and is certainly a carrier of typhus lice. . . .

To some it may seem, I repeat, that persistent attention to such things is nagging, is "bureaucratism." The slovenly and the dissolute love to cover themselves with the disguise of struggling against bureaucratism. "Who cares whether cigarette butts are left on the stairs?" they say. This attitude is so much rubbish. Leaving cigarette butts on the floor with no regard for tidiness shows a lack of respect for the work of others. Those who have no respect for the work of others are careless in their own work. If we really intend to develop institutions based on communal living, it is imperative that every man and woman devote full attention to order and cleanliness and the interests of the house as a whole. Otherwise, we end up (as happens all too often) with a foul, louse-ridden pit, rather than a communal dwelling.

We must wage a tireless and relentless struggle against such slovenliness and lack of culture—by word and deed, by propaganda, and higher standards, by exhortation, and by calling individuals to account for their behavior. Those who tacitly overlook such things as spitting on the stairs or leaving a yard or house looking like a pigsty are poor citizens and unworthy builders of the new society.

In the army, all the positive and negative features of national life are combined in the most vivid way. This also holds true in relation to the problem of training people to be economical. The army, whatever else it does, must improve itself at least some degree in this regard. This can be done through the mutual efforts of all the leading elements in the army itself, from top to bottom, with the cooperation of the best elements of the workers and peasants as a whole.

During the period when the Soviet state apparatus was only beginning to take shape, the army was suffused with the spirit and practices of guerrillaism. We carried on a persistent and uncompromising struggle against the guerrilla partisan mentality, and undoubtedly produced important results. Not only was a centralized leadership and administrative apparatus created but—and this is even more essential—the idea of partisanism itself was severely compromised in the eyes of the working class.

We have before us now a struggle no less serious: the struggle against all forms of negligence, slovenliness, indifference, imprecision, carelessness, lack of individual discipline, extravagance, and wastefulness. All of these are merely varying degrees and shades of the same affliction. At one extreme there is a lack of attentiveness; at the other, conscious misbehavior. This calls for an extensive, day-to-day, persistent, tireless campaign by every means, as was done in the case of the campaign against partisanism: agitation, example, exhortation, and punishment.

The most magnificent plan, without attention to details and to particulars, is mere dabbling. Of what value, for example, is the most carefully considered battle plan if due to sloppiness it arrives too late, or if it is copied incorrectly, or if it is carelessly read? Whoever is true in the small matters will also be true in great ones.

We are poor, but we are wasteful. We are careless. We are sloppy. We are slovenly. These vices have deep roots in our slavish past and can be eradicated only gradually by means of persistent propaganda by deed, by example, and by illustration—and by means of careful control, vigilance, and persistent exactitude.

In order to implement great plans, you must devote great attention to very small trifles! This must be the watchword for all the conscious elements in our country as we enter the new phase of construction and cultural ascent.

'Thou' and 'you'
in the Red Army

JULY 18, 1922

In Sunday's *Izvestia* there was an article about two Red Army men, named Shchekochikhin and Chernyshev, who had behaved as heroes on the occasion of a fire and explosion at Ko-

---

From Izvestia, *July 19, 1922. Translated for this volume from* Collected Works, *Vol. 21, by George Saunders.*

In Russian, the polite form of address is the second person plural, vy. The second person singular, ty, expresses intimacy, but also can be used rudely to express overfamiliarity or disrespect. Adults or older people may use it towards younger people, and under the old regime the nobility used it towards peasants, servants, or any other "underlings," who were still expected to respond in the polite mode. The distinction in English between thou and you has largely disappeared; but readers who know French, Spanish, or German, where such formal-informal distinctions are still alive (tu and vous in French, tu and Usted in Spanish, du and Sie in German), will be familiar with the many ramifications of this convention. In English, the closest parallel to the expression of superiority and subordination in forms of address occurs when the "superior" addresses the other by the first name, and the "subordinate" replies with the polite title "Mr." or "Mrs." and the last name.

lomna. As the article recounts it, the commander of the local garrison approached the soldier Shchekochikhin and asked: "Do you (*ty*) know who I am?"

"Yes, you (*vy*) are the commander of the garrison."

I doubt that the dialogue has been recorded accurately in this case. Otherwise, one would have to conclude that the garrison commander does not use the proper tone in speaking to Red Army soldiers. Of course, Red Army personnel may use the familiar form in speaking to one another as comrades, but precisely *as comrades* and only as comrades. In the Red Army a commanding officer may not use the familiar form to address a subordinate if the subordinate is expected to respond in the polite form. Otherwise an expression of inequality between persons would result, not an expression of subordination in the line of duty.

Of course, the polite and familiar forms are only matters of convention. But definite human relationships are expressed in this convention. In certain cases the familiar form may be used to express close comradely relations. But in which? In those where the relationship is mutual. In other cases, the familiar form will convey disdain, disrespect, a looking down the nose, and a shade of lordly hauteur in one's relations with others. Such a tone is absolutely impermissible in the Red Army.

To some this might seem a trifling matter. But it is not! Red Army soldiers need to respect both themselves and others. Respect for human dignity is an extremely important element of what holds the Red Army together in terms of morale. Red Army soldiers submit to their superiors in the line of duty. The requirements of discipline are inflexible. But at the same time, the soldiers are conscious of themselves as responsible citizens called upon to fulfill obligations of the highest sort. Military subordination must be accompanied by a sense of the civil and moral equality of all, and that sense of equality cannot endure if personal dignity is violated.

Introduction to the Tatar-language edition

OCTOBER 29, 1924

Dear Comrades:

I will, of course, be very pleased by the appearance of my book *Problems of Everyday Life* in the Tatar language. In writing this book, I leaned heavily on the Russian experience, and consequently did not take into account the special features characterizing the ways of life among the Muslim peoples. But because the book only touches upon *fundamental* and *general* problems of everyday life, I trust that much of what is said is applicable to the daily experiences of the Tatar working masses. There is no need to say that the discussion of the problems of daily life is by no means exhausted by my book; rather, the problems have merely been posed and partially outlined.

The central task in the transformation of everyday life is

A letter to the Central Publishing House of the Peoples of the East. Translated for this volume from Collected Works, Vol. 21, *by Marilyn Vogt.*

the liberation of women, forced as they have been into the role of mere beasts of burden by the old conditions of the family, household, and economy. In the East, in the countries of Islam, this task is posed more acutely than anywhere else in the world. If this book succeeds in arousing or intensifying a critical interest in the problems of everyday life among the more advanced Tatar workers and peasants, its translation will have been justified in full.

With communist greetings,
L. Trotsky

Thermidor in the family

1936

The October Revolution honestly fulfilled its obligations in relation to woman. The young government not only gave her all political and legal rights in equality with man, but,

Unlike the preceding articles, which were all written during the twenties, this excerpt from The Revolution Betrayed *was written while Trotsky was in exile in Norway in 1936, and after Trotsky had come to believe that a political revolution against Stalinism was needed in the Soviet Union. The full text is available in a 1937 translation by Max Eastman from Pathfinder Press, New York.*

Thermidor was the month, according to the new calendar proclaimed by the French Revolution, in which the radical Jacobins led by Robespierre were overthrown by a reactionary wing in the revolution, which did not go so far, however, as to restore the feudal regime. Trotsky used the term as a historical analogy to designate the seizure of power by the conservative Stalinist bureaucracy within the framework of nationalized property relations. Since capitalist property relations were not restored, Trotsky advocated unconditional defense of the workers' state against the imperialist governments, while he called at the same time for a political revolution to throw out the Stalinist bureaucracy, whose ruinous policies strengthened the danger of capitalist restoration.

what is more important, did all that it could, and in any case incomparably more than any other government ever did, actually to secure her access to all forms of economic and cultural work. However, the boldest revolution, like the "all-powerful" British Parliament, cannot convert a woman into a man—or rather cannot divide equally between them the burden of pregnancy, birth, nursing, and the rearing of children.

The revolution made a heroic effort to destroy the so-called family hearth—that archaic, stuffy, and stagnant institution in which the woman of the toiling classes performs galley labor from childhood to death. The place of the family as a shut-in petty enterprise was to be occupied, according to the plans, by a finished system of social care and accommodation: maternity houses, child-care centers, kindergartens, schools, social dining rooms, social laundries, first-aid stations, hospitals, sanatoria, athletic organizations, moving-picture theaters, etc. The complete absorption of the housekeeping functions of the family by institutions of the socialist society, uniting all generations in solidarity and mutual aid, was to bring to woman, and thereby to the loving couple, a real liberation from the thousand-year-old fetters.

Up to now this problem of problems has not been solved. The forty million Soviet families remain in their overwhelming majority nests of medievalism, female slavery and hysteria, daily humiliation of children, feminine and childish superstition. We must permit ourselves no illusions on this account. For that very reason, the consecutive changes in the approach to the problem of the family in the Soviet Union best of all characterize the actual nature of Soviet society and the evolution of its ruling stratum.

It proved impossible to take the old family by storm—not because the will was lacking, and not because the family was so firmly rooted in people's hearts. On the contrary, after a short period of distrust of the government and its child-care facilities, kindergartens, and like institutions, the working women, and after them the more advanced peasants, appreciated the immeasurable advantages of the collective care of children as well as the socialization of the whole family economy. Unfortunately society proved too poor and little cultured. The real resources of the state did not correspond to the plans and intentions of the Communist Party. You cannot "abolish" the family; you have to replace it. The actual liberation of women is unrealizable on the basis of "generalized want." Experience soon proved this austere truth which Marx had formulated eighty years before.

During the lean years the workers, wherever possible, and in part their families, ate in the factory and other social dining rooms, and this fact was officially regarded as a transition to a socialist form of life. There is no need of pausing again upon the peculiarities of the different periods: military communism, the NEP, and the first five-year plan.[13] The fact is that from the moment of the abolition of the food-card system in 1935, all the better-placed workers began to return to the home dining table. It would be incorrect to regard this retreat as a condemnation of the socialist system, which in general was never tried out. But so much the more withering was the judgment of the workers and their wives upon the "social feeding" organized by the bureaucracy. The same conclusion must be extended to the social laundries, where they tear and steal linen more than they wash it. Back to the family hearth!

But home cooking and the home washtub, which are now half shamefacedly celebrated by orators and journalists, mean the return of the workers' wives to their pots and pans—that is, to the old slavery. It is doubtful if the resolution of the Communist International on the "complete and irrevocable triumph of socialism in the Soviet Union" sounds very convincing to the women of the factory districts!

The rural family, bound up not only with home industry

but with agriculture, is infinitely more stable and conservative than that of the town. Only a few, and as a general rule, anemic agricultural communes introduced social dining rooms and child-care facilities in the first period. Collectivization, according to the first announcements, was to initiate a decisive change in the sphere of the family. Not for nothing did they expropriate the peasant's chickens as well as his cows. There was no lack, at any rate, of announcements about the triumphal march of social dining rooms throughout the country. But when the retreat began, reality suddenly emerged from the shadow of this bragging.

The peasant gets from the collective farm, as a general rule, only bread for himself and fodder for his stock. Meat, dairy products and vegetables, he gets almost entirely from the adjoining private lots. And once the most important necessities of life are acquired by the isolated efforts of the family, there can no longer be any talk of social dining rooms. Thus the midget farms, creating a new basis for the domestic hearthstone, lay a double burden upon woman.

The total number of steady accommodations in the child-care centers amounted in 1932 to 600,000, and of seasonal accommodations solely during work in the fields to only about 4,000,000. In 1935 the cots numbered 5,600,000, but the steady ones were still only an insignificant part of the total. Moreover, the existing child-care facilities, even in Moscow, Leningrad, and other centers, are not satisfactory as a general rule to the least fastidious demands. "A child-care center in which the child feels worse than he does at home is not a child-care center but a bad orphan asylum," complains a leading Soviet newspaper. It is no wonder if the better-placed workers' families avoid child-care facilities. But for the fundamental mass of the toilers, the number even of these "bad orphan asylums" is insignificant. Just recently the Central Executive Committee introduced a resolution that foundlings and orphans should be placed in private bands for bringing up. Through its highest organ, the bureaucratic government thus acknowledged its bankruptcy in relation to the most important socialist function.

The number of children in kindergartens rose during the five years 1930–35 from 370,000 to 1,180,000. The lowness of the figure for 1930 is striking, but the figure for 1935 also seems only a drop in the ocean of Soviet families. A further investigation would undoubtedly show that the principal and, in any case the better part of these kindergartens appertain to the families of the administration, the technical personnel, the Stakhanovists,[14] etc.

The same Central Executive Committee was not long ago compelled to testify openly that the "resolution on the liquidation of homeless and uncared-for children is being weakly carried out." What is concealed behind this dispassionate confession? Only by accident, from newspaper remarks printed in small type, do we know that in Moscow more than a thousand children are living in "extraordinarily difficult family conditions"; that in the so-called children's homes of the capital there are about 1,500 children who have nowhere to go and are turned out into the streets; that during the two autumn months of 1935 in Moscow and Leningrad "7,500 parents were brought to court for leaving their children without supervision." What good did it do to bring them to court? How many thousand parents have avoided going to court? How many children in "extraordinarily difficult conditions" remained unrecorded? In what way do *extraordinarily* difficult conditions differ from *simply* difficult ones? Those are the questions which remain unanswered. A vast amount of the homelessness of children, obvious and open as well as disguised, is a direct result of the great social crisis in the course of which the old family continues to dissolve far faster than the new institutions are capable of replacing it.

From these same accidental newspaper remarks and from

episodes in the criminal records, the reader may find out about the existence in the Soviet Union of prostitution—that is, the extreme degradation of woman in the interests of men who can pay for it. In the autumn of the past year [1935] *Izvestia* suddenly informed its readers, for example, of the arrest in Moscow of "as many as a thousand women who were secretly selling themselves on the streets of the proletarian capital." Among those arrested were 177 working women, ninety-two clerks, five university students, etc. What drove them to the sidewalks? Inadequate wages, want, the necessity to "get a little something for a dress, for shoes."

We should vainly seek the approximate dimensions of this social evil. The modest bureaucracy orders the statistician to remain silent. But that enforced silence itself testifies unmistakably to the numerousness of the "class" of Soviet prostitutes. Here there can be essentially no question of "relics of the past"; prostitutes are recruited from the younger generation. No reasonable person, of course, would think of placing special blame for this sore, as old as civilization, upon the Soviet regime. But it is unforgivable in the presence of prostitution to talk about the triumph of socialism. The newspapers assert, to be sure—insofar as they are permitted to touch upon this ticklish theme—that "prostitution is decreasing." It is possible that this is really true by comparison with the years of hunger and decline (1931–33). But the restoration of money relations which has taken place since then, abolishing all direct rationing, will inevitably lead to a new growth of prostitution as well as homeless children. Wherever there are privileged, there are pariahs!

The mass homelessness of children is undoubtedly the most unmistakable and most tragic symptom of the difficult situation of the mother. On this subject even the optimistic *Pravda* is sometimes compelled to make a bitter confession: "The birth of a child is for many women a serious menace to their position." It is just for this reason that the revolutionary power gave women the right to abortion, which in conditions of want and family distress, whatever may be said upon this subject by the eunuchs and old maids of both sexes, is one of her most important civil, political, and cultural rights. However, this right of women too, gloomy enough in itself, is under the existing social inequality being converted into a privilege. Bits of information trickling into the press about the practice of abortion are literally shocking. Thus through only one village hospital in one district of the Urals, there passed in 1935 "195 women mutilated by midwives"—among them 33 working women, 28 clerical workers, 65 collective farm women, 58 housewives, etc. This Ural district differs from the majority of other districts only in that information about it happened to get into the press. How many women are mutilated every day throughout the extent of the Soviet Union?

Having revealed its inability to serve women who are compelled to resort to abortion with the necessary medical aid and sanitation, the state makes a sharp change of course and takes the road of prohibition. And just as in other situations, the bureaucracy makes a virtue of necessity. One of the members of the highest Soviet court, Soltz, a specialist on matrimonial questions, bases the forthcoming prohibition of abortion on the fact that in a socialist society where there are no unemployed, etc., etc., a woman has no right to decline "the joys of motherhood." The philosophy of a priest endowed also with the powers of a gendarme. We just heard from the central organ of the ruling party that the birth of a child is for many women, and it would be truer to say for the overwhelming majority, "a menace to their position." We just heard from the highest Soviet institution that "the liquidation of homeless and uncared-for children is being weakly carried out," which undoubtedly means a new increase of homelessness. But here the highest Soviet judge informs us that in a country where "life is happy" abortion should be punished with imprisonment just exactly as in capitalist countries where life is grievous.

It is clear in advance that in the Soviet Union as in the West those who will fall into the claws of the jailer will be chiefly working women, servants, peasant wives, who find it hard to conceal their troubles. As far as concerns "our women," who furnish the demand for fine perfumes and other pleasant things, they will, as formerly, do what they find necessary under the very nose of an indulgent justiciary. "We have need of people," concludes Soltz, closing his eyes to the homeless. "Then have the kindness to bear them yourselves," might be the answer of millions of toiling women to the high judge, if the bureaucracy had not sealed their lips with the seal of silence. These gentlemen have, it seems, completely forgotten that socialism was to remove the cause which impels woman to abortion and not force her into the "joys of motherhood" with the help of a foul police interference in what is to every woman the most intimate sphere of life.

The draft of the law forbidding abortion was submitted to so-called universal popular discussion, and even through the fine sieve of the Soviet press many bitter complaints and stifled protests broke out. The discussion was cut off as suddenly as it had been announced, and on June 27 the Central Executive Committee converted the shameful draft into a thrice-shameful law. Even some of the official apologists of the bureaucracy were embarrassed. Louis Fischer[15] declared this piece of legislation something in the nature of a deplorable misunderstanding. In reality the new law against women—with an exception in favor of ladies—is the natural and logical fruit of a Thermidorean reaction.

The triumphal rehabilitation of the family, taking place simultaneously—what a providential coincidence!—with the rehabilitation of the ruble, is caused by the material and cultural bankruptcy of the state. Instead of openly saying,

"We have proven still too poor and ignorant for the creation of socialist relations among men, our children and grandchildren will realize this aim," the leaders are forcing people to glue together again the shell of the broken family, and not only that, but to consider it, under threat of extreme penalties, the sacred nucleus of triumphant socialism. It is hard to measure with the eye the scope of this retreat.

Everybody and everything is dragged into the new course: lawgiver and litterateur, court and militia, newspaper and schoolroom. When a naive and honest communist youth makes bold to write in his paper: "You would do better to occupy yourself with solving the problem of how woman can get out of the clutches of the family," he receives in answer a couple of good smacks and—is silent. The ABCs of communism are declared a "leftist excess." The stupid and stale prejudices of uncultured philistines are resurrected in the name of a new morale. And what is happening in daily life in all the nooks and corners of this boundless country? The press reflects only in a faint degree the depth of the Thermidorean reaction in the sphere of the family.

Since the noble passion of evangelism grows with the growth of sin, the seventh commandment is acquiring great popularity in the ruling stratum. The Soviet moralists have only to change the phraseology slightly. A campaign is opened against too frequent and easy divorces. The creative thought of the lawgivers had already invented such a "socialistic" measure as the taking of money payment upon registration of divorces, and increasing it when divorces were repeated. Not for nothing we remarked above that the resurrection of the family goes hand in hand with the increase of the educative role of the ruble. A tax indubitably makes registration difficult for those for whom it is difficult to pay. For the upper circles, the payment, we may hope, will not offer any difficulty. Moreover, people possessing nice apartments, automobiles, and other good things arrange their personal affairs without unnecessary publicity and consequently without registration. It is only on the bottom of society that prostitution has a heavy and humiliating character. On the heights of the Soviet society, where power is combined with comfort, prostitution takes the elegant form of mutual services, and even assumes the aspect of the "socialist family." We have already heard from Sosnovsky[16] about the importance of the "automobile-harem factor" in the degeneration of the ruling stratum.

The lyric, academic, and other "friends of the Soviet Union" have eyes in order to see nothing. The marriage and family laws established by the October Revolution, once the object of its legitimate pride, are being made over and mutilated by vast borrowings from the law treasuries of the bourgeois countries. And as though on purpose to stamp treachery with ridicule, the same arguments which were earlier advanced in favor of unconditional freedom of divorce and abortion—"the liberation of women," "defense of the rights of personality," "protection of motherhood"—are repeated now in favor of their limitation and complete prohibition.

The retreat not only assumes forms of disgusting hypocrisy, but also is going infinitely further than iron economic necessity demands. To the objective causes producing this return to such bourgeois forms as the payment of alimony, there is added the social interest of the ruling stratum in the deepening of bourgeois law. The most compelling motive of the present cult of the family is undoubtedly the need of the bureaucracy for a stable hierarchy of relations, and for the disciplining of youth by means of forty million points of support for authority and power.

While the hope still lived of concentrating the education of the new generations in the hands of the state, the government was not only unconcerned about supporting the authority of the "elders," and in particular of the mother and father, but on the contrary tried its best to separate the children from the family, in order thus to protect them from the traditions of a stagnant mode of life. Only a little while ago, in the course of the first five-year plan, the schools and the Communist Youth were using children for the exposure, shaming, and in general "reeducating" of their drunken fathers or religious mothers—with what success is another question. At any rate, this method meant a shaking of parental authority to its very foundations. In this not unimportant sphere too, a sharp turn has now been made. Along with the seventh, the fifth commandment is also fully restored to its rights—as yet, to be sure, without any references to God. But the French schools also get along without this supplement, and that does not prevent them from successfully inculcating conservatism and routine.

Concern for the authority of the older generation, by the way, has already led to a change in policy in the matter of religion. The denial of God, his assistance, and his miracles was the sharpest wedge of all those which the revolutionary power drove between children and parents. Outstripping the development of culture, serious propaganda, and scientific education, the struggle with the churches, under the leadership of people of the type of Yaroslavsky,[17] often degenerated into buffoonery and mischief. The storming of heaven, like the storming of the family, is now brought to a stop. The bureaucracy, concerned about their reputation for respectability, have ordered the young "godless" to surrender their fighting armor and sit down to their books. In relation to religion, there is gradually being established a regime of ironical neutrality. But that is only the first stage. It would not be difficult to predict the second and third, if the course of events depended only upon those in authority.

The hypocrisy of prevailing opinion develops everywhere and always as the square, or cube, of the social contradictions. Such approximately is the historic law of ideology translated into the language of mathematics. Socialism, if it is worthy of the name, means human relations without greed, friendship without envy and intrigue, love without base calculation. The official doctrine declares these ideal norms already realized—and with more insistence the louder the reality protests against such declarations. "On the basis of real equality between men and women," says, for example, the new program of the Communist Youth, adopted in April 1936, "a new family is coming into being, the flourishing of which will be a concern of the Soviet state."

An official commentary supplements the program: "Our youth in the choice of a life-friend—wife or husband—know only one motive, one impulse: love. The bourgeois marriage of pecuniary convenience does not exist for our growing generation" (*Pravda*, April 4, 1936). So far as concerns the rank-and-file working man and woman, this is more or less true. But "marriage for money" is comparatively little known also to the workers of capitalist countries. Things are quite different in the middle and upper strata. New social groupings automatically place their stamp upon personal relations. The vices which power and money create in sex relations are flourishing as luxuriously in the ranks of the Soviet bureaucracy as though it had set itself the goal of outdoing in this respect the Western bourgeoisie.

In complete contradiction to the just quoted assertion of *Pravda*, "marriage of convenience," as the Soviet press itself in moments of accidental or unavoidable frankness confesses, is now fully resurrected. Qualifications, wages, employment, number of chevrons on the military uniform, are acquiring more and more significance, for with them are bound up questions of shoes, and fur coats, and apartments, and bathrooms and—the ultimate dream—automobiles. The mere struggle for a room unites and divorces no small number of couples every year in Moscow. The question of relatives has acquired exceptional significance. It is useful to have as a father-in-law a military commander or an influential communist, as a mother-in-law the sister of a high dignitary. Can we wonder at this? Could it be otherwise?

One of the very dramatic chapters in the great book of the Soviets will be the tale of the disintegration and breaking up of those Soviet families where the husband as a party member, trade unionist, military commander, or administrator, grew and developed and acquired new tastes in life, and the wife, crushed by the family, remained on the old level. The road of the two generations of the Soviet bureaucracy is sown thick with the tragedies of wives rejected and left behind. The same phenomenon is now to be observed in the new generation. The greatest of all crudities and cruelties are to be met perhaps in the very heights of the bureaucracy, where a very large percentage are parvenus of little culture, who consider that everything is permitted to them. Archives and memoirs will someday expose downright crimes in relation to wives, and to women in general, on the part of those evangelists of family morals and the compulsory "joys of motherhood" who are, owing to their position, immune from prosecution.

No, the Soviet woman is not yet free. Complete equality before the law has so far given infinitely more to the women of the upper strata, representatives of bureaucratic, technical, pedagogical and, in general, intellectual work, than to the working women and yet more the peasant women. So long as society is incapable of taking upon itself the material concern for the family, the mother can successfully fulfill a social function only on condition that she has in her service a white slave: nurse, servant, cook, etc. Out of the forty million families which constitute the population of the Soviet Union, 5 percent, or maybe 10, build their "hearthstone" directly or indirectly upon the labor of domestic slaves. An accurate census of Soviet servants would have as much significance for the socialistic appraisal of the position of women in the Soviet Union as the whole Soviet law code, no matter how progressive it might be. But for this very reason the Soviet statistics hide servants under the name of "working woman" or "and others"!

The situation of the mother of the family, who is an esteemed communist, has a cook, a telephone for giving orders to the stores, an automobile for errands, etc., has little in common with the situation of the working woman, who is compelled to run to the shops, prepare dinner herself, and carry her children on foot from the kindergarten—if, indeed, a kindergarten is available. No socialist labels can conceal this social contrast, which is no less striking than the contrast between the bourgeois lady and the proletarian woman in any country of the West.

The genuinely socialist family, from which society will remove the daily vexation of unbearable and humiliating cares, will have no need of any regimentation, and the very idea of laws about abortion and divorce will sound no better within its walls than the recollection of houses of prostitution or human sacrifices. The October legislation took a bold step in the direction of such a family. Economic and cultural backwardness has produced a cruel reaction. The Thermidorean legislation is beating a retreat to the bourgeois models, covering its retreat with false speeches about the sacredness of the "new" family. On this question, too, socialist bankruptcy covers itself with hypocritical respectability.

There are sincere observers who are, especially upon the question of children, shaken by the contrast here between high principles and ugly reality. The mere fact of the furious criminal measures that have been adopted against homeless children is enough to suggest that the socialist legislation in defense of women and children is nothing but crass hypocrisy. There are observers of an opposite kind who are deceived by the broadness and magnanimity of those ideas that have been dressed up in the form of laws and administrative institutions. When they see destitute mothers, prostitutes, and homeless children, these optimists tell themselves that a further growth of material wealth will gradually fill the socialist laws with flesh and blood.

It is not easy to decide which of these two modes of approach is more mistaken and more harmful. Only people stricken with historical blindness can fail to see the broadness and boldness of the social plan, the significance of the first stages of its development and the immense possibilities opened by it. But on the other hand, it is impossible not to be indignant at the passive and essentially indifferent optimism of those who shut their eyes to the growth of social contradictions, and comfort themselves with gazing into the future, the key to which they respectfully propose to leave in the hands of the bureaucracy. As though the equality of rights of women and men were not already converted into an equality of deprivation of rights by that same bureaucracy! And as though in some book of wisdom it were firmly promised that the Soviet bureaucracy will not introduce a new oppression in place of liberty.

How man enslaved woman, how the exploiter subjected them both, how the toilers have attempted at the price of blood to free themselves from slavery and have only exchanged one chain for another—history tells us much about all this. In essence, it tells us nothing else. But how in reality to free the child, the woman, and the human being? For that we have as yet no reliable models. All past historical experience, wholly negative, demands of the toilers at least and first of all an implacable distrust of all privileged and uncontrolled guardians.

Part 2

Education and culture

Alas, we are not accurate enough!

[PUBLISHED DECEMBER 17, 1921]
Accuracy or preciseness is a virtue that is gradually acquired and can serve as a criterion of economic and cultural development for a people, a class, or even an individual. And what we are lacking most of all is precision. Our whole national past was such that we were not trained to be accurate. It can be said without exaggeration that our every disaster, every failure, every social misfortune takes on greater proportions than are to be expected just because of the absence of coordination of operations, which itself is impossible without precision. And for that very reason, our every collective effort yields results far less than could be expected.

The accurate person is not hasty. Hasty people, people who are always late to everything—we have enough of those. But precise people, i.e., people who know what an hour means,

From Izvestia, December 23, 1921. Translated for this volume from Collected Works, Vol. 21, by Marilyn Vogt.

what a minute means, who are able to organize their work and waste neither their time nor anyone else's—of those we have too few. Their number is growing, but only slowly. And this is the greatest source of difficulty in our economic as well as our military work.

All practical work requires an orientation in terms of time and space. Meanwhile, all our past training has failed to teach us the value of time or of space. It has always seemed to us that whatever it is, we probably have enough of it. We are wretched measurers.

Ask any peasant on the country road how many versts it is to the village of Ivanshkov. He will answer: three versts. From experience we know that it could turn out to be seven or eight versts to Ivanshkov. If you are fussy and persistent and begin to cross-examine him as to whether it is exactly three versts, not more, not five or seven, in the majority of cases, your interlocutor will answer: "Who knows how many versts it is?" And, actually, our distances have not been measured out. There are even various proverbs on this score: "The old woman measured with her crutch and waved with her hand," and so forth.

During tours of the front lines we daily encountered extremely haphazard attitudes toward distance and time on the part of local peasants who were acting as guides and also, not infrequently, on the part of commissars and commanders of the army itself.

One could compose a fair-sized notebook of recollections and observations on the question of military guides. We subjected every new guide to a trial by ordeal. Did he actually know the road? How many times had he traveled on it? This method turned out to be extremely important for us in eventually finding out that yesterday or three days ago that same guide had misled us because it turned out he didn't know the road at all. Having stood up under severe cross-questioning, the guide would take his seat, and within half an hour after starting out would be looking anxiously from side to side, mumbling that he had traveled this road only once before, and that was at night.

Doubtless, the source of such an attitude toward one's own or another person's time is the nature of rural Russia. There, the savage weather and the savage official manorial system of enslavement served as a school for training in passivity, patience, and as a result, indifference to time. The ability to stand waiting by someone's door for hours—quietly, patiently, passively—is an age-old feature of the Russian peasant. "Don't worry, he'll wait" is the most familiar "expression" of the nobility's contempt for the peasant's time and the equally contemptuous certainty that the peasant will endure anything since he is not used to valuing his time.

At the present, as 1921 draws to a close, the peasants are not the same as they were before 1861, or before 1914, or before 1917. Vast changes have occurred in their living conditions and in their consciousness. But these changes have still only made inroads into the basic substance of their world view. They have not as yet succeeded in reshaping that view, that is, in transforming ingrained habits and ways.

Industry and manufacturing by their very nature require accuracy. A wooden plow digs up the soil some way or another. But if the cogs of two wheels don't mesh precisely, an entire machine is stopped or destroyed. The proletarian, whose work is started and stopped at the sound of a whistle, is much more able to value time and space than is the peasant. However, our working class gets its replacements from that same peasantry, and so their traits are brought into the factory.

The modern army is a mechanized army. It demands precision in time and space. Without it the necessary combination of weapons systems, technical strength, and technical capacity will not be available. In this area, we are very weak. When it comes to time, we very often miscalculate. To take care of a matter like moving artillery up to a certain place at the right time is very, very difficult work. And not just because the roads are bad (the repair of bad roads can be included in the overall calculation), but because the order comes at the wrong time or is not read in time. Also, we handle the various aspects of preparation not in a synchronized way or parallel fashion, but rather one after another. After you had provided fodder, you remembered that there weren't enough harnesses; later you guessed you'd better request binoculars or maps, and so forth.

"Wasted time is as irrevocable as death," Peter once wrote— Peter, who with every step collided with the laziness, immobility, and negligence of the bearded boyars.[1] The privileged class in its own way reflected the general features of rural Russia. Peter tried his best to teach the military class to regard time as the Germans or Dutch did. The superficial, formal, bureaucratic precision of the czarist machine undoubtedly grew out of Peter's reforms. But this ritualized precision was only a cover for the procrastination that we inherited from the accursed past, together with poverty and illiteracy.

Only the extensive development of a mechanized economy, the correct division of labor, and its correct organization foster habits of precision and accuracy. But on the other hand, the correct organization of today's economy is unthinkable without precision and accuracy. The one is dependent on the other. The one can either assist or oppose the other.

Our political propaganda plays a role in this matter. Of course, it is impossible to eradicate sloppiness and irresponsibility by ceaseless repetition of the word "precision." It is in this area that our propaganda and educational work must be rooted most deeply in our massive experiment in consciously planned construction. Pure, bare repetition takes on an annoying and sometimes unbearable character and in the end not only bypasses one's consciousness but passes right out the other ear. But if continuous repetition is geared to the living experience of the factories, plants, state farms, barracks, schools, and offices, then gradually, little by little (oh, how slowly!), it takes root in people's consciousness and contributes toward improving the practical organization of work. And slightly improved practical work in our institutions in turn facilitates further training in the habits of preciseness and accuracy, two of the most necessary features of a conscious, independent, and cultured individual.

This is the age of aviation, electrification, the telephone and telegraph; the age of socialist revolution, which must transform the entire economy into one synchronized factory where all cogs intermesh with clockwork precision—and in the midst of this era we are wandering about up to our knees, and sometimes much higher up, in the mire of the old, barbaric past. In all matters, large and small, one must say to oneself several times a day: "Alas, we are certainly not accurate enough." However, there is not and cannot be a note of despair in this cry.

Precision is something that will come with time. We will learn it. We will master its secret, and that means we will grow richer, stronger, and wiser, for the one follows from the other.

Youth and the
phase of petty jobs

Twenty-five years have passed very quickly, somehow. And yet a quarter of a century is no small period of time. . . . The initiators of the first congress of the party had been going, I understand, to invite our Nikolayev organization to the congress, but hesitated—we at Nikolayev were youngsters.[2] However, the question solved itself: in January 1897[3] the Nikolayev organization was broken up almost completely, and the congress took place in March. We learned about it in Odessa prison in May; the news was passed on by shouting from one cell-window to the next. And now, twenty-five years

From Pravda, *March 14, 1923. Translated from Trotsky's* Generation of October *(Moscow, 1924) by Brian Pearce.*

This article was written on the occasion of the twenty-fifth anniversary of the first congress of the Russian Social Democratic Labor Party, which was a section of the Second International, and as a contribution to the discussion preceding the twelfth congress of the Russian Communist Party, which was to convene in April 1923.

have passed, and what years! Wars, revolutions, upheavals such as had never happened before in human history. And it seems as though the year 1897 was yesterday; how hard it is to comprehend in one moment this twenty-five-year past, richer in content than the preceding millennium. Would it not be better to give thought to the future?

One's first thought is of the youth, for they are also the future. The generation now leading the party incarnates in itself the invaluable experience of the past twenty-five years, but our revolutionary youth is the volcanic product of the October eruption. Neither the European nor, still less, the world revolution, however quickly it may have begun, is completed in the eyes of the older generation. All the more serious and deep-going is the question of training the shift that stands ready to carry through the work to the end.

In Europe the younger generation of the proletariat, stimulated by the Russian Revolution, continues to live under the conditions of the capitalist regime. The combination of these conditions—the revolutionary example of Russia and the powerful oppression of imperialism—is giving the younger generation of the European proletariat a revolutionary tempering which was lacking in the period of the imperialist war.

The conditions under which our young people are developing are exceptional. They have grown up or are growing up in the circumstances of a victorious revolution which has not been and will not be broken. For our young people the revolution is already not an aim but their way of life. Are there no new dangers in this? In its practical realization the revolution is, so to speak, "broken up" into partial tasks: it is necessary to repair bridges, learn to read and write, reduce the cost of production of shoes in Soviet factories, combat filth, catch swindlers, extend power cables into the country-side, and so on. Some vulgarians from the intelligentsia, from the category of persons who wear their brains askew (for that very reason they consider themselves poets or philosophers), have already taken to talking about the revolution in a tone of the most magnificent condescension: learning to trade, ha, ha! and to sew on buttons, heh, heh! But let these windbags yelp into the empty air.

We ourselves put the question critically—is there not a real danger that our young people, without noticing it, might become shaped and petrified in the atmosphere of Soviet "petty jobs"—without a revolutionary outlook, without a broad historical horizon—and that one unhappy day it may turn out that we and they are talking different languages? The existence of that danger cannot be altogether denied. But the conditions that engender it are opposed by other no less powerful conditions, and above all by the international situation of our country and therefore of our party. From the great task which we have accomplished, the conquest of power, we have passed to "petty" tasks, not directly, but through a long civil war, and not forever, but only for a certain period, which we have taken to calling the breathing-space. The mere fact of the existence of the Red Army testifies first and foremost to this. We are not the only ones on the earth. We are only the extreme left flank of a very long and winding front that stretches across all five continents. In these last few years we have thoroughly smashed that detachment of the hostile forces that directly opposed itself to us—"seriously and for a long time."

But the struggle is still going on throughout the world. And at any moment it may be transferred to our territory; or our direct aid may be called for, in the name of our own defense, in other lands. Understanding of this international character of our tasks must constitute the pivot of the education of our young people. If we are passing through a sort of phase of petty jobs, then the Red Army is the most vital link joining us to the still unaccomplished revolutionary tasks on a world scale. For this reason the attitude of the youth to the

Red Army essentially expresses its practical attitude to the revolution, as to a heroic deed. We saw yesterday what its attitude is in relation to the Red Navy; tomorrow we shall see it in relation to the Air Force. On the other hand, what is sometimes called the demobilization mood is essentially a liquidationist mood. The practical revolutionary schooling that was provided by the underground, schooling in high selflessness, in brotherhood in arms, can be replaced in our condition primarily by the Red Army.

For this purpose it is necessary, let me repeat, that an appreciation of the connection between our domestic work and the struggle of the world working class shall enter into the blood of our youth. This can be achieved only by bringing the world working class movement nearer to us, to a much greater degree than previously. How? Through properly presented, serious, conscientiously thought-out information. The time of sweeping slogans about the specter of communism haunting Europe is past already—and hasn't come yet. It is necessary that our advanced young people follow from day to day, through newspapers, periodicals, and lectures, the progress of the revolutionary movement in all its concreteness, so that they may know its strength and its weakness, its difficulties and its mistakes, its successes and its defeats, its organizations and its leaders. Thanks to prison, exile, and emigration the older generation of our party obtained this international knowledge, was educated in it, and absorbed it. This is its strength, which also enables it to play today the leading role in the Communist International. The younger generation has no need to go to prison or into emigration to get this strength. The task can and must be solved through a plan, by party and state means. Above all, our press must learn to give systematic, concrete, living, continuous information about the struggle of the working class throughout the world. Enough of disconnected, episodic, fragmentary tittle-tattling and hot-air reports! The today of the labor movement must be organically derived for the reader from its yesterday. We need properly presented correspondence from abroad. We must closely follow the European press and give our readers excerpts from it.

It is not a matter of preaching, appealing and exhorting— there is already too much of that, and it is wearisome; young people growing up in an atmosphere of slogans, appeals, exclamations, placards, are in danger of ceasing to react to them. The youth must be given factual information in the right proportions and in the right perspective. They must be given solid elements and methods for independently finding their bearings in the development of the world revolution. As the soldier by vocation moves flags on his map, intensely concentrating on the conditions and chances of battles that are being fought on the other side of the world from himself, so our young people must learn to move the flags of the class front independently on the political map of the world, weigh the forces and resources of the struggle, evaluate the methods employed and verify the worth of the leaders. There is no more powerful means of ideological education against hairsplitting depreciation, against NEP demoralization, and against all other dangers.

But purely practical everyday work in the field of Soviet cultural and economic construction (even in Soviet retail trade!) is not at all a practice of "petty jobs," and does not necessarily involve a hairsplitting mentality. There are plenty of petty jobs, unrelated to any big jobs, in man's life. But history knows of no big jobs without petty jobs. It would be more precise to say—petty jobs in a great epoch, that is, as component parts of a big task, cease to be "petty jobs." After the debacle of the Narodnaya Volya,[4] the Russian intelligentsia, fallen into apathy and prostration, tried to take the road of "petty jobs" of a cultural and philanthropic character. Thus there arose the type of the 1880s, the preacher of cooperative workshops and vegetarianism. After the defeat of the revolution of 1905, Russian Menshevism finally took the road of rejecting a revolutionary program, in the name of "topical demands," that is, petty jobs. Thus was formed the type of the liquidator, soaked through and through with bourgeois ideas and soon turning into a patriot. In Europe during the period between the Franco-Prussian War (1871) and the great imperialist slaughter (1914), the Social Democratic and trade union bureaucracy retreated further and further into day-to-day, purely reformist, detailed work, in practice repudiating revolutionary struggle against capitalism, bowing to the ground before its might. Thus was formed the opportunist, the nationalist, the Scheidemannite.[5] In all these instances we see political and moral surrender to the enemy. "Petty jobs" are openly or tacitly counterposed to a great historical task. They are to be carried out in the chinks of the regime set up by the enemy class.

It is perfectly obvious that it is quite a different sort of topical demands and partial tasks that call for our attention today. Our concern is with the constructive work of a working class which is for the first time building for itself and according to its own plan. This historic plan, though as yet extremely imperfect and lacking in consistency, must embrace all sections and parts of the work, all its nooks and crannies, in the unity of a great creative conception. The hairsplitting of the reformists does not consist in their concern with partial reforms but in the fact that these reforms are confined in advance within the narrow framework assigned for them by a hostile will. If our Soviet reforms have narrow limits, these are the limits of our own economic might, or of our weakness. In the last analysis our heroic barricade fighting too breaks down into details, assembling logs, overturning carts, erecting barriers, and so on. But all these acts were linked by the revolutionary high tension of the fighters, in the name of a great political aim. The unity of a great aim likewise wrests a man from petty-bourgeois hairsplitting, elevates him above the level of mere petty everyday concerns alone, brings inspiration into his life even though his personal share in the common task be of the most modest order. Socialist construction is planned construction on the largest scale. And through all the ebbs and flows, mistakes and turns, through all the twists and turns of the NEP, the party pursues its great plan, educates the youth in the spirit of this plan, teaches everyone to link his particular function with the common task, which today demands sewing on Soviet buttons, and tomorrow readiness to die fearlessly under the banner of communism.

Soviet technology is being raised to the level of revolutionary politics. The fitter, the weaver, the foreman, the engineer are conscious participants in a common economic plan, or must become such. The technical training of young people is not only a matter of specialization but also of preparation to take part in planned construction, in socialist architecture, in revolutionary achievement.

Soviet Russia offers a boundless field for technology. And the proletarian students, if things are presented in the right way, will study agronomics, thermodynamics or electrical technology with the same enthusiasm (indeed, they are already so studying) as our generation showed in studying the organization of strikes, discussion circles, and underground print shops. Specialization is necessary, fruitful, salutary, as an elementary precondition of any advance. But specialization in a workers' state must not lead to a flattering of the individual, to a secluded one-sidedness. We must, and shall, demand serious and thorough specialized training for our young people, and so emancipate them from the basic sin of our generation—that of being know-it-alls and jacks of all trades—but specialization in the service of a common plan grasped and thought out by every individual. The party must in the next few years train a powerful scientific and technical cadre. Soviet technique must be raised to the heights of Communist Party ideas.

The question is not, however, to be exhausted by these general historical notions, for they are decisive only in the so-called "last analysis of history." In practice the relationship between specialization and party ideas is at present more complex and more acute.

Before October too, of course, the Bolsheviks were not only Bolsheviks but also had each their own jobs, their own trades at which they were employed. The difference between now and the pre-revolutionary period, however, is enormous. First of all, the officers of the party were then engaged almost exclusively in party work; they were the people called professional revolutionaries, and their number was fairly considerable. In the second place, the party members who remained at the bench, in office jobs, and so on, devoted to their factory and office work only their physical strength, only their time, not their soul. They lived their active, conscious life outside their employment.

But now? The officers of the party, both central and local, consist with few exceptions of comrades who are charged with most responsible state service, almost always of a specialized kind. The same applies also to a very substantial number of party members who are not formally officers of the party but who make up its fundamental cadres. The communists now bring their entire personalities into their administrative, economic, military, diplomatic, and any other sort of work, for it is not just a matter of a job but of socialist construction; and the more party members specialize the more they develop the taste for specialization—and that must be so, for without specialization it is impossible to achieve anything serious and businesslike in such a colossal "undertaking" as the building of a new state and a new economy. But the danger resulting from this is also great—from fixedly looking at trees one can lose sight of the forest.

Three years ago I had occasion to say that it would be a great achievement for the party when instead of inner-party trends and factions of the old kind we should form groupings of electrifiers, peat-enthusiasts, shale-men, and so on. In general, this idea remains sound today. But the delayed development of the revolution on the world scale means for us a delayed economic development, and this, in its turn, means that purely political questions—the relationships between the workers and the peasants, between the party and the masses—still retain for us, for a long time, their decisive significance. If the party, through being fragmented and absorbed in specialized work, were to lose its sensitivity to every change in the political sphere and its ability rapidly to find its bearings in these questions, it would be threatened with very great dangers. To try to resist this tendency by dragging the party back to primitive methods of solving each and every Soviet question "through the party" would certainly be reactionary Don Quixotism. We would merely overstrain the party by taking that road, obliging it to carry out with its bare hands work for which we already have tools, even if they are not very precise ones. The departmental degeneration of the party, and every other kind, can be countered only by combining a number of methods that can strengthen and rally the party, widen its base, improve the Soviet "tools," and teach the party, that is, ourselves, to wield them better.

It is necessary first and foremost to increase systematically the number of members working at the bench. Industry is now much more stable than it was in the first years of the revolution, and we hope that its stability will grow greater. The recruitment of party members from the factories can and must assume a strictly systematic and at the same time individualized character. We must win separately every worker who is worth winning. The working class youth must become ours to a man. This is the task of all tasks, the key to all locks. The more abundantly the underground springs of the party are nourished, the less the crystallization in the upper strata of the party along the lines of profession and department will threaten the party with bureaucratic ossification.

There must be a raising of the political and theoretical level of the party and, as a most important contribution to this end, an improvement in the party press, which must give better information, become more interesting, more profoundly comprehensive, and in particular must get rid of departmental trivia and monotonous proclamations which neither instruct nor arouse but put to sleep. On this matter it is necessary to speak particularly—concretely, and urgently.

Finally, a very important and most pressing means is the intensification and improvement of party supervision not only in party work but also in Soviet work. Departmentalism, bureaucratism, distortion of human relations by market influences, all these develop a very great force which drags at people, wraps them round and corrupts them. Our party is much more aware of this than its critics from the sidelines. But it does not shirk dealing with these tendencies; it acts against them consciously, in a planned way, with vigilance and implacability. And this not only by its general work but also through specialized organs of supervision, adapted to the specific forms of contemporary party and Soviet work. If a party member has become so "specialized" in his departmental work that he has lost his moral link with the party, there is no point in his remaining in the party. He may be a useful Soviet functionary but he cannot be given a voice in deciding general party policy. The communist who is in danger of suffering such a degeneration must be pulled up with a jerk in good time. This is a very important task, which cannot be accomplished by the automatic action of the Soviet machine. The party, as a party, is organized very solidly in our country. But party members become parts of the Soviet machine in accordance with a quite different principle; there they have a different relationship among themselves and there is a different hierarchy. Between party and Soviet organizations there is a very complex interpenetration which, however, is insufficiently organized so far as the party is concerned. From this comes the need for an independent supervisory organ entrusted with the task of implementing the party line not only in party work but also in Soviet work— an organ which will be authoritative, flexible, comradely, but also, when necessary, ruthless. This question constitutes, as everyone remembers, of course, one of the main themes of Comrade Lenin's two last articles.[6]

The Red Army, seedbed of enlightenment

MAY 26, 1923

The eleventh All-Russian congress on the liquidation of illiteracy, which took place a few days ago, mentioned sympathetically and warmly the work of the Red Army in the cause of the struggle with illiteracy. The greetings of the worker-educators are very dear to us, but must not induce self-deception in us.

Illiteracy in the Red Army has been liquidated only in the rough. The majority of the Red Army soldiers return to the illiterate countryside, where there is an inevitable danger that those who have learned imperfectly will forget completely what they have learned. But we must insure that when each Red Army soldier returns to his village, he will become an active fighter against illiteracy. To reach this goal,

An order to the Red Army and Red Navy from Trotsky, who was then president of the Military Revolutionary Council of the Republic. From Pravda, *May 27, 1923. Translated for this volume from* Collected Works, *Vol. 21, by Iain Fraser.*

apart from correct, organized, planned work on the part of the whole military apparatus, we also require the constant influence of the more literate, more conscious, more educated Red Army soldiers on the backward ones. Illiteracy and semiliteracy must come to be regarded in the Red Army as a disgrace from which everyone strives to rid himself as soon as possible.

The struggle with illiteracy is only the first step in the great struggle against poverty, dirt, coarseness, and all the rest of the inheritance of slavery. Let us remember this every day and hour!

Don't spread yourself too thin!

Dear Comrades:

You complain that you have not been able to read even one-tenth of the books that interest you, and ask how to rationally allot your time. This is a very difficult question, because in the long run each person must make such a decision according to his particular needs and interests. It should be said, however, that the extent to which a person is able to keep up with the current literature, whether scientific, political, or otherwise, depends not only on the judicious allotment of one's time but also on the individual's previous training.

In regard to your specific reference to "party youth," I can only advise them not to hurry, not to spread themselves thin, not to skip from one topic to another, and not to pass

---

A letter to the Kiev comrades. From Pravda, *May 31, 1923. Translated for this volume from* Collected Works, *Vol. 21, by Marilyn Vogt.*

on to a second book until the first has been properly read, thought over, and mastered. I remember that when I myself belonged to the category of "youth," I too felt that there just wasn't enough time. Even in prison, when I did nothing but read, it seemed that one couldn't get enough done in a day. In the ideological sphere, just as in the economic arena, the phase of primitive accumulation is the most difficult and troublesome. And only after certain basic elements of knowledge and particularly elements of theoretical skill (method) have been precisely mastered and have become, so to speak, part of the flesh and blood of one's intellectual activity, does it become easier to keep up with the literature not only in areas one is familiar with, but in adjacent and even more remote fields of knowledge, because method, in the final analysis, is universal.

It is better to read one book and read it well; it is better to master a little bit at a time and master it thoroughly. Only in this way will your powers of mental comprehension extend themselves naturally. Thought will gradually gain confidence in itself and grow more productive. With these preliminaries in mind, it will not be difficult to rationally allot your time; and then, the transition from one pursuit to another will be to a certain extent pleasurable.

With comradely greetings,
L. Trotsky

Tasks of communist education

JUNE 18, 1923

1. The 'new person' and the revolutionist

Comrades! The entire Soviet Union—and we must bear firmly in mind that we are a Union[7]—is now alive with fifth anniversary celebrations. It must be admitted that after you make it past your own fortieth anniversary, you lose your taste for anniversaries just a little. But if any one of our fifth anniversaries deserves attention, and can actually evoke a joyous spiritual upsurge, it is this one, the anniversary of the Communist University, in the words of Sverdlov,[8] the supplier of party youth. . . .

A speech on the fifth anniversary of the Communist University, renamed Sverdlov University. Less than half of this article was printed in English under the same title in Inprecorr (International Press Correspondence), *the press service of the Communist International, August 16, 1923. From* Pravda, *June 24 and 26, 1923. Translated for this volume from* Collected Works, *Vol. 21, by Marilyn Vogt.*

Comrades, it is frequently asserted that the objective of communist education is to rear a new human being. These words are a little too general, too sentimental. True, on anniversaries, sentiment is not only permitted but encouraged. However, on this anniversary, we do not need to permit a formless humanitarian interpretation of the conception "the new human being" or of the objective of communist education. There is no doubt whatever that the person of the future, the citizen of the commune, will be an exceedingly interesting and attractive being with a psychology—the Futurists will pardon me, but I fancy that the person of the future will possess a psychology [*laughter*]—with a psychology, as I was saying, very different from ours. Our present task—unfortunately, if you like—is not the education of the human being of the future. The utopian humanitarian-psychological viewpoint is that first we must educate the "new human beings," and then they will create the new conditions.

We do not believe this. We know that human beings are the product of social conditions, and cannot somehow jump out of them. But we know something else: namely, that there exists a complex, mutually interacting relationship between conditions and human beings. Individuals themselves are the instruments of historical development, and not the least important instruments. So that within this complicated historical interweaving of environment with actively functioning human beings, we ourselves are now creating (and with Sverdlov University as one of our tools) not the abstractly harmonious and perfect citizen of the commune—oh, no. We are forming the real human beings of our epoch, who still have to fight to create the conditions out of which the harmonious citizen of the commune may emerge. This, of course, is a very different thing for the simple reason that, frankly speaking, our great-grandchild, the citizen of the commune, will not be a revolutionist.

At first glance this seems wrong; it sounds almost insulting.

But it is so. In our conception of "revolutionist" we combine our thought, our strength, the sum total of our highest passions. Therefore, the word "revolutionist" is permeated with the highest ideals and morals that have been handed down to us from the whole preceding epoch of cultural evolution. Thus it would seem that we cast an aspersion on future generations when we do not think of them as composed of revolutionists. But we must not forget that the revolutionist is a product of definite historical conditions, a product of class society. The revolutionist is no psychological abstraction. Revolution in itself is no abstract principle, but a material historical fact, growing out of class antagonisms, out of the violent subjugation of one class by another. Thus the revolutionist is a concrete historical type—and consequently a temporary one. We are justly proud of belonging to this type. But by our work we are creating the conditions for a social order in which there will be no class antagonisms, no revolutions, and thus no revolutionists. Of course, the very meaning of the word "revolutionist" could be extended to cover all conscious human activity—such as that aimed at harnessing nature, or expanding technical and cultural gains, or even building bridges to other universes that we cannot now know or imagine. But we, Comrades, have no right to make such an abstraction, such a limitless extension of the term "revolutionist," for we have by no means fulfilled our own concrete historical, political, revolutionary task—the overthrow of class society.

Our society has made a great leap out of capitalist slavery, but even the threshold of a harmonious communist society is not yet in sight. As a consequence—and I do not think it is out of place to emphasize this, and to do so more strongly than ever, on the occasion of Sverdlov University's anniversary—we should in no way see our educational objective to be the creation, under laboratory conditions, of the harmonious communard during this extremely disharmonious transitional phase of society. Such an objective would be pitiful and puerile utopianism. We want to create fighters and revolutionists who will be the guardians and successors of the historical revolutionary traditions that we have not yet completely fulfilled.

2. NEP, imperialist encirclement, and the International

Thus, when we approach the problem as stated in this correct, concrete, and historical way, certain misgivings that one hears even from some comrades (those with—how would you say it?—an overly humanitarian frame of mind), some of these misgivings fade away by themselves. There is concern about the dangers of NEP. Isn't the education of the new individual—they say to us—inconceivable under the NEP? Let me ask this: Under what conditions were we trained? Our generation, having already celebrated its fortieth birthday, and in general our entire party, was trained under capitalism. And our party would not have been brought up as a revolutionary party with its distinctive and unique revolutionary cast, had it not been the product of the conditions of a bourgeois regime multiplied by those of the czarist regime. And if we now have NEP, i.e., market relations, in our country, and if, therefore, there is also the possibility—yes, there is the theoretical possibility!—that capitalism may be restored (if we, as a party, sell out or blunder in a historically significant way)—well, if this danger exists, how does that measure up with your objective of rearing the harmonious citizen of the commune?

If the problem is rather one of training fighters for communism, allow me to ask, in what sense can the market conditions imposed on us by the course of the struggle prevent the young generation from developing a psychology of uncompromising struggle? The Spartans used to show the young people drunken helots and slaves in order to instill in them an aversion to drinking. I don't think that Sverdlov students need such graphic methods in that respect. [*Laughter*] But in respect to social questions, so we will not get the impression that, indeed, we have already completely and decisively crossed the threshold to socialism, history sometimes shows us sober, and sometimes even drunken, NEPmen, the helots of the marketplace. Today it is a semi-illusion, history tells us, but tomorrow the restoration of capitalism can become a reality if our party capitulates in the face of the difficulties of historical development.

In what sense, I ask, could NEP hamper the development of revolutionary fighters? It does not. In fact, it makes our historical tasks more specific and today serves as a most important method for training revolutionary worker and peasant youth by negative example.

NEP, however, is not the only feature reminding us that we still have not entered the peaceful and happy world of the commune. Serving as another reminder are the very high-ranking helots abroad. History gets them drunk from time to time, and they send us notes to remind us that the bourgeoisie, private property, and capital are still powerful facts and factors.

In connection with these high-ranking helots, which for completely understandable reasons of international courtesy I will not name, there is in today's issue of *Yunosheskaya Pravda* [Young People's Truth] a lead article with a most expressive headline, which I also shall not repeat. (Those who are curious are invited to consult the current issue of the paper.)[9] Here these unmentionable gentlemen remind us by their actions that the class struggle has taken both diplomatic and military forms in our experience because we are a proletariat—to use Engels's phrase—organized into a state and surrounded by the bourgeoisie organized into a number of states, and our relationships with other states is nothing but the class struggle taking different forms: i.e., at certain times, openly revolutionary or military forms; and at others, reformist or diplomatic forms. This is not only a metaphor or a figure of speech, but a living and indisputable historical fact! We are conducting an uninterrupted class struggle by means of diplomacy, foreign trade, and military defense. It is a class struggle that extends along our entire border, i.e., along a battlefront 50,000 versts long, considerably exceeding the length of the equator. This is not the least of the factors that on the one hand rule out the possibility of humanitarian abstractions about the new individual and on the other commit us ever so firmly to the hard reality of the revolutionary fighter.

When we were engaged in our internal struggle on the front lines of war, we had friends on the other side of every front—workers and peasants. And today, on the international scale, on the other side of our border of 50,000 versts by land and sea, we have friends striking in the enemies' rear—the world working class movement. Ties with them, for our revolutionary youth, are the fundamental component of a genuine communist education. Of course Marx, of course Engels, of course Lenin, are the basis, the foundation, the bedrock of theory. But with books alone, you will train only bookworms!

Revolutionary fighters can be trained only under conditions in which they are at once based on a bedrock of theory and closely and inseparably linked with the practical reality of the revolutionary class struggle throughout the world. Observing this worldwide struggle with the utmost attention, penetrating its logic, understanding its inner laws, are the primary conditions for training young revolutionaries in our epoch, an epoch in which all of politics and all of culture, even down to their most fiendish and bloody contradictions, are becoming more and more international.

3. The revolutionist and mysticism

Sverdlov University must train revolutionists. What are revolutionists? What are their main characteristics? It must be emphasized that we have no right, even for the sake of reflection, to separate the revolutionists from the class basis upon which they have evolved, and without which they do not exist. The revolutionists of our epoch, who can be linked only with the working class, possess their own special psychological characteristics, qualities of intellect and will. If it is necessary and possible, revolutionists forcefully shatter the historical obstructions. If this is not possible, they make a detour. If it is impossible to make a detour, revolutionists patiently and persistently keep scraping and chipping away. They are revolutionists because they are not afraid to shatter obstacles or to employ relentless force. They know the historical value of these things. It is their constant endeavor to deploy the full capacity of their destructive and creative work; that is, to extract from every given historical situation the maximum that it is capable of rendering toward the advancement of the revolutionary class.

In their activities, revolutionists are limited only by external obstacles and not by internal ones. That is, they must train themselves to evaluate their situation, the material and concrete reality of their entire arena of activity, in its positive and negative aspects, and to draw the correct political balance sheet. But if the revolutionist is internally hampered by subjective hindrances to action, is lacking in understanding or will, is paralyzed by internal discord, by religious, national, ethnocentric, or craft prejudices, then he is at best only half a revolutionist.

Comrades, there are already too many obstacles in the objective conditions for revolutionists to allow themselves the luxury of multiplying the objective obstacles and frictions by subjective ones. Therefore, the education of revolutionists must, above all, mean their emancipation from all legacies of ignorance and superstition, which are frequently preserved even in very "sensitive" consciousnesses. And therefore, we show irreconcilable opposition to anyone who dares to suggest that mysticism or religious sentiments and frames of mind might be compatible with communism.

You know that not long ago one of the prominent Swedish comrades wrote about the compatibility of religion not only with membership in the Communist Party, but even with a Marxist world view.[10] We consider atheism, which is an inseparable element of the materialist view of life, to be a prerequisite for the theoretical education of the revolutionist. Those who believe in another world are not capable of concentrating all their passion on the transformation of this one.

4. Darwinism and Marxism

That is why natural science has such enormous significance at Sverdlov University. Without Darwin, we would not be where we are now. Comrades, I recall how years ago . . . how many would it be? Almost a quarter of a century ago, while in Odessa prison, I picked up Darwin's *Origin of Species by Natural Selection* for the first time. I vividly remember the colossal shock I experienced when reading those books. I don't remember where it was in *The Origin of Species by Natural Selection* that Darwin portrayed the development of the feather if not of a peacock, then of some other kind of well-decorated poultry cock, showing how from the first insignificant formal color deviations were generated the most complicated refinements. I must say that it was only at that moment, when considering the tail of the peacock from a theoretical perspective in Darwin's interpretation, that I felt that I should be an atheist. Because, if nature can carry out such refined and magnificent work by its "blind" methods, why does that work require the interference of outside forces? Several months later, when I read Darwin's autobiography—all this is firmly imbedded in my memory!—where there is a phrase something like this: Although I, Darwin, have rejected the Bible's theory of creation, I still preserve my belief in God—I was deeply affected, for Darwin's sake, not my own. And I still do not know whether this was a conventional lie or a diplomatic tribute to the social opinions of the English bourgeoisie, the most hypocritical in the world; or was it really that in the brains of this old man—one of the most ingenious in the history of humanity—there remained little cells unaffected by Darwinism, where a religious faith was lodged during his childhood when he was studying to be a priest? I decided not to pursue this psychological question, Comrades. But does it matter? Even if Charles Darwin, as he himself asserted, did not lose his belief in God, Darwinism itself is nonetheless entirely irreconcilable with this belief.

In this, as in other respects, Darwinism is a forerunner of Marxism. Taken in a broadly materialist and dialectical sense, Marxism is the application of Darwinism to human society. Manchester liberalism has attempted to fit Darwinism mechanically into sociology. Such attempts have only led to childish analogies veiling malicious bourgeois apologies: market competition was explained by the "eternal" law of the struggle for existence. There is no reason to dwell on such banalities. It is only the inner connection between Darwinism and Marxism that makes it possible to grasp the living flow of existence in its initial connection with inorganic nature; in its further particularization and evolution; in its dynamics; in the differentiation of the necessities of life among the first elementary varieties of the vegetable and animal kingdoms; in its struggles; in its changes; in its growth, as it became more sophisticated in form; in the appearance of the "first" human or humanoid creature, taking up the first tool-like objects; in the development of primitive cooperation, these creatures putting to use tools that they made themselves; in the further stratification of society on the basis of the development of the means of production, that is, of the means of subjugating nature; in class warfare; and finally, in the struggle for the abolition of classes.

To comprehend the world from such a broad materialist point of view signifies the emancipation of one's consciousness for the first time from the legacy of mysticism, securing both feet firmly on the ground. It means knowing that for the future one has no inner subjective hindrances to the struggle, but that the only resistance and opposition is external, and must be undermined in some cases, circumvented in others, smashed in still others—depending on the conditions of the struggle.

5. Theory of revolutionary struggle
How often have we said, "practice wins in the end." This is correct in the sense that the collective experience of a class and of the whole of humanity gradually sweeps away the illusions and false theories based on hasty generalizations. But it may be said with equal truth, "theory wins in the end," when we understand by this that theory in reality comprises the total experience of humanity. Seen from this standpoint, the counterposition between theory and practice vanishes, for theory is nothing other than correctly considered and generalized practice. Theory does not overcome practice, but rather the thoughtless, purely empirical, crude approach to it. We have every right to say "arm yourself with theory since in the last analysis theory wins out." In order to be able to properly evaluate the conditions of the struggle, including the situation of your own class, you need a reliable method for political and historical orientation. This is Marxism, or with respect to the latest epoch, Leninism.

Marx and Lenin—these are our two supreme guides in the sphere of social thought. The ideas of these two men, who embody the materialist and dialectical world view, form the basis of the program of the Sverdlov Communist University. Marx—Lenin! This combination precludes any thought of "academicism." I have in mind those discussions about academicism which were conducted in your schools and later found their way into the columns of the general party press.[11] Academicism in the sense of the belief in the self-contained importance of theory is doubly absurd for us as revolutionaries. Theory serves collective humanity; it serves the cause of revolution.

It is true that in certain periods of our social development, there were attempts to separate Marxism from revolutionary action. This was during the time of the so-called legal Marxism in the 1890s.[12] Russian Marxists were divided into two camps: Legal Marxists from the journalistic salons of Moscow and Petersburg; and the underground fraternity—imprisoned, in penal exile, emigrated, illegal.

The legalists were as a general rule more educated than our group of young Marxists in those days. It is true that there was among us a group of broadly educated revolutionary Marxists, but they were only a handful. We, the youth, if we are honest with ourselves, were in the overwhelming majority pretty ignorant. We were shocked sometimes by some of Darwin's ideas. Not all of us, however, even had occasion to get so far as to read Darwin. Nevertheless, I can say with certainty that when one of these underground, young, 19- or 20-year-old Marxists happened to meet and collide head-on with a legal Marxist, the feeling invariably sprang up among the young people that, all the same, we were more intelligent. This was not simply puerile arrogance. No. The key to this feeling is that it is impossible to genuinely master Marxism if you do not have the will for revolutionary action. Only if Marxist theory is combined with that will and directed toward overcoming the existing conditions can it be a tool to drill and bore. And if this active revolutionary will is absent, then the Marxism is pseudo-Marxism, a wooden knife which neither stabs nor cuts. And that is what it was under the direction of our legal Marxists. They gradually were transformed into liberals.

The willingness for revolutionary action is a precondition for mastering the Marxist dialectic. The one cannot live without the other. Marxism cannot be academicism without ceasing to be Marxism, i.e., the theoretical tool of revolutionary action. Sverdlov University is guarded from academic degeneration because it is a party institution, and will continue to be a garrison in the besieged revolutionary fortress.

6. To the memory of Sverdlov
It is not without reason, Comrades, that your university is named after Sverdlov. We revere Yakov Mikhailovich with deep affection not as a theoretician—that he was not—but as a revolutionary who mastered the Marxist method sufficiently for the needs of revolutionary action. Like the overwhelming majority of us, he did not independently develop a theory of Marxism and he did not carry it on to new scientific conquests, but on the other hand he applied the Marxist method with total confidence in order to deliver material blows to bourgeois society. That is how we knew him and that is how he was until he died. What characterized him most was his genuine fortitude. Without this quality, Comrades, one is not and cannot be a revolutionist. Not in the sense that a revolutionist cannot be a coward. It is too elementary and simple to speak about courage in the physical sense. A revolutionist must have something more; namely, ideological fortitude, audacity in action, resoluteness in matters never before known to history, which experience has yet to verify and which therefore loom as something inconceivable. The idea of the October insurrection after it took place is one thing; but conceiving of the October insurrection before it took place—that is quite another matter. Every great event in a certain sense takes people by surprise. The idea of an October insurrection on the eve of the insurrection—didn't it, after all, seem to be the embodiment of the impossible,

the unrealizable, and didn't more than a few Marxists shy away in horror, although it seemed all the while they were marching to meet it head-on? And the significance of October was disclosed in the fact that, during those days, history weighed classes, parties, and individuals in its hand, and discarded the chaff.

Sverdlov was not discarded. He was a genuine fighter, made of good stuff, and he had adequately mastered the weapons of Marxism in order to firmly and confidently pass through the October days. I saw him under various conditions: in the huge mass meetings, in tense sessions of the Central Committee, serving on commissions, on the Military Revolutionary Committee, and at sessions of the all-Russian congresses of Soviets. I more than once heard his trumpeting orator's voice and his "meeting chamber" voice as a Central Committee member. And, Comrades, I cannot for a moment imagine an expression of embarrassment or confusion on his face, to say nothing of fright. During the most ominous hours he was always the same: with his leather cap on his head, with a cigarette in his mouth, smiling, slender, small, always moving, and above all confident and calm. . . . That's how he was in July 1917, during the bacchanal of the White Guards in Petrograd;[13] he was that way during the most anxious hours before the October insurrection; he was that way during the days of the German invasion after the Brest-Litovsk Treaty was signed;[14] and during the days of the July uprising of the Left Social Revolutionaries [SRs], when one part of the Council of People's Commissars—the Left SR minority—fired from one of Moscow's streets on the other part of the Council of People's Commissars—the Bolshevik majority—in the Kremlin.[15] I remember Yakov Mikhailovich, with his omnipresent leather cap on his head, smiling and asking, "Well, isn't it obviously time to move again from the Council of People's Commissars to the Military Revolutionary Committee?" Even in those hours, when the Czechoslovaks threatened Nizhny Novgorod, and Comrade Lenin lay wounded by an SR bullet, Sverdlov did not waver. His calm and firm confidence never left him. And this, Comrades, is the invaluable, genuine, truly precious quality of the true revolutionary.

We don't know what kinds of days and hours await us, what sorts of battles we must wage, what kinds of barricades we must take and even temporarily relinquish. We have already taken them more than once, lost them, and taken them again. The curve of revolutionary development is a very complicated line. We must be ready for everything. The courageous spirit of Sverdlov must inspire the students of Sverdlov University. Then we could rest assured about the succession of our party's military traditions.

7. The party in the East

I stated earlier, Comrades, that mysticism and religion are incompatible with membership in the Communist Party. This expression was imprecise, and I want to correct it—not because of any sort of abstract images, but because for us, for the Communist Party of the Soviet Republic, this question has tremendous practical significance.

Moscow is the indisputable center of the Union, but we have in the Union a great outlying area, which is settled by nationalities that were previously oppressed and by peoples who are backward due to no fault of their own. The problem of establishing or developing Communist parties in these areas at this time is one of the most important and complex of our problems; and finding the solution to it will be a responsibility on the young shoulders of the students of Sverdlov in the course of their coming work.

We border on the outside world, and first and foremost on the vastly populated East along the borders of these backward Soviet republics. In accordance with the laws and logic of the revolutionary dictatorship, we will not permit even one of the parties that serve openly or in disguise as agents of a bourgeois state to raise its head in any country of the Union. In other words, we will recognize only a Communist Party's right to rule during the transitional revolutionary period. By the same token, in Turkestan, Azerbaidzhan, Georgia, and Armenia, as in all the other areas of our Union, we will invest only a local Communist Party, supported by the poorest strata of workers, with the right to control the fate of the people during the transitional period.

But in that area, the social base—the proletariat—from which our party arose in the cities, to be tempered in battle, is too weak. The proletariat there is weak. There is not even that modest political prerevolutionary history that characterized the Petrograd proletariat. There, only the October Revolution awakened the backward and previously heavily oppressed peasant masses to a conscious or semiconscious political life; and having awakened, they are gravitating toward the Communist Party, as their liberators. Their most advanced elements are striving to move forward into the party's ranks—those who are sincere, revolutionary, but who in the past have been deprived of the schooling of the class struggle, the experience of strikes, uprisings, barricade battles, of study-circle propaganda, a press in their own or in other languages, etc. These are the elements that have just raised themselves out of seminomadic barbarism, from Lamaism, shamanism, or the realm of Islam, and are now knocking on the door of the Communist Party. We are opening the door of our party to these advanced elements of the backward peoples; and it is not surprising if we observe that in Turkestan and in certain other national republics a notable percentage of our party are believers—in some of the parties as many as 15 percent.

Does this have anything in common with the theory that other "leaders" are developing on the compatibility of religion and Marxism? No, it has nothing at all in common. It is one thing if an educated intellectual gentleman, cast by fate into the Communist Party, but feeling dissatisfied, or suffering from ideological belching or heartburn from theoretical indigestion, thinks that from time to time he needs a dose of mystical medicine—to counter ideological heartburn or some other indisposition. This ideological idleness, this vulgar snobbery, rather than being refined, is in fact an aristocratic banality.

But it is quite another thing when it concerns the raw revolutionary recruits from the Turkestan or Azerbaidzhan Republics—pristine, untried by history—who come knocking on our door. We must take them in and train them. Of course, it would be better if we had a proletariat there that had already had experience in strikes and bouts with the church, that had rejected the old prejudices and only then come to communism. That's how it is in Europe and, to a certain degree, it has been and continues to be that way in the center of our country. But the East is lacking all this previous schooling. There our party is the elementary school, and it must fulfill its responsibility accordingly. We will admit into our ranks those comrades who have yet to break with religion not in order to reconcile Marxism with Islam, but rather tactfully but persistently to free the backward members' consciousnesses of superstition, which in its very essence is the mortal enemy of communism.

By every means at the party's disposal, we must help them rework every area of their consciousness, to raise its level until they really have a totally active materialist world view. One of your most important missions, Comrades of Sverdlov University, will be to extend and strengthen the ties between East and West. Remember: we are the source and the bearers of culture for the immense Asian continent. We must first of all realize and unfold our mission with regard to the East within the limits of our own Soviet Union. Even if it is difficult to re-educate ideologically the elder or mature Turks, Bashkirs, or Kirghizes, it is fully possible in relation to the native youth. This is first of all the task of our Young Communists of Sverdlov University.

The revolution stretches out over years, many years. It will be extended and completed only after decades. You will be its continuers. I do not know whether all of you will be its completers. But it will be a source of great happiness, Comrades, that you will be participants, that you will not let yourselves break from the revolutionary ideological continuity, and that, in possessing the theoretical instruments of struggle, you will apply them to an even wider arena. The main objective of Sverdlov University is to train our most reliable means of defense, the representatives of the young generation. Let us always remember: in the end, theory wins!

8. Sverdlov University and Lenin

I have no doubt that in the coming years the ties between Sverdlov University on the one hand, and the Lenin Institute and Marx Institute on the other, will be strengthened. For the younger generation, the way to Marx is through Lenin. The straight road becomes increasingly difficult, for a longer and longer period now separates the rising generation from the genius of those who founded scientific socialism, Marx and Engels. Leninism is the highest embodiment and condensation of Marxism for direct revolutionary action in the epoch of the imperialist death agony of bourgeois society. The Lenin Institute at Moscow must be made an academy of revolutionary strategy. The tie between Sverdlov University and the Institute must be established from the very beginning in order to be further developed and strengthened.

Comrades! At this, our fifth anniversary celebration, we grieve over nothing more than that our esteemed chairman Ilyich [Lenin] is not sitting here among us. The thought of his long and grave illness is always in the back of our minds. But alongside this grief, and easing it, is a feeling of firm confidence that the mighty spirit of Lenin has reliably and firmly penetrated our Communist Party, as well as one of the party's most valuable allies, Sverdlov University. And in this sense, we can say that if our leader and teacher is not here sitting with us today, his revolutionary genius is with us. It is here with us during the anniversary of Sverdlov University. Our revolutionary lungs breathe the atmosphere of that better and higher doctrine that the preceding development of human thought has created. That is why we are so profoundly convinced that tomorrow is ours.

I cannot conclude these greetings from the Central Committee of our party any other way, Comrades, than by sending our general comradely greetings and the enthusiastic love of the students to our teacher Ilyich! [*Applause and singing of the International*]

The newspaper and its readers

JUNE 29, 1923

The strengthening of our party—not so much in its numbers as in its influence on nonparty people, on the one hand, and on the new period of the revolution we have entered on the other—presents the party with tasks that are in part new and in part old ones in a new form, such as those in the field of agitation and propaganda. We must carefully and attentively examine our weapons and means of propaganda. Are they sufficient in content; i.e., do they embrace all problems that need to be illuminated? Do they find an appropriate *form* of expression, accessible to the readers and interesting for them?

This question, along with a series of others, was the subject of discussion in a group of twenty-five Moscow agitators and mass organizers. Their judgments, opinions, and

From Pravda, *July 1, 1923. Translated for this volume from* Collected Works, *Vol. 21, by Iain Fraser.*

estimates were noted down in shorthand. I hope soon to make use of all this material for the press. The journalist comrades will find some bitter reproaches there, and I must in all conscience say that the majority of these reproaches in my opinion are justified. The question of the organization of our printed agitation, above all in the newspapers, has too great a significance for any hushing up to be permissible here. We must speak frankly.

As they say, "Appearances are important."[16] Let's start then with newspaper technique. It has of course become better than it was in 1919–20, but it is still extremely bad. The slovenliness of the layout and the blurring of the print make reading the newspaper very difficult, even for a thoroughly literate reader, and still more so for a semiliterate one. Newspapers intended for wide sale among the workers, like *Rabochaya Moskva* and *Rabochaya Gazeta** are printed extremely badly. The difference between separate issues is very great: sometimes you can read almost all of the newspaper and sometimes you can't even make out half of it. This has made buying a newspaper into a lottery. I take out at random one of the latest numbers of *Rabochaya Gazeta*. I glance at the "Children's Corner": "Tale of a clever cat. . . ." It's completely impossible to read, the print is so blurred; and that's for children! It has to be said straight out: the technique of our newspapers is our disgrace. With our poverty and need for education we yet contrive to spoil a quarter or even a half of a newspaper page by smearing the printing ink. Such a "newspaper" produces in the reader irritation above all; in the less developed reader it produces weariness and apathy, and in the more educated and demanding one—a gritting of the teeth and outright contempt for those who have permitted themselves to make such a mockery of

---

* Incidentally, why is *Rabochaya Gazeta* folded not lengthwise but across? This may suit someone, but certainly not the reader—L.T.

him. Somebody writes these articles, somebody sets them up, somebody prints them—and as a result the reader, following the lines with his finger, makes out from a fifth to a tenth. Shame and disgrace! The last congress of our party devoted special attention to this question of typography. And the question is: how much longer are we going to have to put up with all this?

"Appearances are important; but what matters is what is inside." We have already seen that poor typographical externals sometimes make it difficult to penetrate through to the inside. The more so since in between still stands the layout of the printed matter, the make-up, and the editing. Let's just stay with the editing, since it is especially bad here. Not only in newspapers but even in scientific journals—especially in the journal *Pod Znamenem Marxizma* (Under the Banner of Marxism]—the most amazing misprints and distortions commonly occur. Lev Tolstoy once said that printing books is a weapon for spreading ignorance. Of course, this arrogant, aristocratic assertion is basically false. But—alas!—it is often justified . . . by the proofreading of our press. This cannot be tolerated either! If the printing houses do not have available the necessary cadres of thoroughly literate proofreaders, competent at their business, then these cadres must be specially trained. Remedial courses are necessary for the present proofreaders, including political education courses. The proofreader must understand the text he is editing, otherwise he is not a proofreader but an involuntary spreader of ignorance; and the press, despite Tolstoy's assertion, is a weapon of enlightenment—it must be.

Let us now come closer to the content of the text.

The newspaper exists above all to link people together by informing them of what's happening where. Thus, fresh, ample, interesting *information* is the soul of a paper. A most important role in newspaper information of our day is played by the telegraph and radio. So the reader, accustomed to the newspaper and knowing its significance, first of all turns to the cables and dispatches. In order for the dispatches to really occupy the first place in Soviet newspapers, they must give information about important and interesting facts, and in a form that is comprehensible to the reading masses. But we don't have this. The dispatches in our newspapers are expressed and printed in terms usual for the "big" bourgeois press. If you follow the wire messages from day to day in some of our newspapers, you get the impression that when the comrades in charge of this department submit fresh cables to be set up, they have completely forgotten what they put in yesterday. There is absolutely no day-to-day method in the work. Each wire looks like some sort of chance fragment. The explanations appended to them have a random and in large part unconsidered character. At most the editor of the section puts in brackets beside the name of some foreign bourgeois politician or other "lib." or "cons." This is supposed to mean "liberal" or "conservative." But since three-fourths of the readers won't understand these editorial abbreviations, the explanations more often just confuse them. Cables with information about events in say Bulgaria or Rumania usually reach us via Vienna, Berlin, or Warsaw. The names of these towns put at the head of the cable completely confuse the *mass* reader, who is very weak in geography as it is.

Why do I bring up these details? All for the same reason: they show best of all how little we think of the position of the less-able readers, of their needs, of their helplessness when we make up our newspapers. *The reworking of dispatches in a workers' newspaper is a very difficult and very responsible matter.* It requires attentive, painstaking work. An important dispatch must be thought through from all angles and given a form that will link it directly to what the reading masses more or less already know. The necessary explanations must precede the cables, joining them into groups or fusing them together.

What point is there in a fat headline taking up three lines or more, if it only repeats what is said in the wire itself? These headlines quite often only confuse the reader. A simple report of a second-rate strike is often headlined "It's Begun!" or "The Denouement Is Approaching," while the cable itself talks briefly about a movement of railwaymen, without mentioning causes or aims. On the next day there's nothing about this event; nor on the day after. The next time the reader sees above a dispatch the headline "It's Begun!" he already sees in this a frivolous attitude toward the matter, cheap newspaper sensationalism, and his interest in cables and in the newspaper fades. If the chief of the cable desk clearly remembers what he printed yesterday and the day before, and himself strives to understand the connection between events and between facts, so as to make this connection clear to the readers, then cabled information, even if very imperfect, will have an immeasurable educational value. Hard factual information gradually sinks into the readers' minds. It becomes increasingly easy for them to understand new facts, and they learn to seek and find in the newspaper in the first place the most important information. The readers who learn this take a big step on the road of cultural development at the same time. Our newspapers must apply all their forces to the dispatch section and insure that it is set up as it ought to be. Only in this way—by pressure and example from the papers themselves—can the Rosta correspondents gradually be trained too.[17]

Once a week—best, of course, in the Sunday issue, i.e., on the day when the worker is free—summary *reviews* of the most important events of the week should be given. At the same time this work would be a wonderful means of educating the department chiefs of a newspaper. They would learn to be more careful about finding the interconnections of separate events, and this would have a very beneficial effect in turn on the day-to-day running of the department.

The understanding of international newspaper information is impossible without at least the most basic geographic knowledge. The sketch maps sometimes given by the papers—even in the cases when they can be made out—are of little help to the reader who does not know the relative positions of the parts of the earth and the countries. The question of maps in our situation—i.e., in a situation of imperialist encirclement and the growth of the world revolution—is a very important question of general education. In all or at least in the most important halls where lectures or meetings are held, there should be specially prepared maps with clearly drawn national frontiers and with other graphic indications of economic and political development. Possibly such schematic maps should be set up in some streets or squares, as during the civil war. Means could probably be found for this. In the last year we have been making an immense quantity of banners for all sorts of reasons. Would it not be better to use these funds to equip factories and workshops, and then also villages, with political maps? Every lecturer, orator, propagandist, etc., when he mentions England and its colonies, will be able to point to them immediately on the maps. The same with the Ruhr. It will be to the benefit of the orator above all; he will know more clearly and firmly what he's talking about, since he will himself check up beforehand where everything is. And the listeners, if the question itself interests them, are bound to notice what they were shown—if not the first time, then the fifth or the tenth. And from the moment when the words Ruhr, London, or India stop being just empty sounds to the readers, they will start to have an entirely different attitude to dispatches. It will be a pleasure to find India in the newspaper when they know where it is. They will stand more firmly on their feet, and understand dispatches and political articles better. They will become and will feel themselves more educated. Demonstrative maps thus become a primary element of general political education. Gosizdat should pay serious attention to this problem.[18]

But let's get back to the newspaper. The same general faults we found in the field of international news can be observed again in respect to domestic news, in particular about the activity of Soviet, professional, cooperative, and other institutions. A careless, slovenly, thoughtless attitude to the reader here too is often expressed in "details," but in the kind that make a mess of the whole business. Soviet and other institutions here have abbreviated names, and are sometimes denoted only by initials. Within the institution itself, or in neighboring institutions, this leads to certain conveniences in the sense of saving time and paper. But the broad mass of readers cannot know these arbitrary abbreviations.

Our journalists, reporters, and chroniclers throw about all sorts of incomprehensible Soviet words, like clowns with balls. Here in a prominent place is printed a conversation with Comrade someone or other, "president of the CED." These letters are repeated dozens of times in the article without explanation. You have to be a dyed-in-the-wool Soviet bureaucrat to guess that it's all about the Commune Economy Department. The mass reader will never guess this, and of course will give up the article in annoyance, and maybe even the whole paper. Our newspaper workers should carve on their walls that abbreviations and arbitrary names are good and acceptable within the limits in which they are certain to be understood; but where they just confuse people, recourse to them is criminal and pointless.

A newspaper, we said above, should in the first place inform well. It can only teach through good, interesting, properly organized news. Above all, facts should be explained clearly, to the point, and forcefully; where, what, and how. It is often considered in our country that events and facts are known to the readers by themselves, or can be understood by them with just a hint, or do not have any meaning at all, and that the task of a newspaper consists, as it were, in relating "in connection" with this fact (unknown or incomprehensible to the readers) a number of instructive things which have long been causing a pain in the neck. This happens frequently also because the author of the article or remark himself does not know for sure, and to speak frankly cannot be bothered to check up, find out, read up, lift the phone for some information. And he aims to talk around the matter and says "in connection" with the fact, that the bourgeoisie is the bourgeoisie and the proletariat is the proletariat. Comrade journalists, the reader begs you not to admonish him, not to preach, not to summon, not to urge, but to tell him clearly and to the point, to explain, to clarify—what, where, and how! The lessons and the warnings will follow from this of themselves.

The writer, especially on a newspaper, must start off not from himself, but from the reader. This is a very important difference, and is expressed in the construction of every individual article and of the edition as a whole. In the one case a writer (unskillful, not understanding his job) simply presents the reader with himself, his views, his thoughts, or frequently—nothing but his phrases. In the other, a writer who approaches his task properly leads the reader himself to the necessary conclusions, using for this the everyday experience of the life of the masses.

We shall explain our meaning by an example that came up during the discussions of the Moscow propagandists. This year in our country, as is well known, a violent malaria epidemic is raging. While our traditional epidemic diseases—typhus, cholera, etc.—have declined considerably in recent times, falling even below the prewar level, malaria has taken on unprecedented proportions. Towns, regions, factories have been caught by it. By its sudden appearance, its ebbs and flows, by the chronic character of its attacks, malaria affects not only the health but also the imagination. But our press in general was and is too little interested in this fact. Every article that appeared on the theme of malaria was, as the Moscow comrades related, an object of the greatest interest: the copy of the paper would pass from hand to hand, the article would be read aloud, etc.

It is absolutely clear that our press should not limit itself to the sanitary and propaganda activity of Narkomzdrav[19] but should develop more independent work in this connection. It should begin with the course of the epidemic itself, the regions where it is found, listing the factories, workshops, etc., most affected by it. This by itself will establish a living connection with the most backward masses, and show them that people know about them, are interested in them, that they are not forgotten. Further, malaria should be explained from the scientific and social points of view, showing by dozens of examples its distribution in connection with certain conditions of life and work; the measures being taken by the appropriate organs of the state should be correctly highlighted, the necessary advice should be given and constantly repeated from edition to edition, etc. This is the concrete basis on which propaganda can and must be developed—for example, against religious prejudices. If epidemics, like all diseases in general, are a punishment for sin, why is malaria more common in some works than in others, or in damp places than in dry ones? The factual picture of the distribution of malaria with the necessary explanations is a marvelous weapon of anti-religious propaganda. The force of action of this weapon is the more powerful since the question affects simultaneously broad circles of workers, and very sharply, too.

A newspaper does not have the right not to be interested in what the masses, the people in the street, are interested in. Of course, our newspaper can and must throw light on facts, since it is called upon to educate, elevate, develop. But it will only reach the goal if it starts off from facts, thoughts, and moods that really affect the mass reader.

There is no doubt, for example, that trials and so-called "events"—accidents, suicides, murders, dramas of jealousy, etc.—greatly excite the thoughts and emotions of broad circles of the population. This is not surprising; they are all brilliant bits of vivid life. But our press, as a general rule, shows a great lack of attention to this, commenting at best in a few lines of small type. As a result the people in the street get their news from lower-quality sources, and along with the news, low-quality elucidations. A family drama, a suicide, a murder, a trial with a severe sentence, strike and will go on striking the imagination. "The Komarov trial for a while even overshadowed Curzon," [20] write comrades Lagutin and Kazansky ("Red Star" tobacco factory). Our press must approach all these facts with the greatest attention, explain them, illuminate them, and clarify them.

Here both a psychological, a domestic, and a social approach are necessary. Dozens and hundreds of abstract articles, repeating banal commonplaces about the middle-classness of the bourgeoisie or about the dullness of the petty-bourgeois family structure, do not touch the consciousness of the reader; they are just like ordinary, tedious autumn rain. But a trial based on a family drama, ably told and illuminated in a series of articles, can enthrall thousands of readers and awaken in them new, fresher, and broader thoughts and emotions. After this perhaps some of the readers will feel they would like a general article on the theme of the family, too.

The bourgeois yellow press of the whole world makes murders and poisonings an object of profitable sensation, playing on unhealthy curiosity and in general on the worst human instincts. But it does not at all follow that we should simply turn our backs on human curiosity and on human instincts in general. This would be sheer hypocrisy and bigotry. We are the party of the masses. We are a revolutionary state, and not a holy order or a monastery. Our newspapers ought to satisfy not only desire for knowledge of the highest kind but also natural curiosity: all that is required is that they should uplift and ennoble it by an appropriate selection of material and illumination of the question. This kind of article or note is always and everywhere read very widely. In the Soviet press, however, it is almost absent.

They will say that the necessary literary powers for this do not exist. This is only partly true. Workers appear when the problem is posed correctly and distinctly. Above all we need a serious change in the direction of our attention. Where to? Towards the reader, alive, as he is, the mass reader, awakened by the revolution, but not very literate, poorly educated, striving to get to know much, but often helpless, and always remaining a living person, to whom nothing human is alien. This reader demands attention to himself very insistently, although he may not always be able to express this. But the twenty-five propagandists and mass organizers of the Moscow committee of our party expressed it very clearly for him.

Our young writers and propagandists are far from all able to write so that they can be understood. Maybe this is because they did not have to break through the primeval crust of darkness and lack of understanding. They came into party and agitational literature in a period when a certain circle of ideas, works, and expressions received a durable distribution among fairly broad layers of the workers. The danger of a split between the party and the nonparty masses in the field of agitation is expressed in the exclusiveness of the content of agitation and of its form, in the construction of an almost arbitrary party language, inaccessible to almost nine-tenths not only of the peasants but even of the workers.

But life does not stop even for an hour; new generations are arising one after another. The fate of the Soviet Republic is now being decided to a considerable extent by those who were fifteen, sixteen, or seventeen during the imperialist war and then in the February and October revolutions.[21] This "dominance" of the young coming to replace us will be felt more strongly as we proceed.

With these young people you cannot talk in ready formulas, phrases, expressions, and words which mean something to us "oldsters" because they flow from our experience, but which for them remain almost empty sounds. We must learn to speak with them in their language, i.e., in the language of their experience.

The struggle with czarism, the revolution of 1905, the imperialist war, and both revolutions of 1917 are for us personal experiences, memories, living facts of our own activity. We talk about them in hints, remember, and mentally fill in what we don't completely say. But the young? They do not understand these hints because they do not know the facts, have not lived through them, and cannot get to know them from books or from well-written stories, since there are none. Allusion is enough for the older generation; but the young need a primer. The time has come to prepare a series of such textbooks and primers of revolutionary political education for the young.

Big and small

[PUBLISHED OCTOBER 18, 1923]
Both the great events developing in Germany and the greater events which may grow from the German revolution affect the interests of the Soviet Union in the most direct and immediate way. What about our current everyday tasks; don't they take second place? Won't they disappear altogether? No, they are not disappearing, and they are not going away.

From the preface to The Generation of October. *Printed in* Pravda, *October 18, 1923. Translated for this volume from* Collected Works, *Vol. 21, by Iain Fraser.*

The French invasion of the Ruhr in 1923, because Germany had not paid war reparations on time, combined with a severe economic crisis, produced a revolutionary situation, with the German Communist Party in the leadership. At the time Trotsky wrote this article, the outcome of the situation was unknown. But because the Bolsheviks had pinned their hopes on a victorious revolution in Germany, which would ease the tasks of socialist construction in the Soviet Union and open prospects for revolution in the rest of the industrially advanced world, the events in Germany were the focus of attention during this time.

On the contrary, in the new perspective they acquire a new, enormously increased significance.

Parties, like individual people, really show themselves only in times of great trial. And if Tolstoy's officer was right to think that the brave man is the one who acts as must be, then this is even more true of a party: the truly revolutionary party is the one that can extract from each situation, by the methods appropriate to it, the maximum benefit for the world revolution.

We are now without a doubt coming up to one of these historical turning points that determine future developments for a number of years, and in all probability even for decades. The center of the European and world problem is Germany. Our interest in the fate of Germany has the deepest and the most direct character. If the plunderers of French imperialism, the most reactionary, rapacious, and base of any that history has known, manage for long to break the will of the German people to life and independence, the Soviet Union would stand immeasurably weaker. The question of the fate of Germany is being decided now first of all by the internal struggle of its classes, and it is superfluous to say that everyone who is consciously with us is striving to fathom the internal course of development of the German people, to predict the next stages of the struggle of the German proletariat. All other political interests naturally take second place among our vanguard.

However, the matter is not limited to the vanguard. The overwhelming majority of the population of our country has not learned and could not have learned to think about phenomena on a world scale. But even if we limit ourselves to the vanguard alone, even here there is not at all enough political interest and sympathy for the struggle of the German workers and the fate of the German people. We are not observers but participants in the historical process. And here we must ask ourselves: Is there no contradiction between today's everyday work in the conditions of NEP, between our economic and cultural construction on the one hand, and the sweep of the approaching events on the other? Without an answer to this question, there will be an inescapable ambiguity in the mind of every thinking worker, and there is nothing worse than ambiguity, which can paralyze the will.

Let us try to get to the essence of the matter by a simple example. When I questioned a young student about how his studies were going, he answered half-jokingly, half-seriously: "What studies? There's a revolution approaching in Germany!" Not only young students, but even very many mature workers seem to feel somehow knocked off the rails. Our everyday work, which Comrade Lenin, in his article on cooperation, for want of a better word called "culturizing," seems to be losing its point and weight in face of the approaching great events.

Thus, for example, in one provincial party newspaper I read a very long article proving that it is impossible for us to occupy ourselves with questions of everyday life, since the German revolution is already knocking at the door of history. As an alternative to this, we are encouraged to take our example "by looking at your elders, us, for example, or your late uncle" who showed Spartan hardness, the ability to be selfless, etc. Many of us have more than once had to speak of the necessity for the younger generation to adopt the best elements of the revolutionary past. But to transform the idea of receptivity into didactic preaching about the Spartans who lived on thought alone, without bothering about "everyday life" and other day-to-day matters, is to distort history, to make a living revolutionary tradition into an abstract canon, and to send the young to alien sources to look for answers.

The old, prerevolutionary generations of the intelligentsia, and then the advanced workers, too, formed themselves through taking an interest in everything, including personal and family life. The future revolutionary often began by thinking about personal self-improvement, and spent many sleepless nights in burning arguments about the marital relationships of Chernyshevsky's heroes, etc., etc. Even more so is the present-day youth forming himself in a milieu of great transitions in all social and domestic relations, apart from conditions of developed class struggle. He cannot become a real revolutionary type if he has not thought through the conditions of his own private life and family and domestic relationships from all angles, in their unbreakable connection with social relations, i.e., with the conditions and perspectives of the epoch of social revolution. Unless he thinks things through and works them out in this way, with the aim of practical action and self-transformation, he will become at best a schoolbook Marxist, or more likely not even that, since the blows of life would make the youth seek answers to immediate questions of life in non-Marxist theories.

To counterpose the close prospect of the German revolution to our current practical tasks is to be a phrasemonger and not a revolutionary. To say that now, when a sharp transition is approaching in the fate of Europe, there is no desire to study algebra, can be taken only as a joke, or in the extreme case, as the expression of a quickly passing mood of a young comrade knocked off the rails by the first news of the approaching events. But the party, and even more so the working class, cannot of course counterpose its everyday practical work to the new, grandiose tasks that must arise before us in the relatively near future.

That layer of workers—and young workers in particular—that has already learned to comprehend events on a world scale immediately makes a political response to the German events. But we repeat: this layer is thin. Our cultural work consists now in attracting people to the ideas of communism not only by means of general propaganda and agitation, but also by means of practical work in the economic and domestic fields, connected with the life of the toiling masses. It is useless to try talking about the German revolution to a working woman who has not learned to think critically about her own life and the lives of those close to her. But if we have touched her or can touch her with our cultural and domestic work, then we will construct for her a spiritual bridge from the individual to the social, and the German revolution will become for her a close and kindred thing.

This is even more true of the young. Here is the real application of the words of the gospel: "Whoever is true in the small matters will also be true in great ones." Wherever great events may unfold, whatever form they might have to start with, they will demand of us this time an incomparably higher degree of preparation, more special qualification in all fields than all the tasks we have had to carry out up to now. It would be childishly naive, therefore, to imagine that the coming events demand a jump back from our present work: studies, the economy, special cultural activity, etc., etc. The only thing that the new circumstances require is that in all fields we work at least twice as hard and twice as well as before.

Big events are a test not only for parties and people but also for a social system as a whole. In this sense, the practical conclusions from the prediction of great events become a major test for the regime, for its leading party, and in particular for its conscious youth. The question is posed by history thus: to what extent will we prove capable of transforming the prediction of great events tomorrow into intense preparatory work today? Ninety percent of this preparatory work involves nothing specific, nothing out of the ordinary. It is a matter of continuing the same work, the same construction, the same organizing, the same learning—only the pace must be different. Now we must work with the concentration that can be seen, for example, in a workers' college student who has fallen behind but pulled himself together in time, a few weeks before the examinations. This concentrated work—above all, for this period—in its greater accuracy and clarity, in its heightened consciousness of responsibility, must express our internal connection with the events whose center is now in central Europe.

"No matter how important and vitally necessary our culture-building may be," we wrote in an article on proletarian culture,[22] "it is entirely dominated by the approach of European and world revolution. We are, as before, merely soldiers in a campaign. We are bivouacking for a day. Our shirt has to be washed, our hair has to be cut and combed, and most important of all, the rifle has to be cleaned and oiled. Our entire present-day economic and cultural work is nothing more than a bringing of ourselves into order between two battles and two campaigns. The principal battles are ahead and may be not so far off." What is more important: the battle or the cleaning and oiling of the rifle, or a search for a draught horse, or explaining to a peasant woman what the Red Army is there for, or learning the geography and history of Germany, or the manufacture of horse blankets, etc., etc.? It is ridiculous and downright absurd to put the question this way. Precisely because there may be great trials ahead, we have to build peasant plows as well and cheaply as possible, weave horse blankets, diligently study the geography and history of Germany and of all other countries, draw the attention of the most backward working man and woman to the conditions of their everyday life, and thus open to their minds the way on to the broad revolutionary road. Each new communal dining hall is an excellent material argument in favor of international revolution.

I have found this correct conception of the connection between big things and small in the "Song of Ten Rubles" by the Young Communist poet Aleksandr Zharov.[23] To those who are inclined to counterpose great upheavals to questions of everyday life and worries about currency, the young poet replies:

> Hey!
> To the fight against filth and smells
> and not with bullets of sharp words!
> Keep your lid on, brother!
> You'll give all you've got!
> And—no sacred cows!
>
> Well, and if the shrill whine
> of an enemy's shell starts overhead—
> I will know how to be patient
> and go
> into the combat that we know so well!

Great events are forming a new generation. We often used to talk about the preparation of successors. In day-to-day learning and work our successors are being prepared slowly and imperceptibly. In great events they will rise up and reveal themselves at once. Theoretical accumulation combined with experience gives the necessary tempering and self-confidence. Boys become youths, and youths—men.

On bibliography

MAY 18, 1924

We very much need a good bibliographical journal. Setting it up is an exceptionally difficult affair. Such a journal must be a source of counsel and information on literature for the reader who needs advice—and the majority do.

Reviewing is the most responsible kind of literature. A good review presupposes that the author has an acquaintance with the subject, and understanding of the place of the given book within a series of other books—and conscientiousness. We do not need two or three hasty thoughts thrown up "about" the book, but a review that acquaints us with the book itself. It is sometimes better to give the detailed contents of the book and two or three quotes than a hasty, dilettante, and unconvincing evaluation. It would be very desirable for your journal to become *an educator*

From Kniga o knigakh [A book about books], May 1924. Translated for this volume by Iain Fraser.

of reviewers, campaigning mercilessly against superficiality, slovenliness, and that specific favoritism which, alas, is an all too common phenomenon in reviewing.

Allow me with these few words to express my support for your undertaking and to wish it every success!

A few words on how to raise a human being

JUNE 24, 1924

When I received the invitation to the meeting to celebrate the first teaching year of the Karl Liebknecht Institute, I found myself in a difficult position. Work in our Soviet Republic is becoming extraordinarily specialized, a larger and larger number of separate regions are being formed, and it is becoming increasingly difficult to keep up with a tenth or a hundredth, much less all, of this work with any degree of attention and conscientiousness. When you have to speak about an establishment such as your institute, which is connected with a factory and workshop school, an establishment of exceptional importance, then you naturally find yourself in difficulties. I therefore ask you in advance not to expect a report on the significance and role of your Institute. I shall

A speech to the anniversary meeting of the Karl Liebknecht Institute. Translated for this volume from Trotsky's Problems of Cultural Work *(1924), by Iain Fraser.*

limit myself only to some considerations of principle, or more exactly considerations concerning the questions of principle that arise when one starts to think about the tasks of your Institute, and in general about the tasks of any education that strives to set up an unbreakable link between physical and mental labor.

In the preparatory class of socialism, we learned long ago that the main curse of capitalist society consisted in the division between mental and physical labor. This division started before capitalism, with the first steps of the development of class society and culture; since that time, the task of management has become ever more bound up with mental labor and is operated through various categories of mental labor. In serving production, mental labor becomes separated from material production. This process goes on throughout the whole development of culture. Capitalism puts mental and physical labor in the greatest contradiction, raising the division to an extraordinary degree of tension. Capitalism transforms physical labor into repellent, automatic labor, and raises mental labor, at the highest level of generalization, into idealistic abstraction and mystical scholasticism.

Here there seems to be a contradiction. You know that scholasticism arose from the church of the Middle Ages. Then, still in the depths of the old feudal society, natural science began to develop and fertilize production. Thus, the development of bourgeois society is closely linked with the development of natural science, and consequently with the struggle against church scholasticism. But at the same time, the more the bourgeoisie grew, the more it feared the application of the methods of science to history, sociology, and psychology. In these fields, bourgeois thought wandered off ever higher into the region of idealism, abstraction, and a new scholasticism; and then, to cover up its traces, it began to introduce elements of idealism and scholasticism into natural science, too.

Science is a part of the historical praxis of man; in its development it strives to grasp the world from all sides, to give an all-embracing orientation to creative man. The division of theory and practice cannot help striking at mental labor with one end of a broken chain, and at physical labor with the other end. We know this from the first pages of the first books about socialism. There we also learned that capitalism, bringing this contradiction to the highest degree of tension, ipso facto prepares the way for the reconciliation of mental and physical labor and for their union on the basis of collectivism.

Our socialist country is striving for the reconciliation of physical and mental labor, which is the only thing that can lead to the harmonious development of man. Such is our program. The program gives only general directions for this: it points a finger, saying "Here is the general direction of your path!" But the program does not say how to attain this union in practice. It cannot say this, since no one could or even now can predict under what conditions, along what lines, socialism will be constructed in all countries and in each individual country, what the state of the economy will be, or by what methods the younger generation will be educated—precisely—in the sense of combining physical and mental labor. In this field, as in many others, we shall go and are going already by way of experience, research, and experiments, knowing only the general direction of the road to the goal: as correct as possible a combination of physical and mental labor.

This factory and workshop school is interesting in that it is one of the practical attempts at a partial solution of this colossal social and educational problem. I do not mean by this that the problem has already been solved or that the solution is very near. On the contrary, I am convinced that to reach the goal we still have considerably further to go than the small distance we have already gone. If we could say that through the factory and workshop school we were actually approaching the combination of mental and physical labor, that would mean that we had already gone perhaps three-quarters or even more of the way to establishing socialism. But there is still a long, long way to go to that. A precondition for combining physical and mental labor is the destruction of class rule. In outline we have done this; power here is in the hands of the workers. But it was only when the working class had taken power into its hands that it understood for the first time how poor and how backward we still are, or, as the Russian critic Pisarev once said, how "poor and stupid" we are. By the word stupidity here we must understand simply cultural backwardness, since by nature we are not stupid at all, and when we have had time to learn we shall stand completely by ourselves.

The working class had to take power into its own hands so that there would be no political obstacles to the construction of the new society. But when it had won power, it found itself faced with another hindrance: poverty and lack of culture. Here is the difference between our position and the position of the proletariat in the advanced capitalist countries. On their road there is a direct obstacle: the bourgeois state, which allows only a definite area of proletarian activity, the area the ruling class considers permissible. The first task in the West is to overthrow class rule, the bourgeois state. There, it is more difficult to solve this problem than here, for the bourgeois state is stronger there than here. But when it has overthrown class rule, the Western proletariat will find itself in a more favorable position with respect to cultural creation than ours.

If now we have run ahead by a few years, this does not at all mean that we shall get to the realm of socialism earlier than the English or German proletariat. No, that has not been proven. On the road to the kingdom of socialism there are a few trenches or barricades. We took the first barricade—

the political one—earlier, but it is altogether possible that the Europeans will catch up on the second or third barricade. The economy, production, is the most difficult barricade, and only when we take it, when we raise the productive forces of socialism, will the cursed distinction between "worker" and "intellectual," which results from the fact that mental labor is separated from physical labor, disappear. It is not at all impossible—on the contrary, it is very probable—that the German proletariat, if it takes power into its hands in the next three years (I am speaking approximately), will with two or three jumps not only catch up with us, but even overtake us, because the "inherited" material basis for cultural creation is considerably richer there than here. Today the working class of Germany marches on paved roads, but its hands and feet are bound in class slavery. We walk in ruts, along ravines, but our hands and feet are free. And that, Comrades, typifies the difference between us and the European proletariat. Under the yoke of capital, it is now powerless even to start solving the problem of physical and mental labor. It does not have the power.

State power is the material capability and the formal right to say to the subject class: there, you have the right to come up to this line, but no further—as we, the ruling class in our country, say to the NEPmen. We are our own authority, but as soon as we look beneath our feet, there are puddles, holes, ditches of all sorts, and we hobble and stumble along; we move slowly. But the European proletariat, freed from the fetters on its hands and feet, will catch up to us; and we will of course welcome this, for they will help us, too, to get to the end of the matter.

I am saying this to point out that with just our own pedagogical measures we shall not complete the full solution of the basic problems of socialist education and the merging of physical with mental labor; but if we make a series of experiments on this road and reach partial successes, then that will already be an enormous plus both for us and for the European proletariat, who will be able to develop these partial successes on a wider scale. Thus, we must work along this road the more energetically, the more persistently, the more stubbornly.

In the field of pedagogics, i.e., in the field of the conscious cultivation of man, people have perhaps been learning even more blindly than in other fields. The social life of man had, as you know, an elemental character: human reason did not immediately start to work through, to think through social life. Peasant production, the peasant family, church life, the "patriarchal"-monarchic state forms were laid down behind people's backs imperceptibly, over hundreds and thousands of years. Only at a certain level, and especially with the appearance of the natural sciences, did people begin to organize production consciously, not according to tradition, but according to planned design (of course, not on a social scale, but on a private one). Then they began to criticize the class structure and the royal power, to demand equality and democracy. Democracy meant the application of the reason of the young and still fresh bourgeoisie to the cause of the construction of the state. Thus, critical thought was transferred from questions of natural science and technology to the state. But social relations in the broad sense continued under the rule of the bourgeoisie to be laid down spontaneously. The proletariat arose spontaneously against capitalist spontaneity. Then conscious criticism arose. On this the theory of socialism was built.

What is socialist construction? It is economic construction according to reason, no longer only within the limits of the enterprise or trust, as under the rule of the bourgeoisie, but within the limits of the society, and then of all humanity. In socialism we have the application of scientific thought to the construction of human society. Just as earlier the bourgeoisie built factories "according to reason," and constructed its state according to (bourgeois) reason, so the working class says: "I will construct the whole of social life from top to bottom according to reason."

But man himself is also an elemental thing. Only gradually does he apply the criticism of reason to himself. The effect of education on man went, as we said, unseen. Only under a socialist society will the conditions for a scientific approach to man be established. And man needs such an approach. For what is man? Not at all a finished and harmonious being; no, his being is still very incoherent. In him there is not only the vestige of the appendix, which is no use to him—only appendicitis comes from it—but also, if you take his psyche, then you will find there as many unnecessary "vestiges" as you like, from which come all sorts of illnesses, all sorts of spiritual appendicitis.

Man, as a type of animal, developed under natural conditions, not according to plan, but spontaneously, and accumulated many contradictions in himself. One of these serious contradictions, not only social but physiological, is reflected in the sexual process, which has a disturbing effect on the young. The problem of how to cultivate and adjust, how to improve and "finish" the physical and spiritual nature of man, is a colossal one, serious work on which is conceivable only under conditions of socialism. We may be able to drive a railway across the whole Sahara, build the Eiffel Tower, and talk with New York by radio, but can we really not improve man? Yes; we will be able to!

To issue a new "improved edition" of man—that is the further task of communism. But for this it is necessary as a start to know man from all sides, to know his anatomy, his physiology, and that part of his physiology which is called psychology.

Vulgar philistines say that socialism is a structure of total stagnation. Rubbish, the crassest rubbish! Only with socialism does real progress begin. Man will look for the first time at himself as if at raw material, or at best, as at a half-finished product, and say: "I've finally got to you, my dear homo sapiens; now I can get to work on you, friend!" To perfect man's organism, using the most varied combinations of methods, to regulate the circulation of the blood, to refine the nervous system, and at the same time to temper and strengthen it, make it more flexible and hardier—what a gigantic and fascinating task!

But this, of course, is the music of the future. What we have to do is lay the first stones in the foundations of socialist society. And the cornerstone is to increase the productivity of labor. Only on this basis can socialism develop. For each new social structure conquers because it increases the productivity of human labor. We will only be able to talk of a real, complete, and invincible victory of socialism when the unit of human power gives us more products than under the rule of private property. One of the most important means to this is the education of cultivated, qualified workers. Such education is now taking place here in this factory and workshop school. To what extent will these schools solve the problem of preparing a "change" in production? I shall not go into that question. That needs the serious test of experience. But let us impress on our memories the fact that the fate of our economy, and hence of our state, depends on the solution of this problem.

The education of qualified workers is one side of the matter; the education of citizens is the other. The socialist republic needs not robots of physical labor, but conscious builders. The educated man of the land of workers and peasants, whatever he may be by profession, with a narrow or broad specialization, must also be armed in one other field. This is the social field. Nothing protects one from the humiliating effect of specialization so well as the Marxist method, as Leninism, i.e., the method of understanding the conditions of the society in which you live, and the method of acting upon those conditions. And when we try to understand the relations between states, we again need the same method of Marxism-Leninism. Without the understanding of the connections between the private and the social, there can be no educated man.

The basic peculiarity of petty-bourgeois thought is that it is specialized in its own narrow sphere, locked in its own closet. There are learned bourgeois intellectuals who, even though they write learned books a thousand pages thick, still go on looking at questions separately, each for itself, without connections, and thus they remain limited petty bourgeois. One must be able to take every question in its development and in its connections with other questions; then the conclusions are so much the more guaranteed to be right. This guarantee is given only by the Marxist school. And therefore whatever the specialization, passing through the school of Leninism is essential for every educated worker, and especially for every future teacher.

The school of Leninism is a school of revolutionary action. "I am a citizen of the first workers' and peasants' republic in the world": that consciousness is the precondition of all the rest. And for us that consciousness is a requirement of self-preservation. We would be utopians, wretched dreamers, or dreamy wretches, if we began to think that we are assured for all eternity of a peaceful development for socialism. Not at all! In the international sense things have become easier for us, that is unquestionable. But do you think, Comrades, that the more the communist movement develops in Europe, the more we will be insured against the dangers of war? Anyone who thinks that is wrong. A dialectical approach is necessary here. While the Communist Party remains more or less dangerous, but not yet frightening, the bourgeoisie, being wary of giving it nourishment, will seek truces with us; but when the Communist Party of a given country becomes a threatening force, when the water starts to come up to the neck of the bourgeoisie, then the danger will grow again for us, too.

It was not for nothing that Vladimir Ilyich warned that we shall still be faced with having to go through a new explosion of the furious hatred of world capital for us. Of course, if we were an isolated state, or the only one in the world, then after conquering power we would have built socialism by a peaceful path. But we are only a part of the world, and the world that surrounds us is still stronger than we are. The bourgeoisie will not give up its position without cruel fights, considerably more cruel than the ones we have already been through. The attacks from the bourgeoisie will take on a fierce character again when the Communist parties start to grow above the head of the bourgeoisie. It would therefore be an unforgivable piece of thoughtlessness to suppose that we will pass to socialism without wars and upheavals. No, they won't let us do that. We'll have to fight. And for that we need hardness, education in the spirit of revolutionary valor. The name that is written on the walls of your Institute—Karl Liebknecht—must not have been written in vain.[24]

I had the good fortune to know Liebknecht over a period of some twenty years. He is one of the finest human figures that lives in my memory. Liebknecht was a real knight of revolutionary duty. He knew no other law in life than the law of the struggle for socialism. The best of German youth has long connected its best hopes, thoughts, and feelings with the figure of Karl Liebknecht, the fearless knight of the proletarian revolution. Education in revolutionary duty is education in the spirit of Karl Liebknecht. We must remember: we still have enormous difficulties to go through. And for that it is necessary for each one of you when you leave the walls of this Institute to have the right to say to yourself: the Karl Liebknecht Institute has made me not only a teacher, but a revolutionary fighter! [*Applause*]

Leninism and library work

JULY 3, 1924

Comrades, let me first extend a welcome to your congress, the first Soviet congress of library workers. This congress, convened by Glavpolitprosvet,[25] has a special significance for our country. Here, a librarian—and everyone who has read the remarks of Vladimir Ilyich on this subject knows this—here, a librarian is not an official dealing with books, but rather he is, must be, must become a cultural warrior, a Red Army soldier fighting for socialist culture. Such a congress of troops of socialist culture I welcome with all my heart! [*Applause*]

Having scarcely begun, Comrades, I have already used the word "culture" two or three times. Just what, then, is culture? Culture is the sum total of all knowledge and skills amassed

A speech to the First All-Union Congress of Librarians. From Pravda, *July 10, 1924. Translated for this volume from* The Generation of October *by Tom Scott.*

by mankind throughout all its preceding history. Knowledge *for* skills! Knowledge of everything that surrounds us, that we may change everything that surrounds us—change it in the interests of mankind. Of course, there exist other, quite different definitions of science and culture—idealistic, abstract, high-flown, false through and through, linked with the "eternal verities" and other such trumpery. We reject all these. We accept the concrete, historical, materialistic definition of culture that Marxism-Leninism teaches us. Culture is the conjunction of the skills and knowledge of historical mankind, the mankind of nations and classes. Knowledge grows out of the activities of man, out of his struggle with the forces of nature; knowledge serves to improve these activities, to spread the methods of combating each obstacle, and to increase the power of man.

If we assess the meaning of culture in this way we shall grasp more easily the meaning of Leninism. For Leninism, too, is knowledge and skills—and also, not knowledge for its own sake but knowledge for skills. In this sense, although not only in this one, Leninism represents the product and consummation of all of man's previous culture. Leninism is the knowledge and ability to turn culture, i.e., all the knowledge and skills amassed in previous centuries, to the interests of the working masses. Therein lies the essence of Leninism.

Man can claim great achievements in many fields. Were it not so, one could not even speak of communism. The most fundamental of these achievements is the acquisition of techniques—once again, knowledge and skills—geared to the direct struggle with the forces of nature, to their subjugation to man. From this base of techniques grow classes, the state, law, science, art, philosophy, and so on and so on—a whole hierarchy of methodological knowledge and skills. Many of these departments and methods of culture are useful in general to man, insofar as they subjugate nature to

him. But there exist some kinds of knowledge and skills—
and not a few—which are of use only to an exploiting class,
i.e., which have the express purpose of supporting exploitation, embellishing it, concealing and masking it—and which
consequently must be rejected as mankind develops further.
In particular, as I have already said, we reject the idealistic,
high-flown, semi-religious interpretation of culture that also
arises from class supremacy and serves to hide the fact that
culture is monopolized by the possessing classes and exists,
in the first instance, for their pleasure.

Leninism adopts a boldly revolutionary and at the same
time thoroughly businesslike approach to culture: it teaches
the working class to pick out from the gigantic store of culture what is most necessary today for its social liberation
and for the reconstruction of society along new lines. Leninism is the knowledge of the construction and development of society and the ability to become rightly oriented
in a historical situation at any given hour, so that one can
correctly and skillfully, and as profoundly as possible, exert
an influence on one's milieu, on social life, in the interests
of the proletarian revolution in the capitalist countries, and
in the interests of the construction of socialism here.

Such is the essence of Leninism. Every teacher, every
worker correspondent, every liquidator of illiteracy, every
librarian must understand this essence and realize it in
himself, if he wishes to become not simply an official of the
Soviet state, but rather a conscious worker for culture who,
with book, article, and newspaper, must penetrate deeper and
deeper into the minds of the masses, as a miner with a pick
penetrates deeper and deeper into layers of coal.

In this context it must be said that all the work, however
partial it may be, which we are carrying out now in the field
of economics and education, can and must be a part of the
Leninist method of orienting in given conditions and of influencing these conditions. In our state, where the working

class is in power, supported by those conscious and thinking elements among our millions of peasants, the fundamental problem is how to use all cultural acquisitions to raise the material and cultural level of the masses. Our country now represents state-organized Leninism. This is the first gigantic experiment of its kind to be carried out—not in a roundabout way, not in the underground, as we have had to struggle in our time, and not by way of revolutionary parties struggling for power, as happens today in the capitalist countries—but by way of the state organization applying the method of Marxism-Leninism, using all cultural acquisitions with the aim of rebuilding society on a socialist basis.

When we created the state, under the leadership of Vladimir Ilyich and by our general efforts, when we created it in a rough form—only then did we realize properly for the first time how much we lag behind, how little culture we have. And the most elementary problems stood before us in all their concrete immensity.

One might ask—and I was recently asked about this—how it is possible to explain the fact that in our culturally backward country the Communist Party is in power, whereas in countries with a high level of culture, e.g., England, it is as yet very weak. I answered this question fully in another report.[26] Here I will only mention the most necessary points. From a superficial, fleeting glance at the problem, one might get the impression that communism somehow stands in inverse ratio to the cultural level of a country, i.e., the higher the cultural level, the weaker communism, and vice versa. Of course, if this conclusion were correct, it would represent the death sentence for communism, which has always been irreconcilably opposed to the Tolstoyan and to every other denial of culture; its fate is wholly linked with that of culture. "This is a question that torments us," a teacher wrote me, and one can understand the psychology of an intellectual approaching communism gradually, with doubts and hesitations, and bothered by the problem of the relationship between communism and culture. But even here, Comrades, Leninism, the theoretical generalization and practical method of that very communism, gives us the key to the understanding of this contradiction.

Why did we take power earlier in Russia, we, the communists? Because we had a weaker enemy—the bourgeoisie. In what way was it weak? It was not as rich and cultured as the English bourgeoisie, which has at its disposal huge funds, both of money and of culture, and also great experience in dealing with the masses and subjugating them politically. This gave it the opportunity, as experience has shown, to hold back the awakening political self-determination of the proletariat. If, for a time, we proved to be more farsighted, stronger, and more intelligent than the workers' parties of the advanced countries—and we were; it can be said without boasting—it was due not to our purely Russian cast of mind, but to the experience of the working classes of the whole world, crystallized in the theory of Marxism, in the theory and practice of Leninism. But why were we the ones to crystallize this theory and turn it into action? Because we were not under the hypnosis of a powerful bourgeois culture. In this lay our revolutionary advantage.

Our bourgeoisie was such a miserable historical epigone that during the last few decades everything grand and important in all classes gravitated not to the bourgeoisie but to the workers. Chernyshevsky stood not with the bourgeoisie but with the peasantry and the working class, insofar as it was distinguishable from the peasantry. A very great man, created by a new kind of history—Lenin—headed here not petty-bourgeois Jacobins, as he would have done had he been born in the eighteenth century in France, but the revolutionary proletariat. The historically backward, pitiful, escheated character of our bourgeoisie made for great independence and valor, gave great scope to the vanguard of the working class. But when, thanks to this, we first came to power and looked at the inheritance left us by czardom and a vanquished bourgeoisie, it turned out that this inheritance was, to say the least, meager. Of course, we knew earlier, before the revolution, that our country was backward, but we only began to feel the practical effects of this after the conquest of power, after October.

And how do things stand in this matter in Europe? In Europe it will be incomparably more difficult for the proletariat to come to power, for the enemy is stronger; but when it does come to power it will be incomparably easier for it to build socialism, for it will receive a much larger inheritance. Greater culture, a greater development of technology—this, ultimately, will have its effect. If we came to power earlier than the English proletariat, this does not mean by itself that we will reach full socialism, still less communism, earlier than they. No: on the political plane, thanks to the historical peculiarities of our development, we have led the working classes of all other countries; but, on the other hand, we are now set against our cultural backwardness and forced to advance slowly, inch by inch.

When will the English proletariat get real power, not in the fashion of MacDonald's Menshevik government, but a dictatorship of the proletariat?[27] It is difficult to predict this; perhaps in five or ten years. Well, how much time will we need to make the whole population literate and provide it with books and newspapers? In the European part of our Union, considerably more than half our adult population is illiterate, about 57 percent. I recently read that in Moscow 20 percent, i.e., one-fifth, of the adult population is illiterate. We will bear this firmly in mind! Here in Moscow just now—and we take great pride in this—the Fifth Congress of the Comintern is in session.[28] The best fighters in the world have come to us to learn—and there is much to learn in Lenin's school!—but go down a Moscow street and watch five people pass, and you will say to yourself: on the average, one of them is illiterate. That's our revolution with all its contradictions!

We can express it graphically thus: The European proletariat has under its feet the soil of culture—let's say solid asphalt. But the owner of the European street is the bourgeoisie, which draws a chalk line along the asphalt (bourgeois legality!) and says: you can walk here but not there. And the part you cannot walk on is ninety or ninety-nine times as big as the part you can. You can do nothing. The bourgeoisie has the power; it is sovereign. In addition, the working class of the capitalist countries has its feet rather well bound (police, courts, prisons), so that it won't cross the forbidden line. So, under its feet is asphalt, but its feet are bound and the road is closed.

In this sense we are free. Power here is in the hands of the working class. There are no measures that we dare not take in the interests of the workers, whether in the field of economics or of culture. We dare all. We have no bosses. We are up against only backwardness and insufficient resources. Our feet are free, not bound; no one draws a chalk line on the road in front of us; but under our feet is not asphalt but a country track, crossed by ravines and puddles. It is quite clear that in the first few years the pace of our journey will not be great. Our work must be extremely tenacious. And meantime, you will see, even the English proletariat will have untied its feet. Once it has overthrown the bourgeoisie, the roads are open to it. And under its feet there is asphalt. Therefore, in about fifteen to twenty years—of course, I take this period only for the illustration—this same English proletariat, whose conservatism we chide often just now, with full justification, will lead us in the field of construction of socialism. Of course we will not take offense at this. Do your duty; lead the way; we have waited a long time for this; we, with you, shall win together! [*Laughter and applause*]

I am speaking of this, Comrades, not to discourage you and myself by the immensity of the problems that confront us, but to explain by the method of Leninism the contradictions between our political achievements and our present cultural-economic possibilities. To understand these contradictions is to find a way to remove them. We will remember that in Leninism knowledge is always the shortest route to getting things right.

We shall discover all along, at every step, contradictions between our slogans and our real possibilities. But our path lies not in the rejection of the slogans, i.e., the rejection of the main problems created by October, but in the systematic, stubborn, unwearying enlargement of our economic-cultural potential. Our poverty dictates to us in the sphere of cultural activity a severely businesslike, economical, prudent, almost Spartan approach: economy, meticulous selection, efficiency.

In the first instance, this applies to newspapers and books. Let's take the jubilee exhibition of Gosizdat. When I visited it, in all truth I was able to say: here's something worth praising; we've had much success in five years! If you take a book of 1918, often haphazard in content, written in a hurry, printed any old way, on grey paper, with a huge number of misprints, unbound, not sewn, and so on, and for comparison take at random one of today's books, more carefully finished, all in more attractive covers, completely lithographed and not typed (perhaps this is already a luxury!), then our progress seems great. However, we can say that all this is only the scales, the exercises, not a real tune on the publishing instrument. And we hope Gosizdat itself realizes this. The number of copies of books we have is still minute in comparison with the country's needs. We still have not managed to make a selection of books that are definitely and absolutely necessary to us. We must hold to our basic course, publishing not so much a great number of titles as a great number of copies of a minimum number of titles that are absolutely necessary for the readers we have in mind. We must start either to print these titles or to pick them from the number already issued. To make such a selection is a huge task which can be completed only collectively, relying on the experience of schools, courses, libraries, correcting and improving available titles, presenting a demand for such improvements and additions. . . . The press runs of basic books, i.e., those especially necessary for a worker-peasant republic, must be something on the order of 100,000, 500,000, a million, and still more. The number issued will be the best criterion of the success of our cultural work.

We print, if I am not mistaken, only three million copies of newspapers a day just now, all told—an altogether insignificant number for our gigantic problems and even for the present needs of the country. Here, a state-centralized approach—based on the activity of all regions—could be of great service in making a correct selection and distribution of books and newspapers indispensable to workers. In this, we must not forget for a moment the qualities of our mass of readers; they don't yet have reading knowledge and skills— the knowledge of which books to read and the skill to find them. And since our reader cannot find his book, our book must find its reader. This is a librarian's task! In the work of enlightenment we will have to supply newspapers for a long time yet, because we will not be able to ignore the need for political orientation, since we are surrounded by capitalist countries and the proletarian revolution is still completely in the future; also, in the given situation, under the given cultural conditions, with the given resources, the newspaper is the most comprehensive weapon for enlightenment, touching the greatest number of people.

Around the newspaper we can and must construct a whole system of cultural-political information and educational activity. We must view the newspaper not as an organ telling us about this and that, but as the workers' instrument of education, as a weapon of knowledge and skill, as a direct, daily, practical expression of Leninism in political and economic educational activity. Our newspapers will aspire to this, but they will not be this for a long time yet. They must become this, and they can become this only by relying on tens of thousands, and subsequently on hundreds of thousands of libraries, reading "huts,"[29] and other cultural-educational cells in all the localities, who not only understand a newspaper from above but who will also be able to put pressure on it from below. This is a very big and important task. But for this it is necessary to supply newspapers as a real weapon of weekly or perhaps (in the near future) daily activity, as an instrument coordinating our educational efforts.

Let us look at the problem more closely. Coming to the fore now in cultural-educational activity—I'm talking about the countryside—is the hut-reader. If there is a newspaper in the middle of the hut, then on the wall there should be a political map. Without this, the newspaper is not a newspaper.

Some time ago I conducted propaganda in favor of political-geographical maps, but without much success as yet. Perhaps this congress will support my initiative in this direction. [*Applause*] Comrades, the newspaper is not only for the peasant but for the worker who is blind, when geographical terms are only names to him, when he doesn't know and cannot imagine the sizes and respective positions of France, England, America, Germany. Of course, we can encourage or awaken the village Young Communists or rural gathering to sing the *Internationale* and send a greeting to the Fifth Congress of the Comintern. This we do magnificently, almost automatically. [*Laughter*] But, Comrades, it is necessary that these workers and peasants who send greetings can, as far as possible, concretely visualize: what this Comintern is, from what countries, where these countries are—if only just a little, by sight. It is necessary that, when they read or hear a news story, they visualize to which living part of our planet it is referring. And if every day, or perhaps once a week, in this same hut-library, while reading, while interpreting a newspaper, the librarian or *izbach* [hut-dweller]—since this marvelous word has come into use there's nothing you can do, so accept it and inscribe it in your dictionary—if, I say, he pokes a finger at the map while explaining a dispatch, by this act alone he will be carrying out real cultural work, for the listener, after looking at the map, will now keep that dispatch in his brain quite differently, more firmly, more surely. For it is a whole epoch in the personal development of a reader when he begins to visualize what England is—this, he will say, is an island separated from Europe—and the commercial and political relationships of England, defining her world position, will become immediately clearer to him. I apologize, however; I don't have to explain to you the use of geography, but I must say that perhaps it is worthwhile repeating it to some of our institutions. [*Laughter*] Here we need pressure, and more pressure. However, I would not like to be misunderstood. I would not in any way put all the responsibility on Gosizdat. Now Gosizdat, and all other publishing houses, are run on a self-supporting basis—i.e., they publish under certain conditions, and must publish what there is a demand for. In this, the open will of the customer plays a significant role, and the customer is the library or the reading room.

One may well reject dozens of books which, in different words, yet in a rather slovenly manner, tell one and the same thing. We have an unknown quantity of such slovenly books on the theme of the day. We can completely reject them if we are making a strict selection, in favor of geographical maps which, since they are hung on the wall, will hang there and teach for months, perhaps for years. For example, I made inquiries everywhere I could before this report to see if there exists a reference book to newspapers, a reference book that can help one to find out about a newspaper. Apparently there is no such thing. I don't know if this was discussed at your congress or not, but the question deserves attention.

I was sent an array of periodicals in which there were articles on how to use a newspaper. Some of them were very useful for a person involved in this kind of work, but not quite what I have in mind, for these contained general methodological information while I have been thinking of a businesslike reference book which, in this same "hut" or library could be placed under the map on the table where the papers lie, an almanac that would give basic geographical, economic, statistical, and other information, clearly expressed and accessible to every literate reader—but there is no such reference book available. What does this mean? It means, Comrade librarians, that you have not yet organized the readers' pressure from below on the writers and publishers.

Comrades, our educational work is monopolized by the state and its leaders, the Communist Party. Could it be otherwise? Under the conditions of the revolution and the dictatorship of the proletariat every deviation from the monopoly of the education of the working masses would be fatal. [*Applause*] At a time when the bourgeoisie, having at its disposal the mighty resources of the whole world, mercilessly dismisses every communist teacher, we, the leaders of the sole workers' state, surrounded by enemies, would be utterly blind or crazy if we opened the door to educational work to the representatives of a bourgeois world outlook. We will strengthen our monopoly of educational work fully and unconditionally until such time as the working class and the peasantry, together with its leader, the Communist Party, dissolve into a socialist community, constituting a part of the world Soviet Republic—which will not be tomorrow, but the day after tomorrow or the day after that. And until that time, the monopoly of power and of educational work, which is the ideological basis of power, must be kept in the hands of the workers' state and its representatives, the Communist Party. [*Applause*]

But at the same time, Comrades, we are sufficiently sober politicians to realize and know that a monopoly of education has its minuses, its negative sides, its dangers. A monopoly of education in the wrong setting can create red tape and routinism. What is the symptom of red tape? Form without content. What is its danger? In this, that life will turn away and seek another direction. How do we avoid the dangers of red tape? By organized and ever-alive pressure from those who want education, i.e., from below. And this can be the role of the librarian, the role of the instructor of the "hut"; generally speaking, the role of lower workers in the field of culture is decisive. Here, from above, we propagandize in favor of geographical maps, but don't give them out. Why? Because they are not asked for. But if from below, from a thousand, two thousand, three thousand libraries and "huts" the cry resounds, "Give us maps!"—then Gosizdat will give them [*applause*] and give them at a suitable price.

This applies to books as well. Are all books that we publish vital and necessary, like bread? I have already spoken about this: only a tenth of them are absolutely necessary. Why is this? Because our publishing work to a huge extent goes along the lines of old inertia, old interests, the old psychology, old habits, the old reader, and we scarcely touch the modern mass reader. Again, from our incomplete statistics, it appears that for every literate peasant the libraries have (if I am mistaken those who know better can correct me)— almost three-quarters of a book—three-quarters of a book in the libraries for every literate peasant!

[*At this point the transcript records the interjection of N. K. Krupskaya: "Less than that." Trotsky responds:*]

In that case I apologize for my overoptimistic statistics. It is completely clear that in such a state of affairs, to choose from ten books, where nine are more or less useful—perhaps less rather than more—to choose the best and most necessary, and publish it in a tenfold quantity of copies—that in itself means a great cultural victory. Why? Because ten books, more or less similar or close to one another or representing a few secondary shades of meaning, will be read or only leafed through by one and the same reader who, if one may say this, will gorge himself on this kind of literature. But if instead of these ten books we publish one, in ten times as many copies, then it will reach a reader who has a real hunger and a real thirst for reading and knowledge.

But even here, as they say, death dogs life. It is very difficult to drag yourself by the hair out of this inertia of publishing work. To overhear the masses, overhear what they think, what they want, to understand all this and mentally jump over all those who bureaucratically think for the masses but don't listen to them—for this the head of a Lenin is necessary. You now have the opportunity to read all that Lenin wrote. I advise you—this is very useful!—to pay special attention to those parts of the books where he was listening to the masses, to what they wanted, what they needed—not only what they wanted but what they had not yet been taught to want. . . . To be able to overhear everything, with a unique mind, is given to people once in a century. But you can hear the masses in an organized and collective fashion through a big, ramified, flexible, and living apparatus which will actively serve the material and spiritual needs of the masses. And that library worker is not a library worker of a socialist country if he is simply in charge of a shelf of books and so does not manage to listen to the requests of his readers and serve as an organ of transmission of what he has heard to higher bodies—to bring pressure to bear on the writer and the publishers. This is the most important work of the new Soviet socialist library worker. [*Applause*]

To the problems already mentioned, of course, are linked many others. The fundamental contradiction of our position is this: power is in the hands of the workers, but the workers are still far from possessing elementary culture. Contradictions stem from this. We have full equality of men and women here. But for a woman to have the real opportunities that a man has here, even now in our poverty, women must equal men in literacy. The "woman problem" here, then, means first of all the struggle with female illiteracy. Because of the low level of culture, many decrees remain on paper. Is there tyranny in this country? Yes, to a high degree. From what does it stem? Not from a situation of class supremacy but from cultural weakness, from illiteracy, from a feeling of defenselessness whose roots lie in the inability to look into things, read widely, make complaints, consult the right sources. And here again one of the fundamental tasks of that very reading hut in the villages, and of the village libraries, is the waging of a merciless struggle against this feeling of defenselessness. One may and one must complain to a librarian.

I found an interesting quotation from Vladimir Ilyich about this: he suggested installing a bureau of complaints in the libraries. At first sight this appears paradoxical, out of place; but even here the psychology of the working masses has been grasped. Whoever from among the workers or peasantry is awake enough to be attracted to a library, for that person the library is a source of something higher—both knowledge and justice. Build a bureau of complaints in the libraries, create surroundings in which every peasant, male or female—and first and foremost those who fear the Soviet official—will feel he can consult the librarian, the "izbach," without feeling he will be let down or have a dirty trick played on him; a librarian who will advise him, write to a newspaper, make public his grievance, defend him. To kill the feeling of defenselessness in a person crushed by

centuries of hard labor means killing tyranny in the same
stroke, and tyranny, it goes without saying, is incompatible
with that regime which we are building but are still a long
way from completing.

In his work the librarian will draw to himself the best
forces of the village, will rely on them and direct his influence
through them. In connection with this I should especially
like to ask librarians to pay great attention to demobilized
Red Army soldiers. In the countryside, they could become
representatives of the collectivized type of agriculture and
agents of cultural work, if there were a center around which
they could group themselves. At present, our countryside
is going through very complicated and profound processes
that are of huge economic and cultural significance. It is becoming stratified, and very soon in the country there will
be a layer of kulaks.[30] And one must clearly understand that
every vanguard peasant activist, everyone who is literate,
knows what Soviet power means, and is able to understand
the laws, has heard agronomical lectures, or has visited an
agricultural exhibition—every such peasant in the countryside can become one of two things: either a representative of
Soviet culture or—a kulak. And what is a kulak? A kulak is,
in the majority of cases, a capable, clever, strong peasant who
uses all his strength to improve his holding at the expense of
others. And our demobilized soldiers, at present representing
in their mass the best elements of our peasantry and capable
of grouping themselves around a school, a cooperative, a
library—even they could become new Europeanized kulaks.
Why? Because they are literate—if they were illiterate, they
were taught to read and write in the army—they are used to
reading newspapers, they know the addresses of Soviet offices,
they know the laws, they know what the Communist Party
is; in a word, these are not grey, dark peasants, although they
are from the same distant corners. In the army they heard
lectures on agronomy, visited various kinds of agricultural

holdings under the auspices of our agricultural educational institutions, and so on. And if in the countryside they are left to themselves, they could use all the advantages they have acquired to benefit only their own holdings, their own profit. This means that unnoticed even by themselves, they could, in two or three years, become European kulaks. The danger is real. But, at the same time, this young and more cultivated peasant, if he is guided into work as soon as he returns from the army, is ready and able to channel all his energy into work in an artel or cooperative and become an invaluable social worker.

Since I have broached the question of soldiers, I will add: if we send you soldiers on whom you can rely in your cultural work, then we expect from you cultural workers in the countryside a more cultured and more qualified youth for the army. You know that we are running the army increasingly along militia lines. In doing this we are first of all cutting down our share of the budget, and the smaller the part swallowed by the army, the more resources we can and must allot to cultural-educational work. But even here the service should be returned. You must give us a more literate and developed country youth. For a militia system presupposes a more receptive Red Army man, who must acquire all the skills of military craft in his preconscription training, solely in the course of regular educational meetings. He must be in no way inferior to a soldier who has had a long training period in the barracks. The librarian, the "izbach," are obvious participants in the construction of the Red Army.

In conclusion, let me once again turn to the newspaper, that most important weapon of political education. I picked up today's issue of *Izvestia*, read through the dispatches, and put myself this problem, from the point of view of this meeting: How will these dispatches be understood by the mass reader? Are they self-explanatory; can they be interpreted correctly? How will a peasant interpret them? From the point of view of our international position, the problem of Poland and Rumania has, as you know, exceptional interest. For this reason I paused at two dispatches in today's issue, concerning just these countries. The wire from Warsaw said, "The Marshalk of the Seim did not accept the interpellation of the Ukrainian club because part of this interpellation was written in Ukrainian." I am not talking about the complicated structure of the dispatch itself—I am fighting a long civil war with Rosta and the editors of the dispatch on this score. [*Laughter*] However, I cannot conceal the danger that this dispatch is printed in the same unintelligible way in all the newspapers. I think that not only will the literate peasant fail to understand it put like this, but also, perhaps, the "izbach." For he will not know who this "Marshalk" is, and it will have to be explained to him that he is president of the "Seim," i.e., parliament, and that he did not accept the interpellation (inquiry) only because a part of this document was written in Ukrainian.

Let us suppose that you and I are in a hut reading room, and in front of us hangs a map with Poland marked on it. You can point out to everyone that Poland is on our border and cuts us off from Germany. Near the map there is a reference book that tells us how many Ukrainians are in Poland, the total number of the national minorities; and the peasant will learn that in Poland the national minorities constitute almost half the population—about 45 percent. If we now tell him that in Poland the Ukrainians have submitted a motion to their "democratic" parliament, a part of which was written in "Ukrainian," that is, in their native language, and that the democratic president of a democratic parliament of a democratic republic refused to accept the motion on these grounds, then we have enriched the listener with a clear picture of Poland.

No better agitational speech is required than a sensible and calm exposition of these four lines of the dispatch. Then follows the dispatch concerning Rumania. Here we read: "In Bessarabia practically all schools of the national minorities have been closed. In Bukovina not only have all mixed schools been destroyed but all Ukrainian ones." As you see, this dispatch, too, concerns oppression of nationalities. In every issue there are dispatches characterizing class or national oppression in the capitalist countries, the resistance of the oppressed, and so on. All this is an invaluable school, especially for our youth. Around these dispatches, as around a pivot, we can organize magnificent educational work; but clear exposition is essential, or 90 percent of this most valuable material will pass unnoticed by 99 percent of our literate population. Above all, reference books are needed, and there are almost none. And, at the same time, we are printing numerous speeches and reports on approximately the same theme, emphasizing things that by and large would be understood without this repetition. Serious progress must be made in this field. The book must go to the people.

Imagine that we have 50,000 hut readers, or even 100,000, and that in every hut there is a newspaper. Not three, not five newspapers, as we Soviet officials are accustomed to reading, but one newspaper with the most important information clearly and exactly set out. On the wall hangs a map, with all the states visible on it, and there is a reference book giving the population of every country, national and class composition, and so forth. The "izbach," having received a new issue, arms himself with the reference book and clarifies the news, having gathered around as many people as possible—above all, demobilized soldiers. Such a hut reading room will be an irreplaceable school of Leninism, bringing up citizens in the countryside who know how to orient themselves in the international situation so that they can consciously have an effect on it, if necessary, perhaps even with gun in hand. First of all we must train librarians to direct the reading rooms, to be "izbachs," and we must establish close links between the center and these scattered breeding-grounds of culture. This is possible, and it can and will be realized. Only then can our cultural construction establish indispensable levers for itself on the spot. Only then will our October Revolution unfold to the masses all its creative content.

Will this be soon? This, of course, depends on the objective situation but also, to a not insignificant extent, on our own skill. We have a diabolical enemy called red tape. This enemy, which reflects our lack of culture, necessitates a constant struggle. We are acquiring at present district huts, district libraries, district organizers. This is good. Let these district huts, libraries, and organizers be mobilized for the struggle against red tape. [Applause] I have no doubt, Comrades, that you understand that I am not talking about some red-colored tape [laughter], but about our own all-Russian, all-Union red tape—confound it! [Laughter]

I have more on this problem for you. Today, in that very same newspaper, I read a dispatch to the effect that in Tiflis the Transcaucasian cinema was awarded a red banner for putting on "The Red Devils." Of course, there is nothing wrong in recognizing the good work of the cinema. On the contrary, this is fine. The cinema is a powerful weapon, and when we attain a position in certain places whereby in the district huts there is a district cinema, this will signify that we are no longer far from socialism, for a better ally in its construction than the cinema I cannot imagine. But I don't want to draw your attention to this, but rather to how we feebly express greetings and reward services: always we present a red banner. We have now a multitude of celebrations on the occasion of second, third, and fifth anniversaries, and each time the red banner is awarded. Why is this? If we count up how much of our resources are spent on awarding red banners, it turns out to be considerable. But what if the cry were to be: let us not award red banners at such celebrations—for us even a few is too many—but assign these resources to acquiring books through a district library fund. On every book thus acquired and delivered to the district library there will be on the binding (there must be a binding) a stamp saying that this book was acquired in recognition of the services of (perhaps) that same Transcaucasian cinema for showing "The Red Devils," or for something else. It seems to me that this would be better, more interesting, more cultured.

Of course, banners as a symbol of revolutionary struggle are indispensable, but to begin awarding banners in routine fashion, as something obligatory and at the same time totally unnecessary, is absurd and harmful. Why shouldn't librarians raise their voices and newspapermen support them in the cry, "Henceforth let us record all successes, or recollections of successes, or recollections of large-scale failures, by devoting more resources to cultural-educational work in the countryside." Let us make the center of attention this same district hut—in need of books, a reference book, a geographical map, a book of Lenin. We will give it these. And on every such book we will put the corresponding stamp. And, in addition, this will be a short lesson in Soviet history for the reader. . . .

Comrades, if your congress, through various channels, gives such lively jolts to the prevailing opinion at our center, which is inclined to dilly-dally over things, then by this alone the congress will have carried out serious and important work. Whatever happens, we must destroy the practices and habits of serfdom and intellectual haughtiness, expressed in the words of our old satirist, "A writer writes now and then, but a reader reads now and then." No, our writers, publishers, librarians, and readers must all go into the same harness. And this can only be done by organized pressure from below, by control from above, by checks and selections. The reader must become more active and bolder, and demand more. The librarian must show him how to do this. He must teach the reader not just to suffer what is written for him, but to demand that he be given what he needs, and curse the editor—politely, of course [*laughter*], when he doesn't give what is needed. You, Comrades, are the intermediaries, the key factors, the agents of this creative interaction between top and bottom. Long live the active intermediaries, the most valuable key factors in the system of Soviet culture! [*Prolonged applause*]

REPLIES TO QUESTIONS

1. Was it worth producing a revolution in our country if the English proletariat will still have to take us in tow in about fifteen years?

I see from this question that the author of the question failed to grasp my meaning, but perhaps I did not explain myself sufficiently clearly.

1. If the revolution had not come about in 1917, then we would have been a European, or even an American colony, and in effect the European proletariat would have had to take us in tow from a position of slavery.

2. The English proletariat will overtake us in the building of socialism only after power is won, and it can only be won with a struggle, i.e., by way of revolution—as we did.

3. Our revolution, as an important historical fact, will greatly facilitate the taking of power and the construction of socialism for the English proletariat. At a superficial glance it seems that this is not so, in view of the fact that hopes for a rapid revolutionary development in Europe were not justified. But one has only to ponder the problem to realize that without our revolution the movement in the West would have developed incomparably more slowly.

4. Whether the English proletariat will take us in tow, when and how they will do this, is difficult to foretell. But

what does this "take in tow" mean? In the given situation this means that the English proletariat, having come to power and having expropriated the bourgeoisie, will accelerate our socialist construction by means of organizational, technical, and all kinds of help. This help, of course, will not be purely philanthropic, since we will ensure socialist construction in England with our wheat, timber, and other raw materials. Would the English proletariat be able to take us "in tow" if we lived in bourgeois conditions? Of course not. Thus, the doubts of the author of the question concerning whether it was worth producing a revolution indicate that he did not consider the question in depth.

2. *Might it not possibly happen that we ourselves will outstrip the European workers not only in the matter of revolution but also in the construction of a socialist culture?*

Of course this possibility cannot be excluded. If the present European order drags on for a long time, with the bourgeoisie already incapable of coping with matters and the proletariat still incapable of taking power; or if the bourgeoisie leads Europe on the road to a new war, which will sap still further the European economy and culture—theoretically speaking, the possibility cannot be excluded that we will achieve very great economic and cultural successes before the Western proletariat gains power and starts on the road to building socialism. Such a perspective suggests consequently an extremely slow tempo of revolutionary development in the rest of Europe while we are having successes in economic and cultural fields. However, nothing makes us think that the European revolution has been postponed for many long years. If it comes, let us say, within the next decade, then everything points to the European proletariat, having overcome its bourgeoisie, overtaking us on the road to founding a new social structure and a new culture. But, of course, we will apply all our forces to seeing that we are not left behind.

3. Why is the work of printing dispatches so disgracefully organized here?

The wording of the question is too severe. We have achieved certain successes in the field of telegraphic information. But by and large telegraphic information is still definitely weak. How is this expressed? In many ways: first, the correspondents, because of old practices and habits, often communicate to us things that do not deserve much attention; second, for the same reason, they do not observe those things that, on the other hand, ought to be of prime interest to our press; third, in their communications the necessary links and continuity are missing; fourth, the dispatches are printed in the form in which they are received, i.e., often in an unintelligible form.

What causes all this? Those same reasons of which we spoke in the report: an insufficient development of our general culture and in particular of the press. And press matters have their own special field of knowledge and skills—their own culture. How do we struggle against the numerous shortcomings? By the same methods we discussed in the report: pressure from the reader, or at least from the intermediary between the reader and the newspaperman: in the present case, the librarian, the director of the reading room. It is necessary to edit telegraphic information directly for its user—the local reader. Dispatches will be presented in an unsatisfactory form so long as only the leaders read them correctly, since they will understand one way or another what is said in the dispatch. But when, through the librarians and the reading rooms, we are training wide circles of workers to read or listen to the reading of the newspapers every day, then the newspaperman, even the most conservative and lazy one, will have to submit to the pressure of the readers' demands and protests. It is the work of the librarian to organize these demands and protests.

The cultural role of the worker correspondent

JULY 23, 1924

The worker correspondent as a small lever in the raising of the cultural level

Comrades! The question of the tasks of the worker correspondent is intimately connected with the question of raising the cultural level of the working class. All of our present problems, large and small, rest on this fundamental task. The communists, the members of the Russian Communist Party, were and remain international revolutionists. But when applying themselves to the tasks of the Soviet Republic, they are above all "culturizers." Before the revolution, the word "culturization" had a pejorative, almost insulting connotation.

This address, delivered July 23, 1924, was first printed in Pravda, *August 14, 1924, and later was included in* Problems of Cultural Work *(Moscow, 1924). Translated for this volume from* Collected Works, Vol. 21, *by Marilyn Vogt.*

"That one is what they call a culturizer," would imply that the person carried little weight. Were we right in thinking that way? Yes, we were, because under czarism and under the conditions of a bourgeois state, the primary cultural work had to be to unite the proletariat for the conquest of power, for only the conquest of power opens up the possibility for genuine, far-reaching cultural work.

In the German Social Democratic movement, the German Mensheviks have a theoretician named Hilferding.[31] The other day, in the theoretical organ of the German Social Democratic Party, he wrote an article the sense of which was this: We, the German Social Democrats, are renouncing revolutionary activity inside the German republic. Henceforth we shall devote our energies to the cultural advancement of the German working class. It appears at first glance that he has said almost the same thing that we are saying: namely, that the main work is cultural work.

How are the two different? The difference is that in Germany the proletariat has not taken state power. Consequently, the cultural work of the German proletariat is limited by the existence of private ownership of the means of production and bourgeois power. And the bourgeoisie, having state power, controls the publishing houses, books, schools, libraries, etc., and allots to the working class only as much of all this as it, the bourgeoisie, considers necessary and on terms advantageous to itself.

It may be said, of course, that we too are not well off in this regard. But why are we poor in schools, books, and newspapers? Because we are poor and culturally backward in general and we have very little of anything. But we do not have class barriers and obstacles on the part of the state; that is, we do not have a state power that has an interest in curtailing the means of cultural development for the proletariat, since in our country there is workers' power.

In one of his last articles, to which I have alluded elsewhere,

Vladimir Ilyich explained: With the conquest of power, the very approach to socialism is abruptly changed. As long as bourgeois supremacy lasts the struggle for socialism means uniting the proletariat for the revolutionary seizure of power. This means that the first thing you must do is force open the gates to the realm of the future! But once power has been taken, it is necessary to raise the cultural level of the working masses, for it is impossible to build socialism on the basis of underdeveloped culture. Of course, for the German proletariat, the problems of cultural work after the conquest of power will be incomparably easier than for us. But we have to work under the conditions we have been placed in by our whole past history, and our history is one of brutal oppression, backwardness, poverty, and a lack of culture. You cannot jump out of your own skin. The heritage of the past has to be overcome. The greatest advantage, the greatest conquest that the revolution has offered up to this time (and the revolution is not an end in itself, as we know, but only a means) has been the awakening of a powerful thirst for culture among the working masses. A sense of shame over our low cultural level and an aspiration to improve ourselves—that is the main thing the revolution has brought about—and on a scale never before seen, encompassing millions and tens of millions.

This thirst for culture is, of course, particularly strong among the youth. There is no doubt that the rate of illiteracy among the youth is declining. We see this among the new military recruits. But there is a stage between illiteracy and literacy when a person is semiliterate or insufficiently literate. Many stay too long in this stage. There are many such partly literate people in the army, as well as among working class youth, and particularly among peasant youth. It is necessary for our newspapers to get hold of such semiliterates, attract them, induce them to read daily, teach them to read, increase their degree of literacy and through literacy to widen their horizons. Which brings us to the question we are discussing today.

The working class has been awakened to the need for culture. And worker correspondents are one of the expressions of this class awakening. This is the fundamental distinction between the worker correspondents' organization and all the other writers' groups. Worker correspondents are the closest, most direct instruments of the newly awakened working class at the grass roots level. This relationship is what determines the meaning of their work, their role, and the scope of their interests, and this is the scale by which they are measured. The worker correspondent is receptive to everything by which the working class lives and breathes. The worker correspondents use their pens like levers. It is a small lever, but there are many worker correspondents, and that means there are many little levers for elevating the culture of the working masses.

The idea and its exposition

Of course, in order to be successful at playing the role of a cultural lever, the worker correspondent must be able to write. This is not easy; not at all. Being able to write, of course, does not just mean being able to understand simple grammar. Most of all it means having the ability to find your own idea, to ask yourself: Well, what do I want to say? Learn, Comrades, to ask yourselves this more firmly and more seriously. This is a difficult thing to do. It is much easier to take up the pen, the ink, the paper, dip the pen in the ink and scribble down this or that, for no other reason than that sometimes the reader reads simply for want of something better to do. There are a few like that. This writing is neither exposition nor worker correspondence. It is true—and there's no use trying to hide it—that many newspaper articles in our press are written according to this prescription. Thus, the affliction of newspaper "officialese" is rather widespread. When a journalist does not have a sense of the reader's needs, and therefore, has only a vague idea of what should be reported, the inevitable commonplaces emerge—cliches and gobble-dygook. I mean no offense by all this. The ability to specify the main idea, to find what is necessary for and needed by a given reader in a given situation—that is the requirement that every writer must place upon himself, including a beginning worker correspondent. I can't overemphasize this point. The first thing is to examine yourself rigorously: What do I want to talk about? For whom? And why? This is a precondition for anything else. The question of *how* to write is also of enormous importance, but it has to come second.

Lately, I have encountered a lot of arguments, intended for the ears of worker correspondents, about style and about syntax. Of course, this is a very important aspect of the work. But you encounter a lot of nonsense in discussions on this topic. For example, some think they are uttering such great words of wisdom when they recommend: "Write simply, the proletarian way." But what does it mean to write "simply"? It is not such a simple thing at all to write simply. That recommendation comes essentially out of the past, from the time when the revolutionary intelligentsia was approaching the masses, and was told: "Write and speak more simply, more clearly, more concretely. . . ." Of course, such advice can be repeated to advantage even today in many cases. But to say to *worker correspondents*: "Write simply; don't go chasing after style," would be to miss the point entirely. "Simplicity" alone is totally inadequate. One needs ability; one needs proficiency. It is necessary to cultivate your manner of exposition, your style. This is work; this is a task; this means studying. How should this be approached? One comes across some rather curious instructions on this score, too. I even encountered one bit of advice with a reference to myself. A certain comrade told worker correspondents for purposes of instruction that in order to develop my style I used to take a special pen, get a certain special kind of paper and . . . "write like mad," as he put it; "the pen would go through the paper . . . and that would be it." [*Applause, laughter*]

I was totally amazed to read these lines. Where do things like this come from? Let me assure you, Comrade worker correspondents, you younger writers, that style is not developed by pen or paper, but by consciousness, by the brain. Ask yourself first of all what you want to say. That is the first prerequisite, in questions of form, exposition, and style as in all others. All people are eloquent in their own way on questions they are familiar with and interested in. Of course, one person's way of writing will be more vivid, another's more bland. Different writers have different temperaments. But even semiliterate people write in a persuasive and meaningful way when they have a clear idea of what they want to say in a given instance and when they write not merely to write but are trying to accomplish something, e.g., if the report is not simply a means for satisfying someone's vanity—"Here it is," someone says, "I, Ivanov, have signed an article"—not that, but the fulfillment of some social responsibility—"I must rebut certain lies or expose some bad situation," or on the other hand, "I must tell people about something deserving merit. . . ." It is the greatest mistake to think that style can be worked out by formal means alone, without the mainspring, without the social goal, that spurs people to action. We revolutionists, in the area of writing, as in others, give first priority to the will to act: to change something, to bring something about, to achieve something. And the effort to develop a writing style must also be subordinated to this end.

What does a report consist of? Of two elements—both equally necessary. One of them is *fact*; the other is *point of view*. Without fact, there is no real reporting. This should be kept firmly in mind. The basis of a news story must be something lively and specific, as well as being timely—

something that just happened, that took place a day or two before or not long before. But the interesting facts can be noted and singled out only if the worker correspondent has a point of view. Moreover, to present the facts to the reader you can have and must have a certain point of view. Only in this way will the report have the proper educational impact. Such a combination of vivid fact with the correct point of view constitutes the essence of the art of writing for the worker correspondent and for the journalist in general.

It is ridiculous, of course, to argue which is more important, fact or opinion. Both are necessary. Don't stifle or suffocate fact with opinion! First, relate the facts as they appear, correctly and in an interesting way. Don't beat the reader over the head with the moral of your story; don't drag the reader by the collar to your conclusion. Let the reader examine the facts as they stand. Lay them out in such a way that the conclusion flows naturally from them. Suggest the conclusion to your readers in such a way that they do not notice your prompting. This, to be sure, is a higher art, which every worker correspondent who wants to become a serious contributor to the press must strive toward. It is only possible to advance along this line one step at a time, assiduously correcting and refashioning your writing, never being satisfied with what you have achieved, learning from others, verifying yourself through your readers, broadening your knowledge, your horizons, and your vocabulary.

In good exposition there must first of all be internal logic. It is necessary to set forth the facts consistently, that is, in developing an idea, to give the readers a chance to go in their own minds through all the steps that will bring them to the proper conclusion. It is not unusual to meet journalists or orators who do not develop their themes consistently but throw their readers and listeners off by detached and disconnected thoughts or facts that are somehow or other related to the theme. Such a sloppy way of writing has a destructive effect on an idea just as physical sloppiness has on a body. When you hear such an orator, even a young one, you say to yourself: "This one will not go far!" since one can only go farther by conscientiously and thoughtfully working out the problems. And this shows itself in the exposition. No matter how simple the problem, if it is well thought out, the exposition will be consistent and fresh. But if it is all reduced to cliches, phrases, and "blathering," put an "X" on it and write "failed."

When you write, picture to yourself as clearly as you can how your article would sound being read aloud in your own shop at the factory, or in the one next to yours, or in some other plant nearby. Imagine a dozen or so workers, or citizens in general, listening to your article. Think calmly and conscientiously about how this article is going to reach them and enter their consciousness. Or from another angle, imagine as clearly as you can that the persons about whom you are writing an exposé for dereliction of duty or improprieties of some sort are reading your article, and ask yourself whether they can say that you have gone too far, exaggerated, distorted, gotten something all wrong, not looked into the matter as carefully as you should have? Ask yourself whether you may actually be guilty of such charges and whether it might not be better to put the article aside and go verify the facts again as carefully as you should. Conscientiousness on the part of a worker correspondent is the most important quality; without it all other qualities are of no benefit. If your reports turn out to be erroneous, exaggerated, or simply false, once, twice, or a third time, that will not only undermine confidence in you, worker correspondent Petrov, but it can undermine confidence in the printed word in general among backward readers. Keep your own reputation as a newspaper reporter in mind, worker correspondent, and beyond that, your responsibility as a guardian of the honor and achievements of the Soviet press!

Of course, all this goes far beyond the problem of composition and style. But all the same the connection is very direct. An astute French writer said long ago: "The style is the man," that is, it is not something external or superficial, but something internal, expressing the nature of the person's development, will, and conscientiousness. . . . In order to cultivate your style, you must cultivate yourself as a thinking and acting human being. And in this process, it is impossible to stand still.

Popular and accessible style

A composition, of course, must always be as accessible as possible. But again this is a very, very complicated question. Accessibility depends not only on the style of the composition, but most of all on the substance of the topic under discussion. As an approach to this theme, let me acquaint you with an open letter to me which was sent to *Rabochaya Gazeta* but which was forwarded to me by the editor. Here is the main passage from the letter:

"I ask the editors of *Rabochaya Gazeta* to print this open letter to L. Trotsky in the paper. As a worker correspondent for our proletarian worker's newspaper, I cannot remain silent about what affects me as a correspondent and as an advocate of cultural improvement. What concerns me is that I often encounter articles by L. Trotsky in the newspaper *Pravda* (which I also subscribe to) about the everyday life of the workers, proletarian culture, art, party policy on art, etc. The articles are very, very important at the present time and the subject matter is interesting, but not to everyone. By this word *everyone* I am referring to all of the workers, that is, not that the articles are uninteresting for the workers; on the contrary, they are very interesting. But, unfortunately, they are not fully comprehensible; and they are incomprehensible only because they are too crammed full of scientific terms and words. For example, in issue no. 209, the article 'Party

Policy in Art' includes 'criteria,' 'metaphysician,' 'dialectic,' 'abstraction,' 'antagonism,' 'individual,' and so forth. All of these demand a certain preparation and higher education on the part of the reader. For the average reader and particularly for the worker they are incomprehensible and of course, therefore, can hardly interest them. Because of this, I would, for my part, request Comrade Trotsky to write such articles more often but to refrain from the above-mentioned foreign words and terms and to substitute for them accessible, popular Russian words, so that these articles can fully bring that spiritual nourishment which our backward working class readers crave so much." Z. Kryachko, September 25.

The letter, as you see, is rather old. I am answering it here, a little late. But time is not important in this matter because the question about using popular language does not have a temporary or ephemeral significance. I will not try to prove that the articles which Comrade Kryachko speaks of were accessible, or that there were not too many foreign words or expressions in them which could have been phrased more comprehensibly. It's possible, even probable, that such sins and oversights are present in these articles. Nevertheless, this is not the crux of the question of the use of popular language.

I have said that style depends to a great extent on how much a person knows and what he or she wishes to say. The basic thing is the thought, and the will to action; it is only as an auxiliary element that style develops and becomes visible. The same is true of popular language. It is not an end in itself, but a means to an end. The manner of presentation must correspond to the subject matter, to the degree of complexity or simplicity inherent in it. Of course, it is possible to cram in altogether too many foreign words and confuse the most elementary idea. But quite often the difficulty lies not in the words nor in the composition in general but in the subject matter itself. Take, for example, Marx's *Capital*. Could he have written it in popular language eliminating foreign words? No. Why? Because the subject is very complicated. If we replace all the foreign words with the native product, *Capital* will certainly not become more comprehensible. Why? Because the theme is complicated. But how does one approach *Capital*? Try reading a number of simpler books. Accumulate knowledge and then take up *Capital*. The main difficulty is the complexity of the topic.

But it is even more than that. If the foreign words in *Capital* were replaced by purely Russian words, the composition would not only fail to become clearer, on the contrary, it would become more complex. Scientific terms (words, designations) denote particular, precise concepts. If these established terms are replaced by some more or less appropriate Russian words, the preciseness of the terms disappears, and the composition becomes more diffuse. It is much better to explain the necessary terms and then repeat them once or twice and in this way introduce them into the consciousness of the reader or listener. If the topic flows directly out of the worker's experience, the composition can be and should always be presented so that even an illiterate person will understand fully. But if the topic does not flow directly out of the individual worker's experience, if the topic is based on an incomparably wider experience, as for example, mathematical or general scientific and philosophical problems, it is quite impossible to make them fully comprehensible by manner of exposition alone. For these preparation is necessary; a carefully selected library is necessary which will be a "stairway" upwards—every book a step.

The first step for the backward worker-readers must naturally be the reports of their local worker correspondent. How do the advanced, politically and theoretically educated workers read a newspaper? They begin with the most important dispatches from the wire services. Their eyes search to discover whether or not there has been a sharpening of the revolutionary struggle somewhere in the world, a parliamentary clash, a change of government, a threat of a new war, etc. Thus, they start out, from the first, with the great circle of events and issues.

And how do the ordinary workers approach the newspaper? They look for notices or reports that concern their shop, their factory, or a neighboring factory, or a nearby club, and finally, their own region or city as a whole. The ordinary workers begin with the small circle—the smaller the circle, the more interested they are, because the facts being related touch upon their own lives that much more directly.

All of our cultural-educational and political-educational problems and contradictions fall in between these two circles. One circle is huge, taking in our whole planet, all its life and its struggles; the other circle is quite small, taking in only what is under our feet. The most advanced elements, the experienced, enlightened, well-read fighters live in the first circle of interests. The interests of the backward workers and the overwhelming majority of the peasantry are confined in the second, i.e., small circle. Between the small circle and the large one there are a whole series of intermediate concentric circles, which can be regarded as steps. The problem of the newspaper is to broaden the interests of the reader, leading them from the small circle, step by step, little by little, to the big circle. Worker correspondents occupy a very important place in this work of educating the reader and broadening the reader's horizons. They are close to their readers, observing them on a day-to-day basis, following the growth of their interests and assisting in this growth, broadening the circle of their news reports and constantly drawing on life and on book learning in order to always be ahead of their reader.

The worker correspondent—a constituent part of the Soviet system

We must always keep in mind the idea that workers who do not read newspapers are not a part of their class or their times. . . . Whatever else you do, you must arouse the workers. If they are not able to read, you must induce them to listen as others read. And for this you must capture their interests, touch their most vital concerns. How? With what most immediately concerns them. They must hear that someone is thinking and writing about them. Who can do this? The worker correspondent. To arouse the slumbering minds of their most backward fellow workers is the first and foremost task for all worker correspondents who take their work seriously.

The water in a pond does not become stale or stagnant if fresh springs flow into it. It is the same with a newspaper, particularly in cases where there is a revolutionary monopoly of the printed word. Remember: there is always the danger of newspaper bureaucratism. The editorial staff has its own separate departments, its own red tape, its own approach and special habits and instructions enforced from the top down. But life is always changing, new layers develop among the masses, new questions and interests arise. If the newspaper sees things from one angle and the reader from another, it is death for the newspaper. The worker correspondent must not allow this to happen. Worker correspondents do not just write for their newspapers about the life of the masses. They watch how the newspaper is received by the masses, not just their own news stories but all the newspaper's departments and all the articles.

Write in the newspaper about the newspaper itself. Watch what kinds of new books and pamphlets are getting a response in the workers' milieu, and write about books in the newspaper. The newspaper is no substitute for the book. Only a book can cover a topic from all angles and provide deeper scientific enlightenment. A worker correspondent who only writes and does not read will not go forward; and whoever does not go forward, moves backward. Worker correspondents must raise their own intellectual levels as compared to their readers by reading and studying. Their reading must be geared to those issues which life has placed in the center of their attention as worker correspondents.

The major objective of the Soviet organization of the state is to draw the broad popular masses into government and to teach them to rule. We must not under any circumstances lose sight of this objective. But the experience of the past few years has shown us that a practical resolution of this problem is much more difficult than we imagined at the beginning of the revolution. We are too backward, ignorant, illiterate, and habitually inert; while the practical problems of economic construction on the other hand are too sharp and pressing. This is the spring from which the tendency toward bureaucratism flows, i.e., the resolution of problems through state offices, without the workers and behind their backs. Here, the newspaper comes in as a powerful corrective to the work of the state apparatus. The newspaper tells how this work is affecting and is perceived at the grass-roots level, how the rank and file responds to this work. To be sensitive to this response and communicate it in the newspaper is the indispensable task of worker correspondents. In this way they can enlist the newspaper readers to check up on the functioning of the state and gradually prepare them for participation in government themselves. Worker correspondents are not simply newspaper reporters. Not at all. They are a new and important component part of the Soviet system. They supplement the activity of the governing agencies, counteracting bureaucratization within them.

Problems of everyday life

The process by which the everyday life of the working masses is being broken up and formed anew is one of the most important matters confronting the worker correspondent—I have already spoken and written about this more than once. But problems of this nature are much more complicated than issues arising in workshops and factories. Here, the correct approach is particularly important. Otherwise it is all too easy to get tangled up.

The problems of everyday life basically come down to those of economic and cultural construction on the one hand and cultural-educational influences on the other. Here it is very important to learn to evaluate one's own work correctly and realistically, without getting carried away. This work consists of two elements of different historical significance. On the one hand, we are gradually introducing the element of collectivism into everyday family living. In this area, despite the modesty of our achievements, *the direction of our work* distinguishes us in a fundamental way from all that has been done in this regard in the capitalist countries. But on the other hand, we are conducting our work in this direction so that the working masses of our country can acquire the cultural habits that are already common for all civilized peoples: literacy, newspaper reading, tidiness, politeness, and so forth. In this way, at the same time that the fundamental course of our cultural work is toward socialism and communism, we must simultaneously work to move huge sections of our cultural front forward if only to the level of culture attained in the advanced bourgeois states. This dual character of our work, wholly determined by the circumstances of our historical past, must be understood properly so that we not make errors concerning the sense and substance of our work.

Thus, for example, several local societies for a new way of life have set themselves the task of working out a "communist ethic." This is understood to include the elimination of rudeness, the struggle against alcoholism, bribe-taking, and other evils.

It is absolutely clear that by posing the question in this way we fall prey to a certain optical illusion. It would seem that rudeness, foul language, alcoholism, and bribe-taking were characteristic of the entire capitalist world, and that we were undertaking for the first time the task of creating a "communist ethic" by cleansing our country of the above-named sins and vices. In fact, as far as rudeness, foul language, bribe-taking, and so forth are concerned, we are the recipients of a terrible legacy from czarist Russia, which on questions of culture lagged behind the European states for many decades and in some respects for centuries. A goodly share of our cultural tasks and consequently of the work of the culturizing worker correspondent consists in liquidating this prebourgeois barbarism. I stress this because it is very important for us to correctly understand what we are doing.

You will recall that Marx said that it is impossible to judge either parties or individuals on the basis of what they think of themselves. Why? Because all past parties, particularly the petty-bourgeois democratic parties, have harbored illusions, concealing the gaps and contradictions in their own program and their own work from themselves. The bourgeois-democratic parties cannot live without illusions. It is precisely by virtue of this that the Mensheviks and SRs, for example, consider themselves "socialists." These illusions conceal the fact that they are actually executing functions in the interests of the bourgeoisie. But for us communists illusions are unnecessary. We are the only party that needs no illusions, self-deception, or false coloring to implement its great historical work. To christen the struggle against rudeness, alcoholism, and bribe-taking with some sort of super-ceremonious name like the "struggle for a communist ethic" or "for proletarian culture," does not mean that the advent of communism is drawing closer. It merely means adorning our rough preliminary work with false labels, which is inappropriate and unseemly for us as Marxists.

I do not mean to belittle the significance of our day-to-day struggle for raising the cultural level of the masses. On the contrary, everything depends on the success of this struggle. At one time we said that the typhus louse could devour socialism. The struggle against bribery, as against lice, does not in and of itself constitute the inculcation of the communist ethic. But it is clear that it is impossible to establish communism on the basis of physical and moral filth.

In both city and village the opinion is held that "a member of the Communist League of Youth may not drink." This is an achievement that must be strengthened and developed. You will frequently encounter a windbag who with a look of profundity will start explaining that the struggle against alcoholism is Tolstoyanism. It is hard to imagine anything more stupid or banal.

For the working masses the struggle against alcoholism is a struggle for physical, spiritual, and most of all, revolutionary survival. We have barely begun to raise ourselves up. We have barely enough to make do. We can raise our wages only very, very slowly. And indeed wages are the basis of everyday life and the basis of cultural progress. Forcing its way into the daily life of the worker, alcohol snatches a large share of wage earnings and in this way undercuts the advance of culture. It is necessary to clearly understand the full extent of the dangers of alcohol under our conditions, in which the country's economic organs have hardly begun to recover after a dangerous illness and everywhere still carry traces of chronic disease. The worker correspondent must be able to intimately relate the struggle against alcoholism to all the conditions of life of a given group of workers, to all their factory, cultural, and domestic circumstances. And any worker correspondent who takes alcoholism lightly, when it is the most malicious enemy of the revolution and of the cultural advance of the masses, is not a real worker correspondent.

In connection with problems of everyday life, I am asked what my attitude is toward the October movement and whether it is a part of the new way of life. Of course, there is no need to exaggerate the significance of the October movement, and it is no more acceptable to bureaucraticize it. It undoubtedly represents a step forward—a sign of progress. Just today I received a letter from Elizavetgrad District, one of the districts in which Makhno was strongest[32] and which suffered some of the worst ordeals at the hands of outlaw bands. There in a village (I forget which one) some ten families have already organized an "Octobrist communal household" even including older people in it. This in itself, I repeat, does not change everyday life, but it is a critical improvement, revealing the aspiration toward new things. That is how we must view it.

Religious belief in our country often persists, not so much in people's heads, in their consciousness and convictions, as in their way of life, their customs and circumstances. This is why you cannot always be successful with scientific arguments alone. But to make up for it you can deal some very hard knocks to religious prejudices by showing how they manifest themselves in life. You should watch with a clear and critical eye, as christenings, weddings, or funerals are held in church and describe them simply, or with a chuckle, if you have a knack that way. Reports on religious life can and should play a much greater role in the struggle against the role of the church in everyday life than do the intricate and far-fetched caricatures of certain of our graphic artists.

The question of sex

Much is said about the problem of sex in everyday life. Interest in this problem is especially strong among our youth, for understandable reasons. Written questions on this subject are submitted at every kind of meeting. The problem is raised not theoretically, i.e., not in the sense of the Marxist elucidation of the development of the forms of the family and of social and sexual relations, but practically: how to live now, how things are today.

This is a difficult problem. It is impossible under our conditions to give a categorical solution to a problem which in practice is posed so sharply, in such a point-blank way, since the sexual problem takes in the entire knot of problems of our society and of domestic relations; and it is still very, very tangled up. I cannot untangle it here, not even theoretically. This would take a very long time and this problem is not on the agenda for today. But I will indicate the main features because the worker correspondent can in no way be indifferent to relationships, conflicts, and difficulties arising out of the basic complex of sociosexual relations.

It goes without saying that we are examining the sexual problem openly, without mysticism, without conventional lies and hypocrisy—and, of course, without cynicism. The young generation must be informed in a timely way about both the physiology and the social hygiene of sex. *There must be sexual as well as political literacy.* This is the minimum that we must provide. But, of course, this is still far from resolving the contradictions connected with the sexual aspects of life under the transitional conditions in our country.

The housing problem has a tremendous influence in this area as it does in general in all areas concerning private life. The creation of housing conditions worthy of civilized human beings is a necessary prerequisite for great progress in terms of culture and humaneness as well as of sexual relations. The same applies to social facilities for meals, for the feeding and rearing of infants, and for the situation of children in general. It is clear that all work toward reorganizing everyday life along socialist lines will create more auspicious conditions for the resolution of the present sexual contradictions.

The process of awakening and developing the personality is and will continue to be parallel with this. Being cultured is above all a matter of internal discipline. When we say that on the way to total socialism and communism the state as an apparatus of constraint will gradually disappear, we are also saying that the source of the discipline necessary for the new society will become wholly internal rather than external. It will depend on the degree of culture of each individual citizen. Just as people in a chorus sing harmoniously not because they are compelled to but because it is pleasant to them, so under communism the harmony of relationships will answer the personal needs of each and every individual. For sexual relations this means on the one hand, freedom from external bonds and constraints; and on the other hand, submitting oneself to the internal discipline of one's personality—its richer spiritual life and higher needs.

Of course, this perspective is still a rather remote one. But all the same it shows us the path we must take to find the way out of the present sharp and painful contradictions in the area of sexual relations. *Public work aimed at reorganizing everyday life and individual efforts aimed at heightening the standards of personality in all respects*—this is the basic prescription that can be given in response to the ever so many inquiries submitted on matters of sex. Moreover, this is the point of view with which the worker correspondent must approach these problems.

Portrayal of morals and manners and the new literature

Thus, through the worker correspondent, the everyday life of the workers should tell about itself and reflect upon itself. We have had many arguments about what the objectives of the new proletarian literature should be. Some literary circles have tried to convince us that revolutionary literature should not "reflect" but "transform" and, therefore, that the portrayal of morals and manners has no place in revolutionary works of art.

This approach is a very obvious example of a left-wing

"infantile disorder." There is not a grain of Marxism in it. How can you transform something without first reflecting it? How can you influence everyday life without knowing it in detail? Some people (some of the Communist-Futurists) go so far as to say that revolutionary literature must give us a "standard"—models and norms, so to speak—of what should be. But this is clearly a lifeless, idealistic, professorial, scholastic point of view. It artificially divides the world into two parts: what is and what should be. They say, let the conservatives portray what is, and we—oh, what revolutionaries these are!—we will show what should be.

When you read this sort of philosophizing, you say to yourself: It's as though neither Marx nor Lenin had ever existed for these people. No, don't philosophize, ladies and gentlemen: we desperately need a reflection of workers' lives and their everyday existence going from the simple reports by worker correspondents all the way up to artistic generalizations. There is no doubt that the development of a network of worker correspondents who are broadening their horizons and the range of their interests and developing their literary techniques—all these things combined will create the basis for the new and more comprehensive literature of our transitional epoch.

With that let me again return to the discussion of proletarian literature in order to get to the heart of the matter. Some comrades accuse me of allegedly being "against" proletarian literature. At best—or rather, at worst—this can be understood to mean that I am to some degree opposed to worker correspondents as well, since they are the sole first-hand, local literary voice of the proletariat. Through the worker correspondent the proletariat looks around itself, looks at itself, and relates what it sees. If the worker correspondent does not serve this function—then he or she is not a worker correspondent and should be reduced in rank.

In what sense, Comrades, have I spoken "against" proletarian literature? I have not spoken against proletarian literature, but against the fact that detached circles of writers hang signs over their doors saying: "In this little office proletarian literature is being developed. You need go no further." *No!* Creating a proletarian culture will not be that easy. It is a much more intricate and complicated task than that. Proletcult is carrying out excellent work as far as teaching and learning to write, teaching and learning dramatic composition, music, and art.[33] But when literary circles are carelessly created from a dozen young writers connected with the proletariat only by their frame of mind, and when they say, "Proletarian literature—that is what we represent; all the rest can go to the devil . . ." then we must object. You are being too hasty! You are mistaking your wishes for reality. We don't object because we are "against" proletarian literature. What nonsense! We object because it is impossible to create proletarian literature—if it is understood to represent not a literary circle but the [proletarian] class—by such simple and easy means. You have before you first of all the task of raising the cultural level of the backward masses who, unfortunately, still do not even understand literature.

Comrades, we speak of "bourgeois literature." Why do we call it bourgeois? Where was this taken from? How was it composed? The bourgeois class is rich; therefore, it is educated. It has free time, since it exploits the proletariat. It devotes its free time to all sorts of pleasures including literature, art, etc. How are bourgeois writers trained? They are quite often the sons of the petty, middle, or big bourgeoisie, who study at bourgeois schools, live in bourgeois families, frequent bourgeois salons, where they meet bourgeois deputies, engineers, merchants, and musicians, delighting in the small talk of the bourgeoisie itself. Thus they always have "their own" social atmosphere, in which they live and breathe. They take hints from one another. The writer, the artist must have an accumulation of day-to-day impressions. Where do they accumulate them? In the bourgeois environment. Why? Because they swim in this atmosphere like a fish in water. This is *their* environment—rich and cultured. And the things that they absorb, the things that they inhale and become intoxicated with from this bourgeois sphere—these things they reproduce in their poems, narratives, and novels. Here, simply and briefly speaking, is the process of creation of bourgeois literature. It does not spring up full-blown. It was created over a period of centuries.

The bourgeoisie has ruled for hundreds of years. Even before it took power, it was a wealthy and educated class for its time. And the entire artistic fraternity, including newspaper reporters—what were they called, burzhkor, perhaps?[34]—these same bourgeois correspondents fed on everything seen and heard in the bourgeois families, salons, stores, etc. So what was the main condition for the development of bourgeois literature? The main condition was that bourgeois writers and in general the artistic worker and the bourgeoisie themselves lived in one and the same day-to-day setting and were roughly characterized by an identical cultural level. Literature, science, and art are particularly rich in those countries where the bourgeoisie was rich and powerful, where it had developed and ruled for a long time, ideologically subjugating a great circle of people, where it had great scientific and literary traditions. In our case, in the process of creating our classical, aristocratic, belated, bourgeois literature, our writers lived only with the class which was able to feed, support, and inspire its writers.

If we were to ask ourselves, Comrades, whether at the present time, today, our proletariat could create such conditions for its own artists, writers, and poets—yes or no?—I would answer: unfortunately, it is still not possible. Why? Because the proletariat is still the proletariat. In order to send beginning proletarian writers or artists to school to study, to develop, we must under present conditions tear them away from production, from the factory, and even partly from the day-to-day life of the working class in general. Until that time, while the proletariat remains a proletariat, even the intelligentsia which emerges from the bosom of the working class will inevitably be to a greater or lesser degree out of touch with it.

Although Marx and Lenin were not workers, they were nevertheless able, by the genius of their intellect, to understand the course of development of the working class and to express it in scientific terms. But in order for poets and novelists to feel the frame of mind of the broad working class masses and express it in literature and poetry, they must be constantly and inseparably linked with the working masses in day-to-day life, in daily experiences. And this is not the case now and really cannot be the case until we have created the prerequisites for a new, genuinely mass culture. And these conditions are: first, literacy; second, genuine literacy, and not semiliteracy; and third, a universally well-informed population. And this assumes general material security, i.e., such conditions of life that people have vast amounts of leisure—not only for relaxation, but for self-education and self-training. In other words, this assumes material and spiritual advancement to such a level that the working class in its vast majority, and not just its leading elements, becomes proficient in all human culture.

Is the road to this big or little, long or short? It is as long or short as our entire road to complete and developed socialism, since the only way to raise the entire proletariat, and after it the peasant masses, to a cultural level at which there would no longer be an enormous cultural gap between readers and writers, artists and spectators, is by strengthening and developing socialism. And what kind of culture will this be? Proletarian culture? No, it will be socialist culture because the proletariat, as distinguished from the bourgeoisie, cannot and does not want to remain the ruling class forever. On the contrary, the proletariat took power in order to cease being the proletariat as soon as possible. Under socialism there is no proletariat; rather there is a vast and cultured producers' cooperative, and consequently, a cooperatively produced, or socialist, art.

Of course, among the young literary groups emerging now from the ranks of the proletariat or coming to the proletariat, there are talented or at least promising poets, novelists, etc. But their work so far represents such a drop in the bucket that there can be no question of satisfying the proletariat with this art alone. We must do everything possible to help these first shoots of proletarian artistic creativity, but at the same time it is impossible to allow such scandalous violations of perspective as when a small young literary group declares itself the vehicle for "proletarian literature." Such a self-evaluation rests upon a false understanding of the entire course of the cultural-historical development of the proletariat, which still has a very, very great need of schooling in bourgeois art, of acquiring for itself the best of what was created by that art, of raising its own artistic level and thereby ensuring the conditions for a genuine mass socialist art. In this process each separate literary-proletarian group can have its own little place, but none can have a monopoly.

Of course, the proletariat approaches bourgeois art in its own proletarian way, just as it does the mansions of the nobility. Indeed, the proletariat does not derive its class point of view from art; on the contrary, it carries its point of view to art. And here too the worker correspondent should provide assistance. He must become the intermediary between the broad masses on the one hand, and literature and art in general on the other. What do working men read? What do working women read? What kind of artistic works do they like? How do they read them? Will they apply the conclusions to their own lives? The worker correspondent must spy on, overhear, and relate all of this.

The wall newspapers which hang in this hall, and which the worker correspondents have played such an active role in creating, represent of course a very valuable achievement in the process of our struggle to raise the cultural level of the masses. Their tremendous significance is in their local origin. And we take note of, praise, and reward—mainly with a collection of Lenin's works—those factory writers and artists who best composed and decorated their wall newspapers. At the same time, Comrades, these wall newspapers, printed by hand, remind us of our poverty and our cultural backwardness and of how very much we have to learn in order to catch up culturally with the advanced bourgeois nations, while of course preserving and strengthening our socialist foundations. Our press, including our wall newspapers, expresses immeasurably higher ideas than those "ideas" that are developed by the bourgeois press. But if you take, let's say, an English paper from the standpoint of variety of material, skill, and attractiveness of presentation, illustration, and technique, you will have to say: How far ahead of us they are! They have, besides the large newspapers, numerous small, special newspapers devoted to the particular interests or needs of a trade, a corporation, or a neighborhood, and reflecting all aspects of its life. Meanwhile, we have to create wall newspapers by hand, which we bring out only once a month and sometimes not that often.

Or compare our press with the American press! In all the Soviet Union we now have less than five hundred newspapers with a general circulation of two and a half million. In North America there are roughly 20,000 newspapers with a circulation of more than 250 million, i.e., approximately one hundred times more than we have. And the population of the United States is smaller than ours by 20 million! We must always keep these figures in mind. It is impossible to forget about our own backwardness. This, incidentally, is where cultural backwardness gets its sinister strength: it lulls the consciousness; but what we need is an ever-vigilant consciousness. Only then will we conquer all our enemies including the most powerful one, our own lack of culture.

On criticism and exposure

In conclusion I would like to speak once more about criticism and exposure of all our cases of malfunctioning. This is easy and difficult at the same time. It is easy because malfunctions are many. You don't have to search for them; all you have to do is look around. It is difficult because the reasons for malfunctioning are very complex, and it is not always easy to discover them immediately.

We are always in the process of "working things out." The very expression "It will work out" is, as we know, quite current among us. Vladimir Ilyich disliked these words very much and would always repeat them ironically: "It will work out . . . which means, it hasn't worked out, and nobody knows when it will work out." Frequently the expression "It will work out" conceals incompetence, self-seeking, and thoughtlessness, but it also can reflect difficult objective conditions and all sorts of shortages and deficiencies. To separate the objective reasons for malfunction from the subjective ones, misfortune from guilt, is very difficult. Thus, it is not easy to give a general evaluation of a situation in a factory, a school, or a military department: Are things improving? Were there great successes? Should you praise or blame the leader? It is possible to take any given factory and upon inspecting it give two contradictory pictures: in one case, one could enumerate all the facts and incidentals concerning malfunctioning, disorganization, irrational utilization of labor or materials, and so forth, and still be left with a great many such facts. But it is possible to deal with this in another way: gather together all the improvements, any kind of achievements in the last two or three years, and such improvements are also numerous. If you gather these together, closing your eyes to all the flaws, you get a very comforting picture.

That is why, under our complex and difficult transitional conditions, inspectors and consequently also worker correspondents so easily fall victim to their own subjective weaknesses, their own critical arbitrariness, and even more, to ill will. And when those who have been inspected or reprimanded in the press see that the conclusions of an inspection are based only on surface impressions or personal bias, they are clearly not spurred on by such an examination or investigation; on the contrary, it kills their spirit and thus defeats the whole purpose.

Worker correspondents must avoid this danger like the plague. Of course, they will often make mistakes in judgment and evaluation. There is a possibility of error in every business, and in newspaper work more than any other. But partiality, arbitrariness, and irresponsibility are things a worker correspondent cannot and must not allow. While fighting against arbitrariness, worker correspondents must in no way become sources of arbitrariness in their sympathies, evaluations, and conclusions. A sense of responsibility for carrying out our work must play a leading role in all their activities. The worker correspondent is an organ of the social conscience, one that watches, exposes, demands, persists. It cannot be otherwise. The worker correspondent writes about cases of malfunctioning and expects them to be eliminated. But they are not always eliminated immediately.

This, then, opens up the only genuine sphere of activity for the worker correspondents. It is very easy after a failure to throw up your hands. But worker correspondents who are fighters act otherwise. They know that it is much easier to find malfunctioning than to eliminate it. They also know that a newspaper makes itself felt, not all at once, but by repeating, keeping pressure on, day after day. Worker correspondents take advantage of all new opportunities and find new ways, using new circumstances or details, to expose these instances of malfunctioning. Moreover, they continue to study the problem themselves, approaching it first from one angle, and then from another, in order to more clearly understand its roots and to strike more accurately at its main cause.

A worker correspondent needs self-control; a worker correspondent needs the temperament of a fighter. Even in the larger political arena we do not win everything immediately. We went through decades of underground struggle, followed by 1905, then defeat, and again the underground; then came 1917, the February revolution, the civil war. . . . Our party displayed the greatest tenacity in the revolutionary struggle and through this, it conquered. Worker correspondents must be totally imbued with the spirit of the Communist Party—the spirit of struggle, tenacity, and revolutionary commitment. The worker correspondent must be a communist, must live not just by the letter, but also by the spirit of Lenin's teachings, which means constant criticism and self-criticism. Don't believe everything you hear; don't live by rumors; confirm figures, confirm facts; study, criticize, strive; struggle against arbitrariness and the feeling that there is no defense against injustice; persist, press your views, broaden your field of ideological understanding; go forward and push others forward—only then will you be *genuine and true* worker correspondents! [*Thunderous applause*]

On stenography

OCTOBER 27, 1924
I owe so much to stenography and stenographers that I find it difficult to know how and where to start. My close working connection with stenographers starts with the October Revolution. Up till then I never had the chance to take advantage of this wonderful skill—at least, not counting the trial of the first Petersburg Soviet of Workers' Deputies (1906), when stenographers noted down the testimony and speeches of the accused, including myself.

Looking back on these seven years of revolution, I am completely unable to imagine how it would have been possible to get through them without the constant help of stenographers. I always watched with grateful amazement while my young friend Glazman, now dead, used to write under rapid dictation on speeding trains, over weeks, months, and

Written for Voprosy Stenografi *(1924), and translated for this volume from* Collected Works, *Vol. 21, by Iain Fraser.*

years, orders and articles, and take minutes of the decisions of meetings, and thus carry out a huge part of the work that without him would never have been carried out at all. Taking shorthand on a train at full speed is a really heroic task. And when I received from Glazman or his colleagues articles for our newspaper *V Puti* [On the Road], orders or notes of speeches made from the steps of carriages, I always silently "blessed" the wonderful skill of stenography.

All the pamphlets and books written by me since 1917 were first dictated and then corrected from shorthand notes. This method of working admittedly also has certain negative features. When you write by yourself, you construct your sentences better and more accurately. But on the other hand, your attention gets too taken up with the details of expression and the very process of writing, and you easily lose sight of the overall picture. When you dictate, individual omissions are unavoidable, but the general construction gains tremendously in consistency and logic. And the individual omissions, inaccurate formulations, etc., can be corrected afterwards on the shorthand record. This is the method I have mastered. I can now say with full conviction that in these years I would not have written a third of what I have done without the constant help of the stenographer comrades.

At first I experienced a certain embarrassment; it's as if you're working under surveillance—you can't slack off, your co-worker is waiting. But then I got used to it, accustomed myself to the system and began to find in it a force of discipline. When two people are sawing wood with a handsaw, they have to work rhythmically; when you learn how, it makes the work very much easier. It's the same with shorthand: thought becomes disciplined and works more rhythmically in harmony with the stenographer's pencil.

In our journal, some contributors express the hope that in the more or less near future ordinary cursive writing will be supplanted by shorthand. I do not undertake to judge how feasible this is. My colleagues whom I consulted on this point expressed doubt: the better, they say, a man writes shorthand for himself, the more difficult it tends to be for others to read his notes. I repeat, I do not undertake to judge this. But even in its present form, when stenography is a complicated, delicate specialization, the profession of a relatively small number of persons, its social role is invaluable and will without fail increase. In the first Soviet years, stenography mainly served politics. This is a field in which it will go on doing a lot. But at the same time it will increasingly serve economic tasks, science, art, and all branches of socialist culture. In a certain sense it can be said that the cultural growth of our society will be measured by the place that stenography has in it. The education and training of young stenographers is a task of primary importance. I hope that this task will be carried out successfully. But for now I'll finish these quick lines with a big hearty *thank you* to stenography and stenographers.

Next tasks for
worker correspondents

We must struggle to raise the cultural level

We must struggle to raise the cultural level, beginning with A in a literal sense, that is, with ABC. On Monday in Moscow the congress of the Down With Illiteracy Society opens. We put forward that slogan quite a while ago, yet there is still plenty of illiteracy to be found, illiteracy in the most straightforward sense of the word, and we must not forget this; and must not forget that there are ten million persons in our country who cannot read *Rabochaya Gazeta*.

We are going to enlarge *Rabochaya Gazeta*, and that will be a good thing, but even in its present small size it is beyond the mental reach of ten million grown men and

---

A speech to the All-Union Conference of Worker Correspondents of Rabochaya Gazeta. *From* Pravda, *January 20, 1926. Translated from* Collected Works, *Vol. 21, by Brian Pearce.*

women. And yet, Comrades, we want to build socialism. If socialism is to be built in an illiterate country, a heroic effort will be needed from the advanced people, in order to raise the dark backward masses, first of all and at the very least to the level of ordinary literacy.

The first task—to abolish illiteracy

As I was leaving to come here, I glanced through the latest mail, which had been placed on my desk. It included some emigre White Guard newspapers. In these were accounts of the New Year celebrations. At one party, some emigres belonging to the Nationalists, or the Cadets, proposed a toast to the letter *yat*.[35] There are a lot of young people here, and I am afraid that many of you will not know what sort of personage is meant. The letter *yat*, together with the hard sign, *fita*, and *izhitsa*, were the estate of nobles in our alphabet, suppressed by the October Revolution. They were unnecessary letters, superfluous and nobly parasitic. They were abolished. And in Paris one of the leaders of the emigres (I have forgotten his name) proposes a New Year's toast to the letter *yat*. Well, there you are, it is a symbolic toast. We on our part can, at the New Year—and today, if I'm not mistaken, is the old Russian New Year's Day—declare that we hand over *yat*, the hard sign, *fita*, and *izhitsa* to the emigrants, whole and entire. In the Ukraine, I believe, they call this giving somebody "the hole from the doughnut."

But now all the remaining letters, which are really needed—not the noble parasitic ones, but the functional proletarian ones that we need in our work—in the year ahead of us, in the next two or three years, must at all costs be made the possession of everybody in our country. We should not have such a disgraceful situation as grown-up peasant men and women, working men and women, not knowing how to read and write. And it is the worker correspondent who must be the real moving force in this work. The abolition of illiteracy is our first task in the struggle for culture.

Women in the fight against drunkenness

But, Comrades, in this struggle we have another fierce adversary whom we must overcome if we are to be able to advance. I speak of alcoholism, of drunkenness. Various forms and methods of struggle against drunkenness have been tried and will be tried in the future. But the basic method is to bring about the cultural progress of the masses themselves, to develop in them a stubborn fighting vanguard in the battle against alcoholism.

In this connection, the first place must be taken by the women, and of course the worker correspondents must make their contribution to this movement. The period that lies ahead must be a period of heroic struggle against alcoholism. The working masses still live very poorly, but nevertheless not so poorly as in past years. We can observe a weariness of the nerves, both from the revolutionary upsurge of the recent past and from the present revolutionary lull, which demands stubborn everyday work. People's nerves are badly worn. There is a great demand for different sorts of stimulants or, conversely, sedatives. The demand for alcohol, for intoxicating, artificially stimulating drink, is very strong among the workers in the towns.

And, Comrades, the worker correspondent who sets a bad example in this matter is not worthy of the name of worker correspondent. A worker correspondent must be a fighter against drunkenness. This is no laughing matter. History will subject us to a hard test in this matter. If we do not give a rebuff to drunkenness, starting in the towns, then we shall drink away socialism and the October Revolution.

This evil must be exposed and scourged. Together with cultural progress in general, we need to enlist for the fight against drunkenness particular people, the youngest, most militant, and best elements of the working class, in the first place working women, for nothing bears so hard upon the working woman, and especially upon the working mother, as drunkenness. Nothing threatens the physical and moral health of the rising generation of the working class as drunkenness does. Without a fight against it there can be no real social service by worker correspondents.

The worker correspondent in the fight for quality in production

The third question is the question of quality in production. I have a lot of notes on this subject.

What do we mean by quality in production? Quality in production means that what you do, you do well, remembering that you are doing it for the community, for society as a whole. So far as the reports sent in by worker correspondents are concerned, quality means conscientiousness. Don't write from hearsay, and don't exaggerate. Again, the newspaper itself will exaggerate; such errors do occur. Fight against this kind of thing!

In the matter of quality of production, of course, mistakes are made in both directions. Sitting here is a correspondent who caught me out in a mistake regarding the cars produced at the AMO factory. The fact is that I was led into error and supposed that things were worse at that factory than proved to be actually the case.

More often, though, the mistakes made are of the other sort, mistakes of bragging, of boasting. Don't you see, we have made the October Revolution, and we will show up the Germans, the French, and the Americans—with cars and machines, too, with textile goods, with anything you care to mention. People who talk like this forget that our cultural level is low, that we even have illiteracy, that drunkenness still plays a big and cruel role in our people's life, and that at present we produce worse than capitalist economies produce.

Every article is the product not only of living human labor, but also of accumulated dead labor, i.e., of machinery and equipment. At present we are weak in the latter, and we have to put forth all our efforts to catch up with the capitalist countries economically. We must never forget that we are building socialism amidst capitalist encirclement.

How is one social system distinguished from another? How must socialism be distinguished from capitalism? Socialism must provide more products per unit of labor than capitalism provides. If we don't achieve that, then we ourselves will have to admit that socialism is of no use to us.

Socialism, after all, does not consist only in the abolition of the exploiters. If people lived more prosperously under the exploiters, more abundantly and freely, and were materially more secure; if they lived better with exploiters than without, then they would say "Bring back the exploiters."

This means that our task is, without exploiters, to create a system of material prosperity, general security, and all-round cultured existence, without which socialism is not socialism. The October Revolution merely laid down the state foundations for socialism; only now are we laying the first bricks. And when we ask ourselves whether we are at this moment producing more goods per unit of labor-power than are produced in other countries, the answer can only be: at present, no, we are producing considerably less—in comparison with America, monstrously less. This question will decide everything. They tried to crush us with their armies, but they failed; they used blockade and famine, but that failed, too. And now we have gone out onto the world market—and this, you know, means that the world market is also creeping up on us. We import foreign goods and export our own. Thereby has begun direct and immediate competition between our fabrics and

British ones, our machines and American ones, our grain and North America's.

The question of quality is a question of competition

What does competition mean? In the language of the capitalist market it means comparison between the quality of our work and the work of the capitalist countries. This question is a perfectly clear and simple one. If we stitch one pair of shoes in two days, for example, and these shoes wear out in one year, while the Americans, thanks to better technology, correct division of labor, and greater specialization, stitch a pair in half a day, and these shoes last the same length of time, it means that in this branch of industry the Americans are four times as powerful as we are.

Under the capitalist system, every society is divided into different classes with a very great variety of incomes, and the goods produced reflect this structure of society. As we have seen, the old alphabet included some aristocratic letters: well, there are aristocrats among goods, too, which are adapted to privileged tastes. We, of course, need in the next few years to produce mass goods, democratic goods. This does not mean crudely and badly made goods that cannot satisfy human tastes; but that the basic quality of goods for us is still their durability. And we must now learn to compare our economy with Europe's, not just by superficial appearances or by hearsay. Nor is it enough now to make comparisons with prewar levels. The prewar economy of czarism was backward and barbarous—that was why the czarist government was routed in the war: it relied upon a backward economy. We need to compare our economy with that of the countries of Europe, so as first to catch up with them and then to surpass them.

I repeat, we have to make comparisons not on the basis of superficial appearances or of hearsay. People say that we work "almost" as the Germans, the French, and others work. I am ready to declare a holy war on that word "almost." "Almost" means nothing. We need exact measurement. This is very simple. We need to take the cost of production; we need to establish, for example, what it takes to make a pair of shoes, to establish how long the goods last and how long they take to produce, and then we will have what we need to make comparisons with other countries. In scientific terminology, this is called finding the comparative coefficient.

I have often quoted the example of the electric light bulb. It reveals the heart of the problem more clearly than anything else. It is easy to measure a light bulb, to estimate what it costs, how many hours it will burn compared with a foreign-made one, how much electric power it uses and how much light it gives. If we work all that out we get a perfectly precise comparative coefficient. If, say, it proves that one of our bulbs is only half as good as a foreign one, then the coefficient will be 1:2. The social utility of our bulb will be equal to one-half. If we take such comparative coefficients for shoes, for machines, for fabrics, for nails, for matches, etc., and compare them together, we get what is called in statistics the average weighted coefficient, which will show how far behind we are. It may turn out that our weighted coefficient in relation to America is 1:10, i.e., that we work only one-tenth as well as America. I give this figure only for illustration, but I think that it is not far from the truth, for in the U. S. they have more than forty times as much mechanical labor-power as we have.

In our country we have less than one unit of mechanical labor-power per head of population, while over there they have more than forty. That is why the national income in America is eight to ten times as big as ours. There the population numbers 115 million, whereas we have 130 million, and yet there they turn out in a year eight to ten times as many products of agriculture, stockbreeding, and industry. These basic figures must hit the worker correspondent in the eye, but they ought not to call forth any feeling of dejection. There are no grounds for that. The U.S. arose and grew up on virgin territories under the capitalist system; we have a people liberated by the revolution, living in a country of unlimited natural resources, and working for themselves and only for themselves.

No communist conceit and no worker correspondent conceit

Thus, our opportunities are very much greater. But, while recognizing our opportunities, we ought at the same time to see clearly the degree to which we are backward: bragging, conceit, communist conceit, worker correspondent conceit, can have no place here at all. We must clearly and truthfully evaluate what exists.

Recently, I had the following experience. I won't mention any names, lest once again I get caught out by some worker correspondent—though this time I'm well shod. It concerns cars and rubber. We held a run to test out cars and tires. The report on the results of this test was sent to a newspaper. In this report it was stated that our rubber had proved to be definitely worse than foreign rubber, and in some cases was quite useless. And now I take up the newspaper—I won't name it, but, out of respect for our visitors, I will say that it is not *Rabochaya Gazeta*. I don't make any promises. Perhaps later on I will name this paper; for the moment I am only making a preliminary reconnaissance. [*Laughter*] What was published in this paper? They said that our rubber was not in any way inferior to foreign rubber, and in some cases was even superior to it.

In my opinion, Comrades, this is downright shamelessness. Of course, we live in a socialist state. Corporal punishment is forbidden here; corporal punishment is a disgraceful thing; but if we were to allow corporal punishment for anything at all, then it should be for stunts of this sort. Because to deceive yourself, to deceive public opinion, means to ruin the cause of socialism. Naturally, people will offer thousands of arguments in justification for such things. They will say that we musn't let the outside world know of our shortcomings, that this matter has a military significance, and so forth. Rubbish! You can't hide rubber. There are plenty of foreigners here. And a foreigner will take our rubber, weigh it in a laboratory and evaluate it, both mechanically and technically, from all angles, with complete accuracy. Whom, then, are we deceiving? We are deceiving our own working men who read this paper, we are deceiving our own working women, we are deceiving the very managers in charge of our industries. We are deceiving the peasants, the army. We are deceiving ourselves. And by so doing we are ruining the cause of socialist construction. We must burn out our mendacity with a red-hot iron, and our propensity to boast, which takes the place of real, stubborn, relentless struggle to raise the level of our technology and our culture. This also forms part of the task of the worker correspondent in the fight for quality in production.

Weak sides of our newspapers

Comrades, I want to add only a few more words regarding a section which is fearfully weak in all our publications, all our newspapers. I refer, Comrades, to the section dealing with the world labor movement. This section must at all costs be strengthened and enlarged. If we were to examine not merely the ordinary worker, not only the ordinary party member, but even the worker correspondent, to see if he knows the basic facts about the life of the German or the French Communist Party, or about the British trade unions, I am convinced that the outcome of such an examination would be poor. And this is not the fault of the worker correspondent; it is our fault, the fault of the newspapermen—I, too, belong in that shop to some extent and take part of the blame upon myself. If you take the communist press of the prewar, prerevolutionary period—in those days it was the Social Democratic press—you find that incomparably more space was allotted to this section. And the advanced elements of the working class were not only educated on their own internal political experience, but, as they climbed upward, they penetrated into the life of the world working class. Things are a lot worse here in this respect today. Of course, there are vast objective causes operating: we have great tasks on hand, we have begun to build a new economy, to raise millions of people to a higher level.

Our forces, our attention, are absorbed in internal construction, but all the same it is now not 1918, not 1919, not even 1920, but 1926. The eight-hour working day is in our country the fundamental precondition for the mental culture of the working class. One can study; there is spare time available for self-education. And, of course, we shall not surrender the eight-hour day on any account. On the contrary, we have to raise the level of technology, through increasing the productivity of labor, so as to be able over the years to pass from the eight-hour to the seven-hour day, then to the six-hour day, the five-hour day, and so on. But for the present we have the eight-hour working day, as one of the most precious conquests of the October Revolution and as the most important precondition for raising the level of our working class culturally and with respect to knowledge of international politics.

More attention to the world working class movement

We are too dependent on the world revolution, on the European revolution, to dare to turn our backs upon it. What we need is for concrete facts about the life of the working class to penetrate through the newspapers into the minds of our advanced people. They should find news about familiar figures in the newspapers; they should follow the activity, say, of the parliamentary group in the German Communist Party, the changes in policy, the radicalization, the turn to the left of the British trade unions. The advanced workers, and through them the wider mass of the workers, should understand the ebbs and flows in the European and world revolutionary movement.

We cannot restrict ourselves in relation to the world revolution to mere waiting and nothing else. I think that those of you who engage in local agitational work will have noticed more than once that when one speaks to the masses about the European revolution, they yawn, they don't feel it, they don't sense its internal development; in short, the European revolution has been turned for them into an empty phrase. And yet it is not at all just a phrase: the European revolution is growing, but it has its ebbs and flows, its mistakes and its successes. In the course of this experience the leading strata of the working class are being prepared and formed.

This process must be followed, and it is the workers' press that must follow it first and foremost. Worker correspondents must see to it that German and French worker correspondents occupy an appropriate place in our press, so that there may be a real international exchange of news between worker correspondents on the basic questions of our economic construction and of the world proletarian revolution. No onesidedness, no narrowness or craft exclusiveness can be allowed for worker correspondents on even a single question, beginning with frozen meat and flared skirts and ending with the European revolution. There, Comrades, in that little space between flared skirts and frozen meat and the world revolution—is defined the range of interests of worker correspondents. And only that worker correspondent is worthy of the name who strives to embrace all of these various interests and the entire complexity of the struggle and of culture throughout the world. [*Stormy applause*]

For freedom in education

JULY 10, 1938
I sincerely thank the editors of *Vida* for having asked me to express my opinion on the tasks of Mexican educators. My knowledge of the life of this country is still insufficient for me to formulate concrete judgments. But there is a general consideration which I can state here:

In backward countries, which include not only Mexico but to a certain extent the USSR as well, the activity of schoolteachers is not simply a profession but an exalted mission. The task of cultural education consists in awakening and developing the critical personality among the oppressed and downtrodden masses. The indispensable condition for this is that the educator himself must possess a personality

This letter to Vida, *the newspaper of the teachers of Michoacan, Mexico, was written while Trotsky was in his final place of exile in Mexico. From* IV Internacional, *August 1938. Translated for this volume from the Spanish by Iain Fraser.*

developed in the critical sense. A person who does not have seriously worked-out convictions cannot be a leader of the people. That is why a regime that is totalitarian in all its forms—in the state, in the trade union, in the party—strikes irreparable blows at culture and education. Where convictions are imposed from above like a military command, the educator loses his mental individuality and cannot inspire either children or adults with respect or trust in the profession he exercises.

This is at present happening not only in the fascist countries, but also in the USSR. The bases created by the October Revolution are still—fortunately—not completely destroyed. But the political system has already definitively assumed a totalitarian character. The Soviet bureaucracy which has done violence to the revolution wants the people to consider it infallible. It is to the schoolteacher that it has entrusted this task of deceiving the people as priests do. To stifle the voice of criticism, it has introduced the totalitarian system into the education workers' trade unions. The police functionaries put at the head of the unions wage a furious campaign of slanders and repression against educators with a critical mind, accusing them of being counterrevolutionaries, "Trotskyists," and "fascists." Those who do not yield, the GPU suppresses. What is more, the Soviet bureaucracy is striving to extend the same system to the whole world. In every nation it has its agents who are seeking to establish the totalitarian system inside the trade unions of those countries. This is the terrible danger which is threatening the cause of revolution and threatening culture, particularly in the young, backward countries, where the population is all too ready, even as it is, to bow the knee to feudalism, clericalism, and imperialism.

The most fervent wish I can express is for Mexican education not to be subjected to a totalitarian system in its trade unions, with the lies, slanders, repressions, and strangling of critical thought this brings in its train. Only an honorable and tenacious ideological struggle can secure the elaboration of firmly rooted, serious convictions. Only education armed with these convictions is capable of winning unshakable authority and completing its great historical mission.

Part 3

Science and technology

Science in the task
of socialist construction

NOVEMBER 23, 1923

I am extremely distressed that a passing illness threatens to prevent me from fulfilling my obligation to address the Congress of Scientific Workers. The questions on the agenda of the congress are of enormous interest. But of still greater interest—I venture to say—is the fact of the congress itself, which, in accordance with its objective significance, must facilitate and expedite the adaptation of scientific thought to the innumerable, boundless tasks of the new society that are placed before us by our historical destiny.

The expression just used about the "adaptation" of scientific thought to new tasks may give rise to apprehensions among some people about the creation of a bureaucratic science of a new, Soviet type. I have nothing of this sort in mind. I do

A message to the First All-Russian Congress of Scientific Workers. From Pravda, *November 24, 1923. Translated for this volume from* Collected Works, *Vol. 21, by Frank Manning and George Saunders.*

not and could not. The proletariat needs that kind of science, and only that kind, which correctly perceives the objective world in its material and dynamic reality. Only classes that have outlived themselves need to give science a goal incompatible with its intrinsic nature. Toiling classes do not need an adaptation of scientific laws to previously formulated theses. But all of us very much need a new orientation on the part of scientists: the adjustment of their attention, their interests, and their efforts to the tasks and demands of the new social structure.

These tasks are immense, because on the one hand we are a terribly backward country, and because on the other we are conducting the struggle against our backwardness, not in the limited interests of a privileged minority, but in the name of the material and spiritual development of the whole nation, including its most sluggish and backward peasant layers. Just what are the reasons for our hopes of victory?

The first reason is that the popular masses have been roused to activity and to critical thought. Through the revolution, our people opened a window onto Europe for themselves— by "Europe" we mean culture—just as, over two hundred years ago, the Russia of Peter the Great opened not a window, but a peephole onto Europe for the elite of the aristocratic-bureaucratic system. Those passive qualities of meekness and humility, which were proclaimed by government—paid or intentionally idiotic ideologues as the peculiar, unchanging, and sacred qualities of the Russian people, but which were in fact only the expression of the people's slavelike subjugation and cultural alienation—these wretched, shameful qualities received a death blow in October 1917. This does not mean, of course, that we no longer bear within us the heritage of the past. We do, and will continue to for a long time. But a great transformation, not only material but also psychological, has been accomplished. No longer does anyone dare to recommend to the Russian people that they base their destiny on meekness, humility and long-suffering. No; from now on, the virtues which are penetrating ever deeper into the people's consciousness are critical thought, activism, and collective creativity. And our hope for the success of our work is based above all else on this very great achievement of the national character.

Another phenomenon is closely connected with this change. Some real or imaginary "spiritual aristocrats" have been pleased to worry themselves on the grounds that the coming to power of the working class would signify the supremacy of ignorant narrow-mindedness or, more bluntly, smug boorishness. The harsh experience of these six years, with all its pluses and minuses, has shown one thing—at least to those who have not deliberately closed their eyes—that the stronger the workers' state becomes, the keener and more impatiently the toiling masses perceive our technical, scientific, and cultural backwardness and the more persistently they seek to overcome this backwardness, thereby creating a fundamental precondition for giving our scientific thought maximum scope in the more or less near future. It may be said that the workers' state—at least to the extent that it is left in peace—is an organized struggle for civilization and culture, and consequently for science as the most important lever of culture. This is why I think that despite all our present backwardness, there is nothing utopian in the formulation of our basic aim—the creation of a new, socialist culture.

Socialist construction is in its very essence conscious, planned construction, combining—on a hitherto unprecedented scale—technology, science, and carefully thought-out social forms and methods of utilizing them. In precisely this vein I have allowed myself to speak about the adaptation of scientific work to the new, i.e., socialist, tasks of our social development.

One method for this adaptation is overcoming not only the

parochialism of science in general, but also the fragmented divisions within science itself. Without the specialization of scientific thought there is no progress; but there are limits beyond which this specialization begins to undermine the basic foundation of science itself. Under the bourgeois system, impenetrable partitions have frequently arisen between the separate scientific disciplines and been felt as barriers to the development of scientific thought in general. This overcoming of parochialism is all the more correct in relation to socialist society, which must subject all the processes of its construction, in parallel fashion, to scientific supervision, leadership, and control.

Our various economic crises are largely a result of the fact that we have not yet learned to carry out this work as we should. To the extent that scientific thought will correctly evaluate and weigh the various factors (technical, economic, etc.) and thus create the conditions for their planned coordination, crises will be more and more relegated to the past, thus clearing the arena for the growth of a well-thought-out and internally harmonious socialist economy and culture. And inasmuch as representatives of the different divisions of our scientific arsenal have been brought together at this congress, the congress in and of itself is an extraordinarily valuable fact of scientific culture. It is a step on the road to combining professional specialization with an all-encompassing synthesis of the processes and problems of our life and work.

Socialist construction in general may be characterized as an attempt to rationalize human relationships, i.e., to subordinate them to reason armed with science. All scientific disciplines grew out of the needs of human society and serve these needs in one way or another. Socialism therefore needs all the sciences. But at the same time, socialism, as a constructive social movement, has its own theory of social development that is an independent science ranking with the other sciences and, I dare think, not the least important among them. If biology today is unthinkable without Darwinism, of course with all the subsequent advances and modifications of it; if scientific psychology today is unthinkable without the theory and methodology of conditioned reflexes—then how much more is social science unthinkable today outside of and without Marxism. Without this theory it is impossible today to properly understand and evaluate our own successes and failures on the new road, and it is impossible to find our way in the chaos that constitutes the capitalist world today.

I am prompted to raise this question particularly by the recently published collection of our Academician Pavlov's work of the past twenty years on conditioned reflexes. This truly remarkable book does not need a recommendation at a Russian scientific congress, especially from an ignoramus, which the author of the present letter is in questions of physiology. And if I make mention here of the labor of our deep thinker and scholar, then it is only because I feel compelled to oppose Pavlov—and to do so just as determinedly as I am prepared to do in following him step by step through his system of reflexes. For, though only in passing, he has tried to establish certain interrelations between questions of physiology and questions of social relationships.

Academician Pavlov considers that only knowledge of "the mechanism and laws of human nature"—with the help of objective, i.e., purely materialist, methods—can assure "true, full, and stable human happiness." The task of properly accommodating man on earth is thus placed entirely on the shoulders of psychophysiology.

Let the mind conquer for human life and activity not only all the dry land of the earth, but also its watery depths, as well as the atmosphere surrounding the terrestrial globe. Let the mind transport its enormous energy from one place on earth to another with ease for its multifaceted goals. Let it overcome space in order to broadcast its thoughts, words, etc., etc.—still and all, the human being to whom this mind belongs is guided by certain dark forces acting within him and causes himself incalculable material losses and inexpressible suffering with wars and revolutions and all their horrors, reminiscent of the relations among beasts. Only the ultimate science, the exact science of man himself—and the most accurate possible approach to it on the part of all-powerful natural science—will lead man out of the present darkness and cleanse him of the present shame in the sphere of relations among people.

That cruelty, perfidy, treachery, and violence in the sphere of relations among people constitute shame, we will not argue with the author of the lines we have cited. But we cannot in any way agree with the view that natural science—powerful, but by no means "all-powerful"—is capable, by delving into the laws of human nature, of altering social relationships, cleansing them of their present shame.

This way of posing the question, which assumes that the motive forces behind social relationships are to be found not in the objective, material conditions of their development, but in the evil ("dark") qualities of the individual human being is essentially idealistic and is therefore basically in contradiction with those materialist methods that find their brilliant application in the theory of conditioned reflexes itself.

If it be accepted that the cause of social phenomena lies in the nature of the individual human being, as a rather stable system of absolute and conditioned reflexes, what then determines the changes in the social structure, its evolution according to certain laws, and the revolutionary leaps that are inevitable phases in this evolution? The point is that society, as an objectively conditioned, productive combination of people, by no means functions according to the same laws that the reflexes of the individual human organism follow. Of course, without the human need for food and so on there would be no social production. But social production is not at all regulated by those laws that determine the assimilation of protein by the human organism. Society is governed by social laws that are just as much subject to objective, i.e., materialist, regulation as the laws which govern the work of a dog's salivary glands.

It could be demonstrated beyond any question—this is a very interesting and important methodological problem— that Marxism, in relation to social phenomena, occupies the very same position that Darwinism does in relation to the vegetable and animal world, and that reflexology does in relation to psychology. The fathoming of the secrets of conditioned reflexes will without a doubt enrich both individual and social pedagogy, providing new, powerful means of influencing the human character. But in what direction? Under what conditions? For what goals? This depends on the social environment. We know, for example, that psychological technique, which can be approached seriously only on the basis of reflexology, is used, and not unsuccessfully, in military affairs by helping to carry out the selection of personnel and of the individual qualities that make someone more suited for artillery, aviation, or chemical warfare. In other words, extending our knowledge of individual human natures allows us to further organize the business of the annihilation of man by man, i.e., that very business that all of us, together with Pavlov, consider the worst shame of contemporary human culture.

In this regard, physiology shares the fate of all the natural sciences in general. While increasing the power of man over nature and while arming man with new technological methods and means, natural science makes man himself all the more powerful, and consequently all the more destructive, in the arena of war between nations and classes. If the

workers had agreed to accept the conclusion that their liberation would come through natural science—without class
war and revolution—then, undoubtedly, the bourgeoisie
at a certain level of development of natural science would
have put to work those methods of psychological technique
that would have strengthened the reflexes of subjugation in
the exploited and those of domination in the exploiters. But
fortunately, the laws of social development have excluded
the possibility that the toiling masses would turn down the
road of naive pedagogical idealism. They will go onward to
their liberation along that one path which has been determined by history.

Not so long ago the military use of poisonous substances
was considered impermissible according to the so-called
norms of so-called international law. This was in that period when chemistry still could not offer anything serious
in this department. We know, however, how radically views
regarding poisonous substances changed in the course of
the imperialist war, especially toward its close. Chemistry
is one of those sciences which will play a leading role in
the process of the further material and spiritual flowering
of human culture. But at the present time this in no way
prevents chemistry, while contributing new methods to agriculture and industry, i.e., the task of preserving human
life, from serving with all its powers the task of the mutual
extermination of man by man. And even if we citizens of
the Soviet Union had succeeded in purging ourselves, one
and all, of every kind of foulness, we still would not have
freed ourselves thereby from the imperialist encirclement
that we feel pressing hard upon us on all our frontiers, and
would not in the least have made ourselves secure from the
poisonous substances that are being prepared by chemists
in the service of the bourgeoisie of the most powerful and
civilized countries.

It is shameful, thrice shameful, that relations between

people are still decided by means of nickel-plated bits of lead, by dynamite explosions, and by waves of poison gas. But so long as these methods prevail in the world, a world which hitherto has not been constructed as we would like or according to our plans, we do not want to remain and we dare not remain unarmed, if we believe in that great task that historical fate has entrusted to our generation. The workers' state, we have already said, is an organized struggle for culture and civilization; but this peaceful struggle can be waged with firm hope of success only if the workers' state tirelessly and devotedly defends its own borders.

As in the field of peaceful construction, so in that of defense do the toiling masses of our country need the cooperation of science. If none of the scientific disciplines can leap over the conditions imposed by social organization, if natural science serves not only to subjugate nature but also to help people exterminate each other, then let Soviet science, while guiding the planned utilization of the natural wealth of our country, help us at the same time to defend the frontiers of our constructive and cultural work from our irreconcilable and ruthless foes. Let Soviet science give us gases and countergases such as will deprive the civilized beasts of prey of all desire to make attempts on our independence and labor.

If I single out chemistry so emphatically, it is because the savage methods of chemical warfare are more and more being pushed to the forefront, demanding the greatest attention on our part. Theoretical and practical elaboration of questions in chemistry and creation of the necessary network of laboratories and industrial enterprises are together not only a paramount task from the point of view of our industrial activities, but also a question of life and death—I do not exaggerate in the least—in the sphere of our defense.

But this matter, of course, is not limited to chemistry. For defense we need aviation, heavy industry in general, a powerful network of railroads, the indefatigable working out of technical questions, and science in all of its branches and applications. So long as relations among people have not been cleansed of the shame of wars; so long as we must pave the road to the future and secure it for ourselves with blood— we are willing and able to fight well. And in this field we strongly rely on the comprehensive assistance of scientific thought, which has put its social orientation on the side of the toiling masses and their workers' state.

The Red Army and the Red Navy warmly greet your congress!

Dialectical materialism
and science

INTRODUCTION

APRIL 18, 1938

This speech was delivered in 1925, at a time when the author still firmly hoped that Soviet democracy would overcome the tendencies toward bureaucratism, and create exceptionally favorable conditions for the development of scientific thought. Because of a combination of historical causes, this

In 1925, Trotsky was chairman of the technical and scientific board of industry, and in that capacity he delivered this speech before the Mendeleyev Congress. It was published in Ekonomicheskaya Zhizn, *September 18, 27, and 29, 1925. In 1938 Trotsky wrote an introduction to the English translation of his speech, which finally appeared in the February 1940* New International, *the theoretical journal of the Socialist Workers Party. Both the 1938 introduction and the 1925 speech are reprinted here.*

Dimitri Mendeleyev (1834–1907) was a Russian chemist who developed the periodic table of the elements. He was the author of The Principles of Chemistry.

hope has not yet materialized. On the contrary, the Soviet state in the intervening thirteen years has fallen victim to complete bureaucratic ossification and has assumed a totalitarian character equally baneful to the development of science and of art.

Through the cruel irony of history, genuine Marxism has now become the most proscribed of all doctrines in the Soviet Union. In the field of social science, shackled Soviet thought has not only failed to utter a single new word, but on the contrary has sunk to the depths of pathetic scholasticism. The totalitarian regime likewise exercises a disastrous influence upon the development of the natural sciences.

Nevertheless, the views developed in this speech retain their validity, even in the section that deals with the interrelations between the social regime and scientific thought. However, they should be viewed not in the light of the present Soviet state, a product of degeneration and disintegration, but rather in the light of that socialist state that will arise from the future victorious struggle of the international working class.

DIALECTICAL MATERIALISM AND SCIENCE

SEPTEMBER 17, 1925

The continuity of cultural heritage

Your congress convenes amid the celebrations of the bicentenary of the founding of the Academy of Sciences. The connection between your congress and the Academy is made all the firmer by the fact that Russian chemistry occupies by no means the last place in the achievements that have brought fame to the Academy. Here it is perhaps proper to pose the question: what is the inner historical significance of the elaborate academic celebrations? They have a significance far beyond mere visits to museums, theaters, and banquets. How can we estimate this significance? Not merely by the fact that foreign scientists, kind enough to come here as our guests, have had the opportunity of ascertaining that the revolution, far from destroying scientific institutions, has on the contrary developed them. This evidence acquired by the foreign scientists possesses a meaning of its own. But the significance of the academic celebrations is far greater and deeper. I would formulate it as follows: *The new state, a new society based on the laws of the October Revolution, takes possession triumphantly—before the eyes of the whole world—of the cultural heritage of the past.*

Since I have inadvertently referred to heritage, I must make clear the sense in which I use this term, so as to avoid any possible misunderstandings. We would be guilty of disrespect to the future, dearer to all of us than the past, and we would be disrespectful of the past, which in many of its aspects merits profound respect—if we were to talk loosely about heritage. Not everything in the past is of value for the future. Furthermore, the development of human culture is not determined by simple concretion; there have been periods of organic growth as well as periods of rigorous criticism, sifting, and selection. It would be difficult to say which of these periods has proved more fruitful for the general development of culture. At all events, we are living in an epoch of sifting and selection.

Roman jurisprudence, from the time of Justinian, had established the law of inventorial inheritance. In contrast to pre-Justinian legislation, which established the right of an heir to accept inheritance provided only he likewise assumed responsibility for all obligations and debts, inventorial inheritance gave the inheritor a certain degree of choice. The revolutionary state, representing a new class, is a kind of inventorial inheritor in relation to the accumulated store of culture. Let me state frankly that not all of the 15,000 volumes published by the Academy during its two centuries of existence will enter into the inventory of socialism!

There are two aspects of by no means equal merit to the scientific contributions of the past which are now ours and upon which we pride ourselves. Science as a whole has been directed toward acquiring knowledge of reality, research into the laws of evolution, and discovery of the properties and qualities of matter, in order to gain greater mastery over it. But knowledge did not develop within the four walls of a laboratory or a lecture hall. No, it remained a function of human society and reflected the structure of human society. For its needs, society requires knowledge of nature. But at the same time, society demands an affirmation of its right to be what it is, a justification of its particular institutions— first and foremost, the institutions of class domination—just as in the past it demanded the justification of serfdom, class privileges, monarchical prerogatives, national exceptionalism, etc. Socialist society accepts with utmost gratitude the heritage of the positive sciences, discarding, as is the right of inventorial choice, everything that is useless in acquiring knowledge of nature but only useful in justifying class inequality and all other kinds of historical untruth.

Every new social order appropriates the cultural heritage of the past, not in its totality but only in accordance with its own structure. Thus, medieval society embodied in Christianity many elements of ancient philosophy, subordinating them, however, to the needs of the feudal regime and transforming them into scholasticism, the "handmaiden of theology." Similarly, bourgeois society inherited, among other things from the Middle Ages, Christianity, but subjected it either to the Reformation, that is, revolt in the shape of Protestantism, or pacification in the shape of adaptation of Catholicism to the new regime. In any case, Christianity of the bourgeois epoch was brushed aside to the degree that the road had to be cleared for scientific research, at least within those limits which were required for the development of the productive forces.

Socialist society, in its relation to scientific and cultural inheritance in general, holds to a far lesser degree an attitude of indifference, or passive acceptance. It can be said that the greater the trust of socialism in sciences devoted to direct study of nature, the greater is its critical distrust in approaching those sciences and pseudo-sciences which are linked closely to the structure of human society, its economic institutions, its state, laws, ethics, etc. Of course, these two spheres are not separated by an impenetrable wall. But at the same time, it is an indisputable fact that the heritage embodied in those sciences which deal not with human society but with "matter"—in natural sciences in the broad sense of the term, and consequently of course in chemistry—is of incomparably greater weight.

The need to know nature is imposed upon men by their need to subordinate nature to themselves. Any digressions in this sphere from objective relationships, which are determined by the properties of matter itself, are corrected by practical experience. This alone seriously guarantees natural sciences, chemical research in particular, from intentional, unintentional, or semideliberate distortions, misinterpretations, and falsifications. Social research primarily devoted its efforts toward justifying historically arisen society, so as to preserve it against the attacks of "destructive theories," etc. Herein is rooted the apologetic role of the official social sciences of bourgeois society; and this is the reason why their accomplishments are of little value.

So long as science as a whole remained a "handmaiden of theology," it could produce valuable results only surreptitiously. This was the case in the Middle Ages. It was during the bourgeois regime, as already pointed out, that the natural sciences gained the possibility of wide development.

But social science remained the servant of capitalism. This is also true, to a large extent, of psychology, which links the social and natural sciences, and philosophy, which systematizes the generalized conclusions of all sciences.

I said that *official* social science has produced little of value. This is best revealed by the inability of bourgeois science to foresee tomorrow. We have observed this in relation to the first imperialist world war and its consequences. We have seen it again in relation to the October Revolution. We now see it in the complete helplessness of official social science in the evaluation of the European situation, the interrelations with America and with the Soviet Union; in its inability to draw any conclusions regarding tomorrow. Yet the significance of science lies precisely in this: to know in order to foresee.

Natural science—and chemistry occupies a most important place in that field—indisputably constitutes the most valuable portion of our inheritance. Your congress stands under the banner of Mendeleyev, who was and remains the pride of Russian science.

To know so that we may foresee and act

There is a difference in the degree of foresight and precision achieved in the various sciences. But it is through foresight—passive, in some instances, as in astronomy, active as in chemistry and chemical engineering—that science is able to verify itself and justify its social purpose. An individual scientist may not at all be concerned with the practical application of his research. The wider his scope, the bolder his flight, the greater his freedom from practical daily necessity in his mental operations, the better. But science is not a function of individual scientists; it is a public function. The social evaluation of science, its historical evaluation, is determined by its capacity to increase man's power and arm him with the power to foresee and master nature. Science is knowledge that endows us with power. When Leverrier on the basis of the "eccentricities" in the orbit of Uranus concluded that there must exist an unknown celestial body "disturbing" the movement of Uranus; when, on the basis of his purely mathematical calculations, he requested the German astronomer Galle to locate a body wandering without a passport in the skies at such and such an address; when Galle focused his telescope in that direction and discovered the planet called Neptune—at that moment the celestial mechanics of Newton celebrated a great victory.

This occurred in the autumn of 1846. In the year 1848 revolution swept like a whirlwind through Europe, demonstrating its "disturbing" influence on the movement of peoples and states. In the intervening period, between the discovery of Neptune and the revolution of 1848, two young scholars, Marx and Engels, wrote *The Communist Manifesto*, in which they not only predicted the inevitability of revolutionary events in the near future, but also analyzed in advance their component forces, the logic of their movement—up to the inevitable victory of the proletariat and the establishment of the dictatorship of the proletariat. It would not at all be superfluous to juxtapose this prognosis with the prophecies of the official social science of the Hohenzollerns, the Romanovs, Louis Philippe, and others in 1848.[1]

In 1869, Mendeleyev, on the basis of his research and reflection upon atomic weight, established his Periodic Table of the Elements. To the atomic weight, as a more stable criterion, Mendeleyev linked a series of other properties and traits, arranged the elements in a definite order, and then through this order revealed the existence of a certain disorder, namely, the absence of certain elements. These unknown elements or chemical units, as Mendeleyev once called them, should occupy specific vacant places in that order, in accordance with the logic of elemental periodicity. Here, with the authoritative gesture of a research worker confident in himself, Mendeleyev knocked at one of nature's hitherto closed doors, and from within a voice answered: "Present!" Actually, three voices responded simultaneously, for in the places indicated by Mendeleyev there were discovered three new elements, later called gallium, scandium, and germanium.

A marvelous triumph for thought, analytical and synthesizing! In his *Principles of Chemistry* Mendeleyev vividly characterizes scientific creative effort, comparing it with the projection of a bridge across a ravine. For this it is unnecessary to descend into the ravine and to fix supports at the bottom; it is only necessary to erect a foundation on one side and then project an accurately designed arc which will then find support on the opposite side. Similarly with scientific thought. It can base itself only on the granite foundation of experience, but its generalizations can rise above the world of facts like the arc of a bridge, in order later, at another point calculated in advance, to meet the former. At the moment in scientific thought when a generalization turns into prediction—and prediction is triumphantly verified through experience—at that moment, human thought is invariably supplied with its proudest and most justified satisfaction! Thus it was in chemistry with the discovery of new elements on the basis of the Periodic Table.

Mendeleyev's prediction, which later produced a profound impression upon Frederick Engels, was made in the year 1871, the year, that is, of the great tragedy of the Paris Commune in France. The attitude of our great chemist to this event can be gathered from his general hostility towards "Latinism," its violence and revolutions. Like all official thinkers of the ruling classes, not only in Russia and in Europe but throughout the world, Mendeleyev did not ask himself: What is the real driving force behind the Paris Commune? He did not see that the new class growing in the womb of the old society was here exercising in its movement as "disturbing" an influence upon the orbit of old society as the unknown planet did upon the orbit of Uranus. But a German exile, Karl Marx, at that time did analyze the causes and inner mechanics of the Paris Commune, and the rays of his scientific torch penetrated to the events of our own October and shed light upon them.

We have long found it unnecessary to resort to a more mysterious substance, called phlogiston, to explain chemical reactions. As a matter of fact, phlogiston served merely as a generalization for the ignorance of alchemists. In the sphere of physiology, the time has long since passed when a need was felt for a special mystical substance, called the vital force, the phlogiston of living matter. *In principle* we now possess sufficient knowledge of physics and chemistry to explain physiological phenomena. In the sphere of the phenomena of consciousness we are no longer in need of a substance labeled the "soul," which in reactionary philosophy performs the role of the phlogiston of psychophysical phenomena. Psychology is for us in the *final analysis* reducible to physiology, and the latter—to chemistry, mechanics, and physics. This is far more viable than the "theory of phlogiston" in the sphere of social science, where this phlogiston appears in different costumes, now disguised as "historical mission," now disguised as changeless "national character," now as the disembodied idea of "progress," now as "critical thought," and so on ad infinitum. In all these cases, an attempt has been made to discover some supersocial substance to explain social phenomena. It is hardly necessary to repeat that these ideal substances are only ingenious disguises for sociological ignorance. Marxism rejected superhistorical essences, just as physiology has renounced the vital force, or chemistry, phlogiston.

The essence of Marxism consists in this, that it approaches society concretely, as a subject for objective research, and analyzes human history as one would a colossal laboratory record. Marxism appraises ideology as a subordinate integral element of the material social structure. Marxism examines the class structure of society as a historically conditioned form of the development of the productive forces; Marxism deduces from the productive forces of society the interrelations between human society and surrounding nature, and these in turn are determined at each historical stage by man's technology, his instruments and weapons, his capacities and methods for struggle with nature. Precisely this objective approach arms Marxism with the insuperable power of historical foresight.

Consider the history of Marxism even if only on the national scale of Russia, and follow it not from the standpoint of your own political sympathies or antipathies but from the standpoint of Mendeleyev's definition of science: to know so that we may foresee and act. The initial period of the history of Marxism on Russian soil is the history of a struggle for correct sociohistorical prognosis (foresight) as against the official governmental and official oppositional viewpoints. In the early 1880s—that is, at a time when official ideology existed as the trinity of absolutism, orthodoxy, and nationalism—liberalism daydreamed about a Zemstvo Assembly, i.e., a semiconstitutional monarchy, while the Narodniks combined feeble socialistic fantasies with economic reaction. At that time Marxist thought predicted not only the inevitable and progressive work of capitalism, but also the appearance of the proletariat in an independent historical role—the proletariat gaining hegemony in the struggle of the popular masses, the proletarian dictatorship leading the peasantry behind it.

There is no less a difference between the Marxist method of social analysis and the theories against which it fought than there is between Mendeleyev's Periodic Table with all its latest modifications on the one side and the mumbo-jumbo of the alchemists on the other.

Natural science and Marxism

"The cause of chemical reaction lies in the physical and mechanical properties of compounds." This formula of Mendeleyev is completely materialist in character. Chemistry, instead of resorting to some new supermechanical and superphysical force to explain its phenomena, reduces chemical processes to the mechanical and physical properties of its compounds.

Biology and physiology stand in a similar relationship to chemistry. Scientific, materialist physiology does not require a special superchemical vital force (as is the claim of Vitalists and neo-Vitalists) to explain phenomena in its field. Physiological processes are reducible in the last analysis to chemical ones, just as the latter are to mechanics and physics.

Psychology is similarly related to physiology. It is not for nothing that physiology is called the applied chemistry of living organisms. Just as there exists no special physiological force, so it is equally true that scientific, materialist psychology has no need of a mystic force—soul—to explain phenomena in its field, but finds them reducible in the final analysis to physiological phenomena. This is the school of the academician Pavlov; it views the so-called soul as a complex system of conditioned reflexes, completely rooted in the elementary physiological reflexes which in their turn find their root, through the potent stratum of chemistry, in the subsoil of mechanics and physics.

The same can also be said of sociology. To explain social phenomena it is not necessary to adduce some kind of eternal source, or to search for origins in another world. Society is a product of the development of primary matter, like the earth's crust or the amoeba. In this manner, scientific thought with its methods cuts like a diamond drill through the complex phenomena of social ideology to the bedrock of matter, its component elements, its atoms with their physical and mechanical properties.

Naturally, this does not mean to say that every phenomenon of chemistry can be reduced *directly* to mechanics; and even less that every social phenomenon is directly reducible to physiology and then—to laws of chemistry and mechanics. It may be said that this is the uppermost aim of science. But the method of gradual and continuous approach toward this aim is entirely different. Chemistry has its special approach to matter, its own methods of research, its own laws. Without the knowledge that chemical reactions are reducible *in the final analysis* to mechanical properties of elementary particles of matter, there is not and cannot be a finished philosophy linking all phenomena into a single system; similarly, on the other hand, the mere knowledge that chemical phenomena are themselves rooted in mechanics and physics does not provide in itself the key to even one chemical reaction. Chemistry has *its own keys*. One can choose among them only from experience and generalization, through the chemical laboratory, chemical hypothesis, and chemical theory.

This applies to all sciences. Chemistry is a powerful pillar of physiology, with which it is directly connected through the channels of organic and physiological chemistry. But chemistry is no substitute for physiology. Each science rests on the laws of other sciences only in the so-called *final instance*. But at the same time, the separation of the sciences from one another is determined precisely by the fact that each science covers a particular field of phenomena, i.e., a field of complex combinations of elementary phenomena and laws that require a special approach, special research technique, special hypotheses and methods.

This idea seems so indisputable in relation to the sciences of mathematics and natural history that to harp on it would be like forcing an open door. It is otherwise with social science. Outstanding trained naturalists who, in the field, say, of physiology, would not proceed a step without taking into account rigidly tested experiments, verification, hypothetical generalization, latest verification, and so forth, approach social phenomena far more boldly, with the boldness of ignorance, as if tacitly acknowledging that in this extremely complex sphere of phenomena it is sufficient merely to have vague propensities, day-to-day observations, family traditions, and even a stock of current social prejudices.

Human society has not developed in accordance with a prearranged plan or system, but empirically, in the course of a long, complicated, and contradictory struggle of the human species for existence, and, later for greater and greater mastery over nature itself. The ideology of human society took shape as a reflection of and an instrument in this process—belated, desultory, piecemeal, in the form, so to speak, of conditioned social reflexes, which are in the final analysis reducible to the necessities of the struggle of collective man against nature. To arrive at judgments upon laws governing the development of human society on the basis of their ideological reflection, on the basis of so-called public opinion, etc., is almost equivalent to forming a judgment upon the anatomical and physiological structure of a lizard on the basis of its sensations as it lies basking in the sun or crawls out of a damp crevice. True enough, there is a very direct bond between the sensations of a lizard and its organic structure. But this bond is a subject for research by means of objective methods.

There is, however, a tendency to become most subjective in judging the structure and laws that govern the development of human society, to judge in terms of the so-called consciousness of society, that is, its contradictory, disjointed, conservative, unverified ideology. Of course, one can become insulted and raise the objection that social ideology is, after all, at a higher elevation than the sensation of a lizard. It all depends on one's approach to the question. In my opinion there is nothing paradoxical in the statement that from the sensations of a lizard, if it were possible to bring them into proper focus, one could draw much more direct conclusions concerning the structure and function of its organs than one could draw concerning the structure of society and its dynamics from such ideological reflections as, for example, religious creeds that once occupied and still continue to occupy so prominent a place in the life of human society; or from the contradictory and hypocritical codices of official morality; or, finally, from the idealistic philosophic conceptions that, in order to explain complex organic processes occurring in man, seek to place responsibility upon a nebulous, subtle essence called the soul, endowed with the qualities of impenetrability and eternity.

Mendeleyev's reaction to problems of social reorganization was one of hostility and even scorn. He maintained that from time immemorial nothing had yet come from the attempt. Mendeleyev instead expected a happier future to arise through the positive sciences, and above all chemistry, which would reveal all of nature's secrets.

It is of interest to juxtapose this point of view to that of our remarkable physiologist Pavlov, who is of the opinion that wars and revolutions are something accidental, arising from people's ignorance, and who conjectures that only a profound knowledge of "human nature" will eliminate both wars and revolutions.

Darwin can be placed in the same category. This highly gifted biologist demonstrated how an accumulation of small *quantitative* variations produces an entirely new biologic "quality," and by that token he explained the origin of species. Without being aware of it, he thus applied the method of dialectical materialism to the sphere of organic life. Darwin, although unenlightened in philosophy, brilliantly applied Hegel's law of transition from quantity into quality. At the same time, we very often discover in this same Darwin, not to mention the Darwinians, utterly naive and unscientific attempts to apply the conclusions of biology to society. To interpret competition as a "variety" of the biological struggle for existence is like seeing only mechanics in the physiology of mating.

In each of these cases we observe one and the same fundamental mistake: the methods and achievements of chemistry or physiology, in violation of all scientific boundaries, are transplanted into human society. A scientist would hardly carry over without modification the laws governing the movement of atoms into the movement of molecules, which is governed by other laws. But many scientists have an entirely different attitude upon the question of sociology. The historically conditioned structure of society is very often disregarded by them in favor of the anatomical structure of things, the physiological structure of reflexes, the biological struggle for existence. Of course, the life of human society, interlaced with material conditions, surrounded on all sides by chemical processes, itself represents in the final analysis a combination of chemical processes. On the other hand, society consists of human beings whose psychological mechanism is resolvable into a system of reflexes. But public life is neither a chemical nor a physiological process, but a social process which is shaped according to its own laws, and these in turn are subject to an objective sociological analysis whose aims should be to acquire the ability to foresee and to master the fate of society.

Mendeleyev's philosophy

In his commentaries to the *Principles of Chemistry*, Mendeleyev states: "There are two basic or positive aims to the scientific study of objects: that of forecast and that of utility. . . . The triumph of scientific forecasts would be of very little significance, if they did not in the end lead to direct and general usefulness. Scientific foresight, based on knowledge, endows human mastery with concepts by means of which it is possible to direct the substance of things into a desired channel." And further, Mendeleyev adds cautiously: "Religious and philosophical ideas have thrived and developed for many thousands of years, but those ideas that govern the exact sciences capable of forecasting have been regenerated for only a few centuries and have thus far encompassed only a limited sphere. Scarcely two hundred years have passed since chemistry became part of these sciences. Truly, there lies ahead of us a great deal in respect both to prediction and to usefulness to be derived from these sciences."

These cautious, "insinuating" words are very noteworthy on the lips of Mendeleyev. Their half-concealed meaning is clearly directed against religion and speculative philosophy. Mendeleyev contrasts them to science. Religious ideas—he says in effect—have ruled for thousands of years and the benefits derived from these ideas are not very many; but you can see for yourselves what science has contributed in a short period of time and from this you can judge what its future benefits will be. This is the unquestionable meaning of the foregoing passage, included by Mendeleyev in one of his commentaries and printed in the finest type on page 405 of his *Principles of Chemistry*. Dimitri Ivanovich Mendeleyev was a very cautious man and did not intend to quarrel with official public opinion!

Chemistry is a school of revolutionary thought, not because of the existence of a chemistry of explosives (explosives are far from always being revolutionary), but because chemistry is, above all, the science of the transmutation of elements; it is hostile to every kind of absolute or conservative thinking cast in immobile categories.

It is very instructive that Mendeleyev, obviously under the pressure of conservative public opinion, defended the principle of stability and immutability in the great processes of chemical transformation. This great scientist insisted with remarkable stubbornness on the immutability of chemical elements and their nontransmutation into one another. He felt the need for firm pillars of support. He said: "I am Dimitri Ivanovich, and you are Ivan Petrovich. Each of us possesses his own individuality even as the elements."

Mendeleyev more than once scornfully denounced dialectics. By this he understood not the dialectic of Hegel or Marx, but the superficial art of toying with ideas, half-sophistry, half-scholasticism. Scientific dialectic embraces general methods of thought that reflect the laws of development. One of these laws is the change of quantity into quality. Chemistry is thoroughly permeated with this law. Mendeleyev's whole Periodic Table is built entirely on it, deducing qualitative difference in the elements from quantitative differences in atomic weights. Engels evaluated the discovery of new elements by Mendeleyev precisely from this viewpoint. In his sketch *The General Character of Dialectics as a Science,* Engels wrote:

> Mendeleyev showed that in a series of related elements arranged according to their atomic weights there were several gaps that indicated the existence of other, hitherto undiscovered elements. He described in advance the general chemical properties of each of these unknown elements and foretold approximately their relative and atomic weights, and their atomic place. Mendeleyev, unconsciously applying Hegel's law of change of quantity into quality, accomplished a scientific feat which in its audacity can be placed alongside Leverrier's discovery of the yet unknown planet Neptune by computing its orbit.

The logic of the Periodic Table, although later modified, proved stronger than the conservative limits that its creator tried to place upon it. The kinship of elements and their mutual metamorphoses can be considered as proved empirically from the hour when, with the help of radioactive elements, it became possible to resolve the atom into its components. In Mendeleyev's Periodic Table, in the chemistry of radioactive elements, the dialectic celebrates its own most outstanding victory!

Mendeleyev did not have a finished philosophical system. Perhaps he lacked even a desire for one, because it would have brought him into inevitable conflict with his own conservative habits and sympathies.

A dualism upon basic questions of knowledge is to be observed in Mendeleyev. Thus it would seem that he tended toward agnosticism, declaring that the "essence" of matter must forever remain beyond our cognition because it is "alien to our knowledge and spirit" (!). But almost immediately he offers us a remarkable formula for knowledge, which at a single stroke brushes agnosticism aside. In the very same note, Mendeleyev says: "By accumulating gradually their knowledge of matter, men gain mastery over it, and to the degree in which they do so they make ever more precise predictions, verifiable factually, and *there is no way of seeing how there can be a limit to man's knowledge and mastery of matter.*" It is self-evident that if there are no limits to knowledge and mastery of matter, then there is no unknowable "essence."

Knowledge that arms us with the ability to forecast all possible changes in matter, and endows us with the necessary power of producing these changes—such knowledge does in fact exhaust the essence of matter. The so-called unknowable "essence" is only a generalization of our inadequate knowledge about matter. It is a pseudonym for our ignorance. Dualistic demarcation of unknown matter from its known properties reminds me of the jocular definition of a gold ring as a hole surrounded by precious metal. It is obvious that if we gain knowledge of the precious metal of phenomena and are able to shape it, then we can remain completely indifferent to the "hole" of the substance; and we gladly make a present of it to the archaic philosophers and theologians.

Major miscalculations

Despite his verbal concessions to agnosticism ("unknowable essence") Mendeleyev is unconsciously a dialectical materialist in his methods and his higher achievements in the sphere of natural science, especially chemistry. But his materialism appears as though encased in a conservative shell, shielding its scientific thought from too sharp conflicts with official ideology. This does not imply that Mendeleyev artificially created a conservative covering for his methods; he was himself sufficiently bound to the official ideology, and therefore undoubtedly felt an inner compulsion to blunt the razor edge of dialectical materialism.

It is otherwise in the sphere of sociological relationships. The warp of Mendeleyev's social philosophy was conservative, but from time to time remarkable surmises, materialist in their essence and revolutionary in their tendency, are woven into this warp. But alongside of these surmises there are miscalculations, and what miscalculations!

I shall confine myself to only two. Rejecting all plans for social reorganization as utopian and "Latinist," Mendeleyev envisaged a better future only in connection with the development of scientific technology. But he had his own utopia. According to Mendeleyev, better days would come when the governments of the major powers of the world realized the need of being strong and arrived at sufficient unanimity among themselves about the need of eliminating all wars, revolutions, and the utopian principles of all anarchists, communists, and other "mailed fists," incapable of understanding the progressive evolution occurring in all mankind. The dawn of this universal concord was already to be perceived in the Hague, Portsmouth, and Morocco conferences.[2]

These instances represent major miscalculations on the

part of a great man. History subjected Mendeleyev's social utopia to a rigorous test. From the Hague and Portsmouth conferences blossomed the Russo-Japanese war, the war in the Balkans, the great imperialist slaughter of nations, and a sharp decline in European economy; while from the Moroccan conference in particular arose the revolting carnage in Morocco, which is now being completed under the flag of defense of European civilization.

Mendeleyev did not see the inner logic of social phenomena—or, more precisely, the inner dialectic of social processes—and was therefore unable to foresee the consequences of the Hague conference. But, as we know, the significance of science lies, first and foremost, in foresight. If you turn to what the Marxists wrote about the Hague conference in the days when it was arranged and convoked, then you will easily convince yourselves that the Marxists correctly foresaw the consequences. That is why in the most critical moment of history they proved to be armed with the "mailed fist." And there is really nothing lamentable in the fact that the historically rising class, armed with a correct theory of social knowledge and foresight, finally proved to be likewise armed with a fist sufficiently mailed to open a new epoch of human development.

Permit me to cite another miscalculation. Not long before his death, Mendeleyev wrote: "I especially fear for the quality of science and of all enlightenment and general ethics under 'state socialism.'" Were his fears well founded? Even today, the more farsighted students of Mendeleyev have begun to see clearly the vast possibilities for the development of scientific and technicoscientific thought, thanks to the fact that this thought is, so to speak, nationalized, emancipated from the internecine wars of private property, no longer required to lend itself to bribery of individual proprietors, but intended to serve the economic development of the nation as a whole. The network of technicoscientific institutes now being established by the state is only a tiny and—so to speak—material symptom of the limitless possibilities that have been disclosed.

I do not cite these miscalculations in order to cast a slur on the great renown of Dimitri Ivanovich. History has passed its verdict on the main controversial issues, and there is no basis for resuming the dispute. But permit me to state that the major miscalculations of this great man contain an important lesson for students. From the field of chemistry itself there are no *direct* and *immediate* outlets to social perspectives. The objective method of social science is necessary. Marxism is such a method.

Whenever any Marxist attempted to transmute the theory of Marx into a universal master key and ignore all other spheres of learning, Vladimir Ilyich would rebuke him with the expressive phrase "Komchvanstvo" ("communist swagger"). This would mean in this particular case—communism is not a substitute for chemistry. But the converse theorem is also true. An attempt to dismiss Marxism with the supposition that chemistry (or the natural sciences in general) is able to decide all questions is a peculiar *"chemist* swagger," which in point of theory is no less erroneous and in point of fact no less pretentious than *communist* swagger.

Great surmises

Mendeleyev did not apply a scientific method to the study of society and its development. A very careful investigator who repeatedly checked himself before permitting his creative imagination to make a great leap forward in the sphere of generalization, Mendeleyev remained an empiricist in sociopolitical problems, combining conjectures with an outlook inherited from the past. I need only say that his surmise was truly Mendeleyevian, especially where it touched directly upon the scientific industrial interests of the great scientist.

The very gist of Mendeleyev's philosophy might be defined as *technicoscientific optimism*. This optimism, coinciding with the line of development of capitalism, Mendeleyev directed against the Narodniks, liberals, and radicals, against the followers of Tolstoy, and in general against every kind of economic retrogression. Mendeleyev believed in the victory of man over all of nature's forces. From this arises his hatred of Malthusianism.

This is a remarkable trait in Mendeleyev. It passes through all his writings, the purely scientific, the sociopublicistic, as well as his writings on questions of applied chemistry. Mendeleyev greeted with pleasure the fact that the annual increase in Russia's population (1.5 percent) was higher than the average growth in the whole world. Computing that the population of the world would in 150–200 years reach 10 billion, Mendeleyev saw no cause for any alarm. He wrote:

> Not only 10 billion but a population many times that size will find nourishment in this world, not only through the application of labor but also through the persistent inventiveness which governs knowledge. It is in my opinion sheer nonsense to fear lack of nourishment, provided the peaceful and active communion of the masses of the people is guaranteed.

Our great chemist and industrial optimist would hardly have listened with sympathy to the recent advice of Professor Keynes of England, who told us during the academic celebrations that we must busy ourselves with limiting the increase in population. Dimitri Ivanovich would have only repeated his old remark: "Or do the new Malthuses wish to arrest this growth? In my opinion, the more, the merrier." Mendeleyev's sententious shrewdness very often expressed itself in such deliberately oversimplified formulas.

From the same viewpoint—industrial optimism—Mendeleyev approached the great fetish of conservative idealism, the so-called national character. He wrote:

> Wherever agriculture in its primitive forms predominates, a nation is incapable of permanent, regular, and continuous labor, but is able to work only fitfully and in a harvest-time manner. This reflects itself clearly in the customs in the sense that there is a lack of equanimity, calmness, and thriftiness; fidgetiness is to be observed in everything, a happy-go-lucky attitude prevails, along with it extravagance—there is either miserliness or squandering. . . . Wherever factory industry, side by side with agriculture, has developed on a large scale, where one can see before one's eyes, in addition to sporadic agriculture, the regulated, continuous, uninterrupted labor in the factories, there obtains a correct appraisal of labor, and so on.

Of special value in these lines is the outlook on national character not as some primordial fixed element created for all time, but as a product of historical conditions, and more precisely social forms of production. This is an indubitable, even if only a partial approach to the historical philosophy of Marxism.

In the development of industry Mendeleyev sees the instrumentalities of national reeducation, the elaboration of a new, more balanced, more disciplined and self-controlled national character. If we actually contrast the character of the peasant revolutionary movements with the movement of the proletariat and especially the role of the proletariat in October and today, then the materialist prediction of Mendeleyev will be illumined with sufficient clarity.

Our industrial optimist expressed himself with remarkable lucidity on the elimination of the contradictions between city and country, and every communist will accept his formulation on this subject. Mendeleyev wrote:

> Russian people have begun to migrate to cities in large numbers. . . . My view is that it is sheer nonsense to fight against this development; this process will terminate only when the city, on the one side, will spread out to include more parks, gardens, etc.—i.e., the aim in the cities will be not only to render life as healthy as possible for all but also to provide sufficient open spaces, not only for children's playgrounds and for sport, but for every form of recreation—and on the other hand, in the villages and farms, etc., the nonurban population will so multiply as to require the building of many-storied houses; and there will arise the need for water-works, street lighting, and other city comforts. In the course of time all this will lead to the whole countryside (sufficiently densely populated) becoming inhabited, with dwellings being separated by, so to speak, the kitchen gardens and orchards necessary for the production of foodstuffs and with factories and plants for manufacturing and altering these products. [D.I. Mendeleyev, *Towards an Understanding of Russia*, 1906]

Here Mendeleyev testifies convincingly in favor of the old thesis of socialism: the elimination of the contradiction between city and country. Mendeleyev, however, does not here pose the question of changes in social forms of economy. He believes that capitalism will automatically lead to the leveling out of urban and rural conditions through the introduction of higher, more hygienic, and more cultural forms of human habitation. Herein lies Mendeleyev's mistake. It appears most clearly in the case of England, to which Mendeleyev referred with such hope. Long before England could eliminate the contradictions between city and country, her economic development had already landed in a blind alley. Unemployment corrodes her economy. The leaders of English industry see the salvation of society in emigration, in forcing out the surplus population. Even the more "progressive" economist, Mr. Keynes, told us only the other day that the salvaging of the English economy lies in Malthusianism! . . . For England, too, the road of overcoming the contradictions between city and country leads through socialism.

There is another surmise made by our industrial optimist. In his last book, Mendeleyev wrote:

> After the industrial epoch, there will probably follow in the future a most complex epoch, which, according to my view, would denote a facilitation, or *an extreme simplification of the methods of obtaining food, clothing, and shelter.* Established science should aim at this extreme simplification, towards which it has already been partly directed in recent decades.

These are remarkable words. Although Dimitri Ivanovich elsewhere makes reservations—against the realization, God forbid, of the utopia of socialists and communists—in these words he nevertheless outlines the technicoscientific perspectives of communism. A development of the productive forces that would lead us to attain extreme simplification of the methods of obtaining food, clothing, and shelter would also clearly lead us to reduce to a minimum the element of coercion in the social structure. With the elimination of completely useless greediness from social relations, the forms of labor and distribution will assume a communist character. In the transition from socialism to communism no revolution will be necessary, since the transition wholly depends upon the technical progress of society.

Utilitarian and "pure" science

Mendeleyev's industrial optimism constantly directed his thought towards practical industrial questions and problems. In his purely theoretical works, we find his thought directed through the same channels to the problems of economy. There is a dissertation by Mendeleyev devoted to the question of diluting alcohol with water, a question which is of economic significance even today.[3] Mendeleyev invented a smokeless powder for the needs of state defense. He occupied himself with a careful study of petroleum, and that in two directions—one, purely theoretical, the origin of petroleum; and the other, technico-industrial uses. Here we should always bear in mind Mendeleyev's protest against using petroleum simply as a fuel: "Heating can be done with banknotes!" exclaimed our chemist. A confirmed protectionist, Mendeleyev took a leading part in elaborating tariff policies and wrote his "Sensible Tariff Policy," from which not a few valuable directives can be quoted even from the standpoint of socialist protectionism.

Problems of northern sea routes stirred his interest shortly before his death. He recommended to young investigators and navigators that they solve the problem of opening up the North Pole. He held that commercial routes must necessarily follow. "Near that ice there is not a little gold and other minerals, our own America. I should be happy to die at the Pole, for there at least no one 'putrefies.'" These words have a very modern ring. When the old chemist reflected upon death, he thought about it from the standpoint of putrefaction and dreamed incidentally of dying in an atmosphere of eternal cold.

Mendeleyev never tired of repeating that the goal of knowledge was "usefulness." In other words, he approached science from the standpoint of utilitarianism. At the same time, as we know, he insisted on the creative role of disinterested pursuit of knowledge. Why should anyone in particular seek for commercial routes by roundabout ways involving the North Pole? Because the Pole is a problem of disinterested research capable of arousing scientific research-sport passions. Is there not a contradiction between this and the affirmation that science's goal is usefulness? Not at all. Science is a function of society and not of an individual. From the sociohistoric standpoint, science is utilitarian. But this does not mean that each scientist approaches problems of research from a utilitarian point of view. No! Most often scholars are motivated by their passion for knowledge, and the more significant a man's discovery the less he is able, as a general rule, to foresee its possible practical applications. Thus the disinterested passion of a research worker does not contradict the utilitarian meaning of each science any more than the personal self-sacrifice of a revolutionary fighter contradicts the utilitarian aim of those class needs which he serves.

Mendeleyev was able to combine perfectly his passion for knowledge for its own sake with incessant preoccupation about raising the technical power of mankind. That is why the two wings of this congress—the representatives of theoretical and of applied branches of chemistry—stand with equal right under the banner of Mendeleyev. We must educate the new generation of scientists in the spirit of this harmonious coordination of pure scientific research with industrial tasks. Mendeleyev's faith in the unlimited possibilities for knowledge, prediction, and mastery of matter must become the scientific credo for the chemists of the socialist homeland. The German physiologist Du Bois Reymond once envisaged philosophic thought as departing from the scene of the class struggle and crying out: *"Ignorabimus!"*—that is, we shall never know, we shall never understand! And scientific thought, linking its fate with the fate of the rising class, replies, "You lie! The impenetrable does not exist for conscious thought! We will reach everything! We will master everything! We will rebuild everything!"

Culture and socialism

1. TECHNOLOGY AND CULTURE

Let us recall first of all that culture meant originally a ploughed, cultivated field, as distinct from virgin forest and virgin soil. Culture was contrasted with nature, that is, what was acquired by man's efforts was contrasted with what was given by nature. This antithesis fundamentally retains its value today.

Culture is everything that has been created, built, learned, conquered by man in the course of his entire history, in distinction from what nature has given, including the natural history of man himself as a species of ani-

From Krasnaya Nov *(6), 1926. Published in the Autumn 1962* Labour Review, *in an English translation by Brian Pearce.*

mal. The science that studies man as a product of animal evolution is called anthropology. But from the moment that man separated himself from the animal kingdom—and this happened approximately when he first grasped primitive tools of stone and wood and armed the organs of his body with them—from that time there began the creation and accumulation of culture, that is, all kinds of knowledge and skill in the struggle with nature and subjugation of nature.

When we speak of the culture accumulated by past generations, we think first and foremost of material achievements in the form of tools, machinery, buildings, monuments, and so on. Is this culture? Undoubtedly it is culture, the material forms in which culture is deposited: material culture. It creates, on the basis provided by nature, the fundamental setting of our lives, our everyday way of living, our creative work. But the most precious part of culture is its deposit in the consciousness of man himself—those methods, habits, skills, acquired abilities of ours which have developed out of the whole of pre-existing material culture and which, while drawing on this pre-existing material culture, also improve upon it. We will then consider it as firmly established that culture has grown out of man's struggle with nature for existence, for the improvement of his conditions of life, for the enlargement of his power. But out of this same basis classes also have grown. In the process of adapting itself to nature, in conflict with the hostile forces of nature, human society has taken shape as a complex organization of classes. The class structure of society has determined to a decisive degree the content and form of human history, that is, its material relations and their ideological reflections. This means that historical culture has possessed a class character.

Slave-owning society, feudal serf-owning society, bourgeois society—each engendered a corresponding culture, different at different stages and with a multitude of transitional forms. Historical society has been an organization for the exploitation of man by man. Culture has served the class organization of society; exploiters' society has given rise to an exploiters' culture. But does this mean that we are against all the culture of the past?

There exists, in fact, a profound contradiction here. Everything that has been conquered, created, and built by man's efforts and that serves to enhance man's power is culture. But since it is not a matter of individual man but of social man, since culture is a social-historical phenomenon in its very essence, and since historical society has been and continues to be class society, culture is found to be the basic instrument of class oppression. Marx said: "The ruling ideas of an epoch are essentially the ideas of the ruling class of that epoch." This also applies to culture as a whole. And yet we say to the working class: master all the culture of the past, otherwise you will not build socialism. How is this to be understood?

Over this contradiction many people have stumbled, and they stumble so frequently because they approach the understanding of class society superficially, half-idealistically, forgetting that fundamentally it is the organization of production. Every class society has been formed on the basis of definite modes of struggle with nature, and these modes have changed in accordance with the development of technology. What is the basis of bases—the class organization of society or its productive forces? Without doubt the productive forces. It is precisely upon them, at a certain level of their development, that classes are formed and re-formed. In the productive forces is expressed the materialized economic skill of mankind, our historical ability to ensure our existence. On this dynamic foundation there arise classes, which by their interrelations determine the character of culture.

And here, first and foremost, we have to ask ourselves, regarding technology: is it *only* an instrument of class oppression? It is enough to put such a question for it to be answered at once: no, technology is the fundamental conquest of mankind, although it has also served, up to the present, as an instrument of exploitation; yet it is at the same time the fundamental condition for the emancipation of the exploited. The machine strangles the wage-slave in its grip. But he can free himself only through the machine. Therein is the root of the entire question.

If we do not let ourselves forget that the driving force of the historical process is the growth of the productive forces, liberating man from the domination of nature, then we shall find that the proletariat needs to master the sum total of the knowledge and skill worked out by humanity in the course of its history, in order to raise itself up and rebuild life on principles of solidarity.

"Does culture advance technology or does technology advance culture?" asks one of the written questions lying before me. It is wrong to put the question that way. Technology cannot be counterposed to culture for it is its mainspring. Without technology, there is no culture. The growth of technology advances culture. But the science and general culture that have arisen on the basis of technology constitute a powerful aid to further growth of technology. Here we have a dialectical interaction.

Comrades, if you want a simple but expressive example of the contradiction contained in technology itself, you will not find a better one than railways. If you take a look at Western European passenger trains you will see that they have carriages of different "classes." These classes remind us of the classes of capitalist society. The first-class carriages are for the privileged upper circles, the second-class for the middle bourgeoisie, the third for the petty-bourgeoisie, and the fourth for the proletariat, which was formerly called, with good reason, the Fourth Estate. In themselves railways constitute a colossal cultural-technical conquest by mankind which has very greatly transformed the face of the earth in the course of a single century. But the class structure of society also influences the structure of the means of communication. And our Soviet railways are still a long way from equality—not only because they make use of carriages inherited from the past, but also because the NEP merely prepares the way for equality; it does not accomplish it.

Before the railway age, civilization was hemmed in by the shores of the seas and the banks of the great rivers. The railways opened up whole continents to capitalist culture. One of the fundamental causes, if not the most fundamental cause, of the backwardness and desolation of our Russian countryside is the lack of railways, concrete roads, and access roads. In this respect the majority of our villages exist in precapitalist conditions. We must overcome our great ally which is at the same time our greatest adversary—our great spaces.[4]

Socialist economy is planned economy. Planning presupposes communication first and foremost. The most important means of communication are roads and railways. Every new railway line is a path to culture, and in our conditions also a path to socialism. Besides, with improvement in the technique of communications and in the country's prosperity, the social profile of our railway trains will change: the separation into "classes" will disappear; everybody will travel in "soft" carriages . . . that is, if when that time comes people are still traveling by rail and don't prefer to use airplanes, which will be available to one and all.

Let us take another example, the instruments of militarism, the means of extermination. In this sphere, the class nature of society is expressed in an especially vivid and repulsive way. But there is no destructive (explosive or poisonous) substance the discovery of which would not in itself be a valuable scientific and technical achievement. Explosive and poisonous substances are used also for creative and not only for destructive purposes, and open up new possibilities in the field of discovery and invention.

The proletariat can take power only by breaking up the old machinery of the class state. We have carried out this task as decisively as anybody ever has. However, in building the new machinery of state we have found that we have to utilize, to a certain fairly considerable extent, elements of the old. The further socialist reconstruction of the state machine is inseparably linked with our political, economic, and cultural work in general.

We must not destroy technology. The proletariat has taken over the factories equipped by the bourgeoisie in that state in which the revolution found them. The old equipment is still serving us to this day. This fact most graphically and directly shows us that we do not renounce the "heritage." How could it be otherwise? After all, the revolution was undertaken, first and foremost, in order to get possession of that heritage.

However, the old technology, in the form in which we took it over, is quite unsuitable for socialism. It constitutes a crystallization of the anarchy of capitalist economy. Competition between different enterprises, chasing after profits, unevenness of development between different branches of the economy, backwardness of certain areas, parcelization of agriculture, plundering of human forces: all this finds in technology its expression in iron and brass. But while the machinery of class oppression can be smashed by a revolutionary blow, the productive machinery that existed under capitalist anarchy can be reconstructed only gradually. The completion of the restoration period, on the basis of the old equipment, has only brought us to the threshold of this tremendous task. We must carry it through at all costs.

2. THE HERITAGE OF SPIRITUAL CULTURE

Spiritual culture is as contradictory as material culture. And just as we take from the arsenals and storehouses of material culture and put into circulation not bows and arrows, not stone tools or the tools of the Bronze Age, but the most improved tools available, of the most up-to-date technology, in this way also must we approach spiritual culture as well.

The fundamental element in the culture of the old society was religion. It possessed paramount importance as a form of human knowledge and human unity; but this form first of all reflected man's weakness in the face of nature and his helplessness within society. We utterly reject religion, along with all substitutes for it.

It is different with philosophy. We have to take from the philosophy created by class society two invaluable elements—materialism and dialectics. It was in fact from the organic combination of materialism and dialectics that Marx's method was born and that his system arose. This method lies at the base of Leninism.

If we pass on to science in the strict sense of the word, here we find it quite obvious that we are confronted with a huge reservoir of knowledge and skill accumulated by mankind during our long life. True, one can show that in science, the aim of which is the cognition of reality, there are many tendentious class adulterations. That is quite true. The railways give expression to the privileged position of some and the poverty of others; but this applies even more to science, the material of which is a great deal more flexible than the metal and wood out of which they make railway carriages.

But we have to reckon with the fact that scientific work is basically nourished by the need to obtain knowledge of nature. Although class interests have introduced and are still introducing false tendencies even into natural science, nevertheless this falsification process is restricted by the limits beyond which it begins directly to prevent the progress of technology. If you examine natural science from the bottom upward, from the field of accumulation of elementary facts up to the highest and most complex generalizations, you will see that the more empirical a piece of scientific research is, the closer it is to its material, to facts, the more indubitable are the results that it produces. The wider the field of generalization, the nearer natural science approaches to questions of philosophy, the more it is subjected to the influence of class inspiration.

Matters are more complicated and worse in the case of the social sciences and what are called the "humanities." In this sphere too, of course, what is fundamental is the striving to know that which exists. Thanks to this fact we have, incidentally, the brilliant school of classical bourgeois economists. But class interest, which speaks very much more directly and imperatively in the social sciences than in natural science, soon called a halt to the development of economic thought of bourgeois society.

In this field, however, we communists are equipped better than in any other. Socialist theoreticians, awakened by the class struggle of the proletariat, basing themselves on bourgeois science and also criticizing it, finally created in the teachings of Marx and Engels the powerful method of historical materialism and the peerless application of this method in *Capital*. This does not mean, of course, that we are insured against the influence of bourgeois ideas in the field of economics and sociology generally. No, the most vulgar professorial socialist and petty-bourgeois-Narodnik tendencies burst out at every step into currency among us, from the old "treasure chests" of knowledge, finding a nutrient medium for themselves in the unformed and contradictory relations of the transitional epoch. But in this sphere we have the indispensable criteria of Marxism, verified and enriched in the works of Lenin. And we will give an even more triumphant rebuff to the vulgar economists and sociologists the less we shut ourselves up in the experience of the passing day, the more widely we embrace world development as a whole, distinguishing its fundamental trends beneath mere conjunctural changes.

In questions of law, morality, and ideology in general, the situation of bourgeois science is even more lamentable than in the field of economics. A pearl of genuine knowledge can be found in these spheres only after digging through dozens of professional dunghills.

Dialectics and materialism are the basic elements in the Marxist cognition of the world. But this does not mean at all that they can be applied to any sphere of knowledge, like an ever-ready master key. Dialectics cannot be imposed upon facts; it has to be deduced from facts, from their nature and development. Only painstaking work on a vast amount of material enabled Marx to advance the dialectical system of economics to the conception of value as social labor. Marx's historical works were constructed in the same way, and even his newspaper articles likewise. Dialectical materialism can be applied to new spheres of knowledge only by mastering them from within. The purging of bourgeois science presupposes a mastery of bourgeois science. You will get nowhere with sweeping criticism or bald commands. Learning and application here go hand in hand with critical reworking. We have the method, but there is enough work for generations to do.

Marxist criticism in science must be not only vigilant but also prudent, otherwise it can degenerate into mere sycophancy, into Famusovism.[5] Take psychology, even. Pavlov's reflexology proceeds entirely along the paths of dialectical materialism. It conclusively breaks down the wall between physiology and psychology. The simplest reflex is physiological, but a system of reflexes gives us "consciousness." The accumulation of physiological quantity gives a new "psychological" quality. The method of Pavlov's school is experimental and painstaking. Generalizations are won step by step: from the saliva of dogs to poetry, that is, to the mental mechanics of poetry, not its social content—though the paths that bring us to poetry have as yet not been revealed.

The school of the Viennese psychoanalyst Freud proceeds in a different way. It assumes in advance that the driving force of the most complex and delicate of psychic processes is a physiological need. In this general sense it is materialistic, if you leave aside the question whether it does not assign too big a place to the sexual factor at the expense of others, for this is already a dispute within the frontiers of materialism. But the psychoanalyst does not approach problems of consciousness experimentally, going from the lowest phenomena to the highest, from the simple reflex to the complex reflex; instead, he attempts to take all these intermediate stages in one jump, from above downwards, from the religious myth, the lyrical poem, or the dream, straight to the physiological basis of the psyche.

The idealists tell us that the psyche is an independent entity, that the "soul" is a bottomless well. Both Pavlov and Freud think that the bottom of the "soul" is physiology. But Pavlov, like a diver, descends to the bottom and laboriously investigates the well from there upwards, while Freud stands over the well and with a penetrating gaze tries to pierce its ever-shifting and troubled waters and to make out or guess the shape of things down below. Pavlov's method is experiment; Freud's is conjecture, sometimes fantastic conjecture. The attempt to declare psychoanalysis "incompatible" with Marxism and simply turn one's back on Freudianism is too simple, or, more accurately, too simplistic. But we are in any case not obliged to adopt Freudianism. It is a working hypothesis that can produce and undoubtedly does produce deductions and conjectures that proceed along the lines of materialist psychology. The experimental procedure in due course will provide the tests for these conjectures. But we have no grounds and no right to put a ban on the other procedure, which, even though it may be less reliable, yet tries to anticipate the conclusions to which the experimental procedure is advancing only very slowly.*

By means of these examples I wished to show, if only partially, both the heterogeneity of our scientific heritage and the complexity of the paths by way of which the proletariat can advance to mastery of it. If it is true that in economic construction problems are not solved by decree and we have to "learn to trade," so also in science the mere issuing of bald commands can achieve nothing but harm and disgrace. In this sphere we have to "learn to learn."

Art is one of the ways in which man finds his bearings in the world; in this sense the heritage of art is not distinguished from the heritage of science and technology—and it is no less contradictory than they. Unlike science, however, art is a form of cognition of the world, not as a system of laws but as a group of images, and at the same time it is a way of inspiring certain feelings and moods. The art of past centuries has made man more complex and flexible, has raised his mentality to a higher level, has enriched him in an all-around way. This enrichment is a precious achievement of culture. Mastery of the art of the past is, therefore, a necessary precondition not only for the creation of new art, but also for the building of the new society, for communism needs people with highly developed minds. However, can the art of the past enrich us with an artistic knowledge of

---

* This question has, of course, nothing in common with the cultivation of a sham Freudianism as an erotic indulgence or place of "naughtiness." Such claptrap has nothing to do with science and merely expresses decadent moods; the center of gravity is shifted from the cortex to the spinal cord.—L.T.

the world? It can, precisely because it is able to give nourishment to our feelings and to educate them. If we were groundlessly to repudiate the art of the past, we should at once become poorer spiritually.

One notices nowadays a tendency here and there to put forward the idea that art has as its purpose only the inspiration of certain moods, and not at all the cognition of reality. The conclusion drawn from this is: with what sort of sentiments can the art of the nobility or of the bourgeoisie infect us?

This is radically false. The significance of art as a means of cognition—including for the mass of people, and in particular for them—is not at all less than its "sentimental" significance. The ancient epic, the fable, the song, the traditional saying, the folk-rhyme provide knowledge in graphic form; they throw light on the past, they generalize experience, they widen the horizon, and only in connection with them and thanks to this connection is it possible to "tune in." This applies to all literature generally, not only to epic poetry but to lyric poetry as well. It applies to painting and to sculpture. The only exception, to a certain degree, is music, the effect of which is powerful but one-sided! Music too, of course, relies upon a particular knowledge of nature, its sounds and rhythms. But here the knowledge is so deeply hidden, the results of the inspiration of nature are to such an extent refracted through a person's nerves, that music acts as a self-sufficient "revelation." Attempts to approximate all forms of art to music, as to the art of "infection,"[6] have often been made and have always signified a depreciation in art of the role of the intelligence in favor of formless feeling, and in this sense they were and are reactionary. . . . Worst of all, of course, are those works of "art" which offer neither graphic knowledge nor artistic "infection" but instead advance exorbitant pretensions. In our country no few such works are printed, and, unfortunately, not in the students' books at art schools, but in many thousands of copies. . . .

Culture is a social phenomenon. Just because of this, language, as the vehicle of intercourse between men, is its most important instrument. The culture of language itself is the most important condition for the growth of all branches of culture, especially science and art. Just as technology is not satisfied with the old measuring apparatus but is creating new ones, micrometers, voltameters, and so on, striving for and attaining ever greater accuracy, so in the matter of language, of skill in choosing the appropriate words and combining them in the appropriate ways, constant, systematic, painstaking work is necessary in order to achieve the highest degree of accuracy, clarity, and vividness. The foundation for this work must be the fight against illiteracy, semiliteracy, and near-illiteracy. The next stage of this work is the mastering of Russian classical literature.

Yes, culture was the main instrument of class oppression. But it also, and only it, can become the instrument of socialist emancipation.

3. THE CONTRADICTIONS IN OUR CULTURE

Town and country

What is special about our position is that we—at the point where the capitalist West and the colonial-peasant East meet—have been the first to make a socialist revolution. The regime of proletarian dictatorship has been established first in a country with a monstrous inheritance of backwardness and barbarism, so that among our people whole centuries of history separate a Siberian nomad from a Moscow or Leningrad worker. Our social forms are transitional to socialism and consequently are incomparably higher than capitalist forms. In this sense we rightly consider ourselves the most advanced country in the world. But technology, which lies at the basis of material and every other kind of culture, is extremely backward in our country in comparison with the advanced capitalist countries. This constitutes the fundamental contradiction of our present reality.

The historical task that follows from this is to raise our technology to the height of our social formation. If we do not succeed in doing this, our social order will inevitably decline to the level of our technological backwardness. Yes, in order for us to appreciate the entire significance of technological progress it is necessary to tell ourselves frankly: if we do not succeed in filling the Soviet forms of our social order with the appropriate productive technology, we shall shut off the possibility of our transition to socialism and we shall be turned back to capitalism—and to what sort of capitalism? Semiserf, semicolonial capitalism. The struggle for technology is for us the struggle for socialism, with which the whole future of our culture is bound up.

Here is a fresh and very expressive example of our cultural contradictions. There recently appeared in the papers a report that our Leningrad Public Library holds first place for the number of books: it now possesses 4,250,000 books! Our first feeling is a legitimate feeling of Soviet pride: our library is the first in the world! To what are we indebted for this achievement? To the fact that we have expropriated private libraries. Through nationalizing private property we have created a richer cultural institution, accessible to everyone. The great advantages of the Soviet order are indisputably shown in this simple fact.

But at the same time our cultural backwardness is expressed in the fact that in our country the percentage of illiterates is greater than in any other European country. The library is the biggest in the world, but as yet only a minority of the population reads books. And that is how things are in almost every respect. Nationalized industry, with gigantic and far from fantastic schemes for Dnieprostroi, the Volga-Don canal and so on—and the peasants do their threshing with chains and rollers. Our marriage laws are permeated with the spirit of socialism—and physical violence still plays no small part in our family life. These and similar contradictions result from the entire structure of our culture, at the meeting point of West and East.

The basis of our backwardness is the monstrous predominance of the country over the town, of agriculture over industry, while in the country itself, moreover, the most backward implements and modes of production predominate. When we speak of historical serfdom we above all have in mind estate relations,[7] the bondage of the peasant to the landlord, and the czarist official. But, Comrades, serfdom has a deeper foundation under it: the bondage of man to the soil, the dependence of the peasant on the elements.

Have you read Gleb Uspensky?[8] I fear that the younger generation does not read him. His works should be republished, or at least his best ones, and there are some splendid things among them. Uspensky was a Narodnik. His political program was utopian through and through. But Uspensky, a writer about the morals and manners of country life, was not only a splendid artist but also a remarkable realist. He was able to appreciate the peasant's way of life and his mentality as derived phenomena, which had developed on an economic basis and were wholly determined by it. He was able to appreciate that the economic basis of the countryside was the bondage of the peasant in his labor-process to the soil and in general to the forces of nature. You should certainly read at least his *Power of the Land*. With Uspensky, an artist's intuition takes the place of Marxist method, and in its results in many respects it rivals the latter. For this reason, Uspensky the artist was constantly engaged in mortal conflict with Uspensky the Narodnik. From the artist we must still learn, even now, if we want to understand the many survivals of serfdom in peasant life, especially in family life, which often slop over into urban life as well; it is enough to listen to certain notes which are being sounded in the current discussion about problems of the marriage laws!

Capitalism throughout the world has brought to an extreme tension the contradiction between industry and agriculture, town and country. In Russia, owing to the lag in our historical development, this contradiction is quite monstrous in character. After all, our industry had already begun to strive to imitate Western European and American models, while our countryside remained in the depths of the seventeenth century and even more remote times. Even in America, capitalism has proved obviously unable to raise agriculture to the level of industry. This is a task which has entirely passed to socialism's responsibility. In our conditions, with the colossal predominance of country over town, the industrialization of agriculture is the most important sector of socialist construction.

By the industrialization of agriculture we mean two processes, which only in combination can, in the last analysis, finally wipe out the frontier between town and country. Let us dwell a little longer on this question which is so important for us.

The industrialization of agriculture consists, on the one hand, in the separation from the rural household economy of a whole series of branches of the preliminary processing of industrial raw material and foodstuffs. All industry in general has emerged from the countryside, through the handicrafts and the work of the village craftsman, through the detachment of particular branches from the closed-in system of domestic economy, through specialization, the creation of the appropriate apprenticeship and technology and later also machine production. Our Soviet industrialization must, to a considerable extent, proceed along this path, the path of the socialization of a whole series of production processes that lie between agriculture in the strict sense of the word and industry. The example of the United States shows that here immeasurable possibilities are open to us.

But the question is not exhausted by that. The overcoming of the contradiction between agriculture and industry presupposes the industrialization of arable and pastoral farming, horticulture, and so on. It means that these branches of production, too, must be placed on a basis of scientific technology: the use of machines on a large scale and in the right combination, tractorization and electrification, proper rotation of crops, laboratory testing of methods and results, correct organization of the whole production process with the most expedient use of labor power, and so on. Of course, even highly organized cultivation will differ from engineering. But for that matter there are profound differences within industry itself, between different branches. If today we have the right to counterpose agriculture to industry as a whole, this is because agriculture is carried on in scattered units by primitive methods, with servile dependence of the producer on natural conditions, and in circumstances of an extremely uncivilized way of living for the peasants. It is not enough to socialize, that is, to transfer to factories, particular branches of present-day agriculture, such as butter-making, cheese-making, the production of starch and molasses, and so on. It is necessary to socialize agriculture itself, that is, to wrest it from its present parcelization and in place of the present wretched pecking of the soil to set up scientifically organized wheat and rye "factories," cattle and sheep "factories," and so on. That this is possible is shown in part by the capitalist experience already available, in particular the agricultural experience of Denmark, where even the chickens are subjected to planning and standardization, laying eggs to order in huge quantities, of uniform size and color.

The industrialization of agriculture means the elimination of the present fundamental contradiction between town and country and so between peasant and worker: as regards their role in the country's economy, their living conditions, their cultural level, they must come closer together in proportion as the frontier between them disappears. A society in which mechanized cultivation forms an equal part of the planned economy, in which the town has absorbed into itself the advantages of the country (spaciousness, greenery) while the country has been enriched with the advantages of the town (paved roads, electric light, piped water supply, drains), that is to say, where the antithesis of town and country has itself disappeared, where the peasant and the worker have been transformed into participants of equal worth and equal rights in a single production process—such a society will also be a genuine socialist society.

The road to this society is long and hard. The most important landmarks along this road are mighty electric power stations. They will bring to the country light and transforming power: against the power of the land, the power of electricity!

Not long ago we opened the Shatura power station, one of our best constructions, erected on a peat bog. From Moscow to Shatura is only about a hundred kilometers. You might say the two places could shake hands. And yet what a difference in conditions! Moscow is the capital of the Communist International. But you go a few dozen kilometers and you are in the backwoods, with snow-laden fir trees, frozen marshes, and wild beasts. Dark hamlets of log huts are dozing in the snow. From the carriage window you can sometimes see the tracks of wolves. Where the Shatura station stands today, a few years ago, when they began construction work there, elks had their homes. Today the distance between Moscow and Shatura is covered by an elegant series of metal masts, which carry cables with a current of 115,000 volts. And under these masts vixens and she-wolves will this spring bring forth their cubs. That is what our entire culture is like—made up of extreme contradictions, of the highest achievements of technology and generalizing thought, on the one hand, and on the other, of the primeval conditions of the taiga.

Shatura lives on peat, as though on pasture. Truly, all the wonders created by the childish imaginings of religion and even the creative fantasy of poets pale before this simple fact: machines that occupy very little space are eating up an age-old bog, transforming it into invisible power and returning it along lightweight cables to that very industry which created and set up these machines.

Shatura is a thing of beauty. Gifted and devoted builders made it. Its beauty is not put on, is not an affair of tinsel decoration, but grows from the inherent properties and needs of technology itself. The highest and the only criterion of technology is fitness for purpose. The test of functional fitness is economic efficiency. And this presupposes the most complete correspondence between part and whole, means and end. Economic and technological criteria fully coincide with aesthetic ones. One may say, and it will not be a paradox, that Shatura is a thing of beauty because a kilowatt-hour of its power is cheaper than a kilowatt-hour of power from other stations situated in similar conditions.

Shatura stands on a bog. We have many bogs in the Soviet Union, very many more than we have power stations. We have also many other kinds of fuel which await transformation into motive power. In the south, the Dnieper flows through a very rich industrial area, spending the mighty force of its head of water to no purpose, bounding over age-old rapids, and waiting for us to bridle its flow with a dam and compel it to give light, motion, wealth to towns, factories, and fields. Let us compel it!

In the United States of America they generate 500 kilowatt-hours of power per head of population every year, while here we generate only 20 kilowatt-hours, that is, one twenty-fifth as much. Mechanical motive power in general is only one-fiftieth as much per person here as in the United

States. The Soviet system shod with American technology will be socialism. Our social order offers a different, incomparably more expedient application for American technique. But American technology for its part will transform our order, liberating it from the heritage of backwardness, primitiveness, and barbarism. From the combination of the Soviet order with American technology there will be born a new technology and a new culture—technology and culture for all, without favorite sons or stepsons.

The 'conveyor' principle of socialist economy

The principle of socialist economy is harmony, that is, continuity based on inner concord. What is the conveyor? An endless moving belt that brings to the worker or takes from him everything required by the course of his work. It is now well known how Ford uses a combination of conveyors as a means of internal transport: transmission and supply. But the conveyor is something bigger than that: it constitutes a method of regulating the production process itself, in that the worker is obliged to harmonize his movements with the movement of the endless belt. Capitalism uses this circumstance for higher and more perfected exploitation of the worker. But this use of the conveyor is connected with capitalism, not with the conveyor itself.

In which direction is the development of methods of regulating labor in fact proceeding, in the direction of piecework or in the direction of the conveyor method? Everything points to the conveyor. Piecework, like every other form of individual control over work, is characteristic of capitalism in the first periods of its development. This procedure ensures the maximum physiological loading of each individual worker, but not the coordination of the efforts of different workers. Both of these tasks are accomplished automatically by the conveyor. A socialist organization of the economy must endeavor to bring about a reduction in the physiological load on each individual worker, in accordance with the growth in technical power, while safeguarding at the same time the coordination of the efforts of different workers. This will be the significance of the socialist conveyor as distinct from the capitalist one. Speaking more concretely, the whole problem here consists in regulating the movement of the belt in accordance with a given number of working hours, or, conversely, in regulating working time in accordance with a given speed of the belt.

Under the capitalist system, the conveyor is used within the confines of an individual enterprise as a method of internal transport. But the principle of the conveyor is in itself very much broader. Each separate enterprise receives from outside raw material, fuel, auxiliary materials, supplementary labor-power. The relations between the separate enterprises, however gigantic they may be, are regulated by the laws of the market—limited, to be sure, in many instances, by all sorts of long-term agreements. But every factory taken separately, and still more society as a whole, is interested in raw material being supplied in good time, not accumulating wastefully in the stores, but also not causing stoppages in production; that is, in other words, it is interested in this material being supplied on the conveyor principle, in complete accord with the rhythm of production. For this there is no need to imagine a conveyor necessarily in the form of an endless moving belt. The forms of the conveyor can be endlessly varied. A railway, if it is working to plan, that is, without cross-hauls, without seasonal piling up of loads, in short, without elements of capitalist anarchy—and under socialism that is just how it will work—is like a mighty conveyor, ensuring the service of factories in good time with raw material, fuel, materials, and personnel. The same applies to steamships, trucks, etc. All kinds of means of communication form elements of transport within the production system from the point of view of the planned economy as a whole. An oil pipeline is a form of conveyor for liquids. The wider the network of oil pipelines the less need there is for reservoirs, the less oil is transformed into dead capital.

The conveyor system does not at all presuppose that enterprises are located very close together. On the contrary, modern technology makes it possible to scatter them—not, of course, in chaotic and casual fashion, but strictly taking into account the most advantageous location for each separate factory. The possibility of a wide scattering of industrial enterprises, without which the town cannot be dissolved in the country or the country in the town, is ensured to a very great degree by the use of electricity as motive power. A metal cable is the most perfect conveyor of power, making it possible to divide motive power into the smallest of units, setting it to work and switching it off by merely turning a knob. It is precisely by these characteristics that the power "conveyor" clashes most sharply with the partitions erected by private property. Electricity at its present level of development is the most "socialist" sector of technology; and no wonder, for it is the most advanced sector.

Gigantic land-improvement systems, for the in-draught or drainage of water, constitute, from this standpoint, the water conveyors of agriculture. The more completely chemistry, engineering, and electrification liberate cultivation from the effects of the elements, giving it the highest degree of planned regularity, the more completely will present-day agriculture be included within the system of the socialist conveyor which regulates and coordinates the whole of production, beginning with the subsoil (extraction of ore and coal) and the soil (plowing and sowing).

Old man Ford tries to build a sort of social philosophy upon his experience with the conveyor. In this attempt of his we see an extremely curious combination of experience on an exceptionally large scale in the field of production management with the insufferable narrowness of a smug philosopher who has become a multimillionaire while remaining merely a petty-bourgeois with a lot of money. Ford says, "If you want wealth for yourself and well-being for your fellow citizens, act like me." Kant demanded that everyone should act in such a way that his conduct could serve as the norm for others. In the philosophical sense Ford is a Kantian. But in practice the "norm" for Ford's 200,000 workers is not Ford's conduct but the gliding past of his automatic conveyor: it determines the rhythm of their lives, the movement of their hands, feet, and thoughts. For "the well-being of your fellow citizens" it is necessary to separate Fordism from Ford and to socialize and purge it. This is what socialism does.

"But what about the monotony of labor, depersonalized and despiritualized by the conveyor?" I am asked in one of the written questions sent up. This is not a serious fear. If you think and discuss it through to the end, it is directed against the division of labor and against machinery in general. This is a reactionary path. Socialism and hostility to machinery have never had and will never have anything in common.

The fundamental, main, and most important task is to abolish poverty. It is necessary that human labor shall produce the maximum possible quantity of goods. Grain, shoes, clothing, newspapers, everything that is necessary must be made available in such quantities that no one may fear that there will not be enough. Poverty must be abolished, and with it, greed. Prosperity and leisure must be won, and with them the joy of living, for everyone. A high productivity of labor cannot be achieved without mechanization and automation, the finished expression of which is the conveyor. The monotony of labor is compensated for by its reduced duration and its increased easiness. There will always be branches of industry in society that demand personal creativity, and those who find their calling in production will make their way to them. What we are concerned with here is the basic type of production in its most important branches, until at least a fresh chemical and power revolution in technology sweeps aside mechanization as we know it today. But it is for the future to worry about that. A voyage in a boat propelled by oars demands great personal creativity. A voyage in a steamboat is more "monotonous" but more comfortable and more certain. Moreover, you can't cross the ocean in a rowboat. And we have to cross an ocean of human need.

Everyone knows that physical requirements are very much more limited than spiritual ones. An excessive gratification of physical requirements quickly leads to satiety. Spiritual requirements, however, know no frontiers. But in order that spiritual requirements may flourish it is necessary that physical requirements be fully satisfied. Of course, we cannot and we do not put off the struggle to raise the spiritual level of the masses until we are rid of unemployment, the problems of waifs and strays, and poverty. Everything that can be done must be done. But it would be a miserable and contemptible daydream to imagine that we can create a truly new culture before we have ensured *prosperity, plenty, and leisure for the masses.* We must and will test our progress by its reflection in the everyday life of the workers and peasants.

The cultural revolution

It is now, I think, clear to everybody that the creation of a new culture is not an independent task to be carried out separately from our economic work and our social and cultural construction as a whole. Does trade belong to the sphere of "proletarian culture"? From the abstract standpoint one would have to answer this question in the negative. But the abstract standpoint is valueless. In the transitional epoch, and especially in the initial stage we are in now, products assume, and will continue for a long time yet to assume, the social form of *commodities.* And we have to know how to deal properly with commodities, that is, how to buy them and sell them. Unless we do, we shall not advance from the initial stage to the next stage. Lenin told us to learn to trade, and recommended that we learn from the examples provided by Western European culture. Trading culture forms, as we now realize very well, a most important part of the culture of the transitional period. Whether we should call the trading culture of the workers' state and the cooperatives "proletarian culture" I don't know; but that it is a step towards socialist culture is beyond dispute.

When Lenin spoke of the cultural revolution, he saw its fundamental content as raising the cultural level of the masses. The metric system is a product of bourgeois science. But teaching this simple system of measurement to a hundred million peasants means carrying out a big revolutionary-cultural task. It is almost certain that we shall not achieve it without the aid of tractors and electric power. At the foundation of culture lies technology. The decisive instrument in the cultural revolution must be a revolution in technology.

In relation to capitalism, we say that the development of the productive forces is pressing against the social forms of the bourgeois state and bourgeois property. Having accomplished the proletarian revolution we say: the development of the social forms is pressing against the development of the productive forces, that is, technology. The big link to carrying through the cultural revolution is the link of industrialization, and not literature or philosophy at all. I hope that these words will not be understood in the sense of an unfriendly or disrespectful attitude to philosophy and poetry. Without generalizing thought, and without art, man's life would be bare and beggarly. But that is just what the lives of millions of people are to an enormous extent at the present time. The cultural revolution must consist in opening up to them the possibility of real access to culture and not only to its wretched fag-ends. But this is impossible without creating great material preconditions. That is why a machine that automatically manufactures bottles is at the present time a first-rate factor in the cultural revolution, while a heroic poem is only a tenth-rate factor.

Marx once said about philosophers that they had interpreted the world sufficiently; the task was to turn it upside down. There was no lack of esteem for philosophy in those words of his. Marx was himself one of the greatest philosophers of all time. These words meant only that the further development of philosophy, as of all culture in general, both material and spiritual, requires a revolution in social relations. And so Marx appealed from philosophy to the proletarian revolution, not against philosophy but on its behalf. In this same sense we can now say: it is good when poets sing of the revolution and the proletariat, but a powerful turbine sings even better. We have plenty of songs of middling quality, which have remained the property of small circles, but we have terribly few turbines. I don't wish to imply by this that mediocre verses hinder the appearance of turbines. No, that cannot be said at all. But a correct orientation of public opinion, that is, an understanding of the real relationship between phenomena, the how and why of things, is absolutely necessary.

The cultural revolution must not be understood in a superficially idealistic way or as something which is an affair for small study groups. It is a question of changing the conditions of life, the methods of work, and the everyday habits of a great nation, of a whole family of nations. Only a mighty tractor system which for the first time in history will enable the peasant to straighten his back; only a glass-blowing machine that produces hundreds of bottles and liberates the lungs of the old-time glass-blower; only a turbine of dozens and hundreds of thousands of horsepower; only an airplane available to everyone—only these things together will ensure the cultural revolution, not for a minority but for all. And only such a cultural revolution will deserve the name. Only on that basis will a new philosophy and a new art come to flower.

Marx said: "The ruling ideas of an epoch are essentially the ideas of the ruling class of that epoch." This is true also in relation to the proletariat, but it means something quite different from what it means in relation to other classes. The bourgeoisie, when it had seized power, tried to perpetuate this power. All its culture was adapted to this purpose. The proletariat, having taken power, must unquestionably try to shorten as much as possible the duration of its rule, to bring nearer the classless socialist society.

The culture of morals

To trade in a cultured way means, in particular, not to deceive, that is, to break with our national tradition in trading matters: "If you don't deceive you won't sell."

Lying, deceit—this is not merely an individual sin but a function of the social order. Lying is a method of struggle, and consequently is derived from the contradiction between interests. The fundamental contradictions result from relations between classes. True, one can say that deceit is older than class society. Animals already show cunning and deceive others in the struggle for existence. A considerable part was played by deceit—military cunning—in the life of primitive tribes. This sort of deceit resulted more or less directly from the zoological struggle for existence. But from the time when "civilized," that is, class society appeared, lying became frightfully complicated; it became a social function, was refracted along class lines, and also entered into the body of human "culture." That, however, is a part of culture which socialism will not take over. Relations in socialist society, that is, the higher development of socialist society, will be thoroughly transparent and will not require such auxiliary methods as deceit, lies, falsification, forgery, treachery, and perfidy.

However, we are still a long way from that. In our relationships and morals there are still very many lies of both serf-owning and bourgeois origin. The highest expression of serf-owning ideology is religion. The internal relations of feudal-monarchical society were based on blind tradition and were elevated into the form of religious myths. Myths are imagined, false interpretations of natural phenomena and social institutions and the connections between them. However, not only the deceived, that is, the oppressed masses, but also those in whose name the deception was carried out, the rulers, mostly believed in the myths, and were honestly guided by them. An objectively false ideology, woven out of superstitions, does not in itself necessarily mean subjective mendacity. Only in proportion as social relations become more complicated—that is, as the bourgeois order develops and religious mythology comes into ever-greater contradiction with it—does religion become a source of greater and greater trickery and deliberate deception.

Developed bourgeois ideology is rationalistic and directed against mythology. The radical bourgeoisie tried to get on without religion and to build a state upon reason, not tradition. This was expressed in democracy with its principles of liberty, equality, and fraternity. Capitalist economy, however, created a monstrous contradiction between everyday reality and democratic principles. In order to make up for these contradictions, higher-grade lying was needed. Nowhere is there such political lying as in bourgeois democracies. This is now not the objective "lying" of mythology, but consciously organized deception of the people by means of a combination of methods of exceptional complexity. The technique of lying is cultivated no less than the technology of electricity. The most lying press is found in the most "developed" democracies, in France and the United States.

But at the same time, and this must be frankly admitted, in France they trade more honestly than here, and at all events with incomparably more attention to the customer's requirements. Having attained a certain level of prosperity, the bourgeoisie renounces swindling methods of primary accumulation, not from any abstract moral notions but for material reasons: petty deceit, counterfeiting, grabbing, do harm to the reputation of an enterprise and undermine its future prospects. The principles of "honest" trade, derived from the interests of trade itself at a certain level of its development, enter into morals, become "moral" rules, and are watched over by public opinion. True, the imperialist war brought colossal changes in this sphere too, throwing Western Europe a long way back. But the postwar "stabilization" efforts of capitalism have overcome the more malignant manifestations of the reversion to savagery in trade. In any case, if you take our Soviet trade in its total scope, that is, from the factory to the consumer in the remote village, then you will have to recognize that we still trade in an incomparably less cultured way than the advanced capitalist countries. This results from our poverty, from the insufficient supply of goods, from our economic and cultural backwardness.

The regime of the proletarian dictatorship is irreconcilably hostile both to the objectively false mythology of the Middle Ages and to the conscious falsity of capitalist democracy. The revolutionary regime is vitally interested in laying bare social relations, not in covering them up. This means that it is interested in political truthfulness, in saying what is. But one must not forget that the regime of revolutionary dictatorship is a transitional regime and therefore a contradictory one. The existence of powerful enemies obliges us to resort to military cunning, and cunning is inseparable from falsehood. It is only necessary that the cunning used in the struggle against foes not be employed for the deluding of one's own people, that is, of the working masses and their party. This is a fundamental requirement of revolutionary policy, which runs like a red thread through all of Lenin's work.

But while our new state and social forms create the possibility and necessity of a higher degree of truthfulness than has hitherto been attained in relations between rulers and ruled, this cannot at all be said as yet about our relationships in everyday life, on which our economic and cultural backwardness, and in general the entire heritage of the past, continue to weigh very heavily. We live much better than we did in 1920. But the lack of the necessary good things of life still sets its mark heavily on our life and on our morals, and will continue to do so for a number of years. From this will result contradictions big and small, big and small disproportions, struggle connected with these contradictions, and—connected with this struggle—cunning, lies, deceit. There is only one way out: raising the level of technology in both production and trade. A correct orientation in this direction must already in itself help to improve "morals." The interaction of improved technology and morals will advance us along the road to a social order of civilized cooperators, that is, to socialist culture.

Radio, science, technology, and society

A new epoch of scientific and technical thought

Comrades, I have just come from the Turkmenistan jubilee celebrations. This sister republic of ours in Central Asia today commemorates the anniversary of its foundation. It might seem that the subject of Turkmenistan is remote from that of radio technology and from the Society of Friends of Radio, but in fact there is a very close connection between them.

Just because Turkmenistan is *far* it ought to be *near* to the participants in this congress. Given the immensity of our federated country, which includes Turkmenistan—a

A speech at the First All-Union Congress of the Society of Friends of Radio. The address was given in the Polytechnical Museum, and was broadcast. From Krasnaya Nov *(2), 1927. Translated for the December 1957* Labour Review *from* Collected Works, *Vol. 21, by Leonard Hussey.*

land covering five to six hundred thousand versts, bigger than Germany, bigger than France, bigger than any European state, a land where the population is scattered among oases, where there are no roads—given these conditions, radio communication might have been expressly invented for the benefit of Turkmenistan, to link it with us.

We are a backward country; the whole of our Union, including even the most advanced parts, is extremely backward from the technical standpoint; and at the same time we have no right to remain in this backward state, because we are building socialism, and socialism presupposes and demands a high level of technology. While constructing roads through the countryside, improving them, and building bridges to carry them (and how terribly we need more such bridges!), we are obliged at the same time to catch up with the most advanced countries in the field of the latest scientific and technical achievements—among others, first and foremost, that of radio technology. The invention of the radiotelegraph and radiotelephone might have occurred especially to convince the bilious sceptics among us of the unlimited possibilities inherent in science and technology, to show that all the achievements that science has registered so far are only a brief introduction to what awaits us in the future.

Let us take the last twenty-five years—just a quarter of a century—and recall what conquests in the sphere of human technology have been accomplished before our eyes, the eyes of the older generation to which I belong. I remember—and probably I am not the only one among those present to do so, though the majority here are young people—the time when motor cars were still rarities. There was no talk, even, of the airplane at the end of the last century. In the whole world there were, I think, 5,000 motor cars, whereas now there are about twenty million, of which eighteen million are in America alone—fifteen million cars and three million trucks. The motor car has before our eyes become a means of transport of first-class importance.

I can still recall the confused sounds and rustlings which I heard when first I listened to a phonograph. I was then in the first form at secondary school. Some enterprising man who was traveling around the cities of south Russia with a phonograph arrived in Odessa and demonstrated it to us. And now the gramophone, grandchild of the phonograph, is one of the most commonplace features of domestic life.

And aircraft? In 1902, that is, twenty-three years ago, the British man of letters, Wells (many of you will know his science-fiction novels), published a book in which he wrote, almost in so many words, that in his personal opinion (and he considered himself a bold and adventurous fantast in technical matters) approximately in the middle of this present twentieth century there would be not merely invented but also to some degree perfected, a flying machine heavier than air that could be used for operations of war. This book was written in 1902. We know that aircraft played a definite part in the imperialist war—and there are still twenty-five years to go to midcentury!

And cinematography? That's also no small matter. Not so very long ago it didn't exist; many present will recall that time. Nowadays, however, it would be impossible to imagine our cultural life without the cinema.

All these innovations have come into our lives in the last quarter of a century, during which men have, in addition, accomplished also a few trifles such as imperialist wars, when cities and entire countries have been laid waste and millions of people exterminated. In the course of this quarter-century more than one revolution has taken place, though on a smaller scale than ours, in a whole series of countries. In twenty-five years, life has been invaded by the motor car, the airplane, the gramophone, the cinema, radiotelegraphy and radiotelephony. If you remember only the fact that, according to the hypothetical calculations of scholars, not less than

250,000 years were needed for man to pass from a simple hunter's way of life to stock-breeding, this little fragment of time, twenty-five years, appears as a mere nothing. What does this fragment of time show us? That technology has entered a new phase, that its rate of development is getting continually faster and faster.

Liberal scholars—now they are no more—commonly used to depict the whole of the history of mankind as a continuous line of progress. This was wrong. The line of progress is curved, broken, zigzagging. Culture now advances, now declines. There was the culture of ancient Asia, there was the culture of antiquity, of Greece and Rome, then European culture began to develop, and now American culture is rising in skyscrapers. What has been retained from the cultures of the past? What has been accumulated as a result of historical progress? Technical processes, methods of research. Scientific and technical thought, not without interruptions and failures, marches on. Even if you meditate on those far-off days when the sun will cease to shine and all forms of life die out upon the earth, nevertheless there is still plenty of time before us. I think that in the centuries immediately ahead of us, scientific and technical thought, in the hands of socialistically organized society, will advance without zigzags, breaks, or failures. It has matured to such an extent, it has become sufficiently independent and stands so firmly on its feet, that it will go forward in a planned and steady way, along with the growth of the productive forces with which it is linked in the closest degree.

A triumph of dialectical materialism

It is the task of science and technology to make matter subject to man, together with space and time, which are inseparable from matter. True, there are certain idealist books—not of a clerical character, but philosophical ones—wherein you can read that time and space are categories of our minds, that they result from the requirements of our thinking, and that nothing actually corresponds to them in reality. But it is difficult to agree with this view. If any idealist philosopher, instead of arriving in time to catch the nine p.m. train, should turn up two minutes late, he would see the tail of the departing train and would be convinced by his own eyes that time and space are inseparable from material reality. The task is to diminish this space, to overcome it, to economize time, to prolong human life, to register past time, to raise life to a higher level and enrich it. This is the reason for the struggle with space and time, at the basis of which lies the struggle to subject matter to man—matter, which constitutes the foundation not only of everything that really exists, but also of all imagination.

Our struggle for scientific achievements is itself only a very complex system of reflexes, i.e., of phenomena of a physiological order, which have grown up on an anatomical basis that in its turn has developed from the inorganic world, from chemistry and physics. Every science is an accumulation of knowledge, based on experience relating to matter, to its properties; an accumulation of generalized understanding of how to subject this matter to the interests and needs of man.

The more science learns about matter, however, the more "unexpected" properties of matter it discovers, the more zealously does the decadent philosophical thought of the bourgeoisie try to use the new properties or manifestations of matter to show that matter is not matter. The progress of natural science in mastering matter is paralleled by a philosophical struggle against materialism. Certain philosophers and even some scientists have tried to utilize the phenomena of radioactivity for the purpose of struggle against materialism: there used to be atoms, elements, which were the basis of matter and of materialist thinking, but now this atom has come to pieces in our hands, has broken up into electrons, and at the very beginning of the popularity of the electronic theory a struggle has even flared up in our party around the question whether the electrons testify *for* or *against* materialism. Whoever is interested in these questions will read with great profit to himself Vladimir Ilyich's work on *Materialism and Empirio-Criticism*. In fact neither the "mysterious" phenomena of radioactivity nor the no less "mysterious" phenomena of wireless transmission of electromagnetic waves do the slightest damage to materialism.

The phenomena of *radioactivity*, which have led to the necessity of thinking of the atom as a complex system of still utterly "unimaginable" particles, can be directed against materialism only by a desperate specimen of vulgar materialist who recognizes as matter only what he can feel with his bare hands. But this is sensualism, not materialism. Both the molecule, the ultimate chemical particle, and the atom, the ultimate physical particle, are inaccessible to our sight and touch. But our organs of sense, although they are the instruments with which knowledge begins, are not at all, however, the last resort of knowledge. The human eye and the human ear are very primitive pieces of apparatus, inadequate to reach even the basic elements of physical and chemical phenomena. To the extent that in our thinking about reality we are guided merely by the everyday findings of our sense organs, it is hard for us to imagine that the atom is a complex system, that it has a nucleus, that around this nucleus electrons move, and that from this there result the phenomena of radioactivity.

Our imagination in general accustoms itself only with difficulty to new conquests of cognition. When Copernicus discovered in the sixteenth century that the sun did not move around the earth but the earth around the sun, this seemed fantastic, and conservative imagination still to this day finds it hard to adjust itself to this fact. We observe this in the case of illiterate people and in each fresh generation of schoolchildren. Yet we, people of some education, despite the fact that it appears to us, too, that the sun moves round the earth, nevertheless do not doubt that in reality things happen the other way around, for this is confirmed by extensive observation of astronomical phenomena.

The human brain is a product of the development of matter, and at the same time it is an instrument for the cognition of this matter; gradually it adjusts itself to its function, tries to overcome its limitations, creates ever new scientific methods, imagines ever more complex and exact instruments, checks its work again and yet again, step by step penetrates into previously unknown depths, changes our conception of matter, without, though, ever breaking away from this basis of all that exists.

Radioactivity, as we have already mentioned, in no way constitutes a threat to materialism, and it is at the same time a magnificent triumph of dialectics. Until recently scientists supposed that there were in the world about ninety elements, which were beyond analysis and could not be transformed one into another—so to speak, a carpet for the universe woven from ninety threads of different qualities and colors. Such a notion contradicted materialist dialectics, which speaks of the unity of matter and, what is even more important, of the transformability of the elements of matter. Our great chemist, Mendeleyev, to the end of his life was unwilling to reconcile himself to the idea that one element could be transformed into another; he firmly believed in the stability of these "individualities," although the phenomena of radioactivity were already known to him.

But nowadays no scientist believes in the unchangeability of the elements. Using the phenomena of radioactivity, chemists have succeeded in carrying out a direct "execution" of eight or nine elements, and along with this, the execution of the last remnants of metaphysics in materialism, for now the transformability of one chemical element into another has been proved experimentally. The phenomena of radioactivity have thus led to a supreme triumph of dialectical thought.

The phenomena of radio technology are based on wireless transmission of electromagnetic waves. *Wireless* does not at all mean *nonmaterial* transmission. Light does not come only from lamps but also from the sun, being also transmitted without the aid of wires. We are fully accustomed to the wireless transmission of light over quite respectable distances. We are greatly surprised though, when we begin to transmit sound over a very much shorter distance, with the aid of those same electromagnetic waves which underlie the phenomena of light. All these are phenomena of matter, material processes—waves and whirlwinds—in space and time. The new discoveries and their technical applications show only that matter is a great deal more heterogeneous and richer in potentialities than we had thought hitherto. But, as before, nothing is made out of nothing.

The most outstanding of our scientists say that science, and physics in particular, has in recent times arrived at a turning point. Not so very long ago, they say, we still approached matter, as it were, "phenomenally," i.e., from the angle of observing its manifestations; but now we are beginning to penetrate ever deeper into the very interior of matter, to learn its structure; and we shall soon be able to regulate it "from within." A good physicist would, of course, be able to talk about this better than I can. The phenomena of radioactivity are leading us to the problem of releasing intra-atomic energy.

The atom contains within itself a mighty hidden energy, and the greatest task of physics consists in pumping out this energy, pulling out the cork so that this hidden energy may burst forth in a fountain. Then the possibility will be opened up of replacing coal and oil by atomic energy, which will also become the basic motive power. This is not at all a hopeless task. And what prospects it opens before us! This alone gives us the right to declare that scientific and technical thought is approaching a great turning point, that the revolutionary epoch in the development of human society will be accompanied by a revolutionary epoch in the sphere of the cognition of matter and the mastering of it. . . . Unbounded technical possibilities will open out before liberated mankind.

Radio, militarism, superstition

Perhaps, though, it is time to get closer to political and practical questions. What is the relation between radio technology and the social system? Is it socialist or capitalist? I raise the question because a few days ago the famous Italian, Marconi, said in Berlin that the transmission of pictures at a distance by means of Hertzian waves is a tremendous gift to pacifism, foretelling the speedy end of the militarist epoch. Why should this be? These ends of epochs have been proclaimed so often that the pacifists have got all ends and beginnings mixed up. The fact that we shall be able to see at a great distance is supposed to put an end to wars! Certainly, the invention of a means of transmitting a living image over a great distance is a very attractive problem, for it is insulting to the optic nerve that the auditory one is at present, thanks to radio, in a privileged position in this respect. But to suppose that from this there must result the end of wars is merely absurd, and shows only that in the case of great men like Marconi, just as with the majority of people who are specialists in a particular field—even, one may say, with the majority of people in general—scientific thinking lays hold of the brain, to put the matter crudely, not as a whole, but only in small sectors.

Just as inside the hull of a steamship impenetrable partitions are placed so that in the event of an accident the ship will not sink all at once, so also in man's consciousness there are numberless impenetrable partitions: in one sector, or even in a dozen sectors, you can find the most revolutionary scientific thinking; but beyond the partition lies philistinism of the highest degree. This is the great significance of Marxism, as thought that generalizes all human experience: that it helps to break down these internal partitions of consciousness through the integrity of its world outlook.

But to get closer to the matter in hand—why, precisely, if one can see one's enemy, must this result in the liquidation of war? In earlier times whenever there was war the adversaries saw each other face to face. That was how it was in Napoleon's day. Only the creation of long-distance weapons gradually pushed the adversaries further apart and led to a situation in which they were firing at unseen targets. And if the invisible becomes visible, this will only mean that the Hegelian triad has triumphed in this sphere as well—after the thesis and the antithesis has come the "synthesis" of mutual extermination.

I remember the time when men wrote that the development of aircraft would put an end to war, because it would draw the whole population into military operations, would bring to ruin the economic and cultural life of entire countries, etc. In fact, however, the invention of a flying machine heavier than air opened a new and crueler chapter in the history of militarism. There is no doubt that now, too, we are approaching the beginning of a still more frightful and bloody chapter. Technology and science have their own logic—the logic of the cognition of nature and the mastering of it in the interests of man. But technology and science develop not in a vacuum but in human society, which consists of classes. The ruling class, the possessing class, controls technology and through it controls nature. Technology in itself cannot be called either militaristic or pacifistic. In a society in which the ruling class is militaristic, technology is in the service of militarism.

It is considered unquestionable that technology and science undermine superstition. But the class character of society sets substantial limits here too. Take America. There, church sermons are broadcast by radio, which means that the radio is serving as a means of spreading prejudices. Such things don't happen here, I think—the Society of Friends of Radio watches over this, I hope? [*Laughter and applause*] Under the socialist system science and technology as a whole will undoubtedly be directed against religious prejudices, against superstition, which reflect the weakness of man before man or before nature. What, indeed, does a "voice from heaven" amount to when there is being broadcast all over the country a voice from the Polytechnical Museum? [*Laughter*]

We must not lag behind!

Victory over poverty and superstition is ensured to us, provided we go forward technically. We must not lag behind other countries. The first slogan which every friend of radio must fix in his mind is: Don't lag behind!

Yet we are extraordinarily backward in relation to the advanced capitalist countries; this backwardness is the main inheritance that we have received from the past. What are we to do? If, Comrades, the situation were to be such that the capitalist countries continued to develop steadily and go forward, as before the war, then we should have to ask ourselves anxiously: shall we be able to catch up? And if we do not catch up, shall we not be crushed? To this we say: we cannot forget that scientific and technical thought in bourgeois society has attained its highest degree of development in that period when, economically, bourgeois society is getting more and more into a blind alley and is beginning to decay. European economy is not going forward. In the last fifteen years, Europe has become poorer, not richer. But its inventions and discoveries have been colossal. While ravaging Europe and devastating huge areas of the continent, the war at the same time gave a tremendous impetus to scientific and technical thought, which was suffocating in the clutches of decaying capitalism.

If, however, we take the material accumulations of technology, i.e., not that technology which exists in men's heads, but that which is embodied in machinery, factories, mills, railways, telegraphic and telephone services, etc., then here above all it is plain that we are fearfully backward. It would be more correct to say that this backwardness would be fearful for us if we did not possess an immense advantage in the Soviet organization of society, which makes possible a planned development of technology and science while Europe is suffocating in its own contradictions.

Our present backwardness in all spheres must not, however, be covered up, but must be measured with a severely objective yardstick, without losing heart but also without deceiving oneself for a single moment. How is a country transformed into a single economic and cultural whole? By means of communications: railways, steamships, postal services, the telegraph, and the telephone—and now radiotelegraphy and radiotelephony. How do we stand in these fields? We are fearfully backward. In America the railway network amounts to 405,000 kilometers, in Britain to nearly 40,000, in Germany to 54,000, but here to only 69,000 kilometers—and that with our vast distances! But it is much more instructive to compare the loads that are carried in these countries and here, measuring them in ton-kilometers, i.e., taking as the unit one ton transported over one kilometer's distance. The United States last year carried 600 million ton-kilometers, we carried 48.5 million, Britain 30 million, Germany 69 million: i.e., the U.S. carried ten times as much as Germany, twenty times as much as Britain, and two or three times as much as the whole of Europe along with ourselves.

Let us take the postal service, one of the basic means of cultural communication. According to information provided by the Commissariat of Posts and Telegraphs, based on the latest figures, expenditure on postal communications in the U.S. last year amounted to a billion and a quarter rubles, which means 9 rubles 40 kopeks per head of population. In our country, postal expenditure comes to 75 million, which means 33 kopeks per head. There's a difference for you— between 9 rubles 40 kopeks and 33 kopeks![9]

The figures for telegraph and telephone services are still more striking. The total length of telegraph wires in America is 3 million kilometers, in Britain half a million kilometers, and here 616,000 kilometers. But the length of telegraph wires is comparatively small in America because there they have a lot of *telephone* wires—60 million kilometers of them, whereas in Britain there are only 6 million and here only 311,000 kilometers. Let us neither mock at ourselves, Comrades, nor take fright, but firmly keep these figures in mind; we must measure and compare, so as to catch up and surpass, at all costs! [*Applause*] The number of telephones— another good index of the level of culture—is in America 14 million, in Britain a million, and here 190,000. For every hundred persons in America there are thirteen telephones, in Britain a little more than two, and in our country one-tenth, or, in other words, in America the number of telephones in relation to the number of inhabitants is 130 times as great as here.

As regards radio, I do not know how much we spend per day on it (I think the Society of Friends of Radio should work this out), but in America they spend a million dollars, i.e., 2 million rubles a day on radio, which makes about 700 millions a year.

These figures harshly reveal our backwardness. But they also reveal the importance that radio, as the cheapest form of communication, can and must have in our huge peasant country. We cannot seriously talk about socialism without having in mind the transformation of the country into a single whole, linked together by means of all kinds of communications. In order to introduce it we must first and foremost be able to talk to the most remote parts of the country, such as Turkmenistan. For Turkmenistan, with which I began my remarks today, produces cotton, and upon Turkmenistan's labors depends the work of the textile mills of the Moscow and Ivanovo-Voznesensk regions. For direct and immediate communication with all points in the country, one of the most important means is radio—that is, of course, if radio in our country is not to be a toy for the upper strata of the townspeople, who are established in more privileged conditions than others, but is to become an instrument of economic and cultural communication between town and country.

Town and country

Let us not forget that between town and country in the USSR there are monstrous contradictions, material and cultural, which as a whole we have inherited from capitalism. In that difficult period we went through, when the town took refuge in the country and the country gave a pood of bread in exchange for an overcoat, some nails, or a guitar, the town looked quite pitiful in comparison with the comfortable countryside. But in proportion as the elementary foundations of our economy have been restored, in particular our industry, the tremendous technical and cultural advantages of the town over the country have reasserted themselves. We have done a great deal in the sphere of politics and law to mitigate and even out the contrasts between town and country. But in technique we have really not made a single big step forward so far. And we cannot build socialism with the countryside in this technically deprived condition, with the peasantry culturally destitute. Developed socialism means above all technical and cultural leveling as between town and country, i.e., the dissolving of both town and country into homogeneous economic and cultural conditions. That is why the mere bringing closer together of town and country is a question of life and death for us.

While creating the industry and institutions of the town, capitalism held the country down and could not but do this: it could always obtain the necessary foodstuffs and raw materials not only from its own countryside but also from the backward lands across the ocean or from the colonies, produced by cheap peasant labor. The war and the postwar disturbances, the blockade and the danger that it might be repeated, and finally the instability of bourgeois society, have compelled the bourgeoisie to take a closer interest in the peasantry. Recently we have heard bourgeois and Social Democratic politicians more than once talk about the link with the peasantry. Briand, in his discussion with Comrade Rakovsky about the debts, laid emphasis on the needs of the small landholders, and in particular the French peasants.[10] Otto Bauer, the Austrian "Left" Menshevik, in a recent speech spoke about the exceptional importance of the "link" with the countryside. Above all, our old acquaintance, Lloyd George—whom, true, we have begun to forget a little—when he was still in circulation organized in Britain a special land league in the interests of the link with the peasantry.[11] I don't know what form the link would take in British conditions, but on Lloyd George's tongue the word certainly sounds knavish enough. At all events, I would not recommend that he be elected patron of any rural district, nor an honorary member of the Society of Friends of Radio, for he would without fail put over some swindle or other. [Applause]

Whereas in Europe the revival of the question of the link with the countryside is on the one hand a parliamentary-political maneuver, and on the other a significant symptom of the tottering of the bourgeois regime, for us the problem of economic and cultural links with the countryside is a matter of life and death in the full sense of the word. The technical basis of this linkage must be electrification, and this is directly and immediately connected with the problem of the introduction of radio on a wide scale. In order to *approach* the fulfillment of the simplest and most urgent tasks, it is necessary that all parts of the Soviet Union be able to talk to each other, that the country be able to listen to the town, as to its technically better-equipped and more cultured elder brother. Without the fulfillment of this task the spread of radio will remain a plaything for the privileged circles of the townspeople.

It was stated in your report that in our country three-quarters of the rural population do not know what radio is, while the remaining quarter know it only through special demonstrations during festivals, etc. Our program must provide that every village not only should know what radio is but should have its own radio receiving station.

The diagram attached to your report shows the distribution of members of your society according to social class. Workers make up 20 percent (that's the small figure with the hammer); peasants 13 percent (the still smaller figure with the scythe); office workers 49 percent (the respectable figure carrying a briefcase); and then comes 18 percent of "others" (it's not stated who they are exactly, but there is a drawing of a gentleman in a bowler hat, with a cane and a white handkerchief in his breast pocket, evidently a NEP-man). I don't suggest that these people with handkerchiefs should be driven out of the Society of Friends of Radio, but they ought to be surrounded and besieged more strongly, so that radio may be made cheaper for the people with hammers and scythes. [*Applause*] Still less am I inclined to think that the number of members with briefcases should be mechanically reduced.

But it is necessary, though, that the two basic groups be increased, at all costs! Twenty percent workers—that's very little; 13 percent peasants—that's shamefully little. The number of people in bowler hats is nearly equal to the number of workers (18 percent) and exceeds the number of peasants, who make up only 13 percent! It is a flagrant breach of the Soviet constitution. It is necessary to take steps to ensure that in the next year or two peasants become about 40 percent, workers 45 percent, office workers 10 percent, and what are called "others"—5 percent. That will be a normal proportion, fully in keeping with the spirit of the Soviet constitution.

The conquest of the village by radio is a task for the next few years, very closely connected with the task of eliminating illiteracy and electrifying the country, and to some extent a precondition for the fulfillment of these tasks. Each province should set out to conquer the countryside with a definite program of radio development. Place the map for a new war on the table! From each provincial center first of all, every one of the larger villages should be conquered for radio. It is necessary that our illiterate and semiliterate village, even before it manages to master reading and writing as it ought, should be able to have access to culture through the radio, which is the most democratic medium of broadcasting information and knowledge. It is necessary that by means of the radio the peasant shall be able to feel himself a citizen of our Union, a citizen of the whole world.

Upon the peasantry depends to a large extent not only the development of our own industry—that is more than clear—but upon our peasantry and the growth of its economy also depends, to a certain degree, the revolution in the countries of Europe. What worries the European workers—and that not by accident—in their struggle for power, what the Social Democrats utilize cleverly for their reactionary purposes, is the dependence of Europe's industry upon countries across the oceans as regards foodstuffs and raw materials. America provides grain and cotton; Egypt, cotton; India, sugarcane; the islands of the Malay Archipelago, rubber; etc., etc.

The danger is that an American blockade, say, might subject the industry of Europe, during the most difficult months and years of the proletarian revolution, to a famine of food-stuffs and raw materials. In these conditions an increased export of our Soviet grain and raw material of all kinds is a mighty revolutionary factor in relation to the countries of Europe. Our peasants must be made aware that every extra sheaf that they thresh and send abroad is so much additional weight in the scales of the revolutionary struggle of the European proletariat, for this sheaf reduces the dependence of Europe upon capitalist America.

The Turkmenian peasants who are raising cotton must be linked with the textile workers of Ivanovo-Voznesensk and Moscow and also with the revolutionary proletariat of Europe. A network of radio receiving stations must be established in our country such as will make it possible for our peasants to live the life of the working people of Europe and the whole world, to participate in it from day to day. It is necessary that on that day when the workers of Europe take possession of the radio stations, when the proletariat of France take over the Eiffel Tower and announce from its summit in all the languages of Europe that they are the masters of France [applause], that on that day and hour not only the workers of our cities and industries but also the peasants of our remotest villages may be able to reply to the call of the European workers: "Do you hear us?"—"We hear you, brothers, and we will help you!" [Applause] Siberia will help with fats, grain, and raw materials, the Kuban and the Don with grain and meat. Uzbekistan and Turkmenistan will contribute their cotton. This will show that our radio communications have brought nearer the transformation of Europe into a single economic organization. The development of a radiotelegraphic network is, among so many other things, a preparation for the moment when the people of Europe and Asia shall be united in a Soviet Union of Socialist Peoples. [Applause]

Part 4

The materialist outlook

Youth fills the breach

[PUBLISHED MARCH 5, 1920]
In history, counterrevolution often came in the wake of revolution. One reason for this is that the revolutionary class exhausted itself in the heat of the struggle—the best, self-sacrificing elements perished in battle, and a still greater number wore out their physical and moral strength in the cruel, tense struggle. From this stemmed the inevitable decline of the movement. The party of counterrevolution took advantage of this eminently suitable moment. It took the offensive, inflicted a decisive blow on the ranks of the revolutionaries, and for a long time thereafter controlled the battlefield.

From Derevenskaya Kommuna, *March 5, 1920. Published in the February 20, 1970,* Militant, *in a translation by Tom Scott.*

The grim and severe tone of this article and Work: The Basis of Life *are understandable in the light of the bitter civil war that was raging during this period.*

Our revolution consumes an incredible amount of working class strength. On all fronts, in all battles, hundreds and thousands of the best die. Tens of thousands of proletarians, who were tempered in the underground struggle with czarism and who now constitute the ranks of the vanguard party, are dispersed in the soviets and the trade unions, working under intense pressure. They do not spare their energy or their blood. This layer of advanced workers is the basic capital of the revolution. It is being dispersed quickly, and without it the revolution is weakened and impoverished.

What is the way out? To make both the ideas of communism and struggle by working class youth into customs. As some wear themselves out and die, others must mature ideologically—young and fresh ones—and temper themselves in the atmosphere of revolutionary struggle.

This organization of youth is our reserve. Without plentiful reserves, the very best armies are doomed to perish. But even a weak army that has reserves to regenerate it will inevitably be victorious.

In other European countries, the proletarian struggle for power is just beginning to flare up. But everywhere, especially in Germany, this struggle has already consumed innumerable victims. How many more are there to be? As it enters the last decisive battle, the proletariat of Europe and of the whole world must assure itself a constant influx of reinforcements and fresh strength. Such a role falls to the youth, organized internationally.

Communism is the struggle for the future, for the happiness of future generations. Our immediate future is embodied in the younger generation. Drawing it into the struggle means that tomorrow is provided for. The more widely and more powerfully the youth movement develops, the firmer is our confidence that counterrevolution will not overcome us.

We have great reserves. The organization of youth throughout the world and, above all, here in Russia, fosters many tens of thousands of fighters, each of whom, when the time comes, will take his place in the common ranks, replacing the comrades who have fallen in battle. The movement which has the working class youth behind it is indestructible.

All hail to youth which fills the breach!

Work: The basis of life

APRIL 20, 1920

Russia is wretched, despoiled, weakened, exhausted. The plunderers all over the world think—or want to think—that Russia is lying on her deathbed. But no. We, the toilers, will raise her, strengthen her, heal her—by our stubborn, strenuous, coordinated work, the basis of human life. Now, when the land and the factories belong to the people, the labor of each one of us is no longer enriching individual parasites as it used to, but is going to the general good of the toilers themselves.

We will remember: work is the basis of life. And the poorer now our life is, the more disrupted is transport, the scantier are provisions, the stronger is desolation, dirt, and disease—the greater intensity and conscientiousness must characterize our work. The negligent, unconscientious worker is now

---

From Petrogradskaya Pravda, *May 1, 1920. Translated for this volume from Trotsky's* How the Revolution Armed Itself, *Vol. 2, by Iain Fraser.*

the worst enemy of the socialist society—the idle servant of the gospels, who buries his talents in the ground. The person who does not come to work on time, wastes time to no purpose in the workshop, busies himself in it with outside matters, or simply takes days off work, is the enemy of socialist Russia, and is undermining her future.

Working men and women! Let our precept in these difficult times be stern and unrelenting struggle with self-seeking, with slovenliness, with carelessness, and with absenteeism—with this labor desertion. Let us tirelessly work together with millions of hands to forge a happier fate for the generations to come.

Long live work—the liberator, the basis of life!

Attention to theory!

FEBRUARY 27, 1922

Dear Comrades,

The idea of publishing a journal to introduce progressive proletarian youth to the materialist conception of the world seems to me to be in the highest degree valuable and fruitful.

The older generation of workers and communists, which is now playing the leading role in the party and in the country, awoke to conscious political life ten, fifteen, twenty, or more years ago. Their thought started its critical work on

A letter to the first issue of a new Soviet youth publication, Pod Znamenem Marxizma *(Under the Banner of Marxism), January-February 1922. The publication was to be a militant materialist, atheist organ in the education of Soviet youth. About Trotsky's letter, Lenin said: "Comrade Trotsky has already said everything necessary, and said it very well, about the general purposes of* Pod Znamenem Marxisma. . . ." *Published in the September 1969* Young Socialist *in a translation by John Fairlie from* Collected Works, Vol. 21.

the policeman, the timekeeper, and the foreman, worked up
to czarism and capitalism, and then, most often in prison
and exile, turned to questions of the philosophy of history
and the scientific cognition of the world. Thus, before the
revolutionary proletarian reached the very important questions of the materialist explanation of historical development, he had already managed to accumulate a certain sum
of ever-widening generalizations, from the particular to the
general, on the basis of his own experience of life.

The young worker of the present day awakens in the environment of the Soviet state, which is itself a living criticism
of the old world. The general conclusions which were given to
the older generation of workers in struggle, and which were
reinforced in consciousness with the strong nails of personal
experience, are now received by the workers of the younger
generation ready made, directly from the hands of the state
in which they live, from the hands of the party that rules
this state. This means, of course, a gigantic step forward in
the sense of creating the conditions for further political and
theoretical education of the toilers. But at the same time, on
this incomparably higher historical level reached by the work
of the older generation, new problems and new difficulties
arise for the generation of the young.

The Soviet state is a living contradiction of the old world,
of its social order, of its personal relations, of its outlooks
and beliefs. But at the same time the Soviet state itself is
still full of contradictions, gaps, lack of coordination, vague
fermentation—in a word, of phenomena in which the inheritance of the past is interwoven with the shoots of the future.
In such a deeply transitional, critical, and unstable epoch
as ours, the education of the proletarian vanguard requires
serious and reliable theoretical foundations. To prevent the
great events, mighty surges and ebbs, rapid changes of tasks
and methods of the party and the state from disorganizing
the consciousness of the young worker and from breaking

down his will even before he crosses the threshold of his independent responsible work, it is necessary to arm his thought and his will with the materialist attitude.

To arm his *will*, and not only his *thought*, we say, since in an epoch of great worldwide upheavals more than at any other time our will is capable not only of collapsing, but also of being tempered—but only on condition that it is supported by scientific understanding of the conditions and causes of historical development.

On the other hand, precisely in this kind of epoch of great change like ours—especially if it is prolonged, i.e., if the tempo of revolutionary events in the West turns out to be slower than might be hoped—it is very probable that attempts will be made by various idealistic and semi-idealistic philosophical schools and sects to gain control of the consciousness of the working youth. Caught unawares by events—without previous rich experience of practical class struggle—the thought of the working youth may prove defenseless against the various doctrines of idealism, which are in essence a translation of religious dogmas into the language of sham philosophy. All these schools, for all the variety of their idealistic, Kantian, empiriocritical and other appellations, amount in the last analysis to making consciousness, thought, and cognition precede matter, and not the other way around.

The task of the materialist education of working youth consists in revealing to them the basic laws of historical development, and deriving from these basic laws the highest and most important one, namely, the law that says that the consciousness of people is not a free, independent psychological process, but a function of the material economic basis; that it is conditioned by it and serves it.

The dependency of consciousness on class interests and relations, and of the latter on the economic organization, appears most plainly, most openly, and most harshly in a revolutionary epoch. With this irreplaceable experience we must help working youth to strengthen in their consciousness the fundamentals of the Marxist method.

But this is not all. Human society itself, both by its historical roots and by its contemporary economy, extends into the world of natural history. We must see contemporary man as a link in the whole development that starts from the first tiny organic cell, which came in its turn from the laboratory of nature, where the physical and chemical properties of matter act. The person who has learned to look with a clear eye on the past of the whole world, including human society, the animal and vegetable kingdoms, the solar system, and the endless systems around it, will not start to hunt for keys to the secrets of the universe in ancient "holy books," those philosophical fairy tales of primitive infantilism. And the person who does not admit the existence of mystical heavenly forces, capable at will of intruding upon personal or social life and directing it to this side or that, who does not believe that want and suffering will find some kind of higher reward in other worlds, will stand more firmly and stably on our earth, will more boldly and more confidently seek support for his creative work in the material conditions of society.

The materialist world outlook not only opens a wide window on the whole universe, but it also strengthens the will. It is also the only thing that makes contemporary man a man. He still depends, it is true, on difficult material conditions, but he already knows how to overcome them, and takes part consciously in the construction of the new society, based at once on the highest technical skill and the highest solidarity.

Giving proletarian youth a materialist education is a supreme task. And to your journal, which wants to take part in this work of education, I wish success with all my heart.

With communist and materialist greetings,
L. Trotsky

The curve of
capitalist development

JUNE 21, 1923
In his introduction to Marx's *Class Struggles in France*,
Engels wrote:

> In judging the events and series of events of day-to-day
> history, it will never be possible for anyone to go right
> back to the final economic causes. Even today, when the
> specialised technical press provides such rich materials,
> in England itself it still remains impossible to follow day
> by day the movement of industry and trade in the world
> market and the changes which take place in the methods
> of production, in such a way as to be able to draw the
> general conclusion, at any point of time, from these very
> complicated and ever changing factors: of these factors,

*Subtitled "A Letter to the Editors in Place of the Promised Article"; from
Book IV,* Vestnik Sotsialisticheskoi Akademii, *April-July 1923. Published
in English in the May 1941* Fourth International.

the most important, into the bargain, generally operate a long time in secret before they suddenly and violently make themselves felt on the surface. A clear survey of the economic history of a given period is never contemporaneous; it can only be gained subsequently, after collecting and sifting of the material has taken place. Statistics are a necessary help here, and they always lag behind. For this reason, it is only too often necessary, in the current history of the time, to treat the most decisive factor as constant, to treat the economic situation existing at the beginning of the period concerned as given and unalterable for the whole period, or else to take notice of such changes in this situation as themselves arise out of events clearly before us, and as, therefore, can likewise be clearly seen. Hence, the materialist method has here often to limit itself to tracing political conflicts back to the struggles between the interests of the social classes and fractions of classes encountered as the result of economic development, and to show the particular political parties as the more or less adequate political expression of these same classes and fractions of classes.

It is self-evident *that this unavoidable neglect of contemporaneous changes in the economic situation, of the very basis of all the proceedings subject to examination, must be a source of error.* [*The Class Struggles in France, 1848–1850,* by Karl Marx (International Publishers, New York) pp. 9–10. Our emphasis—L.T.]

These ideas which Engels formulated shortly before his death were not further developed by anyone after him. To my recollection they are rarely even quoted—much more rarely than they should be. Still more, their meaning seems to have escaped many Marxists. The explanation for this fact is once again to be found in the causes indicated by Engels, which militate against any kind of finished economic interpretation of *current* history.

It is a very difficult task, impossible to solve in its full scope, to determine those subterranean impulses which economics transmits to the politics of today; and yet the explanation of political phenomena cannot be postponed, because the struggle cannot wait. From this flows the necessity of resorting in daily political activity to explanations which are so general that through long usage they become transformed into truisms.

As long as politics keeps flowing in the same forms, within the same banks, and at about the same speed, i.e., as long as the accumulation of economic quantity has not passed into a change of political quality, this type of clarifying abstraction ("the interests of the bourgeoisie," "imperialism," "fascism") still more or less serves its task: not to interpret a political fact in all its concreteness, but to reduce it to a familiar social type, which is, of course, intrinsically of inestimable importance.

But when a serious change occurs in the situation, all the more so a sharp turn, such general explanations reveal their complete inadequacy, and become wholly transformed into empty truisms. In such cases it is invariably necessary to probe analytically much more deeply in order to determine the qualitative aspect, and if possible also to measure quantitatively the impulses of economics upon politics. These "impulses" represent the dialectical form of the "tasks" that originate in the dynamic foundation and are submitted for solution in the sphere of the superstructure.

Oscillations of the economic conjuncture (boom-depression-crisis) already signify in and of themselves periodic impulses that give rise now to quantitative, now to qualitative changes, and to new formations in the field of politics. The revenues of possessing classes, the state budget, wages, unemployment, proportions of foreign trade, etc., are intimately bound up with the economic conjuncture, and in their turn exert the most direct influence on politics. This alone is enough to make one understand how important and fruitful it is to follow step by step the history of political parties, state institutions, etc., in relation to the cycles of capitalist development. By this we do not at all mean to say that these cycles explain *everything:* this is excluded, if only for the reason that cycles themselves are not fundamental but derivative economic phenomena. They unfold on the basis of the development of productive forces through the medium of market relations. But cycles explain a *great deal,* forming as they do through automatic pulsation an indispensable dialectical spring in the mechanism of capitalist society. The breaking points of the trade-industrial conjuncture bring us into a greater proximity with the critical knots in the web of the development of political tendencies, legislation, and all forms of ideology.

But capitalism is not characterized solely by the periodic recurrence of cycles—otherwise what would occur would be a complex repetition and not dynamic development. Trade-industrial cycles are of different character in different periods. The chief difference between them is determined by quantitative interrelations between the crisis and the boom period within each given cycle. If the boom restores with a surplus the destruction or constriction during the preceding crisis, then capitalist development moves upward. If the crisis, which signals destruction, or at all events contraction of productive forces, surpasses in its intensity the corresponding boom, then we get as a result a decline in economy. Finally, if the crisis and boom approximate each other in force, then we get a temporary and stagnating equilibrium in economy. This is the schema in the rough.

We observe in history that homogeneous cycles are grouped in a series. Entire epochs of capitalist development exist when a number of cycles is characterized by sharply delineated booms and weak, short-lived crises. As a result we have a sharply rising movement of the basic curve of capitalist development. There are epochs of stagnation when this curve, while passing through partial cyclical oscillations, remains on approximately the same level for decades. And finally, during certain historical periods the basic curve, while passing as always through cyclical oscillations, dips downward as a whole, signaling the decline of productive forces.

It is already possible to postulate a priori that epochs of energetic capitalist development must possess features—in politics, in law, in philosophy, in poetry—sharply different from those in the epochs of stagnation or economic decline. Still more, a transition from one epoch of this kind to a different one must naturally produce the greatest convulsions in the relationships between classes and between states. At the Third World Congress of the Comintern we had to stress this point [1]—in the struggle against the purely mechanistic conception of capitalist disintegration now in progress. If periodic replacements of "normal" booms by "normal" crises find their reflection in all spheres of social life, then a transition from an entire boom epoch to one of decline, or vice versa, engenders the greatest historical disturbances; and it is not hard to show that in many cases revolutions and wars straddle the borderline between two different epochs of economic development, i.e., the junction of two different segments of the capitalist curve. To analyze all of modern history from this standpoint is truly one of the most gratifying tasks of dialectical materialism.

Following the Third World Congress of the Comintern, Professor Kondratiev approached this problem—as usual, painstakingly evading the formulation of the question adopted by the congress itself—and attempted to set up alongside of the "minor cycle," covering a period of ten years, the concept of a "major cycle," embracing approximately fifty years.[2] According to this symmetrically stylized construction, a major economic cycle consists of some five minor cycles, and furthermore, half of them have the character of boom, and the other half that of crisis, with all the necessary transitional stages. The statistical determinations of major cycles compiled by Kondratiev should be subjected to careful and not over-credulous verification in respect both to individual countries and to the world market as a whole. It is already possible to refute in advance Professor Kondratiev's attempt to invest epochs labeled by him as major cycles with the same "rigidly lawful rhythm" that is observable in minor cycles; it is an obviously false generalization from a formal analogy.

The periodic recurrence of minor cycles is conditioned by the internal dynamics of capitalist forces, and manifests itself always and everywhere once the market comes into existence. As regards the large segments of the capitalist curve of development (fifty years) which Professor Kondratiev incautiously proposes to designate also as cycles, their character and duration are determined not by the internal interplay of capitalist forces but by those external conditions through whose channel capitalist development flows. The acquisition by capitalism of new countries and continents, the discovery of new natural resources, and, in the wake of these, such major facts of "superstructural" order as wars and revolutions, determine the character and the replacement of ascending, stagnating, or declining epochs of capitalist development.

Along what path then should investigation proceed?

To establish the curve of capitalist development in its non-periodic (basic) and periodic (secondary) phases and breaking points in respect to individual countries of interest to us and in respect to the entire world market—that is the first part of the task. Once we have the fixed curve (the method of fixing it is, of course, a special question in itself and by no means a simple one, but it pertains to the field of economic-statistical technique), we can break it down into periods, depending upon the angle of rise and decline in reference to an axis on a graph. In this way we obtain a pictorial scheme of economic development, i.e., the characterization of the "very basis of all the proceedings subject to examination" (Engels).

Depending upon the concreteness and detail of our investigation, we may require a number of such schemas: one relating to agriculture, another to heavy industry, and so on. With this schema as our starting point, we must next synchronize it with political events (in the widest sense of the term) and we can then look not only for correspondence—or to put it more cautiously, interrelationship between definitely delineated epochs of social life and the sharply expressed segments of the curve of capitalist development—but also for those direct subterranean impulses which unleash events. Along this road it is naturally not at all difficult to fall into the most vulgar schematization and, above all, to ignore the tenacious internal conditioning and succession of ideological processes—to become oblivious of the fact that economics is decisive only in the *last analysis*. There has been no lack of caricature conclusions drawn from the Marxist method! But to renounce on this account the above indicated formulation of the question ("it smells of economism") is to demonstrate complete inability to understand the essence of Marxism, which looks for the causes of changes in social superstructure in the changes of the economic foundation, and not anywhere else.

At the risk of incurring the theoretical ire of opponents of "economism" (and partly with the intention of provoking their indignation) we present here a schematic chart which depicts arbitrarily a curve of capitalist development for a period of ninety years along the above-mentioned lines. The general direction of the basic curve is determined by the character of the partial conjunctural curves of which it is composed. In our schema three periods are sharply demarcated: twenty years of very gradual capitalist development (segment *A-B*);

CURVE OF CAPITALIST DEVELOPMENT

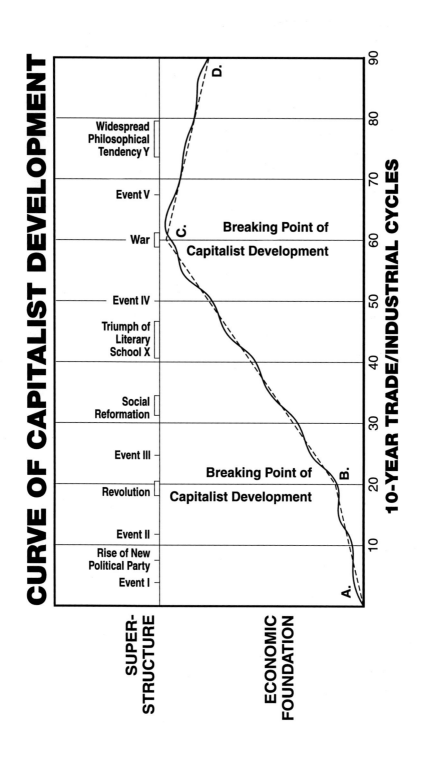

SUPER-STRUCTURE

ECONOMIC FOUNDATION

Event I
Rise of New Political Party
Event II
Revolution
Event III
Social Reformation
Triumph of Literary School X
Event IV
War
Event V
Widespread Philosophical Tendency Y

Breaking Point of Capitalist Development

Breaking Point of Capitalist Development

A.
B.
C.
D.

10-YEAR TRADE/INDUSTRIAL CYCLES

10   20   30   40   50   60   70   80   90

forty years of energetic upswing (segment B-C); and thirty years of protracted crisis and decline (segment C-D). If we introduce into this diagram the most important historical events for the corresponding period, then the pictorial juxtaposition of major political events with the variations of the curve is alone sufficient to provide the idea of the invaluable starting points for historical materialist investigations. The parallelism of political events and economic changes is of course very relative. As a general rule, the "superstructure" registers and reflects new formations in the economic sphere only after considerable delay. But this law must be laid bare through a concrete investigation of those complex interrelationships of which we here present a pictorial hint.

In the report to the Third World Congress, we illustrated our idea with certain historical examples drawn from the epoch of the revolution of 1848, the epoch of the first Russian revolution (1905), and the period through which we are now passing (1920–21). We refer the reader to these examples. They do not supply anything finished, but they do characterize adequately enough the extraordinary importance of the approach advanced by us, above all for understanding the most critical leaps in history: wars and revolutions. If in this letter we utilize a purely arbitrary pictorial scheme, without attempting to take any actual period in history as a basis, we do so for the simple reason that any attempt of this sort would resemble far too much an incautious anticipation of those results flowing from a complex and painstaking investigation which has yet to be made.

At the present time, it is of course still impossible to foresee to any precise degree just what sections of the field of history will be illuminated and just how much light will be cast by a materialist investigation which would proceed from a more concrete study of the capitalist curve and the interrelationship between the latter and all the aspects of social life. Conquests that may be attained on this road can be determined only as the result of such an investigation itself, which must be more systematic, more orderly than those historical materialist excursions hitherto undertaken.

In any case, such an approach to modern history promises to enrich the theory of historical materialism with conquests far more precious than the extremely dubious speculative juggling with the concepts and terms of the materialist method that has, under the pens of some of our Marxists, transplanted the methods of formalism into the domain of the materialist dialectic, and has led to reducing the task to rendering definitions and classifications more precise and to splitting empty abstractions into four equally empty parts; it has, in short, adulterated Marxism by means of the indecently elegant mannerisms of Kantian epigones. It is a silly thing indeed endlessly to sharpen and resharpen an instrument to chip away Marxist steel, when the task is to apply the instrument in working over the raw material!

In our opinion this theme could provide the subject matter for the most fruitful work of our Marxist seminars on historical materialism. Independent investigations undertaken in this sphere would undoubtedly shed new light or at least throw more light on isolated historical events and entire epochs. Finally, the very habit of thinking in terms of the foregoing categories would greatly facilitate political orientation in the present epoch, which is an epoch that reveals more openly than ever before the connection between capitalist economics, which has attained the peak of saturation, and capitalist politics, which has become completely unbridled.

I promised long ago to develop this theme for the *Vestnik Sotsialisticheskoi Akademii*. Up to now I have been prevented by circumstances from keeping this promise. I am not sure that I shall be able to fulfill it in the near future. For this reason I confine myself in the meantime to this letter.

Young people, study politics!

Comrades, not long ago, we released from the Red Army on indefinite leave the class of 1901. On this occasion we carried out in a number of places an inquiry among the men being discharged, questioning them as to what they had learned in the Red Army. From among the answers they gave, one in particular struck my attention, a very brief and expressive answer. I have already quoted it at several meetings. One of the Red Army comrades answered thus: "I have learned about the machine gun and about politics."

Remember that answer, Comrades! It is a very good one; in my opinion the thing could not be better put. As a revolutionary soldier he is obliged to know, as Suvorov said long ago,

A speech on the fifth anniversary celebration of the Communist Young Workers' Hostels. From the May-June 1924 Kommunisticheskii Internatsional. *Published in English in the January 1966* Fourth International *(London), in a translation by Brian Pearce.*

his military art; he must know his weapon and how to use it, otherwise he will not be a soldier. In this case, evidently, we are dealing with a machine-gunner, whose weapon is the machine gun. "I have learned about the machine gun, and besides that, I have learned about politics," he says. What does it mean when he says that he has learned about politics? It means that he has learned to understand why he was given a machine gun. So long as he only knows about the machine gun, he is just the slave of the weapon, and cannon fodder in somebody else's hands; but when he knows what purpose under certain conditions that machine gun is to fulfill in the Red Army, he is a revolutionary fighter, a conscious citizen.

This applies not only to a soldier in the revolutionary army, but to every kind of service in our workers' and peasants' country. "What have you learned?" we must ask the young proletarian when he leaves the factory training school. "I have learned about the hammer, the pincers, the plane, and about politics." And about politics!

You know that in bourgeois countries there is a hypocritical and base notion that the army and the younger generation stand outside politics. This very day, in another connection, I have been looking through Volumes 2 and 3 of Comrade Lenin's works. (This is in general, Comrades, a very useful occupation—whether one has any special reason for doing it or not—for everybody who has the opportunity to undertake it.)

It so happens that my eye fell upon a number of Lenin's plain, extremely sharp and merciless observations regarding this base and hypocritical conception about the younger generation being outside politics. We know that the army is in all countries an instrument of politics, or rather, that it serves political ends. When it is said that the army is outside politics, that means: you, soldier, master your machine gun—politics, however, will be looked after by somebody else on your behalf, i.e., obviously, by the ruling class. The bourgeoisie carries out a division of labor. Politics is in its charge; the workers and peasants in the army are cannon fodder, slaves to the machines of destruction. And it is exactly the same so far as the younger generation is concerned, the young workers and peasants, that is. Politics fills the air; *it is not possible to live outside of politics, without politics, any more than one can live without air.*

But the bourgeoisie cannot reveal its political face to the young people. It cannot say: there you are, the twelve- or thirteen-year-old son of a worker; you have been born into the world in order that, after serving an apprenticeship to some trade, you may go into a factory and there to the end of your days create with your sweat, blood, and marrow, surplus value for the lords of life, the bourgeoisie, who, from this surplus value, will create its bourgeois culture, its luxury, art, and learning for its children. The bourgeoisie cannot openly expound such politics to the young workers. It puts over its politics by way of circumlocution and allegories, imperceptibly or half-perceptibly, through its schools, its churches, and its press. And this work of the imperceptible bourgeois education of young people, or rather, the education of young workers and peasants in the interests of the bourgeois state, is concealed behind the slogan: "the younger generation is outside politics." And that is why Vladimir Ilyich so relentlessly and implacably fought against this base hypocrisy.

Young people live in society, they are born into definite conditions, they step forward into life's arena in particular historical circumstances, and the sooner these youngsters open their eyes to the world around them, the better and more profoundly they grasp the conditions in which they live, the easier their path through life will prove to be.

You young comrades are living in a workers' and peasants' state. This does not mean that your path through life is a very easy one in the years of your apprenticeship. But

I think, nevertheless, that it is already considerably better than it was for the elder generation of the working class in their apprenticeship years. I don't know whether anybody in our country has collected together the works of literature— Chekhov's stories, for instance—which deal with the years of apprenticeship, the gloomiest in the life of the working masses. I think that all these stories, sketches, and memoirs of the years of apprenticeship through which every worker has passed, should be collected and published and made one of the reference books for young people. *It is necessary to learn to hate the old order that we have overthrown but that we are still far, far from having got rid of.* It has bequeathed to us monstrous deposits of ignorance, inertness, crudeness, vulgarity; and all this still surrounds us. And it is for you young comrades to sweep away these deposits. That is why it is very important that the work of mastering the hammer, the pincers, and all the other tools and instruments of production must go hand in hand with the mastering of politics.

Today you are celebrating the fifth anniversary of your hostel. This anniversary falls very closely upon the May Day celebration of the international proletariat. Allow me to say a few words about this. This festival, Comrades, was inaugurated thirty-five years ago, as a festival in honor of the eight-hour working day and the international brotherhood of the working people, and as an international demonstration of the workers against militarism. And just now, as I was on my way here, I was looking, for lack of any papers today, through some recently received dispatches from our news agency. A great part of these dispatches, and a very significant part, so as not to exaggerate, deal with the preparations going on in Europe and in other parts of the world for the May Day festival. This preparation consists of the fact that in a number of bourgeois states, including the most democratic, all street processions, demonstrations, and parades by the workers on May Day have been forbidden.

There is an instructive example for you of present-day European politics. Our state, the state which was built under the leadership of the teacher of all of us, Vladimir Ilyich, this workers' and peasants' state, does not call itself democratic in the sense in which France, Germany, and a number of other states are called democratic. We are reproached because we have a regime of dictatorship, an open one, i.e., the rule of the working people who have put down with mailed fist all resistance to the rule of labor. They have democracy over there, and universal freedom. Who rules Britain today? Menshevik Social Democrats. Who plays a very big role in the political life of Germany? Menshevik Social Democrats. In Saxony, one of the German states, there is a Social Democratic government. The government of Berlin is in the hands of the Social Democrats. This very day the Berlin authorities have forbidden the celebration of May Day in the streets of that city. The Saxon Menshevik government has forbidden May Day to be celebrated in the streets throughout Saxony. In Britain it is exactly the same.[3] There is no need to speak of Poland, Hungary, and Rumania, or of France—in that democratic republic, proletarian street demonstrations have been forbidden for several decades. Here is a stark fact. Who inaugurated the celebration of May Day thirty-five years ago? The Social Democrats. Who is at the head of the German Republic? The Social Democrat Ebert. What is the point? The point is that the new revolutionary generation of the working class in Europe is growing more and more thoroughly filled with hatred for the rule of the bourgeoisie, and that over there in Europe, democratic Menshevism is the last instrument the bourgeoisie has for keeping the working masses down.

And we see that those very governments that reproached us communists for openly saying that only the transfer of power into the hands of the working people could abolish the rule of capital, those very same governments that belong to the parties that inaugurated the May Day celebrations, are forbidding the workers to go into the streets with the slogans of international brotherhood and the eight-hour working day. And the same telegrams report that the German Young Communists, the young people of Germany and those of France, too, are nevertheless doing all they can to be able to go out into the streets of their cities with slogans of protest and struggle.

What are these slogans? The slogan laid down for May Day thirty-five years ago—the eight-hour working day—was achieved almost everywhere in Europe after the war; but in recent years the working day has been lengthened. If there were a country that had the right, if there were a working class that had the right to demand of itself and of its sons a working day longer than eight hours, then it would be our country, exhausted and devastated, working not for the bourgeoisie but for itself—and yet in our country the eight-hour working day remains a precondition, based on the laws of the republic, for the moral and spiritual advance and development of the working masses.

And on May Day we hurl this fact in the face of Europe's capitalist, lying, thoroughly hypocritical bourgeois democracy. What sort of democracy is it for the working people if they are merely promised the eight-hour working day? And what of the fraternity of the peoples, respect for the working people of other nationalities, who speak other languages, fraternal feelings which we must absorb from our earliest years, because national chauvinism and national hatred are the poison with which the bourgeoisie pollutes the minds of the working people? I demand to know where this slogan of the May Day celebration has been put into effect more fully than in our country. I have been in Caucasia, that backward region. There are three main republics there and dozens of backward nationalities. That region was bled white by wars.

But now the young generation there is learning to work and to create culture on the basis of cooperation among all the different nationalities. Have not we, the workers' republic, the right to contrast, with justified pride, this backward Caucasia, which has been restored and given new life by the Soviet power, to any of the cultured countries of Europe, where on every frontier there is hatred, enmity, and danger of new armed conflicts?

And the third slogan by which the Social Democrats swore thirty-five years ago, the slogan of struggle against militarism? Now in power in Britain is the Menshevik Labour Government of MacDonald. What is it spending on arms? It is spending 1,150 million gold rubles a year. That is four or five times as much as we spend. Britain has 40 million people, we have 130 million. MacDonald may say that we are the poorer country and so, of course, we spend less. But, Comrades, if we are the poorer, that means that we are threatened by greater danger, for throughout history it has always happened that rich peoples, led by their rich ruling classes, have conquered and subjected poorer and more backward ones. China will not fall upon Britain and the United States, but the wealthy United States and Britain may crush China.

If we did not have Soviet power—the power of the workers and peasants, of the Communist Party boldly marching onward to battle—our country, weakened and exhausted by the imperialist war, would long ago have been torn to pieces by the barbarians of world imperialism. And when those very same Mensheviks reproach us for giving military training to our young people, for building the Red Army, when they tell us: "You, too, are militarists," then it is sufficient for us to contrast the states that surround us with the first republic of labor in the world, surrounded for the last seven years by irreconcilable and ruthless foes.

If they are recognizing us now, and if we are carrying on

negotiations in London today,[4] it must not be supposed that the world bourgeoisie has become better disposed towards the republic of workers and peasants. A change of tactics does not do away with the hatred felt by the bourgeoisie of all countries for the republic where the rising generation of working people is growing up in a new atmosphere, with new ideals—for we are overthrowing the old ideals insofar as we are teaching the young generation to have confidence in the power of the world working class. The world bourgeoisie will never reconcile itself to this. And is it surprising if we feel, and must feel, that we are the camp of emancipated labor? Study the technique of production, and remember that at any moment the workers' and peasants' government, threatened from outside may call you to the colors of the workers' and peasants' Red Army.

Comrades, you know what a frightful misfortune another war would be for our Soviet Republic, which has still not healed its wounds. And when in today's foreign news I read about how we are supposed to be preparing to attack Rumania and Poland, I can only, like any of you, shrug my shoulders in contempt. The world revolution has been delayed. We are waiting patiently and confidently for the fate of Rumania and Poland to be settled along with the fate of the world revolution. We are not inclined to launch into bloody enterprises for the purpose of deciding piecemeal the question of the liberation of all Europe, including Poland and Rumania. It will be decided sooner or later. Our task in this period is to strengthen our economy and to raise the level of our culture, holding on until emancipated Europe's workers come to our aid.

Certainly our situation would be ten times, a hundred times easier if there were a revolutionary workers' government in Britain. It would grant us, on the basis of a comradely, businesslike agreement, a very substantial credit. We should be able immediately to increase our production, flood the market with all kinds of goods for the peasants' use, and in five years raise the level of our agriculture. What would that mean for Britain? It would mean abundant and cheap grain, timber, hides, flax, and all kinds of raw material. The British people, the working people—that is to say, nine-tenths of the total population of Britain—as well as the people of the Soviet Union, would benefit to an extraordinary degree from such businesslike cooperation, and we, Comrades, would be able in a few years to rise to the summit of economic well-being, to a height from which we are still very, very distant. Alas, I do not believe that the present government of Britain, a Menshevik government, is capable of taking such a bold, decisive step.

No, for several years yet, until the coming to real victory of the proletariat, we shall have to learn to stand, in the main, on our own feet. This means that we shall advance, but slowly. We shall be frank with ourselves about this. And when the bourgeois newspapers ask us, and me in particular: "Suppose our ruling classes don't grant you a loan—what will that mean? The collapse of Russia? The collapse of the Soviet power?"—we shall answer them: "How can a gigantic country of 130 million people, who have been awakened for the first time by the revolution, where the young are learning to think critically—how can such a country collapse? A country with inexhaustible natural resources like ours cannot collapse and will not collapse."

The bourgeois press of London, we are told by the latest dispatches, quotes our speeches, in particular my own, as evidence that by our sharp criticism we wish to break off negotiations. That is a slander. An agreement with the British people will be a good thing for us and for the British people. But if the British bourgeoisie thinks that we shall say: "Help, we are collapsing!"—if the British bourgeoisie thinks that we shall agree to any conditions they care to impose, then the British bourgeoisie is wrong.

We have already raised ourselves the two or three first steps and have already shown ourselves and others that we are able to work, to advance the economy and culture of our country. And, if I could, I would say to the City, that center of London, to its banks and bankers, to the MacDonald government, to all the ruling circles of Britain: here, take a look at this, our young generation, the flower of the working class. They are learning to work and to think. Our young generation has passed through the furnace of October, it has grown up in the great school of Lenin. We and our country, so rich in natural wealth, will not perish. With your aid we shall go forward faster, and that will be a great gain for you. Without you we shall go forward slower, but go forward we will, and the reign of labor will come to triumph in our country.

Leninism and workers' clubs

JULY 17, 1924
Comrades, I will be having the opportunity to speak soon at
the Second All-Union Congress of Cultural Workers. Let us
hope that the very fact that such congresses are being held
is a sign of a certain changeover, foretokening a period of
broader and more intense cultural work in all fields.

*A speech to a conference of club personnel, which Trotsky delivered on
July 17, 1924. From* Pravda, *July 23, 1924. Translated for this volume from
Collected Works, Vol. 21, by George Saunders. The section "Antireligious
propaganda" was printed in English in* Labour Speaks for Itself on Religion, *ed. Jerome Davis (Macmillan, New York, 1929).*
    *Workers' clubs are educational and recreational institutions that
first appeared in 1905 but were suppressed by the czarist regime. In
1917 they revived, and were formed at many factories and plants. Their
main function during the civil war was to explain government policies
to rank-and-file workers. Funded by the trade unions, the workers' clubs
are formally independent, with administrative boards elected at general
meetings. They usually include at least a library, an eating room, and a
lecture hall. Some, which have more elaborate facilities, are called "Pal-
aces of Culture."*

Educational work before and after
the conquest of power

For us, questions of cultural work are inseparably connected with politics, with socialist construction. This is as basic as ABC. When we speak of cultural work, and in particular of club work, which is destined to hold a special place within the overall system of our cultural work, what we have in mind in the first place is propaganda work and the practical realization of the basic propositions of Marxism—or to translate into the language of our era, of Leninism.

Just the other day I came across a phrase of Marx's, which I am ashamed to say I had forgotten—a phrase that brings us right to the heart of the question. While still quite young, Marx wrote to the well-known German radical writer Arnold Ruge, "We do not step into the world with a new doctrinaire set of principles, saying: 'Here is the truth; get down on your knees to it!' We develop new foundations for the world out of the world's own foundations."

A superb formulation, and one that is pure Marx. We do not bring truth to the people from the outside, as though truth were something inflexibly fixed and given for all time, and we do not say to the people: "Here is the truth; get down on your knees to it!" No, we take the world as it is, and in a practical way, actively, we extract from the foundations of this living world the means for building a new one.

This is the essence of the Marxist and Leninist method. And the cultural workers of the Soviet Republic need to give this idea a great deal of thought and get the feel of it completely, for in our country Marxism, by way of Leninism, has come to power for the very first time. And that fact, which opens up enormous possibilities for cultural and educational work, entails some serious dangers as well, something that must never be lost sight of. As I have said elsewhere before, our country is *Leninism organized in state form*. Organized in state form—that is to say, holding state power. The state is an organ of coercion, and for Marxists in positions of power there may be a temptation to simplify cultural and educational work among the masses by using the approach of "Here is the truth—down on your knees to it!"

The state, of course, is a harsh thing, and the workers' state has the right, and the duty, to use coercion against the enemies of the working class, a ruthless application of force. But in the matter of educating the working class itself, the method of "Here is the truth—down on your knees to it!" as a method of cultural work contradicts the very essence of Marxism. The techniques and methods of propaganda and education are varied: at one time the party is working underground; at another, it holds state power. But Leninism as a method of thought and a method of educating the workers remains the same, both in the period when the party is fighting for power and after it has attained that objective.

We have to give this idea a great deal of thought. Its full meaning is brought home to us especially clearly if we compare the pattern of a young worker's development under the old bourgeois regime in Russia or in any capitalist country with the kind of development we now have here, given the circumstances and conditions of the Soviet Republic. Previously the worker developed from the factory outward; in the shop where he worked he found, as part of his life experience, the conditions that would help him orient himself not only at the factory but in the society as a whole. Opposing him stood the capitalist who exploited him: class antagonism as the basic principle by which to orient himself in society constantly stared him in the face. And there were times when strikes were called, when the worker had dealings with the police. On the question of housing, he had to deal with the landlord, and finally, as a consumer, he dealt with the exploiting merchant. Thus, within the limited sphere of his everyday life, and starting from his workplace first of all, he encountered the class enemy in all its hypostases, in all its manifestations—and that was sufficient for an elementary orientation under those social conditions. Is the same true for us today? No.

Take for example a young worker, that is, one who has not gone through the school of the capitalist factory of old, one whose active life and work began after October. In a social sense his conditions of labor are immeasurably better; but in material respects that is not always so, not by far. Moreover, at the factory he does not face an enemy who would appear to be the cause of his still difficult material situation. In order for this young worker to understand his place in the factory, he needs to understand his place in society. He ought to give thought to the fact that as part of the working class he is one of the rulers of this country, that the factory belongs to his class, and that he is one part of its collective ownership.

If he lives in a house belonging, let us say, to the Moscow Soviet, or some other soviet, here again he does not have before him a landlord who exploits him. He simply has himself. In order to learn the correct attitude toward his own apartment, toward the stairways of his building, towards the building rules, etc., he must think of himself as a part of the collective ownership.

Thus everything has been turned around on its axis. The worker in bourgeois Russia, as in any capitalist country, had his basic experience at the factory to begin with, and when he first heard the truths of Marxism, they would come to rest directly upon his limited but quite firm class experience of indignation, hatred, and struggle against the exploiters. But now we don't have this. The exploiter stands before us now only on the grand scale, in the form of the world capitalist giant, who uses wars, blockades, and extortionist demands based on the old foreign debt to impede our development. In the plants and factories the situation is quite a new one

now, and in order to get in tune correctly, one must understand one's place in social relations generally. In order to
orient himself correctly on the question of wages—whether
one should or should not increase them under present conditions—or on the question of the productivity of labor—
in order to find his way in all these questions, the worker
must come to know himself in his social position, that is,
to think through all the consequences of the fact that he is
the ruling class.

Thus, to sum up, the starting point for the development
of a worker in a bourgeois country is the factory, the shop,
the workplace, and he proceeds from there, through several
intermediate steps, and arrives at an orientation toward society; whereas, for us, the worker has to gain an understanding of his position in society in order not to go astray at
the factory level. This is a tremendous difference! It entails
a difference in cultural and educational approach, flowing
from the difference in the conditions of individual and class
development. Those generalizations which were sufficient
for the workers under capitalist society could, at least at first,
be quite limited. Today in order to find his place, the worker
needs much broader and more complex generalized ideas.
In compensation for that, however, his experience today is
also much more complex and varied. But this experience is
fragmentary; it needs to be brought together, thought over,
discussed, articulated and formulated. The worker's life experience—his factory experience, his experience at home, his
experience as a member of a cooperative, or as a Red Army
soldier—all this needs to be gathered into a single whole.

When this variegated experience is brought together in
critical fashion in the head of the worker, the latter begins
at once to find the correct orientation in society, and consequently in the factory, and in the communal home, and in
the cooperative, and so on. And here the club serves as one
of the most important points of juncture, where all these

threads of variegated and fragmentary experience intersect, come together in a single whole.

The place of the club in educational work

In our country the Communist Party does the educating. But the party has a complex array of levers and controls at its disposal for this purpose. It works through the government, which it heads, and through the trade unions, whose leadership is likewise in party hands, and through the clubs, whose significance is destined to grow more and more. The club serves as an exceptionally important digestive organ for the collective assimilation of fragmentary experience by the working class, precisely because the club is only *part of the educational system and not part of the system of administration.*

The party is a collective body geared to action—and in our country, it is a collective ruling group as well—and it draws a line between itself and untrained or uneducated elements. Not of course in the sense that it cuts itself off from access to such elements, but rather that it does not allow untrained elements to influence party decisions with their votes. The party sets up stringent rules for admission to its ranks, checks applicants carefully, and so forth. All this is undeniably necessary. The party is in charge of the government. It cannot wait for the backward elements to develop to the point where they understand current events, for the events of today will be yesterday's events tomorrow, and the events of tomorrow will be today's. The party cannot wait. It has to respond actively to the events of the day. It presents slogans and formulations, which to party members and to those workers who follow the party's lead closely are filled with the entire life experience of the past. But for the more backward masses these formulations seem to descend from on high, often enough taking them completely by surprise. In order to comprehend these as their own, the masses have to approach them step by step through their own experience. And here a bridge between the fragmented, partial, inadequate, and as yet unthought-out experience of the worker (and not the worker in general but the particular living worker or group of workers), between that and the political formulations, instructions, and directives of the party—one of the most important bridges between them is—or should be!—the workers' club. This is its basic significance. Everything else flows from this.

Peter the Great is credited with being the author of a phrase which I believe (though I have not checked) he borrowed from earlier military writers. "The manual of arms," said Peter, "has the procedures written out, but not the particulars of time or occasion." That is, when an inexperienced soldier takes the field manual in hand, the overall rules on what to do in various combat situations will sound to him like abstract commands hanging in midair over his head—like some revealed truth that he must get down on his knees to. In order to understand something, one must carry it out and test it out in one's own experience. There are no "particulars of time or occasion" in the manual, as Peter said, that is, no concrete terms or specifications or conditions for applying the general rules. The basic task in military training and instruction is to develop a person's ability to combine regulation orders with concrete times and occasions. The social and educational path of the club leads in the opposite direction, from "particulars of time and occasion"—that is, from the concrete circumstances and specifics experienced by the individual worker, group of workers, entire plant, or entire district—to the book regulations, that is, the general lessons and norms of conduct and operation incumbent upon the class as a whole.

The club does not of course have its own politics, nor does it draw its own generalizations. It gets these from the party, whose creative functions the club nourishes with its own raw experience. The club helps the workers whom it draws into its orbit to think through their experiences and assimilate them in a critical way. At the third youth congress Lenin said: "Communism will become an empty word, a mere signboard, and the Communist a mere boaster, if all the knowledge he has acquired is not digested in his mind."[5] But how to digest it all? On the basis of one's personal experience and that of the group around one, of which one is part, and that of the class as a whole. The club is a bridge from the everyday life of the working man or woman to the life of the citizen, that is, to conscious participation in the constructive work of the state, the party, or the profession to which they belong. But the club does not toss aside the working person who has already joined in on the work of the collective through a trade union, soviet organization, or the party. It helps such already awakened persons to raise their civic and revolutionary qualifications still higher. If the club can be called a school, it is a school of civic awareness, a school for heightening one's qualifications as a citizen.

But not only civic qualifications. Cultural advancement is unthinkable without a rise in the level of our workers' training in technical skills, without the inculcation of the urge for acquiring qualifications as highly skilled, without the development of professional pride. Precisely because communism is not an abstract principle—"Down on your knees, that's all!"—but a method for building a new world proceeding in practical fashion on the basis of the existing world—precisely for that reason one cannot speak seriously of socialism if there is no effort at the same time to achieve the fundamental precondition for socialism by every means, namely, increasing the productivity of labor in our country.

There is no need to close our eyes to what exists—the comments by foreign worker communists about production in our country are not always comforting, not by far: we are still working unskillfully, laxly, sluggishly, and so on. While preserving the eight-hour day as the solid foundation for the cultural development of the proletariat, we must reach a much higher level of labor productivity. To inculcate the desire to become a highly skilled productive worker is one of the club's tasks, in which it works in the closest connection with the trade union. Thus, the course we have taken toward developing good, highly qualified, revolutionary citizens is inextricably bound up with our course toward developing good, highly qualified productive workers.

You know that in Western Europe (and it was partially true for us here as well) a certain section of the highly skilled workers—and in some countries it is quite a considerable section—have a tendency to think of themselves as an aristocracy; they remove themselves from the rest of their class and serve as a base of support for the Social Democrats, Mensheviks, and even more right-wing elements as in America. If we were to suppose such a thing possible in our country, it would signify disastrous negligence in the sphere of working class education, for, to us, for a worker to be highly qualified means that he ought to be so in all ways, that is, not only productively but also politically, and that kind of qualification ought to be the first priority in the work of raising the level of qualification in the working class as a whole, and not only in its upper crust. For that reason the question of developing an inclination among the advanced elements of the working class toward raising their own productive worth, toward understanding the economy as a whole as well as mastering production skills on their own jobs—that is one of the most important tasks facing the club.

And this task obviously cannot be carried out by means of moralizing. In general this method gets you nowhere at all. The problem can be solved, or more precisely, can become solvable, by means of drawing highly qualified workers into discussions at the clubs, workers who at the same time are highly qualified communists, and by arousing in them feelings of professional honor and productive pride, that will be directly linked with the question of the success of our entire socialist economy.

I have said—and this is elementary for us all—that Leninism is not a collection of truths, requiring ritual obeisance, but a method of thinking, requiring continual application in practice. But that does not mean, of course, that Leninism is learned purely empirically, without theory or books. We need books and the club needs books for studying Leninism. A resolution of the thirteenth congress of our party speaks of this: "A most prominent place in the general work of the clubs must be allotted to the propagandizing of Leninism. One of the instruments of our propagandizing must be the club's library, for which an appropriate selection of books is necessary."

Let me say without mincing words that selection must be understood here in the sense of *selecting out,* for a countless number of books on the theme of Leninism have appeared, and they are not all of equal value. It is not easy to write about Leninism. . . . Many of the hastily written booklets are tossed aside like so many husks, while the more valuable ones still need to be reworked in the future. The stringent selection of such books for club use is a very crucial question, which should be resolved only through the collective effort of club and library workers.

I should like, by the way, to give a warning at this point against an error that is now found rather widely, that is, an incorrect attitude toward what is called the *popular* quality of a book. Naturally, one should write as simply as possible, but not to the detriment of the essentials of the subject, not with an artificial simplification of one's theme, not by passing over important aspects of it in silence. The exposition should correspond to the subject matter. Since we wish to heighten the theoretical as well as other qualifications of the advanced workers through the work of the club, we must bring them into the sphere of highly complex ideological interests. Here studying is necessary! There are books that come to one as easily as drinking water but they flow on out like water too—without lodging in one's consciousness. To study Leninism is a big job, and therefore one cannot approach it superficially or light-mindedly; rather, one must work one's way into the field of Leninism wielding pick and shovel. Of course, not every book is useful for everyone. There must be a correlation between the reader's personal experience, general level of development, and abilities, on the one hand, and the level of coverage of Leninism provided by the book. But one cannot take the attitude that Leninism can be presented in a form that can be grasped without any difficulties by anyone. That which can be grasped without any difficulties is generally useless, regardless of the subject. Naturally, a popular style is one of the most important demands we should place on all who write for the working class, but it would be naive to suppose that the manner of presentation can overcome all the difficulties inherent in the substance of a question.

What constitutes a healthy kind of popularization? One in which the exposition corresponds to the theme. *Capital* cannot be written in a more popular style than Marx used if the subject is to be treated in all its depth. Lenin's philosophical work on empiriomonism cannot be developed in a more popular style than Lenin's either. What's the solution? To come to these books through a series of intermediate steps; this is the only way to get to understand them; there is not and cannot be any other way. Engels fought in his later years against a prejudice that has some bearing here, the rather widespread prejudice concerning foreign words.

Naturally, piling one foreign word on top of another, especially ones that are rarely used, is a completely unnecessary mannerism. Still worse, however, are the incomprehensible words of our own manufacture, such as certain Soviet words of three and four elements which uselessly clutter up the text in our newspapers and which can't be found in any foreign dictionary. Abbreviations are acceptable when they are known and understood. There are, too, abbreviations and compound words that are appropriate for a chancellery or government office, but in newspapers or books of general use they simply get in the way. And conversely, there are foreign words, scientific terms, that are necessary for workers. There must be a dictionary in the club, and the director of the club must be a qualified worker; he himself must be moving forward, be studying, and be moving others along with him. But a literature cannot be created for workers only that would be separated by a Chinese wall from all other literature—the kind that uses a certain terminology that includes foreign words. The worker's vocabulary must be enlarged, for vocabulary is the tool kit of thought. The enlargement of the active vocabulary of the worker is also one of the tasks of the club.

Club attendance

We come now to the question of frequency of attendance. The main task of the club, as I have said, is to serve as a bridge from the personal fragmentary experience of life, whether in production, in the family, or anywhere else, to the generalized ideas of Leninism, that is, to the slogans and directives of the Communist Party. This is possible only if this fragmentary experience of life is gathered together into a single whole at the club, and this in turn can be accomplished only if, in general, there is a gathering together at the club, that is, if people come to it. [*Laughter*]

This is an absolutely indispensable precondition, and as you know, it is not always realized in life. I received some very valuable documents and materials from the comrades working in the club field—at Glavpolitprosvet—in particular some statistics on club work. These are very incomplete, like all our Soviet statistics at this point, but they still give some interesting indications. In the Soviet Union we have about 2,500 clubs. Of these, 561 clubs have sent in reports on attendance rates. I don't think we would be mistaken if we voiced the suspicion that it was not the clubs doing most poorly that sent in the reports, but the ones that were not, shall we say, too embarrassed to mention attendance.

The statistical summary states that if the total number of visits is divided by 561—the number of clubs reporting—the average obtained is thirteen visits per day. Yes, all in all, you get thirteen persons per day! If we now suppose that the rest of the clubs have done no worse—and that would be too generous an assumption, since, I repeat, the clubs that sent in reports were probably the ones that had the best attendance records—and if we project our average figure to all of the 2,500 or so clubs, we get a total of about 33,300 persons per day, or a million visits a month, or 12 million a year. We will not multiply any farther, into larger units of time.

This number of visits—12 million—is at first glance quite gratifying, but we are interested really in the number of persons who are actually brought within the purview of the clubs. Of course, if we assume that we have 12 million people, that would mean that each visits the club only once a year. And whoever visits a club once every twelve months, in effect doesn't visit it at all. Let us assume that on the average there is one visit per person each month—that is not very often!—then we would find that all the clubs put together involve one million persons, all told!

In real life things look rather different. There are probably three to four hundred thousand who go to the clubs frequently, two or three times a week; then there are two or three hundred thousand who go on the average of once a week; and then a certain number who stop by the club once a month; and even still after that, there would be a rather large number who look in at the club from time to time, by chance, with someone they know, and so forth. But on the average you would still get a million people, figuring one visit per person per month.

Of course this is a very low figure, appallingly low! One must always keep this figure in mind—not of course as a reproach to those who work in the clubs, by no means that— but as an indication of the still extremely limited scope of our cultural work. This is the same kind of statistic as the ones that depict the level of literacy in our country, or the number of children who cannot be educated because of the lack of schools, and other lamentable figures.

These figures point out to us that much, much more still remains to be done than has been done so far. The question of expanding the scope of the club, of increasing its attractiveness for the masses, is tied up in the most intimate way with the totality of our cultural work.

But I think there is one condition that must be singled out for special consideration as a factor of exceptional importance. Without a correct posing of this question we will not find our way even to the other aspects of the problem of expanding the club's influence. What is involved is the voluntary nature of club work.

Not the slightest hint of compulsion

The thirteenth party congress said on this point: "The club should be organized on a voluntary membership basis, which ensures the maximum active and interested participation by its members." Of course, there is no coercion in this area, at least no obvious or open coercion; but unintended, indirect, hidden forms of coercion can arise. And this problem, in the circumstances we face, is the key to all the others.

Comrades, the working class has before it the state, the party, the unions, the cooperatives, as well as the clubs and so on. By its very nature, the state is an organ of coercion, and in the age of revolution, especially at difficult moments in this age, it is an organ of very strict coercion. We have not yet forgotten that we went through War Communism. And if it comes to the question of saving the republic from external enemies, under onerous conditions, we will not promise never to resort to War Communism again.

The state is an apparatus of coercion. It cannot be otherwise. Unlike the state, the party is a voluntary organization of cothinkers. But our party has the leadership of the state; its fate is closely bound up with the fate of this state. Therefore, certain elements of coercion are unavoidably involved in the role and activity of our party, too.

The union organizations embrace a broader mass than does the party. They do not impose prior conditions for membership beyond the general one of class loyalty. But the unions, too, are directly involved, and from a position of leadership, in regulating the workers' material conditions. Through the factory committees, the unions play a very big role in the life of the factory in practice. An element—to be sure not one of outright command-giving—but a certain element of power-wielding holds true for the trade unions too. Of course, whether this element of power-wielding is felt lightly or harshly depends on the skill, tact, and correctness of line of the factory committee and the trade union as a whole; but still the element exists and is unavoidable.

The situation of the club is quite different. Here is where elements of power-wielding, command-giving, and edict-making cannot and must not be present under any conditions. Here we come back to what I began with: Leninism is not a principle imposed from without, as if to say "Here is the truth—get down on your knees to it." No, that is not Leninism. All workers—and in this case all club members—must be given the chance to proceed from their own experience and work their way up to Leninism.

The club is not an organization for transmitting instructions, and still less is it an organization for asserting authority, not at all. Any hint of that within the club or through it would destroy it. School is compulsory, but the club is free. The principle of total and unconditional voluntariness ought to reign within the club. If the worker observes an attitude of bossiness in the director of the club or in its administrative board, even in the slightest degree, that is a crucial and dangerous error that must be corrected.

Not one bit of coercion! Not even a hint of coercion! No order-giving! Not even a hint of order-giving!

It must be said outright that if workers who have come to the club from the factory sense even the slightest bit of administrative pressure, they will leave on the first occasion for the tavern—and they will be right! Any even partly conscious worker knows how necessary iron discipline is in a revolutionary country surrounded by enemies on all sides. They are willing to make sacrifices along military lines and along the lines of production when collective efforts are needed to defend the country. But when they come to the club—to exchange experiences—they should be able to feel that they are among equals, that things are explained to them in a friendly way, and that consideration will be given to their lack of knowledge in an attentive but simple and unassuming way, that no one will give orders, no one will mock them, that there will not be even a hint of external pressure, that they can feel at home and breathe freely.

Many associations organized on a voluntary basis exist or are being set up in our country today: the Down with Illiteracy organization, a society for the aid to homeless children, one for aid to victims of the world revolution, Vozdukhoflot [a volunteer society to promote the creation of an air force], Dobrokhim [a voluntary society for promoting the chemical industry and military chemistry]; they are also talking about a society to promote the cinema, a society for new conditions of everyday life, and so on, and so on.

It is by far not always that the principle of using only volunteers is actually observed. Very often it comes down to a rather formal selection or a virtual assigning of a group of workers to a new job. This is inadvisable and should not be allowed. Such associations, if we really want them to have an educational function, should be freed unqualifiedly of any compulsory quality, direct or indirect—not because such compulsion is onerous but rather because it might not be noticed.

Take Dobrokhim for example. I pick this organization intentionally because it is a recent and more highly specialized one. I have discussed this subject with several directors of clubs at a small conference and met with total agreement on their part. By discussing Dobrokhim we are not departing from the subject of club work, as you will soon see. The one is connected with the other in the closest possible way. We are setting up Dobrokhim as an association for the promotion of the chemical industry and military chemistry. How should it be set up? If we take the road of allotting quotas to factories, of detailing "volunteers" for this work, nothing will come of it. Naturally, it is possible to elect several people at a general meeting, on a motion by the factory committee or party cell, and to call them the Dobrokhim nucleus. Everything then looks fine in the statistics, but in reality what will they do? I don't know, you don't know, and they themselves sometimes don't know. [*Laughter*]

The point is to seek out people in the factory who really are interested in such matters and bring them into the work. Every plant and workshop surely has an enormous variety of individual personality types. Which type do we seize onto most of all? Primarily the revolutionary worker or administrator. That is demanded of us by the age we live in, the character of our times, the tasks facing the party, the trade unions, and the government.

But among the working masses there are many elements,

who are very valuable in their own way, but who are politically less active than the others. There are workers who are absorbed with production as such, who are caught up in their own specialty, who want to advance themselves in their line of work, to raise their own level of qualification, and who read and study their respective areas of work. There are workers who have great interest in scientific and technical subjects, including chemistry. Those are the ones you must find and draw into the work.

Let's say we were at a factory where there were five thousand workers. Let us find, to begin with, three workers who take an interest in chemistry on their own. That is incomparably better than if a general meeting, on a motion by the factory committee, proposes that several popular workers become experts in chemistry, workers who are already swamped with activities. This road leads nowhere; the people who are appointed this way forget about it after a month or half a year; and the slots are left unfilled.

But if a worker has a lively interest in chemistry—and there are such at every factory—then things will be grounded solidly. How are they to be found? Through the club, and the library: only there are their individual interests expressed—in the kind of books they select, in their conversation, in the kind of lectures they go to hear.

As the tasks of public affairs become more complicated, and more and more highly differentiated, a careful individual selection of workers is necessary, both for big jobs and small. Only in that way can the factory single out active fractions for the various voluntary public organizations from within its own midst. This kind of individual selection of workers and further development of their qualifications according to the kind of interests they have, according to their intellectual artillery, can be guaranteed, under party and trade-union supervision, only with properly and broadly functioning clubs. All these associations should in turn be associated together through the clubs, exchange experience through the clubs, and thereby raise their civic qualifications and other ones as well.

The club and the tavern

I have indicated, Comrades, that if the worker senses an element of coercion at the club, even indirectly, he will go to the tavern instead. But it also happens sometimes that the tavern comes to the club. [*Laughter*]

I know that this is only one part of a large and difficult question, and I do not intend to bring up the question of alcoholism and the struggle against it in all its ramifications at this point—though I think we will soon have to deal with this question exhaustively, for it is very closely tied up with the fate of our economic and cultural work.

But I will touch on that part of the problem connected with clubs, and first of all I will recount a little incident that really shocked me and which, it seems to me, we must publicize in order thereby to get at the truth of the situation more exactly.

This incident involved a club called the Lenin Palace of Labor and the question of a food counter. Here is what Comrade Shagaev told me about it—I have written it down word for word: The lunch counter concession has been given to a private individual! Why? Because the cooperative organization and Narpit[6] *refused to set up a counter unless it sold beer.*

The club knew how to stand up for its own interests and hired a private individual to set up the counter; this person charges MSPO prices [MSPO—the main consumer cooperative], gives club members a 20 percent discount, and pays the club seventy gold rubles a month rent. This is a small incident but it has enormous significance!

A workers' club wants to set up a food counter. Who does it turn to? To the cooperative, and Narpit, that is, to organizations of a public character. And what does the cooperative say? We won't do it without beer; it isn't profitable. What does Narpit say? We won't take it on if there's no beer: we'll lose money. What does the club do? It gives its business to a private individual, who sells to club members at prices 20 percent lower than the government-controlled prices, pays 70 gold rubles per month rent, and, we must assume, still makes a profit.

Comrades, this is the greatest shame and scandal, that the cooperative and Narpit, or those of their agencies involved in this case, should so impermissibly choose to follow the path of least resistance, pushing the club in the direction of turning into a tavern. If the club can attract people simply by offering beer, then there's no need to worry about anything else. Just snare the worker on the fishhook of beer (I don't know if one can properly speak of a "hook of beer," since beer is a liquid; still beer does work just as well as any hook)—snare him and drag him in. Then what is the club there for? This leaves the club totally beside the point. What is the job of the cooperative organization? To learn how to operate a lunch counter at low prices, to make a little profit and support the club. But no, they tell us, why take pains and make life difficult for yourself (that would be acting like a petty private merchant!)? Why does beer exist anyway? Sell beer and your business is guaranteed without a lot of trouble. Such is the path of least resistance, which is equally impermissible for the club and for the cooperative organization, because it puts the whole business in a compromising situation and is totally destructive.

This example is all the more striking because the private trader showed that you can get along without beer altogether.

Incidentally, I don't know what proportion of the figure of 12 million visits to clubs per year, which we have estimated, ought to be credited to visits for beer. At any rate it is clear that a food counter with beer certainly can enhance the statistics for attendance rates. [*Laughter*]

There are some who say: Well, after all, this isn't so terrible. There's a rule for handling such situations—don't allow more than two bottles of beer to be drunk at the food counter by each person. A wise rule—who can deny it?—and yet I don't know how you can make sure that it's followed. You would most likely have to check every member of the club with a manometer for measuring the vapor pressure of beer fumes. [*Laughter*] But a manometer is a pretty expensive toy and is hardly within our clubs' means. Besides, I suspect that enforcing the two-bottle rule would cause the club directors too much trouble, of which they have enough already.

Of course, it is possible to attract the masses to the club by offering beer, but to lure them away from the tavern with the help of beer is tantamount to driving out the devil with the help of Old Nick. [*Laughter*] This will not bring many cultural gains, and, besides that, it simply disguises the fact that the club is unable to attract the masses of its own accord, and that is the worst thing of all. It is not out of abstract moral considerations that we must fight against basing our clubs on a foundation of beer, but precisely because we must inspire the club first of all to attract the masses by its own individual qualities and not by means of the substance Tolstoy had in mind when he said, "From that you can get any and all qualities."

Commemorative campaigns and problems of everyday life

People can be attracted to the club if there is life there, and life means the digesting of everyday experiences in their biggest and most important forms. From this point of view, one can only greet with satisfaction the resolution of the last party congress, which removed or at least modified one of the red tape elements in club work—the innumerable campaigns commemorating dates on the calendar.

Here is what the congress resolution said on this point: "In cutting down on the number of campaigns, reducing them to the most important ones only, it is necessary to consistently and untiringly illuminate the most important international and domestic political events as part of the ongoing work."

Comrade Sukhanov, head of one of the larger Moscow clubs, has actually showed me the list of dates that are supposed to be commemorated by campaigns, and one really cannot help saying: Here the dead overshadows the living, and the past weighs down the ability to respond to the present.

This can be seen especially vividly in one case, which I will cite to show the need for making some shifts in the clubs' calendar of commemorations. A big role in club life is taken up, as you know, by the Paris Commune. Of course the Paris Commune was an event of great historic importance. But everything is relative: the Paris Commune figured much more largely in history before October than it did after. Moreover, since October there have been events of exceptional importance which we have ignored. In Italy they had their own Italian Commune in September 1920, which ended in defeat and the victory of fascism.[7] In March 1921 a heroic uprising took place in Germany.[8] Finally, last year in Germany there was the mighty revolutionary movement of the proletariat, which ended in the cruelest kind of defeat, one without a battle.[9]

We of the older generation to a certain extent trained ourselves for October on the basis of the history of the Commune. Naturally, every revolutionist who is at all educated and every young worker who is now studying must have some conception of the Paris Commune. But it is incomparably more important for a communist of the present day and for a young worker being educated as a communist to know and understand the reasons for the defeat of the revolutionary uprising of the Italian proletariat in September 1920, for the defeat of the revolutionary uprising of the German proletariat in March 1921, and finally, for the defeat of the colossal, unprecedented revolutionary movement of the German proletariat during 1923. And if it is a question of choosing between the Paris Commune and last year's revolutionary movement of the German proletariat, one must vote with both hands for last year. Why? Because this provides a living orientation in the events of the day. Even in the case of young workers, if they have before their eyes the signposts of the October revolution, the Italian uprising, the March uprising in Germany, and last year's revolutionary movement in Germany, they will have a perspective on the current world movement, they will feel the rhythm of events, they will look forward more firmly, confidently, and intelligently to the further development of the revolution, and they will understand the conditions under which it can be victorious or be defeated.

But it is not enough just to bring the calendar for club commemorations *closer* to the present day. It is necessary to keep in step with the events and needs of the present. Here we come to questions of daily life. As I understand it, we are to have a report by Comrade Pletnev on this subject.[10] I will therefore just say a few words without going into it deeply, so that I can polemicize with him a little further on, on the plane of theory and principle.

In the realm of everyday problems, Comrades, we have two extreme points of view, which, I imagine, will be overcome with time. These are, on the one hand, *indifference to problems of daily life*, which is hidden behind various arguments, and which sometimes even goes around openly, and *fantasizing about daily life*, on the other. Sometimes these two extremes get along with each other quite well. Indifference to problems of daily life, as I said, sometimes tries to justify itself theoretically along lines like this: Why should we concern ourselves with problems of everyday life? After all, everyday customs and habits are superstructural, but the base consists of economic production. When the economy changes, everything else will change automatically. . . . This sounds terribly Marxist. But in fact it's just terribly ignorant. [*Laughter*]

All superstructures arise upon economic foundations, and if one is to reason in this way, there is no point in studying politics, for politics too arises upon the foundation of production. But the point is that without politics the base will not be changed, for it is politics that is the instrument for changing the economic base. The same is true of everyday life: customs and habits take shape on the basis of a certain form of production, but they have the characteristic of lagging behind changes in the economy, and it is necessary to drive them forward with a revolutionary whip. And if the revolution is in power, it can do this by means of organized pressure, by the power of example, through propaganda, etc.

Of course we cannot leap over our economic foundation and create some sort of ideal phalansteries in our present state of poverty, but building up the economic preconditions for such communes is something that should be done. That is precisely the task. The opposite extreme, fantasizing about everyday problems, amounts to a desire either to race beyond what is economically possible or to fall into abstractions in general, to turn one's thinking away from the real economic possibilities and to replace collective social work toward transforming everyday life with individual moralizing, that is, by separately pumping individuals full of precise principles about how to be a better human being, a method which usually proves of little avail.

I know of three attempts to establish a Society of Friends of the New Way of Life. . . . In my opinion the very name is unfortunate; it can give the wrong direction to people's thinking. It would be much more modest to say Society for the Improvement of Proletarian Living Habits. Then the name would not concede so much in the direction of creating "proletarian culture."

As I say, I know of three attempts: one, carried out in Moscow, was absolutely stillborn. A proclamation was issued but it met with no response, and that was right and proper, for what was there to respond to? [*Laughter*] Secondly, I received a letter from Kharkov about a Society of Friends of the New Way of Life, apparently from some young comrades who are inspired by the best of intentions but are somewhat guilty, I'm afraid, of idealistic fantasizing. Then, just the other day, I received a similar letter from Kazan, also from young comrades.

In Kharkov the task that was set was to implant communist ethics, aesthetics, etc. All this seemed to be posed too generally, in too wide-ranging and idealistic a fashion. When I began to read the program, it turned out that what they meant by communist ethics was the struggle against drunkenness, sloppiness, foul language, etc. These are most praiseworthy aims, but the signboard of "communist ethic" is too all-embracing. Why, even a cultured bourgeois could come under a heading like that, one who doesn't like dirt, and who hardly ever gets drunk or curses aloud, at least not in public. [*Laughter*]

Now, in Kazan the young comrades have set themselves the task of the "scientific organization of life." Their organizational initials thus were NOZh [*Nauchnaya Organizatsia Zhizni*], that is, the word for knife. I'm afraid, Comrades, that it's not a very good idea for this kind of NOZh to fall into inexperienced hands. [*Laughter and applause*] By this I do not mean to condemn the Kharkov and Kazan comrades' initiative, not at all. But one would wish that this initiative might be steered down a more realistic and practical channel.

Even at the time that I first had occasion to write on this

subject, in my book on problems of everyday life, I expressed serious misgivings: on the one hand, I said, it would be a very tempting idea to organize a society dealing with everyday life, but on the other hand, there was a danger that without having the ground solidly prepared underfoot, such a society would go off in the direction of visionary fantasizing. And it looks like that's what is happening.

By what means can society actually be revolutionized? By acting directly upon its constituent elements. Through Narpit, which sets up public eating facilities. Through housing cooperatives, which ought to transform the domestic foundations of daily life. Through the organization of child-care centers. Through clubs. Through libraries. Through voluntary organizations that take up cultural tasks, say, a society of friends of the film, if we really want to establish something that will move the cinema off of dead center. In other words, it is not enough to organize around the abstract idea of "the new life"; rather a whole series of organizations are necessary that will set themselves definite practical tasks in the sphere of everyday life. Only in that way can we revolutionize life.

These practical, single-purpose organizations cannot accommodate to visionary fantasizing. In this work, you can't help matters along with chattering. If you are Narpit, you must provide food, establish public eating facilities, and afterwards we'll check on how many people come to your dining halls and how well satisfied they are with what you provide. If you are Narpit, and the Lenin Palace asks you to set up a food counter for them, don't go handing them an ultimatum on the beer question, or else you will have to deal with us. The same goes for the cooperative.

We already have the primary tools for affecting everyday life and transforming it. These tools are still weak, they need to be strengthened, developed, brought under public control, and new special-purpose organs need to be created alongside of them in order to affect other aspects of everyday life. Along with all this, in order to bring together the still fragmentary experience of the organizations indicated, we must organize, on *this existing foundation*, a society for improving life, and perhaps even one for "the new life," not in the empty sphere of abstraction, though, but on the foundation of the cooperatives, Narpit, communal homes, etc. And such an organization would be composed of leaders, delegates, and members from these existing organizations and institutions.

In the work of assimilating the experience of various "everyday life" organizations, the workers' club ought to occupy a very important place. The club will bring together within its four walls people who are working separately in one or another field of daily life, whether it be on a factory, district, or citywide level; it will bring them together for discussions and exchange of opinions on the problems they face. Here public opinion will be formed, providing a means for control over and checking on all the institutions and undertakings involved in everyday social life.

This in my opinion is the only realistic way of posing the question of reorganizing everyday life. Along these lines we will overcome both indifference and fantasizing.

Antireligious propaganda

Let us pause once again on the question of antireligious propaganda, as one of the most important tasks in the sphere of everyday life. Here too I quote from the thirteenth congress resolution. It is brief: "Considerable attention should be paid to propaganda promoting the natural sciences (antireligious propaganda)." I don't remember whether this kind of formulation has been used before, putting antireligious propaganda in parenthesis after "propaganda promoting the natural sciences." Even if it was, it has now been authoritatively confirmed. This constitutes a demand for a new and different approach to an old problem.

Under the beneficial influence of the impetus generated by your congress, by the very fact of its being called, I have been forced to look through a great deal of published material which ordinarily I would not have had time to review, in particular the satirical journal *Bezbozhnik* (The Godless), where there are a great many cartoons, sometimes quite effective ones, by some of our best cartoonists, a magazine which surely has its positive role to play within certain, primarily urban, circles, but which nevertheless is hardly following the right track in the struggle against religious superstitions. Issue after issue one finds in its pages an ongoing, tireless duel being conducted with Jehovah, Christ, and Allah, hand-to-hand combat between the talented artist Moor[11] and God. Of course, we are, all of us, on Moor's side completely. But if this was all we were doing, or if this was our main work, then I am afraid the duel would end up as a draw. . . .

At any rate, it is perfectly evident and beyond dispute at the present time that we cannot place our antireligious propaganda on the level of a straightforward fight against God. That would not be sufficient for us. We supplant mysticism by materialism, broadening first of all the collective experience of the masses, heightening their active influence on society, widening the horizon of their positive knowledge, and with this as our basis, we also deal blows at religious prejudice, where necessary.

The problem of religion has colossal significance and is most closely bound up with cultural work and with socialist construction. In his youth, Marx said: "The criticism of religion is the basis of all other criticism." In what sense? In the sense that religion is a kind of fictitious knowledge of the universe. This fiction has two sources: the weakness of man before nature, and the incoherence of social relations. Fearing nature or ignoring it, being able to analyze social relations or ignoring them, man in society endeavored to meet his needs by creating fantastic images, endowing them with imaginary reality, and kneeling before his own creations. The basis of this creation lies in the practical need of man to orient himself, which in turn springs from the conditions of the struggle for existence.

Religion is an attempted adaptation to the surrounding environment in order successfully to meet the struggle for existence. In this adaptation there are practical and appropriate rules. But all this is bound up with myths, fantasies, superstitions, unreal knowledge.

Just as all development of culture is the accumulation of knowledge and skill, so is the criticism of religion the foundation for all other criticism. In order to pave the way for correct and real knowledge, it is necessary to remove fictitious knowledge. This is true, however, only when one considers the question as a whole. Historically, not only in individual cases, but also in the development of whole classes, real knowledge is bound up, in different forms and proportions, with religious prejudices. The struggle against a given religion or against religion in general, and against all forms of mythology and superstition, is usually successful only when the religious ideology conflicts with the needs of a given class in a new social environment. In other words, when the accumulation of knowledge and the need for knowledge do not fit into the frame of the unreal truths of religion, then one blow with a critical knife sometimes suffices, and the shell of religion drops off.

The success of the antireligious pressure which we have exerted during the last few years is explained by the fact that advanced layers of the working class, who went through the school of revolution, that is, acquired an activist attitude toward government and social institutions, have easily shaken off the shell of religious prejudices, which was completely undermined by the preceding developments. But the situation changes considerably when antireligious propaganda extends its influence to the less active layers of the population, not only of the villages, but also of the cities. The real knowledge that has been acquired by them is so limited and fragmentary that it can exist side by side with religious prejudices. Naked criticism of these prejudices, finding no support in personal and collective experience, produces no results. It is necessary, therefore, to make the approach from another angle and to enlarge the sphere of social experience and realistic knowledge.

The means towards this end differ. Public dining halls and nurseries may give a revolutionary stimulus to the consciousness of the housewife and may enormously hasten the process of her breaking off from religion. Chemical crop-dusting methods for destroying locusts may play the same role in regard to the peasant. The very fact that the working man and woman participate in club life, which leads them out of the close little cage of the family flat with its icon and image lamp, opens one of the ways to freedom from religious prejudices. And so on and so forth. The clubs can and must accurately gauge the tenacious power of religious prejudices, and find indirect ways to get around them by widening experience and knowledge. And so, in antireligious struggle, too, periods of frontal assault may alternate with periods of blockading, undermining, and encircling maneuvers. In general, we have just entered such a period; but that does not mean that we will not resume a direct attack in the future. It is only necessary to prepare for it.

Has our attack on religion been legitimate or illegitimate? Legitimate. Has it had results? It has. Whom has it drawn to us? Those who by previous experience have been prepared to free themselves completely from religious prejudices. And further? There still remain those whom even the great revolutionary experience of October did not shake free from religion. And here the formal methods of antireligious criticism, satire, caricature, and the like, can accomplish very little. And if one presses too strongly, one may even get an opposite result. One must drill the rock—it is true, Lord knows, it's hard enough rock!—pack in the dynamite sticks, run back the wires for the fuses, and . . . after a while there will be a new explosion and a new fall-off, that is, another layer of the people will be torn from the large mass. . . . The resolution of the party congress tells us that in this field we must at present pass from the explosion and the attack to a more prolonged work of undermining, first of all by way of promoting the natural sciences.

To show how an unprepared frontal assault can sometimes give an entirely unexpected result, I will cite a very interesting example, which is quite recent, and which I know about from comrades only by word of mouth, since unfortunately it has not been brought to light in the press yet. It comes from the experience of the Norwegian Communist Party. As you probably recall, in 1923 this party split into an opportunist majority under the direction of Tranmael,[12] and a revolutionary minority faithful to the Communist International. I asked a comrade who lived in Norway how Tranmael succeeded in winning over the majority—of course, only temporarily. He gave me as one of the causes the religious character of the Norwegian fishermen. Commercial fishing, as you know, has a very low level of technology, and is wholly dependent upon nature. This is the basis for prejudices and superstitions; and religion for the Norwegian fishermen, as the comrade who related this episode to me wittily put it, is something like a protective suit of clothes.

In Scandinavia there were also members of the intelligentsia, academicians who were flirting with religion. They were, quite justly, beaten by the merciless whip of Marxism. The Norwegian opportunists have skillfully taken advantage of this in order to get the fishermen to oppose the Communist International. The fisherman, a revolutionary, deeply sympathetic with the Soviet Republic, favoring the Communist International with all his heart, said to himself.

"It comes down to this. Either I must be for the Communist International, and go without God and fish [*laughter*] or I must, with heavy heart, break from it." And break he did. . . . This illustrates the way in which religion can sometimes cut with a sharp edge even into proletarian politics.

Of course, this applies in a greater degree to our own peasantry, whose traditional religious nature is closely knit with the conditions of our backward agriculture. We shall vanquish the deep-rooted religious prejudices of the peasantry only by bringing electricity and chemistry to peasant agriculture. This, of course, does not mean that we must not take advantage of each separate technical improvement and of each favorable social moment in general for antireligious propaganda, for attaining a partial break with the religious consciousness. No, all this is as obligatory as before, but we must have a correct general perspective. By simply closing the churches, as has been done in some places, and by other administrative excesses, you will not only be unable to reach any decisive success, but on the contrary you will prepare the way for a stronger return of religion.

If it is true that religious criticism is the basis for all other criticism, it is also no less true that in our epoch the electrification of agriculture is the basis for the liquidation of the peasant's superstitions. I would like to quote some remarkable words of Engels, until a short time ago unknown, concerning the potential importance of electrification for agriculture.

Recently, Comrade Ryazanov has brought out Engels's correspondence with Bernstein and Kautsky for the first time—letters that are extraordinarily interesting.[13] Old Engels proves to be doubly fascinating, as more and more new materials of his come to light, revealing his character ever more clearly, from both an ideological and a personal point of view. I shall now cite his quotation touching directly on the question of electrification and on overcoming the gulf between town and country.

The letter was written by Engels to Bernstein in the year 1883. You remember that in the year 1882 the French engineer, Deprez, found a method of transmitting electrical energy through a wire. And if I am not mistaken, at an exhibition in Munich—at any rate, one in Germany—he demonstrated the transmission of electrical energy of one or two horsepower for about fifty kilometers. It made a tremendous impression on Engels, who was extremely sensitive to any inventions in the field of natural science, technology, etc. He wrote to Bernstein: "The newest invention of Deprez ... frees industry from any local limitations, makes possible the use of even the most distant water power. And even if at the beginning it will be used by the cities only, ultimately it must become *the most powerful lever for the abolition of the antagonism between town and country.*"

Vladimir Ilyich did not know of these lines. This correspondence has appeared only recently. It had been kept under a hat, in Germany, in Bernstein's possession, until Comrade Ryazanov managed to get hold of it. I don't know whether you comrades realize with what strict attention, and yet with what strong affection, Lenin used to pore over the works of his masters and elders, Marx and Engels, finding ever new proof of their insight and penetration, the universality of their thought, their ability to see far ahead of their times. I have no doubt that this quotation—in which Engels, on the day after a method has been demonstrated, basically in laboratory terms, for transmitting electrical energy over long distances, looks over industry's head and sees the village and says that this new invention is a most powerful lever for abolishing the antagonism between town and country—I have no doubt that Lenin would have made this quotation a commonplace of our party's thinking. When you read this quotation, it is almost as if old Engels is conversing from the bottom of the sea (he was cremated and his ashes buried at sea, by his wish) with Lenin on Red Square. . . .

Comrades! The process of eliminating religion is dialectical. There are periods of different tempos in the process, determined by the general conditions of culture. All our clubs must be points of observation. They must always help the party orient itself in this task, to find the right moment or strike the right pace.

The complete abolition of religion will be achieved only when there is a fully developed socialist system, that is, a technology that frees man from any degrading dependence upon nature. It can be attained only under social relationships that are free from mystery, that are thoroughly lucid and do not oppress people. Religion translates the chaos of nature and the chaos of social relations into the language of fantastic images. Only the abolition of earthly chaos can end forever its religious reflection. A conscious, reasonable, planned guidance of social life, in all its aspects, will abolish for all time any mysticism and devilry.

Cultural work and "proletarian culture"

Comrades! The main things that I made notes to myself to say about clubs have been said. Beyond this, I only wish to set this work into a certain perspective, and that perspective, it seems to me, can best be presented if we take a critical approach to the question of clubs as "smithies of proletarian class culture."

I am picking up Comrade Pletnev's formula. If I wish to polemicize with him, it is not because I do not value his cultural work, which, on the contrary, I, like all of you, attribute great importance to, but because I think there is an element in his theoretical posing of this question that presents certain dangers. In his pamphlet on club work—the 1923 edition—Pletnev says: "The club itself, as such, should become, for all its members, a smithy in which proletarian class culture is forged. It is necessary to stress as forcefully as possible that the creation of proletarian culture is a process of class struggle, a consecutive phase of struggle (struggle! I repeat) of the proletariat against bourgeois domination." In an article this year, the same formula is repeated, but with an interesting modification: "The club is the center for the training of proletarian public awareness, where the proletariat forges the *elements* of proletarian class culture." Previously what was said was "proletarian class culture," but here it says *"elements* of proletarian class culture," that is, it is stated slightly more cautiously.

Comrades, it is not out of doctrinairism or pickiness, but for reasons of principle, and by the same token, for reasons of a practical nature, that I am impelled to point out that this is an incorrect way of posing the problem. In the article I have quoted from, Comrade Pletnev is arguing with a trade union worker (I have not read the latter's article) and is giving a general characterization of club work, which in my opinion is quite correctly done, but he concludes with a theoretical formulation that goes halfway toward liquidating the basic thesis of the article.

How is the club actually going to forge a new proletarian class culture? What does that mean? Comrade Lenin wrote about proletarian culture in one of his last articles, "Page from a Diary." Those lines have been quoted many times, and frequently so as to conceal thoughts directly opposite in character to the quotation—a technique that is encountered often enough. Here is what Lenin said: "At a time when we hold forth on proletarian culture and the relation in which it stands to bourgeois culture," it came out that we were cultural ignoramuses in the matter of schools, and so forth. "This shows what a vast amount of urgent spade-work we still have to do to reach the standard of an ordinary West-European civilized country."

Here, in Lenin's way, the emphasis is on "normally civilized," that is to say, *bourgeois.* That, then, is the kind of

level we have to reach first of all! In his article "On Cooperation," Lenin says: "Now the emphasis is changing and
shifting to peaceful, organizational, 'cultural' work." And
further on: "If we leave aside [questions of international
politics and revolution], and confine ourselves to internal
economic relations, the emphasis in our work is certainly
shifting to education."[14] But Comrade Pletnev constantly
uses the term "culture-bearing" (that is, culturization) with
a hint of contempt and counterposes it to the "forging of
proletarian culture."

What is to be understood by the term "proletarian culture?" In what way can the club become the smithy of proletarian culture? In what way? For the club, though a very
important and even vital part of our social fabric, still is only
a part, one that certainly cannot by itself produce anything
that differs qualitatively from what the society as a whole
produces. So in what way can the club become the smithy
of proletarian class culture? And again, the question that
needs to be answered before anything else: What is to be
understood by the term "proletarian culture?"

We are using every means, including the clubs, to build
a socialist economy, a socialist society, and consequently a
socialist, classless culture. But before that has been accomplished, a prolonged transitional period still remains, one
that will also have a culture of its own kind, one that will
be a very ill-formed and very contradictory one for a while.
I would like to think that it is precisely this transitional period that you wish to designate as "proletarian culture." Of
course, terminology can be used in different ways and we
should not quarrel over wording. But it is necessary to settle
on the meanings of terms in order to get to the essence of
the subject without mix-ups.

For the sake of comparison let me take another, parallel
term. We are moving toward a socialist economy through a
transitional era. What should the economy of this transitional

era be called? We call it NEP. Is this a scientific term? Not in the slightest degree. This is a conventional designation for lack of a more appropriate one. Vladimir Ilyich frequently referred to our transitional regime as state capitalism, but in so doing always added the phrase "in quotation marks," or he called it "state capitalism of a very, very particular or peculiar kind." Many people do not understand this qualification, and say *state capitalism* outright, and even call our state trusts and syndicates "organs of state capitalism," which is of course grossly incorrect, as Vladimir Ilyich explained in his article "On Cooperation."

Thus, Lenin proposed a highly conditional term (one in quotation marks!), "state capitalism," for the system transitional to socialism. If you wish, we can call this transitional economic period the period of "forging proletarian economy." I don't like this term since it does not express the essence of the matter (the whole substance being in the transitional state), but if they urge me and offer to use quotation marks, or better, double quotation marks, I am almost ready to say, "O.K., what can you do? If that will make Comrade Pletnev feel better." [*Pletnev from his seat: "Never!" Laughter*] All the better.

But there is really a complete parallel here: proletarian culture, if this term is to be taken seriously, should have a base under it, in the form of proletarian economy—all the more so since culture tends to lag behind the economic base a little. But if you refuse (and that would be fully justifiable!) to designate our transitional economy a "proletarian class economy," then by the same token you have fairly well dug the ground out from under the abstraction of proletarian culture.

What is our economy characterized by? In his booklet on the tax in kind, Lenin explained that our transitional economy contains remnants of patriarchal society, innumerable elements of petty commodity production, that there are private-capitalist elements, state-capitalist elements, and finally, elements of socialist economy. Altogether this constitutes the economy of the transitional period, which can be called "state capitalism" (in quotation marks!) or—as some have proposed—a "market-socialist economy."

It is possible to settle on terminology, but the concepts involved have to be grasped thoroughly. And what does the culture of the transitional period consist of? Of vestiges, still very powerful ones, of the culture of the aristocratic period—and not everything here is useless. We are not going to throw out Pushkin and Tolstoy. We need them. It also consists of elements of bourgeois culture, first of all, of bourgeois technical know-how, which we need even more. We are still living on the basis of bourgeois technical knowledge and to a considerable extent on the basis of bourgeois specialists. For the time being, we have not yet built our own factories, and are working in those we got from bourgeois hands. The culture of the transitional period consists, further, of an overwhelming petty-bourgeois, that is, primarily peasant, lack of culture.

Our culture also consists of the efforts by our party and government to raise the cultural level of the proletariat, and after it, that of the peasantry—if only to the level of a "normally civilized country." It also consists of our socialist construction and, finally, of our ideal of communism, which guides all our constructive work.

There you have the kind of complicated and contradictory elements that are found in the culture (and absence of culture) of the transitional period. How then is the club able to create a proletarian class culture? To me this is absolutely incomprehensible! The club, by connecting and merging together the disconnected experience of the workers, helps them to translate their experience into the language of politics, literature, and art, and in so doing raises the cultural level of certain layers of the proletariat and makes socialist construction easier for them—that is indisputable. But in what way can the club, as such, forge a class culture of the proletariat? This actually involves making major concessions to the laboratory point of view concerning culture. Of course you can pick dozens of capable young workers and by laboratory methods teach them verse composition, painting, and dramatics. Is this useful? Extremely so. But it is necessary for them to conceive of their place and role in the overall economic and cultural development of the country realistically. And to place before them the perspective of creating proletarian class culture by means of the clubs is to start them on a road which can lead them to turning their backs on the masses, i.e., away from the real process of creating a socialist culture, and trying to counterpose the "pure" work of little circles to this process, as has already been attempted before now. Such relapses are possible. But it is obvious that the creation of some sort of proletarian culture by the laboratory methods of Bogdanov has nothing in common with Leninism.[15]

It is true that even Lenin used the expression "proletarian culture" sometimes but it is noteworthy that he only used it in 1919 and 1920, and later, as well as I can remember, he stopped using it precisely because he was afraid he might lend support, even indirectly, i.e., by using a term that was not precise enough, to an incorrect point of view. But in what sense did Lenin refer to proletarian culture? In his speech to the third youth congress in 1920, he said: "Proletarian culture must be *the logical development of the store of knowledge* mankind has accumulated under the yoke of capitalist, landowner, and bureaucratic society." Notice that he said "logical development," and not a hint of the term "combat," nor of "forging" culture in the clubs. Planned, regular development in the economy, in the schools, in the government, in all our work, in all our building toward socialism. Thus, Lenin used the term "proletarian culture" only for the purpose of fighting against the idealist, laboratory-oriented, schematic, Bogdanovist interpretation of it. What we need most of all is literacy—simple literacy, political literacy, literacy in the daily routine, literacy in hygiene, literacy in literature, literacy in the field of entertainment. . . . From literacy in all these fields a general *cultural literacy* will be formed.

They will say, mind you, that this sounds like a nonclass concept. It is nothing of the sort! The proletariat is the ruling class here—and that's precisely what this discussion is about—it is precisely the proletariat that is to extract the most important, urgent, and elementary things from the cultural storehouses accumulated by the other classes. At this point, the proletariat needs to appropriate for itself the primary elements of culture: universal literacy and the four laws of arithmetic. Indeed if the entire country was literate and knew the four laws of arithmetic, we would practically be living under socialism, for socialism, as we have heard, is nothing other than a society of cultured, that is, first of all, literate, cooperative producers.

The proletariat in power is the master of the state. That is what we are talking about, about raising the cultural level of this proletariat. Here the basic class criterion has been provided, not only subjectively but objectively as well. But we cannot take the club and say to it, "Create a proletarian class culture!" because then it would turn its back on the proletariat and close itself off. No, we say to the club, "Raise the cultural and civic level of the illiterate, barely literate, and semiliterate workers and thereby lay the basis for socialist culture." [*Applause*]

That is the correct way to pose the question. And that is why Lenin was not afraid of the word "culturization." It was natural that we used this word with scorn before we won power, for the "culturizers" did not understand the chief preconditions for cultural work on the broad historic scale—the necessity for the overthrow of the bourgeoisie and the conquest of power by the proletariat. But once power has been conquered, culturization becomes the most important part of the work of building socialism. We cannot take a scornful attitude toward this word now. Today the word *culturization*, to us, to revolutionists, to communists of the Soviet Republic, has completely lost that shade of meaning that it had before.

On the basis of the nationalization of industry, under the dictatorship of the proletariat, in a country protected by the monopoly of foreign trade and defended by the Red Army, the main task in building socialism is equivalent to that of filling the new form, step by step, with cultural content. The work of culturizing is for us a fundamental revolutionary task.

But it goes without saying that we cannot close ourselves off within the bounds of a Soviet state protected by the Red Army. The question of the world revolution still stands before us in all its magnitude. There are nations and states— and they are the majority—where the main question is not one of culturization but of conquering power. And for that reason Lenin says, in the article I quoted from, that nine-tenths of our work comes down to culturization—if we abstract ourselves from questions of international politics and revolution.

But we can abstract ourselves from this question only for purposes of argument, in order to clarify the question. We cannot do so politically. That is why our cultural and culturizing work in the clubs and through the clubs should be linked up, to the greatest possible extent, with our international revolutionary work. There should be drive belts leading from all the little pulleys of petty, personal concerns to the giant flywheel of the world revolution. This is precisely why I have pointed to such questions as the events in Italy and Germany. These are milestones of revolutionary development which it is necessary to study so that every worker will get correct bearings in the international situation.

Everything—from the pettiest problems of the factory floor and workshop to the most fundamental problems of the world revolution—should pass through the club. But for this, it is necessary to strengthen the club, to improve it, to raise the level of qualifications of its directors, and to improve the material situation of the club and of those who staff it, and to do this by every possible means.

Lenin wrote that we should raise the teacher to a height such as has never before been attained in the world. This idea also applies totally and completely to those who staff the clubs. Perhaps it would be appropriate for us to conduct an experiment in the near future, by placing first-class workers in charge of a few clubs—an experiment to see what can be accomplished, given our resources, with the human material that we have and with the application of initiative and a broad perspective. If the club is not a smithy where proletarian culture is forged, it is one of the most valuable links in our total system for influencing the working masses and creating a new, socialist culture. To the extent that we can draw ever wider layers of the masses into involvement in public affairs, the club's aim should be to bring them to Leninism, not as to an awe-inspiring truth handed down from on high and demanding "Get down on your knees before me," but as to a generalization of their own experience, an experience which was disconnected and fragmentary, which has been gathered together by the club, generalized politically by the party, defended and strengthened by the authority of the state.

And if we can use workers' clubs to teach every working man and woman to deduce the foundations of the new world from those of the world today, then we will not only make them capable of understanding this world but of transforming it as well, making it a wider world, a more spacious world, a happier world to live in. [*Stormy applause*]

The party in the fields of art and philosophy

JUNE 16, 1933

Dear Comrades:

Your letter poses very important problems, which do not, however, admit, in my opinion, of general and categorical solutions suitable in all cases.

As an organization we have as our point of departure not only definite political ideas, but certain philosophical and scientific methods. We base ourselves on dialectical materialism, from which flow conclusions concerning not only politics and science, but also art. Still, there is a vast difference in our attitude towards these conclusions. We cannot, to any similar degree, exercise the same rigorous control over art, by the very nature of this activity, as over politics. The party is obliged to permit a very extensive liberty

A letter in reply to the American comrades Glee, Ross, and Morris, written at the end of a four-and-one-half-year exile in Turkey. From The Militant, *July 22, 1933.*

in the field of art, eliminating pitilessly only that which is directed against the revolutionary tasks of the proletariat. On the other hand, the party cannot assume an immediate and direct responsibility for the declarations of its various members in the field of art, even when it accords them its tribune. The maintenance of these two rules—the preservation of the liberty necessary for individual creation, and the nonassignment to the party of the responsibility for all its roads—is especially obligatory in those cases where it is a question not of theoreticians in the field of art, but of the artists themselves: painters, men of letters, etc.

In addition, the party must be able to distinguish clearly the line where generalization in the field of art passes directly into the field of politics. Without making any concessions in principle here, the party must confine itself in the case of artists to rectifications, firm but tactical, of any false political conclusions flowing from their artistic views.

Marx expressed this idea in a jocular phrase about Freiligrath: "Poets are queer fish" (*"Die Dichter sind sonderbare Kauze"*). Lenin applied different criteria to Bogdanov, the theoretician and professional politician, and to Gorky, the artist, in spite of the fact that for a certain period of time Bogdanov and Gorky were closely associated in politics. Lenin proceeded from the viewpoint that through his artistic activity and his popularity Gorky could endow the cause of the revolution with benefits far exceeding the harm of his erroneous declarations and actions, which, moreover, the party could always correct in good time and tactfully.

Viewed from this standpoint, philosophical activity lies between art and politics, closer to politics than to art. In philosophy, the party itself occupies a distinct militant position, which is not the case—at least not to the same extent—in the field of art. Objections to the effect that by the "dogmatization" and "canonization" of dialectical materialism the party prevents the free development of philosophical and scientific thought do not deserve serious attention. No factory can work without basing itself upon a definite technological doctrine. No hospital can treat its patients if the physicians do not base themselves on the established teachings of pathology. It would be sheer folly to permit dilettantes to experiment arbitrarily in the factory or in the hospital, on the pretext that they consider themselves "innovators." Innovators must first prove their right to influence practical technology and medicine.

The party must be especially vigilant toward those "innovators" who only warm up stale critical dishes, or towards those who are still in the period of investigating, with uncertain results. But least of all does this signify that in the sphere of philosophy the party can act as if all questions have already been resolved for it, and that it has nothing to expect from the further development of scientific thought. It is not an easy matter to find the correct political line in this field. It is acquired only by experience and by a flexible leadership. Just as in artillery fire, the target is usually hit by a series of shots which fall far and then short of the mark.

It is needless to point out that the question "How do the philosophical views of a certain person or a certain group refract themselves in the field of politics and party organization?" always has a tremendous significance for the elaboration of correct control by the party. Thus Lenin fought mercilessly against Gorky in 1917, when the necessity of a revolutionary overthrow stood above all other considerations. On the other hand, it must be considered as the greatest shame that the Stalinist bureaucracy is transforming Barbusse the *novelist* into a leading *political* figure, in spite of the fact that it is precisely in politics that Barbusse marches arm in arm with Renner, Vandervelde, Monnet, and Paul Louis.[16]

I am very much afraid that I have not given you a satisfactory reply to the practical questions put to me. But what has been said explains, I hope, why I could not give such a reply, which requires a concrete knowledge of the situation and the personal conditions. Just the same, perhaps these brief considerations will at least partially help in the working out of a correct policy in this complicated and responsible field.

With communist greetings,
L. Trotsky

The ABC of dialectical materialism

DECEMBER 15, 1939

Theoretical skepticism and eclecticism

In the January 1939 issue of the *New International,* a long article was published by comrades Burnham and Shachtman:[17] "Intellectuals in Retreat." The article, while containing many correct ideas and apt political characterizations, was marred by a fundamental defect if not flaw. While polemicizing against opponents who consider themselves—without sufficient reason—above all as proponents of "theory," the article deliberately did not elevate the problem to a theoretical height. It was absolutely necessary to explain why the American "radical" intellectuals accept Marxism without

---

An excerpt from In Defense of Marxism, *a collection of articles Trotsky wrote shortly before his death as contributions to a struggle in the Socialist Workers Party. The full text is available from Pathfinder Press, in a 1942 translation by John G. Wright.*

the dialectic (a clock without a spring).

The secret is simple. In no other country has there been such rejection of the class struggle as in the land of "unlimited opportunity." The denial of social contradictions as the moving force of development led to the denial of the dialectic as the logic of contradictions in the domain of theoretical thought. Just as in the sphere of politics it was thought possible everybody could be convinced of the correctness of a "just" program by means of clever syllogisms and society could be reconstructed through "rational" measures, so in the sphere of theory it was accepted as proved that Aristotelian logic, lowered to the level of "common sense," was sufficient for the solution of all questions.

Pragmatism, a mixture of rationalism and empiricism, became the national philosophy of the United States. The theoretical methodology of Max Eastman[18] is not fundamentally different from the methodology of Henry Ford—both regard living society from the point of view of an "engineer" (Eastman—platonically). Historically the present disdainful attitude toward the dialectic is explained simply by the fact that the grandfathers and great-grandmothers of Max Eastman and others did not need the dialectic in order to conquer territory and enrich themselves. But times have changed and the philosophy of pragmatism has entered a period of bankruptcy just as has American capitalism.

The authors of the article did not show, could not and did not care to show, this internal connection between philosophy and the material development of society, and they frankly explained why.

> The two authors of the present article [they wrote of themselves] differ thoroughly on their estimate of the general theory of dialectical materialism, one of them accepting it and the other rejecting it. . . . There is nothing anomalous in such a situation. Though theory is

doubtless always in one way or another related to practice the relation is not invariably direct or immediate; and as we have before had occasion to remark, human beings often act inconsistently. From the point of view of each of the authors there is in the other a certain such inconsistency between "philosophical theory" and political practice, which might on some occasion lead to decisive concrete political disagreement. But it does not now, nor has anyone yet demonstrated that agreement or disagreement on the more abstract doctrines of dialectical materialism necessarily affects today's and tomorrow's concrete political issues—and political parties, programs, and struggles are based on such concrete issues. We all may hope that as we go along or when there is more leisure, agreement may also be reached on the more abstract questions. Meanwhile there is fascism and war and unemployment.

What is the meaning of this thoroughly astonishing reasoning? Inasmuch as *some* people through a bad method *sometimes* reach correct conclusions, and inasmuch as some people through a correct method *not infrequently* reach incorrect conclusions, therefore . . . the method is not of great importance. We shall meditate upon methods sometime when we have more leisure, but now we have other things to do. Imagine how a worker would react upon complaining to his foreman that his tools were bad and receiving the reply: With bad tools it is possible to turn out a good job, and with good tools many people only waste material. I am afraid that such a worker, particularly if he is on piecework, would respond to the foreman with an unacademic phrase. A worker is faced with refractory materials which show resistance and which because of that compel him to appreciate fine tools, whereas a petty-bourgeois intellectual—alas!—utilizes as his "tools" fugitive observations and superficial generalizations—until major events club him on the head.

To demand that every party member occupy himself with the philosophy of dialectics naturally would be lifeless pedantry. But a worker who has gone through the school of the class struggle gains from his own experience an inclination toward dialectical thinking. Even if unaware of this term, he readily accepts the method itself and its conclusions. With a petty bourgeois it is worse. There are, of course, petty-bourgeois elements organically linked with the workers, who go over to the proletarian point of view without an internal revolution. But these constitute an insignificant minority. The matter is quite different with the academically trained petty bourgeoisie. Their theoretical prejudices have already been given finished form at the school bench. Inasmuch as they succeeded in gaining a great deal of knowledge both useful and useless without the aid of the dialectic, they believe that they can continue excellently through life without it. In reality they dispense with the dialectic only to the extent that they fail to check, to polish, and to sharpen theoretically their tools of thought, and to the extent that they fail to break practically from the narrow circle of their daily relationships. When thrown against great events they are easily lost and relapse again into petty-bourgeois ways of thinking.

Appealing to "inconsistency" as justification for an unprincipled theoretical bloc signifies giving oneself bad credentials as a Marxist. Inconsistency is not accidental, and in politics it does not appear solely as an individual symptom. Inconsistency usually serves a social function. There are social groupings which cannot be consistent. Petty-bourgeois elements who have not rid themselves of hoary petty-bourgeois tendencies are systematically compelled within a workers' party to make theoretical compromises with their own conscience.

Comrade Shachtman's attitude toward the dialectical

method, as manifested in the above-quoted argumentation, cannot be called anything but eclectical skepticism. It is clear that Shachtman became infected with this attitude not in the school of Marx but among the petty-bourgeois intellectuals to whom all forms of skepticism are proper.

Warning and verification

The article astonished me to such an extent that I immediately wrote to Comrade Shachtman:

> I have just read the article you and Burnham wrote on the intellectuals. Many parts are excellent. However, the section on the dialectic is the greatest blow that you, personally, as the editor of the *New International*, could have delivered to Marxist theory. Comrade Burnham says: "I don't recognize the dialectic." It is clear and everybody has to acknowledge it. But you say: "I recognize the dialectic, but no matter; it does not have the slightest importance." Reread what you wrote. This section is terribly misleading for the readers of the *New International* and the best of gifts to the Eastmans of all kinds. Good! We will speak about it publicly.

My letter was written January 20, some months before the present discussion. Shachtman did not reply until March 5, when he answered in effect that he couldn't understand why I was making such a stir about the matter. On March 9, I answered Shachtman in the following words:

> I did not reject in the slightest degree the possibility of collaboration with the antidialecticians, but only the advisability of writing an article together where the question of the dialectic plays, or should play, a very important role. The polemic develops on two planes: political and theoretical. Your political criticism is OK. Your

theoretical criticism is insufficient; it stops at the point at which it should just become aggressive. Namely, the task consists of showing that their mistakes (insofar as they are *theoretical* mistakes) are products of their incapacity and unwillingness to think the things through dialectically. This task could be accomplished with a very serious pedagogical success. Instead of this you declare that dialectics is a private matter and that one can be a very good fellow without dialectical thinking.

By allying himself in *this* question with the antidialectician Burnham, Shachtman deprived himself of the possibility of showing why Eastman, Hook, and many others began with a philosophical struggle against the dialectic but finished with a political struggle against the socialist revolution. That is, however, the essence of the question.

The present political discussion in the party has confirmed my apprehensions and warning in an incomparably sharper form than I could have expected, or, more correctly, feared. Shachtman's methodological skepticism bore its deplorable fruits in the question of the nature of the Soviet state. Burnham began some time ago by constructing, purely empirically, on the basis of his immediate impressions, a nonproletarian and nonbourgeois state, liquidating in passing the Marxist theory of the state as the organ of class rule. Shachtman unexpectedly took an evasive position: "The question, you see, is subject to further consideration;" moreover, the sociological definition of the USSR does not possess any direct and immediate significance for our "political tasks" in which Shachtman agrees completely with Burnham. Let the reader again refer to what these comrades wrote concerning the dialectic. Burnham rejects the dialectic. Shachtman seems to accept, but . . . the divine gift of "inconsistency" permits them to meet on common political conclusions. *The attitude of each of them toward the nature of the Soviet state reproduces point for point their attitude toward the dialectic.*

In both cases Burnham takes the leading role. This is not surprising: he possesses a method—pragmatism. Shachtman has no method. He adapts himself to Burnham. Without assuming complete responsibility for the anti-Marxian conceptions of Burnham, he defends his bloc of aggression against the Marxian conceptions with Burnham in the sphere of philosophy as well as in the sphere of sociology. In both cases Burnham appears as a pragmatist and Shachtman as an eclectic. This example has this invaluable advantage, that the complete parallelism between Burnham's and Shachtman's positions upon two different planes of thought and upon two questions of primary importance, will strike the eyes even of comrades who have had no experience in purely theoretical thinking. The method of thought can be dialectical or vulgar, conscious or unconscious, but it exists and makes itself known.

Last January we heard from our authors: "But it does not now, nor has anyone yet demonstrated that agreement or disagreement on the more abstract doctrines of dialectical materialism necessarily affects today's and tomorrow's concrete political issues. . . ." Nor has anyone yet demonstrated! Not more than a few months passed before Burnham and Shachtman themselves demonstrated that their attitude toward such an "abstraction" as dialectical materialism found its precise manifestation in their attitude toward the Soviet state.

To be sure it is necessary to mention that the difference between the two instances is rather important, but it is of a political and not a theoretical character. In both cases Burnham and Shachtman formed a bloc on the basis of rejection and semi-rejection of the dialectic. But in the first instance that bloc was directed against the opponents of the proletarian party. In the second instance the bloc was concluded against the Marxist wing of their own party. The front of military operations, so to speak, has changed, but the weapon remains the same.

True enough, people are often inconsistent. Human consciousness nevertheless tends toward a certain homogeneity. Philosophy and logic are compelled to rely upon this homogeneity of human consciousness and not upon what this homogeneity lacks, that is, inconsistency. Burnham does not recognize the dialectic, but the dialectic recognizes Burnham, that is, extends its sway over him. Shachtman thinks that the dialectic has no importance in political conclusions, but in the political conclusions of Shachtman himself we see the deplorable fruits of his disdainful attitude toward the dialectic. We should include this example in the textbooks on dialectical materialism.

Last year I was visited by a young British professor of political economy, a sympathizer of the Fourth International. During our conversation on the ways and means of realizing socialism, he suddenly expressed the tendencies of British utilitarianism in the spirit of Keynes and others: "It is necessary to determine a clear economic end, to choose the most reasonable means for its realization," etc. I remarked: "I see that you are an adversary of dialectics." He replied, somewhat astonished: "Yes, I don't see any use in it." "However," I replied to him, "the dialectic enabled me on the basis of a few of your observations upon economic problems to determine what category of philosophical thought you belong to—this alone shows that there is an appreciable value in the dialectic." Although I have received no word about my visitor since then, I have no doubt that this antidialectic professor maintains the opinion that the USSR is not a workers' state, that unconditional defense of the USSR is an "outmoded" opinion, that our organizational methods are bad, etc. If it is possible to place a given person's general type of thought on the basis of his relation to concrete practical problems, it is also possible to predict approximately, knowing his general type of thought, how a given individual will approach one or another practical question. That is the incomparable educational value of the dialectical method of thought.

The ABC of materialist dialectics

Gangrenous skeptics like Souvarine believe that "nobody knows" what the dialectic is.[19] And there are "Marxists" who kowtow reverently before Souvarine and hope to learn something from him. And these Marxists hide not only in the *Modern Monthly*.[20] Unfortunately, a current of Souvarinism exists in the present opposition of the SWP. And here it is necessary to warn young comrades: Beware of this malignant infection!

The dialectic is neither fiction nor mysticism, but a science of the forms of our thinking insofar as it is not limited to the daily problems of life but attempts to arrive at an understanding of more complicated and drawn-out processes. The dialectic and formal logic bear a relationship similar to that between higher and lower mathematics.

I will here attempt to sketch the substance of the problem in a very concise form. The Aristotelian logic of the simple syllogism starts from the proposition that A is equal to A. This postulate is accepted as an axiom for a multitude of practical human actions and elementary generalizations. But in reality A is not equal to A. This is easy to prove if we observe these two letters under a lens—they are quite different from each other. But, one can object, the question is not of the size or the form of the letters, since they are only symbols for equal quantities, for instance, a pound of sugar. The objection is beside the point; in reality a pound of sugar is never equal to a pound of sugar—a more delicate scale always discloses a difference. Again one can object: but a pound of sugar is equal to itself. Neither is this true—all bodies change uninterruptedly in size, weight, color, etc. They are never equal to themselves. A sophist will respond that a pound of sugar is equal to itself "at a given moment." Aside from the extremely dubious practical value of this "axiom," it does not withstand theoretical criticism either. How should we conceive the word "moment"? If it is an infinitesimal interval of time, then a pound of sugar is subjected during the course of that "moment" to inevitable changes. Or is the "moment" a purely mathematical abstraction, that is, a zero of time? But everything exists in time; and existence itself is an uninterrupted process of transformation; time is consequently a fundamental element of existence. Thus the axiom A is equal to A signifies that a thing is equal to itself if it does not change, that is, if it does not exist.

At first glance it could seem that these "subtleties" are useless. In reality they are of decisive significance. The axiom A is equal to A appears on one hand to be the point of departure for all our knowledge, on the other hand the point of departure for all the errors in our knowledge. To make use of the axiom A is equal to A with impunity is possible only within certain *limits*. When quantitative changes in A are negligible for the task at hand, then we can presume A is equal to A. This is, for example, the manner in which a buyer and a seller consider a pound of sugar. We consider the temperature of the sun likewise. Until recently we considered the buying power of the dollar in the same way. But quantitative changes beyond certain limits become converted into qualitative. A pound of sugar subjected to the action of water or kerosene ceases to be a pound of sugar. A dollar in the embrace of a president ceases to be a dollar. To determine at the right moment the critical point where quantity changes into quality is one of the most important and difficult tasks in all the spheres of knowledge, including sociology.

Every worker knows that it is impossible to make two completely equal objects. In the elaboration of bearing–brass into cone bearings, a certain deviation is allowed for the cones which should not, however, go beyond certain limits (this is called tolerance). By observing the norms of tolerance, the cones are considered as being equal (A is equal to A). When the tolerance is exceeded, the quantity goes over into quality; in other words, the cone bearings become inferior or completely worthless.

Our scientific thinking is only a part of our general practice, including techniques. For concepts there also exists "tolerance" which is established not by formal logic issuing from the axiom A is equal to A, but by dialectical logic issuing from the axiom that everything is always changing. "Common sense" is characterized by the fact that it systematically exceeds dialectical "tolerance."

Vulgar thought operates with such concepts as capitalism, morals, freedom, workers' state, etc., as fixed abstractions, presuming that capitalism is equal to capitalism, morals are equal to morals, etc. Dialectical thinking analyzes all things and phenomena in their continuous change, while determining in the material conditions of those changes that critical limit beyond which A ceases to be A, a workers' state ceases to be a workers' state.

The fundamental flaw of vulgar thought lies in the fact that it wishes to content itself with motionless imprints of reality, which consists of eternal motion. Dialectical thinking gives to concepts, by means of closer approximations, corrections, concretizations, a richness of content and flexibility, I would even say a succulence, which to a certain extent brings them close to living phenomena. Not capitalism in general, but a given capitalism at a given stage of development. Not a workers' state in general, but a given workers' state in a backward country in an imperialist encirclement, etc.

Dialectical thinking is related to vulgar thinking in the same way that a motion picture is related to a still photograph. The motion picture does not outlaw the still photograph but combines a series of them according to the laws of motion. Dialectics does not deny the syllogism, but teaches us to combine syllogisms in such a way as to bring our understanding closer to the eternally changing reality. Hegel in his *Logic* established a series of laws: change of quantity into quality, development through contradictions, conflict of content and form, interruption of continuity, change of possibility into inevitability, etc., which are just as important for theoretical thought as is the simple syllogism for more elementary tasks.

Hegel wrote before Darwin and before Marx. Thanks to the powerful impulse given to thought by the French Revolution, Hegel anticipated the general movement of science. But because it was only an *anticipation*, although by a genius, it received from Hegel an idealistic character. Hegel operated with ideological shadows as the ultimate reality. Marx demonstrated that the movement of these ideological shadows reflected nothing but the movement of material bodies.

We call our dialectic *materialist*, since its roots are neither in heaven nor in the depths of our "free will," but in objective reality, in nature. Consciousness grew out of the unconscious, psychology out of physiology, the organic world out of the inorganic, the solar system out of nebula. On all the rungs of this ladder of development, the quantitative changes were transformed into qualitative. Our thought, including dialectical thought, is only one of the forms of the expression of changing matter. There is place within this system for neither God, nor Devil, nor immortal soul, nor eternal norms of laws and morals. The dialectic of thinking, having grown out of the dialectic of nature, possesses consequently a thoroughly materialist character.

Darwinism, which explained the evolution of species through quantitative transformations passing into qualitative, was the highest triumph of the dialectic in the whole field of organic matter. Another great triumph was the discovery of the table of atomic weights of chemical elements and further the transformation of one element into another.

With these transformations (species, elements, etc.) is closely linked the question of classifications, just as important in the natural as in the social sciences. Linnaeus's system (eighteenth century), utilizing as its starting point the immutability of species, was limited to the description and classification of plants according to their external characteristics. The infantile period of botany is analogous to the infantile period of logic, since the forms of our thought develop like everything that lives. Only decisive repudiation of the idea of fixed species, only the study of the history of the evolution of plants and their anatomy prepared the basis for a really scientific classification.

Marx, who in distinction from Darwin was a conscious dialectician, discovered a basis for the scientific classification of human societies in the development of their productive forces and the structure of the relations of ownership which constitute the anatomy of society. Marxism substituted for the vulgar descriptive classification of societies and states, which even up to now still flourishes in the universities, a materialistic dialectical classification. Only through using the method of Marx is it possible correctly to determine both the concept of a workers' state and the moment of its downfall.

All this, as we see, contains nothing "metaphysical" or "scholastic," as conceited ignorance affirms. Dialectical logic expresses the laws of motion in contemporary scientific thought. The struggle against materialist dialectics on the contrary expresses a distant past, conservatism of the petty bourgeoisie, the self-conceit of university routinists and . . . a spark of hope for an afterlife.

Notes

Notes to Part 1

1. The full text of this article begins on page 124.

2. *The New Economic Policy* (NEP) was initiated in 1921 to replace "military communism," which had prevailed during the civil war and which had led to conflict between the government and the peasants as industrial production declined drastically and grain was requisitioned and confiscated from the peasants. NEP was adopted as a temporary measure to revive the economy after the civil war, and allowed a limited revival of free trade inside the Soviet Union, and foreign concessions alongside the nationalized sectors of the economy. The NEPmen—traders, merchants, and others who took advantage of the opportunities for profitmaking under NEP—were viewed as a potential base for restoring capitalism.

3. Trotsky's discussion of the disputes over "proletarian military doctrine" will be found in his *Military Writings* (Pathfinder Press, 1971), and his discussion of "proletarian culture" will be found in *Literature and Revolution* (Ann Arbor, 1960).

4. *Party propagandist* is a translation of the Russian term *agitator*. A creation of the October Revolution, the *agitator* was someone whose job is to explain the party's program and policies to the masses. They maintained offices in all parts of the country, and conducted street lectures, as well as working in offices, shops, and schools. The conference referred to here was just one of the numerous conferences these party propagandists held.

5. *Yuri N. Libedinsky* (1898–1959) was a leader of the Russian Association of Proletarian Writers (RAPP). His novel *The Week*

(1922) describes the crushing of a counterrevolutionary revolt among the peasantry. Libedinsky's works deal mostly with the lives of Communists during the revolution, civil war, and socialist construction.

Gubkom is an abbreviation for *gubiernsky komitet,* or provincial committee. The committees were local party organizations in the provinces.—Translator.

6. *"Young Germany"* was a literary movement that began in the 1830s in Germany, strongly influenced by the mood of social unrest and the rise of industrialization.

Heinrich Heine (1797–1856) was a German lyric poet and literary critic, and one of the best-known members of the "Young Germany" movement.

Ludwig Boerne (1786–1837), a leader of "Young Germany," was a political writer and satirist. He published various journals in which he criticized German theater and German politics, and he emphasized social reforms and political freedom.

7. *Vissarion Belinsky* (1811–1848) was an influential literary critic whose support of socially critical writers affected the course of Russian literature. His writings are regarded by Marxists as an intellectual forerunner of socialist thought in Russia.

Nikolai Chernyshevksy (1828–1889) was an author and critic whose novel *What Is To Be Done?* influenced the Russian populist movement.

Dimitri Pisarev (1840–1868) was a literary critic concerned with family problems and with the ethical aspects of socio-economic reforms.

Nikolai Dobrolyubov (1836–1861) was a journalist and critic and an early revolutionary activist.

8. *The Narodniks* (populists) were an organized movement of Russian intellectuals who conducted activities among the peasantry from 1876 to 1879, when they split into two groups. One was a terrorist group, which was crushed after the assassination of Czar Alexander in 1881. The other was led by Plekhanov, and split again, the

Plekhanov group becoming Marxists while the right wing evolved into the Social Revolutionary Party.

9. *Charles Fourier* (1772–1837) was a French utopian socialist whose experimental cooperative communities were designed to be self-sufficient industrially and agriculturally.

10. *Nikolai Semashko* (1874–1949) was an Old Bolshevik who became People's Commissar of Public Health in 1923.

11. *RSFSR* are the initials for the Russian Soviet Federated Socialist Republic. *Fabzavkom* is an abbreviation of *fabrichno-zavodskoy komitet,* or plant-factory committee.—Translator.

12. *Platon M. Kerzhentsev* (1881–1940) joined the Bolsheviks in 1904. He held various literary and cultural posts in the Soviet state, including a prominent post in Soviet radio and in a government commission for the fine arts. He was president of the Rabkrin Council for the Scientific Organization of Labor from 1923 to 1924. In 1923 he founded a "League of Time," with a journal, *Vremya,* to promote the rationalization of work by measurements in terms of time occupied.

13. The first *five-year plan* for economic development was begun in 1928 after a long debate during which the Stalinists opposed the demand by Trotsky and the Left Opposition for accelerated industrialization and collectivization of the land. After Trotsky's expulsion from the party, however, the bureaucracy veered to the other extreme, instituting speed-ups and forcible collectivization of the land, leading to a period of economic chaos and great hardship for the population.

14. *The Stakhanovist* movement was a special system of speedup in production introduced in the Soviet Union in 1935, which led to great wage disparities and widespread discontent among the workers.

15. *Louis Fischer* (1896–1970), European correspondent for the *Nation,* was an American journalist whom Trotsky accused of being an apologist for Stalinism during the Moscow trials.

16. *Lev S. Sosnovsky* (1886–1937) was one of the early leaders of the Left Opposition, and one of the last inside the Soviet Union to capitulate to the Stalinist faction. Earlier in *The Revolution Betrayed*, Trotsky referred to "the well-known Soviet journalist, Sosnovsky, [who] pointed out the special role played by the 'automobile-harem factor' in forming the morals of the Soviet bureaucracy. . . . The old articles of Sosnovsky . . . were sprinkled with unforgettable episodes from the life of the new ruling stratum, plainly showing to what vast degree the conquerors have assimilated the morals of the conquered" (p. 112).

17. *Emilian Yaroslavsky* (1878–1943) was a leader of "The Society of the Godless," an organization designed to conduct antireligious propaganda. He was a member of the presidium of the Central Control Commission, and was coauthor of the official charges against Trotsky by that body in 1927. He was denounced by Stalin in 1931 for permitting "Trotskyist views" to be smuggled into his textbook history of Bolshevism, because while his book extolled Stalinism, it did not sufficiently glorify Stalin himself.

Notes to Part 2

1. *Peter Alekseevich*, also called Peter the Great (1672–1725) was czar from 1682 until his death. He is best known for introducing some elements of European civilization into Russia.

Boyars were members of a Russian aristocratic order next in rank to the ruling princes, which had many privileges until it was abolished by Peter the Great.

2. The Russian Social Democratic Labor Party's first congress was held under illegal conditions in March 1898. But the new organization was quickly broken up by police repression, and a second congress was not held until 1903, in London, where a split took place between the Bolshevik faction, led by Lenin, and the Menshevik faction, led by Martov. The Bolsheviks, after leading the October 1917 Revolution, took the name of the Russian Communist Party.

Nikolayev, in the Ukraine, was where Trotsky was working to build the revolutionary movement in 1898.

3. A mistake for 1898.—Translator.

4. *Narodnaya Volya* (People's Will) was the terrorist organization of the 1870s.—Translator.

5. *Philipp Scheidemann* (1865–1939) was a leader of the right wing of the German Social Democracy, and a member of the cabinet that crushed the November 1918 revolution.—Translator.

6. *Lenin's last two articles*, "How We Should Reorganize the Workers' and Peasants' Inspection," and "Better Fewer, but Better," are in Lenin's *Collected Works*, Vol. 33 (Progress Publishers, Moscow, 1966), beginning on page 481 and 487, respectively.—Translator.

7. The vote in favor of forming a single union out of the Russian, Ukrainian, Georgian, Armenian, Azerbaidzhan, and Byelorussian Soviet Socialist Republics came on December 30, 1922. In the debates around the form that unity would take, the majority led by Lenin and Trotsky stressed that it had to be voluntary, based on real military and economic advantages for the smaller or more backward or formerly oppressed nationalities, and that the *right of secession* be preserved as protection against encroachments on equality between the nations.—Translator.

8. *Yakov M. Sverdlov* (1885–1919), after 1917, was the chairman of the Central Executive Committee of the Congress of Soviets and secretary of the Central Committee of the Bolshevik Party. He was also the first president of the Russian Soviet Republic.

9. The lead article in that issue was headlined *"Merzartsy"* (Villains).—Translator.

10. In 1923, *Seth Hoeglund* (1884–1956) placed an article in the central paper of the Swedish Communist Party trying to prove that

one could be a communist and a religious believer at the same time. In order to be a member of the Communist Party, he argued, it was enough to agree with its program and submit to its discipline. Between 1923 and 1924 he led a struggle against the Executive Committee of the Comintern on this and other questions, and he was finally expelled in August 1924.

11. A debate developed in *Pravda* at the end of 1921, attempting to explain the turn of the youth toward academicism, or abstract theorizing.—Translator.

12. *Legal Marxists* were a group in prerevolutionary Russia that evolved a form of Marxism that was so abstract and unrevolutionary that they were permitted to function legally under czarism. The group was led by Peter Struve (1870–1944). After the October Revolution, most of the legal Marxists became bitter opponents of the Bolshevik regime.

13. *The July days of 1917* in Petrograd broke out without any direction and led to bloody encounters. The Bolsheviks were declared responsible, their leaders arrested, and their papers shut down.
White Guards, or Whites, was the name given the Russian counterrevolutionary forces following the October Revolution.

14. *Brest-Litovsk* was a town on the Russo-Polish border where a treaty ending hostilities between Russia and Germany was signed by the Soviet delegation on March 3, 1918. The terms were extremely unfavorable to Soviet interests, but the new Soviet government felt that it had to sign because it was unable at that time to fight back. Less than two weeks after the signing, the Germans invaded the Ukraine.

15. *The Social Revolutionary Party* (SRs), founded in 1900, soon became the political expression of the Russian populist currents; prior to the 1917 revolution it had the largest share of influence among the peasantry. Its right wing was led by Kerensky. The Left SRs were in a coalition government with the Bolsheviks after the October Revolution. However, dissatisfied with the treaty of Brest-Litovsk,

and unwilling to accept the Bolshevik policy of making peace with Germany, the Left SRs organized an insurrection in July 1918. They took over a few government offices, just long enough to announce the overthrow of Lenin's government; and they assassinated a few public figures, including the German ambassador, hoping that this would provoke a renewed conflict with Germany. The revolt was quickly crushed. Two months later, a Left Social Revolutionary made an unsuccessful attempt on Lenin's life, wounding him gravely.

16. Literally, the proverb says "People meet according to their clothing, but associate according to their minds."—Translator.

17. *Rosta* was the Russian Telegraphic Agency, which preceded TASS.—Translator.

18. *Gosizdat* was the abbreviation for *Gosudarstvennoe Izdatel'stvo*, the state publishing house in the Soviet Union.

19. *Narkomzdrav* was the abbreviation for *Narodnyi Komissariat Zdravookhpraneniya*, the People's Commissariat of Health.

20. *George Curzon* (1859–1925) was the British minister of foreign affairs from 1919 to 1923. He was one of the chief organizers of foreign military intervention against Soviet Russia. In July 1920, during the Polish-Soviet conflict, he sent a note to the Soviet government demanding that the advance of the Red Army be halted at Poland's 1919 eastern frontier, subsequently known as the Curzon line.

21. The February 1917 revolution in Russia overthrew czarism and established the bourgeois Provisional Government, which ruled until October, when the Soviets, led by the Bolsheviks, came to power.

22. "Proletarian Culture and Proletarian Art," chapter 6 of Trotsky's *Literature and Revolution*, was first printed in *Pravda*, September 14 and 15, 1923.—Translator.

23. *Aleksandr Zharov* (1904–1987) later became a member of the "October group" of young writers who called for fighting "bourgeois attitudes" in poetry and prose.

24. *Karl Liebknecht* (1871–1919) was a leader of the German Social Democracy who opposed World War I and was jailed, along with Rosa Luxemburg, for his antiwar activity. He was freed by the November 1918 uprising and assassinated by officers of the German Social Democratic government in January 1919.

25. *Glavpolitprosvet* was the *Glavnyi Politiko-Prosvetitel'nyi Komitet*, the Chief Committee for Political Education, founded in 1920, which directed the mass communist education of adults, chiefly in the struggle against illiteracy, and sponsored party and soviet schools, clubs, libraries, and reading huts in the early years of the revolution. It merged into the "sector for mass work" of the Commissariat of Enlightenment in June 1930. The president of Glavpolitprosvet throughout was N.K. Krupskaya, whose companion, Lenin, had died earlier in 1924.

26. This is a reference to a speech Trotsky made to the Fifth All-Russian Congress of Medical and Veterinary Workers, on June 21, 1924, entitled "Through What Stage Are We Passing?"—Translator.

27. *Ramsay MacDonald* (1866–1937) was a pacifist socialist during World War I. He became prime minister in the first British Labour government in 1924, and opposed the British General Strike of 1926. He bolted the Labour Party during his second term as prime minister (1929–31) to form a "national unity" cabinet with the Tories (1931–35). MacDonald's career is dealt with in *Leon Trotsky on Britain* (Pathfinder Press, 1973).

28. *The Comintern* (Communist or Third International) was organized under Lenin's leadership as the revolutionary successor to the Second International. In Lenin's time, its congresses were held once a year—the First in 1919, the Second in 1920, the Third in 1921, the Fourth in 1922, despite the civil war and the insecurity of the Soviet Union. Trotsky regarded the theses of the Comintern's first

four congresses to be the programmatic cornerstone of the Left Opposition and then of the Fourth International. The Fifth Congress took place in 1924, when Stalin's machine was already in control. The Sixth Congress did not take place until 1928, and the Seventh was not held until 1935. Trotsky called the Seventh the "liquidation congress" of the Comintern (see *Writings of Leon Trotsky, 1935–36*), and it was in fact the last before Stalin announced the dissolution of the Comintern in 1943 as a gesture to his imperialist allies.

29. *Reading "huts"* were the center for political, educational, and cultural work in the Soviet village in the 1920s. They developed from the "people's homes" set up by the liberals under czarism. The huts were supported financially by the Soviet government and functioned under the authority of Glavpolitprosvet. Each hut contained a library and served as a meeting place for lectures, classes, and cultural events. The name *izbach*, for the person in charge of the hut, was coined in 1922. The huts' major function was the struggle against illiteracy.—Translator.

30. *Kulak* is the Russian term for a wealthy peasant.—Translator.

31. *Rudolph Hilferding* (1877–1941) was a leader of the German Social Democracy prior to World War I. A pacifist during the war, he became a leader of the Independent Social Democrats. Returning to the Social Democratic Party, he served as finance minister in a bourgeois cabinet in 1923 and 1928. He died in a German prison camp during World War II.

32. *Nestor Makhno* (1884–1934) was the leader of small partisan bands of peasants who fought Ukranian reactionaries and German occupation forces during the Russian civil war. He refused to integrate his forces into the Red Army and ultimately came into conflict with it. His forces were finally dispersed by the Soviet government.

33. *Proletcult*, the Organization of Representatives of Proletarian Culture, was set up independently of the Bolshevik Party on the eve of the revolution. It did important work in keeping culture alive during the civil war, and disseminating it among the workers.

It was not a literary movement at first. However, in early 1920 a group of writers emerged from it who called themselves the Forge or Smithy, and who issued a manifesto that they called the "red flag of the platform-declaration of proletarian art." They founded the All-Russian Association of Proletarian Writers (VAPP).

Bogdanov, who dominated Proletcult, argued that the dictatorship of the proletariat was advancing on three parallel but distinct lines: political, economic, and cultural. Its political organ was the party, its economic organ the trade unions, and its cultural organ Proletcult. He said that the proletariat should create its own culture as previous ruling classes had done, and that Proletcult should be the supreme voice in this cultural construction.

To Lenin and Trotsky, this was an anti-materialist view. They argued that literature was part of the cultural superstructure that necessarily lags behind politics and economics, and that the Russian proletariat had to assimilate the culture of previous epochs before it could go on to create something new. Lenin fought successfully to have Proletcult made subordinate to the People's Commissariat of Education. However, after Lenin's death, VAPP became an instrument of the growing Soviet bureaucracy, and at its first All-Union Conference of Proletarian Writers in 1925, it pressed its claims to become the organ of a party dictatorship in literature. The same conference resulted in the creation of a new Russian Association of Proletarian Writers (RAPP). VAPP was revived after 1928 as the All-Union Association of Proletarian Writers.

34. *Burzhkor.* Trotsky is making a play on words. Throughout the Russian text, the abbreviation *rabkor,* from the early Soviet period, is used for "worker correspondent." This is a contraction of the Russian words *rabochiy* (worker) and *korrespondent* (correspondent). With the word *burzhkor* (bourgeois correspondent), Trotsky is creating an imaginary parallel with the bourgeois world, using a contraction of the Russian words *burzhuanzhnyi* and *korrespondent.*—Translator.

35. *Cadets* was the popular name for the Russian Constitutional Democrats, a bourgeois party committed to a constitutional monarchy

and moderate liberalism, led by Miliukov, which briefly dominated the Provisional Government after February 1917.

Notes to Part 3

1. *Hohenzollern* was the name of the German royal family that provided Prussian kings and German emperors until 1918.

Romanov was the name of the dynasty that ruled Russia from 1613 until the revolution in 1917.

Louis Philippe (1773–1850) was the king of France from 1830 until he was overthrown in 1848.

2. Two international peace conferences held in 1899 and 1907 at *the Hague* in the Netherlands were called for the purpose of limiting armaments and ensuring the peaceful settlement of international disputes.

The Treaty of *Portsmouth*, signed in Portsmouth, New Hampshire, ended the Russo-Japanese war in 1905.

In 1906, representatives of fifteen powers signed the Act of Algeciras, in *Morocco*, establishing the principle of Morocco's integrity and an open door policy for the European powers.

3. This is an ironic reference to the resumption of the state sale of vodka.

4. Trotsky here refers to the value of Russia's enormous distances and expanses for the purpose of defense, as shown in the wars of intervention.—Translator.

5. *Famusovism* is an expression derived from Famusov, a character in Griboyedov's play *The Folly of Being Wise* (1824). He is a high official whose sole interest is in living up to his rank; he has a horror of anything that may give offense to authority and so disturb his comfortable situation. Trotsky here hits at people who rejected the work of Freud and his followers in a sweeping, indiscriminate way, not on scientific grounds but because they knew it was looked upon with disfavor by the party leadership.—Translator.

6. Here Trotsky challenges Tolstoy's ideas on art and their revival by Bukharin, in *Historical Materialism*.—Translator.

7. *Estate relations* are the relations between different "estates," or social groups with different legal status and rights.—Translator.

8. *Gleb Uspensky* (1840–1902) was a Russian novelist of peasant life in the 1870s and 1880s.—Translator.

9. A kopek is one one-hundredth of a ruble. In 1925, the ruble was worth about 51¢ in American money.

10. This is a reference to the Franco-Soviet negotiations regarding payment of czarist debts to French creditors.—Translator.

Christian Rakovsky (1873–1941), who was the Soviet representative in France for negotiations, had been a leading figure in the Balkan revolutionary movement before the Russian Revolution. In 1918 he became chairman of the Ukrainian Soviet, and later served as ambassador to London and Paris. An early leader of the Russian Left Opposition, he was deported to Siberia in 1928. In 1934 he capitulated. In 1938 he was one of the major defendants in the third Moscow trial, where he was sentenced to twenty years' imprisonment.

Aristide Briand (1862–1932) was expelled from the French Socialist Party in 1906 for accepting an office in the Clemenceau cabinet. He was head of the wartime coalition cabinet from 1915 to 1917, and was the French representative to the League of Nations from 1925 to 1932.

Otto Bauer (1881–1938) was a leader of the Austrian Social Democracy after World War I. He was the chief theoretician of Austro-Marxism.

11. Trotsky's reference here is to the Land and Nation League, founded in 1923.—Translator.

David Lloyd George (1863–1945), an author of the Versailles Treaty, was head of the British government during World War I. He began as a reformer, but ended as the engineer of military intervention against the Soviet state. When that failed, he became an advocate of establishing economic ties with the Soviet Union.

Notes to Part 4

1. The full text of Trotsky's "Report on the World Economic Crisis and the New Tasks of the Communist International" is in Vol. 1 of *The First Five Years of the Communist International*, 2nd ed. (Pathfinder Press, 1973).

2. *Nikolai D. Kondratiev* was a professor at the Agricultural Academy and the head of the Business Research Institute of Moscow after the revolution. His theory of fifty-year, self-adjusting economic cycles provoked wide controversy during the twenties. In 1930 he was arrested as the alleged head of an illegal Peasants Labor Party and exiled to Siberia.

3. The TASS wires presumably misled Trotsky on this point. There was no ban on workers' May Day demonstrations in Britain in 1924, and these duly took place.—Translator.

4. Italy's recognition of the Soviet Union, in November 1923, began a series of recognitions by the great powers. At the time Trotsky was speaking, an Anglo-Soviet conference was in progress in London—Translator.

5. The full text of Lenin's speech "The Tasks of the Youth Leagues," delivered at the Third All-Russian Congress of the Russian Communist League of Youth, October 2, 1920, is in Lenin's *Collected Works*, Vol. 31 (Progress Publishers, Moscow, 1966).—Translator.

6. *Narpit* was an abbreviation for *Narodnoe pitanie* (Food for the people), a special organization to promote public eating facilities, especially at factories, supported by the trade unions, government, and cooperative societies.

7. From the end of World War I the revolutionary movement in Italy grew, and in September 1920 the workers seized the factories and industries. The Social Democrats took fright and jumped back. The proletariat was left leaderless. By November the first major fascist demonstration was held. The Social Democratic leaders hoped

to reclaim the confidence of the bourgeoisie against the fascists, and restrained the workers from resisting Mussolini's bands. But the bourgeoisie swung over to the fascists. At the last minute, the Social Democrats called a general strike, but the workers, demoralized and confused, did not respond, and the fascists were able to consolidate their stranglehold. This development is explained in the section "Lessons of the Italian Experience," in *The Struggle Against Fascism in Germany*, by Leon Trotsky (Pathfinder Press, 1971).

8. In March 1921, the German Communist Party issued a call for an armed insurrection to seize power, in connection with struggles in the central German mining districts against the Social Democratic reaction. The action was crushed after two weeks. The Comintern's Third Congress repudiated the action and theory of "galvanizing" the workers put forward by the ultralefts.

9. A revolutionary situation developed in Germany in late 1923, due to a severe economic crisis and the French invasion of the Ruhr. A majority of the German working class turned toward support of the Communist Party. But the CP leadership vacillated, missed an exceptionally favorable opportunity to conduct a struggle for power, and permitted the German capitalists to recover their balance before the year was ended. The Kremlin's responsibility for this wasted opportunity was one of the factors that led to the formation of the Russian Left Opposition at the end of 1923.

10. *Valerian F. Pletnev* (1886–1942) was a member of the Bolshevik Party since 1904. From December 1920 until 1932 he was president of the Central Committee of Proletcult. In February 1921 he was also appointed the head of the Glavpolitprosvet arts department. His 1922 articles in *Pravda* were attacked both by Krupskaya and by Lunacharsky.

11. *Moor* was the pseudonym of Dimitri S. Orlov (1883–1946), a prominent caricaturist and cartoonist. After the October Revolution, he worked for the State Publishing House. In 1920 he did posters for the Red Army and the Chief Political Administration, and in

1921 to combat the famine. After 1922, he was a regular cartoonist for *Pravda*.—Translator.

12. *Martin Tranmael* (1879–1967) was the leader of the Norwegian Labor Party and editor of its major newspaper. After resisting the demands of the Executive Committee of the Comintern to expel dissidents, he broke completely with the International and later helped bring the Norwegian Labor Party into affiliation with the Socialist International.

13. *Friedrich Engels* (1820–1895) was Marx's closest collaborator and the cofounder with him of modern scientific socialism. His letters were published by the Marx and Engels Institute in the *Marx and Engels Archive*, Vol. I (1924).

The letters were edited by *David B. Ryazanov* (1870–1938), a historian and philosopher, who joined the Bolsheviks in 1917. He organized the Marx and Engels Institute and later withdrew from political activity. But his scholarly and scrupulous attitude toward party history made him offensive to Stalin, who ordered him to be implicated with the defendants at the 1931 trial of a so-called "Menshevik Center," which was accused of plotting to restore capitalism in the Soviet Union. He was dismissed as director of the Marx and Engels Institute and exiled.

Eduard Bernstein (1850–1932) was the first theoretician of "revisionism" in the German Social Democracy. In his *Evolutionary Socialism* he taught that socialism would come about through the gradual democratization of capitalism, and that the workers' movement had to abandon the class struggle in favor of class collaboration with the "progressive" bourgeoisie.

Karl Kautsky (1854–1938) was regarded as the outstanding Marxist theoretician until World War I, when he abandoned internationalism and opposed the Russian Revolution.

14. The full texts of Lenin's "Page from a Diary" and "On Cooperation" are in his *Collected Works*, Vol. 33 (Progress Publishers, Moscow, 1966), and begin on page 472 and page 467, respectively.—Translator.

15. *Aleksandr A. Bogdanov* (1873–1928) became a Bolshevik in 1903. In 1908 he led a "boycottist" tendency, which contended that the party must work strictly through illegal organizations during that period of reaction. He was expelled from the Bolshevik Party in 1909. After the October Revolution, he became an organizer and leader of Proletcult. After 1921, he devoted himself to scientific and medical work.

16. *Henri Barbusse* (1873–1935) was a pacifist novelist who joined the French Communist Party, wrote biographies of Stalin and Christ, and sponsored amorphous antiwar and antifascist congresses used by the Stalinists as showcase substitutes for genuine struggle.

Karl Renner (1870–1950) was a leader of the Austrian Social Democracy. He supported World War I, and became president of Austria from 1931 to 1933 and 1945 until his death. He is the author of various works on economics, government, law, and socialism.

Emile Vandervelde (1866–1938) was a Belgian Social Democratic reformist who served as president of the Second International, 1929–36.

Georges Monnet (1898–1980) was French minister of agriculture in Leon Blum's first cabinet, 1936–37, and in Blum's second cabinet, 1938.

Paul Louis (1872–1948), the French journalist and author of books on labor history, was a member of the small centrist group, the Party of Proletarian Unity.

17. *James Burnham* (1905–1987) was a leader of the Socialist Workers Party in the United States, who broke with the SWP in 1940 and later became a propagandist for McCarthyism and other ultraright movements and an editor of the right-wing publication *National Review*.

Max Shachtman (1903–1972) was a leader in the American Communist Party and a founder and leader of the Trotskyist movement. He split from the SWP in 1940 because of differences over defense of the Soviet Union. In 1958 he joined the Socialist Party.

18. *Max Eastman* (1883–1969) was an early supporter of the Left Opposition, although he was not a member of any party. He

translated several of Trotsky's books and was the first to acquaint the American public with the issues of the Trotsky-Stalin struggle. In the mid-1930s he began a retreat from Marxism, repudiating socialism altogether in 1940. He became an anticommunist and an editor of *Reader's Digest*.

19. *Boris Souvarine* (1893–1984) was a founder of the French Communist Party and was one of the first serious biographers of Stalin. He was repelled by Stalinism in the twenties and was the only foreign delegate to the 13th congress of the Russian CP to defend Trotsky against the Stalinist slanders. He was expelled from the French party shortly thereafter. In the thirties he turned against Leninism. For Trotsky he was a prototype of the cynicism and defeatism that characterized the renegades from Bolshevism.

20. *Modern Monthly* was an independent radical journal edited by V.F. Calverton between the 1920s and the 1940s. It featured diverse political commentary, as well as literary criticism and fiction. Trotsky wrote for it in the early thirties, but he later dissociated himself from it because he felt that it did not have a sufficiently intransigent position on the Moscow trials.

Index

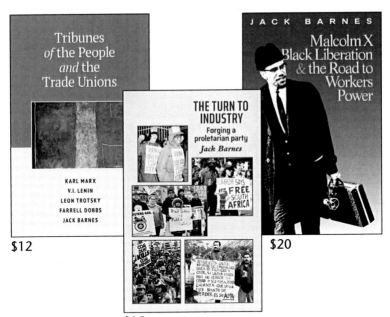

Three books to be read as one . . .

. . . about building the only kind of party worthy of the name "revolutionary" in the imperialist epoch.

- A party that's working class in program, composition, and action.
- A party that recognizes, in word and deed, the most revolutionary fact of our time:

That working people—those the bosses and privileged layers who serve them fear as "deplorables," "criminals," or just plain "trash"—have the power to create a different world as we organize and act together to defend our own interests, not those of the class that grows rich off exploiting our labor. That as we advance along that revolutionary course, we'll transform ourselves and awaken to our capacities—to our own worth.

Three books about building such a party in the US and throughout the capitalist world. Also in Spanish and French.

ART AND REVOLUTION
Writings on Literature, Politics, and Culture
Leon Trotsky

"Art can become a strong ally of revolution only insofar as it remains faithful to itself," wrote Trotsky in 1938. $15

SOCIALISM AND MAN IN CUBA
Ernesto Che Guevara, Fidel Castro

"Man truly reaches his full human condition when he produces without being compelled by physical necessity to sell himself as a commodity," wrote Guevara in 1965. $5. Also in Spanish, French, Farsi, and Greek.

JOHN COLTRANE AND THE JAZZ REVOLUTION OF THE 1960S
Frank Kofsky

An account of John Coltrane's role in spearheading innovations in jazz that were an expression of the new cultural and political ferment that marked the rise of the mass struggle for Black rights. $23

THEIR MORALS AND OURS
The Class Foundations of Moral Practice
Leon Trotsky

Participating in the revolutionary workers movement "with open eyes and an intense will—only this can give the highest moral satisfaction to a thinking being," Trotsky writes. He explains how morality is rooted in the interests of contending social classes. With a reply by the pragmatist philosopher John Dewey and a Marxist response to Dewey by George Novack. $10

THE CUBAN REVOLUTION AND ITS IMPACT FROM AFRICA TO THE US

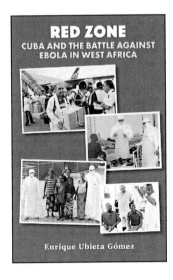

Red Zone
Cuba and the Battle against Ebola in West Africa

ENRIQUE UBIETA GÓMEZ

When three African countries were hit in 2014–15 by the largest Ebola epidemic on record, Cuba's revolutionary government responded to an international call and sent what no other country even pretended to provide: more than 250 volunteer doctors, nurses, and other medical workers. This firsthand account of their actions shows the kind of men and women only a socialist revolution can produce. $17. Also in Spanish.

Cuba and Angola: The War for Freedom
HARRY VILLEGAS ("POMBO")

Cuba and Angola
Fighting for Africa's Freedom and Our Own
FIDEL CASTRO, RAÚL CASTRO, NELSON MANDELA

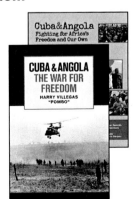

Two books that tell the story of Cuba's unparalleled contribution to the fight to free Africa from the scourge of apartheid. And how, in the doing, Cuba's socialist revolution was also strengthened. $10 and $12. Also in Spanish.

From the Escambray to the Congo
In the Whirlwind of the Cuban Revolution
VÍCTOR DREKE

Dreke was second in command of the internationalist column in the Congo led in 1965 by Che Guevara. He recounts the creative joy with which working people have defended their revolutionary course—from Cuba's Escambray mountains to Africa and beyond. $15. Also in Spanish.

How Far We Slaves Have Come!

South Africa and Cuba in Today's World

NELSON MANDELA, FIDEL CASTRO

Speaking together in Cuba in 1991, Mandela and Castro discuss the role of Cuba in the history of Africa and Angola's victory over the invading US-backed South African army. That victory accelerated the fight to bring down the racist apartheid system. $7. Also in Spanish and Farsi.

Cuba and the Coming American Revolution

JACK BARNES

This is a book about the struggles of working people in the imperialist heartland, the youth attracted to them, and the example set by the Cuban people that revolution is not only necessary—it can be made. It is about the class struggle in the US, where the revolutionary capacities of workers and farmers are today as utterly discounted by the ruling powers as were those of the Cuban toilers. And just as wrongly. $10. Also in Spanish, French, and Farsi.

Che Guevara: Economics and Politics in the Transition to Socialism

CARLOS TABLADA

Quoting extensively from Guevara's writings and speeches on building socialism, this book presents the interrelationship of the market, economic planning, material incentives, and voluntary work. Guevara shows why profit and other capitalist categories cannot be yardsticks for progress in the transition to socialism. $17. Also in Spanish, French, and Greek.

CAPITALIST CRISIS AND THE FIGHT FOR WORKERS POWER

Are They Rich Because They're Smart?

Class, Privilege, and Learning under Capitalism

JACK BARNES

In battles forced on us by the capitalists, workers will begin to transform our attitudes toward life, work, and each other. We'll discover our worth, denied by the rulers and upper middle classes who insist they're rich because they're smart. We'll learn in struggle what we're capable of becoming. $10. Also in Spanish, French, Farsi, and Arabic.

The Clintons' Anti-Working-Class Record

Why Washington Fears Working People

JACK BARNES

What working people need to know about the profit-driven course of Democrats and Republicans alike over the last thirty years. And the political awakening of workers seeking to understand and resist the capitalist rulers' assaults. $10. Also in Spanish, French, Farsi, and Greek.

Is Socialist Revolution in the US Possible?

A Necessary Debate among Working People

MARY-ALICE WATERS

An unhesitating "Yes"—that's the answer given here. Possible—but not inevitable. That depends on what working people *do*. $7. Also in Spanish, French, and Farsi.

THE COMMUNIST INTERNATIONAL IN LENIN'S TIME

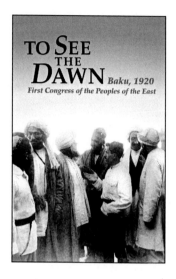

To See the Dawn
Baku, 1920—First Congress of the Peoples of the East

How can peasants and workers in the colonial world achieve freedom from imperialist exploitation? By what means can working people overcome divisions incited by their national ruling classes and act together for their common class interests? These questions were addressed by 2,000 delegates to the 1920 Congress of the Peoples of the East. $17

Workers of the World and Oppressed Peoples, Unite!
Proceedings and Documents of the Second Congress, 1920

The debate among delegates from 37 countries takes up key questions of working-class strategy and program and offers a vivid portrait of social struggles in the era of the October revolution. 2 vol. set. $45

Lenin's Struggle for a Revolutionary International
Documents, 1907–1916; The Preparatory Years

The debate among revolutionary working-class leaders, including V.I. Lenin and Leon Trotsky, on a socialist response to World War I. $30

Other volumes in the series:

The German Revolution and the Debate on Soviet Power (1918–1919). $27

Founding the Communist International (March 1919). $25

EXPAND YOUR REVOLUTIONARY LIBRARY

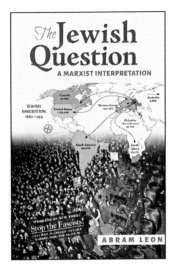

The Jewish Question

A Marxist Interpretation

ABRAM LEON

Why is Jew-hatred still raising its ugly head? What are its class roots—from antiquity through feudalism, to capitalism's rise and current crises? Why is there no solution under capitalism without revolutionary struggles that transform working people as we fight to transform our world? The author, Abram Leon, was killed in the Nazi gas chambers. This 2020 edition has a revised translation, new introduction, and 40 pages of illustrations and maps. $17. Also in Spanish and French.

Che Guevara Talks to Young People

Guevara challenges the youth of Cuba and the world to work. To become disciplined. To join the vanguard on the front lines of struggles, small and large. To become a different kind of human being as they fight together with working people of all lands to transform the world. $12. Also in Spanish and Greek.

The Communist Manifesto

KARL MARX AND FREDERICK ENGELS

Communism, say the founding leaders of the revolutionary workers movement, is not a set of ideas or preconceived "principles" but workers' line of march to power, springing from a "movement going on under our very eyes." $5. Also in Spanish, French, Farsi, and Arabic.

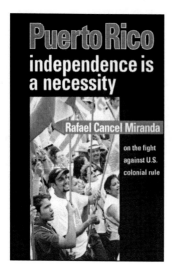

Puerto Rico: Independence Is a Necessity

RAFAEL CANCEL MIRANDA

One of the five Puerto Rican Nationalists imprisoned by Washington for more than 25 years and released in 1979 speaks out on the brutal reality of US colonial domination, the example of Cuba's socialist revolution, and the ongoing struggle for independence. $5. Also in Spanish and Farsi.

The History of the Russian Revolution

LEON TROTSKY

How, under Lenin's leadership, the Bolshevik Party led millions of workers and farmers to overthrow the state power of the landlords and capitalists in 1917 and bring to power a government that advanced their class interests at home and worldwide. Unabridged, 3 vols. in one. Written by one of the central leaders of that socialist revolution. $30. Also in French and Russian.

Maurice Bishop Speaks

The Grenada Revolution and Its Overthrow, 1979–83

The triumph of the 1979 revolution in the Caribbean island of Grenada under the leadership of Maurice Bishop gave hope to millions throughout the Americas. Invaluable lessons from the workers and farmers government destroyed by a Stalinist-led counterrevolution in 1983. $20

February 1965:
The Final Speeches

MALCOLM X

Our revolt is not "simply a racial conflict of Black against white, or a purely American problem. Rather, we are seeing a global rebellion of the oppressed against the oppressor, the exploited against the exploiter." Speeches and interviews from the last three weeks of Malcolm X's life. $17

50 Years of Covert Operations in the US

Washington's Political Police and the American Working Class

LARRY SEIGLE, FARRELL DOBBS, STEVE CLARK

How class-conscious workers have fought against the drive to build the "national security" state essential to maintaining capitalist rule. $10. Also in Spanish and Farsi.

Genocide against the Indians

GEORGE NOVACK

Why did the leaders of the Europeans who settled in North America try to exterminate the peoples already living there? How was the campaign of genocide against the Indians linked to the expansion of capitalism in the United States? Noted Marxist George Novack answers these questions. $5. Also in Farsi.

Lenin's Final Fight
Speeches and Writings, 1922–23

V.I. LENIN

In 1922 and 1923, V.I. Lenin, central leader of the world's first socialist revolution, waged what was to be his last political battle—one that was lost following his death. At stake was whether that revolution, and the international communist movement it led, would remain on the revolutionary proletarian course that brought workers and peasants to power in October 1917. $17. Also in Spanish, Farsi, and Greek.

Socialism: Utopian and Scientific
FREDERICK ENGELS

"To make man the master of his own form of social organization—to make him free—is the historical mission of the modern proletariat," writes Engels. Here socialism is placed on a scientific foundation, the product of the lawful operations of capitalism itself and the struggles of the working class. $10. Also in Farsi.

Portraits, Political and Personal
LEON TROTSKY

Literary and biographical sketches of Rosa Luxemburg, H.G. Wells, Engels, Lenin, Stalin, and others. $17

Humanism and Socialism
GEORGE NOVACK

The relationship between humanism—the rational, secular expression of the ideals of the democratic revolution—and scientific socialism. $12

Women in Cuba:
The Making of a Revolution
Within the Revolution

VILMA ESPÍN, ASELA DE LOS SANTOS,
YOLANDA FERRER

The integration of women into the
ranks and leadership of the Cuban
Revolution was inseparable from its
working-class course from the start.
This is the story of that revolution and
how it transformed the women and
men who made it. $17. Also in Spanish
and Greek.

Thomas Sankara Speaks
The Burkina Faso Revolution,
1983–87

Under Sankara's guidance, Burkina Faso's
revolutionary government led peasants, workers,
women, and youth to expand literacy; to sink
wells, plant trees, erect housing; to combat
women's oppression; to carry out land reform;
to join others in Africa and worldwide to free
themselves from the imperialist yoke. $20. Also in
French.

Socialism on Trial
Testimony at Minneapolis Sedition Trial

JAMES P. CANNON

The revolutionary program of the working class,
presented in response to frame-up charges of
"seditious conspiracy" in 1941, on the eve of US
entry into World War II. The defendants were
leaders of the Minneapolis labor movement and
the Socialist Workers Party. $15. Also in Spanish,
French, and Farsi.

WOMEN'S LIBERATION AND SOCIALISM

Cosmetics, Fashions,
and the Exploitation of Women
Joseph Hansen, Evelyn Reed, Mary-Alice Waters

How big business reinforces women's second-class status and uses it to rake in profits. Where does women's oppression come from? How has the entry of millions of women into the workforce strengthened the battle for emancipation, still to be won? $12. Also in Spanish, Farsi, and Greek.

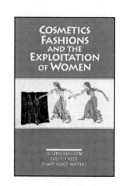

Woman's Evolution
From Matriarchal Clan to Patriarchal Family
Evelyn Reed

Assesses women's leading and still largely unknown contributions to the development of human civilization and refutes the myth that women have always been subordinate to men. "Certain to become a classic text in women's history."
—*Publishers Weekly.* $25. Also in Farsi.

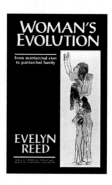

Abortion Is a Woman's Right!
Pat Grogan, Evelyn Reed

Why abortion rights are central not only to the fight for the full emancipation of women, but to forging a united and fighting labor movement. $5. Also in Spanish.

Communist Continuity and
the Fight for Women's Liberation
Documents of the Socialist Workers Party, 1971–86

How did the oppression of women begin? Who benefits? What social forces have the power to end women's second-class status? 3 volumes, edited with preface by Mary-Alice Waters. $12

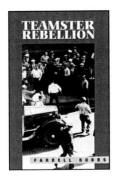  

New International

A MAGAZINE OF MARXIST POLITICS AND THEORY

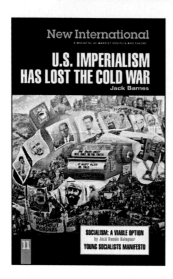

U.S. Imperialism Has Lost the Cold War

JACK BARNES

The collapse of regimes across Eastern Europe and the USSR claiming to be communist did not mean workers and farmers there had been crushed. In today's sharpening capitalist conflicts and wars, these toilers are joining working people the world over in the class struggle against exploitation. In *New International* no. 11. $14. Also in Spanish, French, Farsi, and Greek.

In Defense of Land and Labor

"Capitalist production develops by simultaneously undermining the original sources of all wealth—the soil and the worker."
—*Karl Marx, 1867*

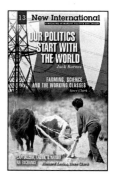

THREE ARTICLES

IN *NEW INTERNATIONAL* NO. 13

• **Our Politics Start with the World**
  JACK BARNES

• **Farming, Science, and the Working Classes**
  STEVE CLARK

IN *NEW INTERNATIONAL* NO. 14

• **The Stewardship of Nature Also Falls to the Working Class**
  JACK BARNES, STEVE CLARK, MARY-ALICE WATERS

$14 each issue

WWW.PATHFINDERPRESS.COM

PATHFINDER AROUND THE WORLD

UNITED STATES
(and Caribbean, Latin America, and East Asia)
Pathfinder Books, 306 W. 37th St., 13th Floor
New York, NY 10018

CANADA
Pathfinder Books, 7107 St. Denis, Suite 204
Montreal, QC H2S 2S5

UNITED KINGDOM
(and Europe, Africa, Middle East, and South Asia)
Pathfinder Books, 5 Norman Rd.
Seven Sisters, London N15 4ND

AUSTRALIA
(and Southeast Asia and the Pacific)
Pathfinder Books, Suite 103, 124-128 Beamish St.
Campsie, Sydney
Postal address: P.O. Box 73, Campsie, NSW 2194

NEW ZEALAND
Pathfinder Books, 188a Onehunga Mall Rd.
Onehunga, Auckland 1061
Postal address: P.O. Box 13857, Auckland 1643

pathfinderpress.com

Visit our website for all our titles, to place orders,
and to join the

PATHFINDER READERS CLUB

25% off all titles
30% off books of the month

JOIN NOW!

$10 a year

Valid at pathfinderpress.com
and local book centers